ptual
A Person-Centered Approach to Psychospiritual Maturation

Jared D. Kass

A Person-Centered Approach to Psychospiritual Maturation

Mentoring Psychological Resilience and Inclusive Community in Higher Education

Jared D. Kass
Concord, MA, USA

ISBN 978-3-319-86282-8   ISBN 978-3-319-57919-1 (eBook)
DOI 10.1007/978-3-319-57919-1

© The Editor(s) (if applicable) and The Author(s) 2017
Softcover reprint of the hardcover 1st edition 2017
This work is subject to copyright. All rights are solely and exclusively licensed by the Publisher, whether the whole or part of the material is concerned, specifically the rights of translation, reprinting, reuse of illustrations, recitation, broadcasting, reproduction on microfilms or in any other physical way, and transmission or information storage and retrieval, electronic adaptation, computer software, or by similar or dissimilar methodology now known or hereafter developed.
The use of general descriptive names, registered names, trademarks, service marks, etc. in this publication does not imply, even in the absence of a specific statement, that such names are exempt from the relevant protective laws and regulations and therefore free for general use.
The publisher, the authors and the editors are safe to assume that the advice and information in this book are believed to be true and accurate at the date of publication. Neither the publisher nor the authors or the editors give a warranty, express or implied, with respect to the material contained herein or for any errors or omissions that may have been made. The publisher remains neutral with regard to jurisdictional claims in published maps and institutional affiliations.

Cover credit: © Akihiro Nakayama

Printed on acid-free paper

This Palgrave Macmillan imprint is published by Springer Nature
The registered company is Springer International Publishing AG
The registered company address is: Gewerbestrasse 11, 6330 Cham, Switzerland

In Memoriam
Dr. Carl R. Rogers
1902–1987
Mentor
to an entire generation
of educators and mental health clinicians
with humanistic values
committed to the positive development of a peaceful and just society

Acknowledgements

Thanks to my intellectual, clinical, and life partner, Lynn Kass. If readers find any wisdom or maturity in this book, it is the result of our shared quest for psychospiritual depth and understanding. Thanks also to our son, Jesse, who has travelled this road with us. His scientific and sociopolitical knowledge have contributed to thoughtful conversations related to this book.

Thanks to my parents and our extended Kass-Shapiro-Siegel-Berkson clan. You have been sources of love, support, and fortitude when our families faced difficult times.

Thanks to Cantor Lawrence Avery, who tutored me in Jewish prayer when I was a high school student. These prayers became part of my daily contemplative practice: a resource for resilience, meaning, and celebration in times of sadness and joy.

Thanks to Leo Marx, my faculty tutor at Amherst College during my senior year as an Independent Scholar. Exploring the work of Ralph Waldo Emerson was my introduction to American Transcendentalism and the Perennial Philosophy at the core of my interfaith studies.

Thanks to the Danforth and Woodrow Wilson Foundation Graduate Fellowship programs for supporting my doctoral research, and the Union for Experimenting Colleges and Universities, then directed by Goodwin Watson, for their commitment to interdisciplinary doctoral studies.

Thanks to Carl Rogers and my professional colleagues on the Person-Centered Approach Project: primary catalysts of my current professional work.

Thanks to Herb Benson and my professional colleagues at the Section on Behavioral Medicine, Beth Israel and New England Deaconess Hospitals: catalysts for my understanding of the connection between body, mind, and spirit. Thanks also to Laurance Rockefeller, whose generous support for Herb Benson's work funded my research on contemplative spirituality, psychological resilience, and health.

Thanks to my clinical colleagues at Greenhouse, a counseling center for personal and social change, and to its founding members. In a society that pursues loneliness and reinforces social inequality, we have been a modest voice for constructive change.

Thanks to the Steering Committee of the Boston Clergy and Religious Leaders Group for Interfaith Dialogue: Tess Browne, Steve Ellis, Claire Kashuck, Brian Kelley, Ted Klein, Claire O'Rourke, Ji Hyang Padma, Carl Scovel, and Don Wells. You have a special place in my heart.

Thanks to the Division of Counseling and Psychology at Lesley University: the nurturing ground for this project. Deepest thanks to Susan Gere for her wise leadership and support of my work. Special thanks to Honor McClellan, Paul Crowley, Eleanor Roffman, Mary Ann Gawelek, Rick Reinkraut, Janice Cooke, Jill Ritchie, Yishiuan Chin, Thema Bryant-Davis, Meg Connor, Karen Cullen, Priscilla Dass-Brailsford, Carmen Dominguez, John Gearin, Maggie Giles, Irle Goldman, Lisa Tsoi Hoshmand, Joan Klagsbrun, Merlin Langley, Dalia Llera, Kathleen Meier, Adam Meiselman, Sue Motulsky, Jen Pappas, Rakhshanda Saleem, Catherine Stalberg, Donna San Antonio, Jill Mattuck Tarule, and Sidney Trantham.

Thanks to the research team that contributed to this project: Sue Lennox and Jon Baxter, Research Fellows; Jenn Crane, Jennifer Fulkerson, Kerry Gough, Barbara Schmitz, and Michelle Stakutis, Research Assistants.

Thanks to Lesley University for supporting this project through faculty development grants and sabbatical leave.

Very special thanks to the Lesley University students with whom I have worked. Our learning has been reciprocal. We have explored person-centered psychospiritual maturation together, and your dedication to this learning process has revealed its depths. Particular thanks to graduates who have become co-teaching colleagues, including:

Jessica Newman, Elizabeth Barragato, Peter Boteas, John Ciervo, Karen Enegess, Richard Fried, Lucia Gates, Joe Mageary, Dan Simone, Anna Stothart, Lauren Walsh, Sasha Juravleva Watkins, and Ann Whelan. Equally special thanks to graduates who have become clinical colleagues, including: Carmen Aldinger (health-promoting schools), Alma Macy and Robert Macy (contributions to peacock feather exercise), Laury Rappaport (mindfulness and the arts), Jill Valle (contributions to anonymous sharing exercise), as well as John Badenhausen, Anne Barton, Lynn Bishop, Erinn Ridge Buxton, Kristen Cahill, Jarrett Clayman, Ming Chang, Doug DiMartile, David Dionisio, Mary Flannery, Kym Goldsmith, Karen Grimes, Elise Hoblitzelle, Valina Jackson, Jennifer Johnston, Brandon Jones, Caroline Kellough, Glenn Klein, Mallory Kroll, Renee LaFountain, Martha Maness, Kathleen Miller, Rachel Benson Monroe, Christine Page, Molly Payne, Angelo Pezzote, Ken Sherman, Grace Stevens, Jenn Terner, Angela Wilson, and many others! We have become a vibrant professional network and learning community.

Immense gratitude to the foundations and programs that provided external funding and support for projects that contributed to my professional development, research program, and the writing of this book: the Templeton Foundation, Danielsen Institute at Boston University, Higher Education Center for Alcohol and Other Drug Abuse Prevention (funded by USDOE), Pew Charitable Trusts (through a program grant to William Miller at the University of New Mexico), and the Center for Contemplative Mind in Society (funded and supported by the American Council of Learned Societies, the John Cummings Foundation, and Fetzer Institute).

Finally, deep thanks to Rachel Krause Daniel at Palgrave MacMillan for her commitment to my work, and to Kyra Saniewski, John Stegner, Rachel Crawford, Subasree Sairam, and Lavanya Diaz for invaluable help with the production of this book.

Endorsements from Professional Leaders

Praise for A Person-Centered Approach to Psychospiritual Maturation

'Jared Kass has given new meaning to "higher education" and challenged administrators and educators to reexamine how universities address the unmet needs of students who seek grounding in what it means to be truly human. He creates a holistic, multidimensional, and inspirational view of how every person can develop the capacity to become a fully functioning adult who can contribute to breaking the "chain of pain" that litters all human history. I was truly overwhelmed by the scope of scholarship and wisdom.

As did his mentor, Carl Rogers, Kass urges us and the students in his course to a deeper and broader understanding of the human person. His unique contribution is to ground that vision in current research investigating neuroscience, culture, stress, and the existential search for meaning. His maturational model can empower us to transcend traditions of greed, conflict, social malaise, and depersonalization, and confront the isms that afflict our global society and infect our youth.

Using his biopsychosocial view of development, Kass created a college course of self-inquiry that can guide the interested student along a personal journey toward "psychospiritual maturation." The course addresses important dimensions of growth that can encourage positive behavior changes in specific areas of academic achievement, reduction of self-destructive attitudes and behaviors, and promotion of interpersonal harmony. However, from my perspective, this course offers the opportunity for a more complete transformation that addresses core spiritual and existential crises of students and offers a strong foundation for a life well-lived.

Want to see how it works? The last several sections offer both research data supporting the effectiveness of the course and compelling stories to document the awakening that can occur in this type of course. I cannot wait to get copies for our president and provost.'

—Carlo DiClemente, Ph.D., Professor of Psychology,
University of Maryland. Author, *Addiction and Change:
How Addictions Develop and Addicted People Recover*

'Higher education currently faces two critical challenges: growing numbers of students entering college with psychological and substance abuse issues and the difficulties of creating inclusive campus communities given the cultural, racial and economic divisions in society. Kass presents a scientifically based intervention that can benefit students in all academic disciplines. His curriculum, Know Your Self, is a person-centered pedagogical process that addresses student needs for psychospiritual growth and development. This book is a must read for student affairs professionals who strive to design effective spiritual formation programs and work to create inclusive campus communities, and for faculty who struggle with helping students address their interpersonal and psychological distress and make meaning of a world fraught with strife.'

—Mary Ann Gawelek, Ph.D., President, Lourdes University.
Former Provost, Seton Hill University

'In an era in which many of us feel untethered from traditional moorings, Dr. Kass makes an important contribution with his exploration of psychospiritual development. He examines the importance of psychospiritual connectedness for both individual and community health and well-being. Moreover, he suggests a pragmatic educational framework that can help us all develop the kind of multidimensional resilience that can see us through troubled times.'

—Gregory Fricchione, M.D., Associate Chief of Psychiatry,
Director, Benson-Henry Institute for Mind-Body Medicine,
Massachusetts General Hospital; Mind Body Medical Professor of
Psychiatry, Harvard Medical School. Author, *Compassion and Healing in
Medicine and Society: On the Nature and Use of Attachment Solutions to
Separation Challenges*

'This text will breathe life into institutions of higher education by providing a roadmap to enhanced well-being for students entering adulthood in the midst of intergenerational "chains of pain." Kass provides an insightful, interdisciplinary, campus-based intervention to empower students to break internal and collective chains through the integration of psychology, spirituality, cultural studies, and biology. From contemplative practice and community building to qualitative and

quantitative investigation, this rich text explores topics that are often neglected on campuses—personal development, social justice, and spirituality.'
—Thema Bryant-Davis, Ph.D., Associate Professor of Psychology, Pepperdine University. Author, *Thriving in the Wake of Trauma: A Multicultural Guide*

'Jared Kass extends the rich discoveries of his mentor, Carl Rogers, in education that develops not only knowledge but wisdom and character. This is an idea-provoking book for faculty and student life professionals for helping students mature in ways that address not only their own suffering but that of humanity.'
—William R. Miller, Ph.D., Emeritus Distinguished Professor of Psychology and Psychiatry, University of New Mexico. Author, *Motivational Interviewing: Helping People Change and Lovingkindness*

'This book is an excellent resource for administrators and faculty across disciplines concerned with student development, and committed to transforming higher education. Educational professionals interested in deepening commitments to health, social justice, and peace for all on campus will resonate with Kass' insights and challenges. This project moves higher education beyond engaged participation toward campus life that supports the psychospiritual maturation of students and the building of inclusive communities. This rich and provocative book will inform the field in years to come.'
—The Rev. Sheryl Kujawa-Holbrook, Ed.D., Ph.D., Vice-President for Academic Affairs and Professor of Practical Theology, Claremont School of Theology. Author, *God Beyond Borders: Interreligious Learning among Faith Communities*

'From the walls of the Temple of Apollo in Delphi to classrooms and campuses across the United States, "Know Your Self" speaks ancient and contemporary truths reweaving a holistic vision for teaching and learning that rescues education from centuries of deconstruction and fragmentation. In this remarkable book, Jared Kass offers an approach to education that invites the identity forming narratives of each student into the classroom so that students of diverse identities are recognized in such a way that the learning environment becomes a place of reflection and discovery, of dialogue and interaction, of encounter and conversation. This work is an essential resource for all who teach and learn, and a blessing for all who believe in education as a pathway to personal and social transformation.'
—The Rev. Victor H. Kazanjian, Jr., M.Div., Executive Director, United Religions Initiative; former Dean, Intercultural Studies and Religious and Spiritual Life, Wellesley College. Editor, *Education as Transformation: Religious Pluralism, Spirituality, and a New Vision for Higher Education in America*

'For four decades, Jared Kass has led the teaching and scholarship of mind-body-spirit approaches to training counselors. His book presents an integrative model promoting the maturational value of articulating diverse worldviews, acknowledging psychosocial trauma, and the healing power of community. He shares his unique curriculum for higher education drawing on knowledge from psychology and contemplative studies. Students who take his course attest that it is a life-changing opportunity and demonstrate both heightened personal and intellectual growth.'

—Susan Gere, Ph.D., Director and Professor, Division of Counseling and Psychology, Graduate School of Arts and Social Sciences, Lesley University

'This remarkable prevention-oriented synthesis teaches us skills and attitudes that markedly enhance health and well-being.'

—Herbert Benson, M.D., Distinguished Mind-Body Medical Institute Professor of Medicine, Harvard Medical School. Author, *The Relaxation Response*

'It will be the lucky student who starts college and early on encounters the remarkable Know Your Self curriculum which Jared Kass has proposed in this book. The depth and range of the philosophical and psychological concepts, combined with the use of self-examination and experiential learning, provides a path to maturation that should be a part of all college students' experience.'

—Jimmie Holland, M.D., Wayne E. Chapman Chair in Psychiatric Oncology, Memorial Sloan-Kettering Cancer Center; Professor of Psychiatry, Weill Cornell School of Medicine. Author, *The Human Side of Cancer: Living with Hope, Coping with Uncertainty*

'Jared Kass demonstrates a lifelong passion for the study of person-centered spiritual maturation and provides educators concerned with the psychological resilience of students in higher education, critical insight for mentoring the next generation and the communities they inhabit. His work encourages us to honor the wisdom of contemplative practices from the spiritual traditions to build diverse and inclusive communities where all human potential can flourish.'

—Cheryl A. Giles, Psy.D., Francis Greenwood Peabody Senior Lecturer, Pastoral Care and Counseling, Harvard Divinity School. Editor, *The Arts of Contemplative Care: Pioneering Voices in Buddhist Chaplaincy and Pastoral Work*

'Professor Kass sees the big picture of social—cultural development—in both its pain and promise. He also recognizes the stem cell moment of emerging adulthood in the human life span. This book is an invitation to Higher Education to meet him at that crossroad and to consider a stretch of soul and curriculum.

Grounded in both research and significant practice, this book is an informing, highly-valuable, thought-provoking read.'

—Sharon Daloz Parks, Ph.D.,Whidbey Institute. Author, *Big Questions, Worthy Dreams: Mentoring Emerging Adults in Their Search for Meaning, Purpose, and Faith*

'Life itself is a university is the memorable conclusion of this remarkable book that breathes new spirit into our efforts to understand and promote the development of college students. In this deep and beautifully written work, Kass introduces readers to Know Your Self, an exciting program to facilitate the journey of emerging adults into greater wholeness as physical, psychological, social, and spiritual beings. Built on a foundation of strong science, the wisdom of multiple religious traditions, and Kass' own work with Carl Rogers, Herbert Benson, interfaith dialogue, and the lived experiences of many college students, Know Your Self deserves wide dissemination within institutes of higher education.'

—Kenneth Pargament, Ph.D., Professor Emeritus, Department of Psychology, Bowling Green State University. Editor-in-Chief, *APA Handbook of Psychology, Religion, and Spirituality;* Author, *Spiritually Integrated Psychotherapy: Understanding and Addressing the Sacred*

Contents

Acknowledgements — vii

Endorsements from Professional Leaders — xi

Part I Conceptual Foundations—Person-Centered Psychospiritual Maturation: A Missing Ingredient in Higher Education

1 Prologue to an Experiment in Higher Education: Mentoring Psychospiritual Maturation, Breaking Humanity's *Chain of Pain* — 3

2 Recognizing Student Needs for Psychospiritual Development: A Preliminary Case Study — 21

3 Higher Education: Model for Constructive Change? Or Mirror of Humanity's *Chain of Pain*? — 33

4 My Professional Journey: Becoming a Person-Centered Mentor with a Psychospiritual and Social Justice Orientation — 55

5	Person-Centered Psychospiritual Maturation: A Multidimensional Model	87

Part II Research Project—Mentoring Psychological Resilience and Inclusive Community Through Person-Centered Psychospiritual Maturation

6	The *Know Your Self* Curriculum: Overview and Research Results	133
7	Establishing Foundations for Person-Centered Learning and Inclusive Community-Building: Group Case Study #1	155
8	Approaching Sociocultural Differences and Interpersonal Conflict as Catalysts for Psychospiritual Growth: Group Case Study #2	181
9	From Self-Regulation to Psychospiritual Exploration: An Introduction to the Deep Structure of Contemplative Mind: Group Case Study #3	203
10	Individual Case Studies of Psychospiritual Maturation: Autobiographical Inquiry and the Deep Wisdom of Contemplative Mind	225

Students Examine
Social-Emotional Impairments to Academic Performance	226
Procrastination	226
Pressure to Overachieve and Somatic Symptoms of Stress	231
Health-Compromising Attitudes and Behaviors	238
Unhealthy Diet	238
Cigarette Smoking	245
Alcohol Dependence	252
Negative Body Image and Depression	258
Impaired Relational Skills	266
Sexual Promiscuity	266
Fear of Intimate Relationships	274

Existential Struggles and Spiritual Alienation   285
   Existential Coping with a Chronic Illness   285
   Alienation from God and Religious Tradition   295
Concluding Analysis   306
   Growth in the Five Dimensions of Psychospiritual Maturation   306

11   The Learning Community: An Inclusive Environment for Person-Centered Psychospiritual Growth: Group Case Study #4   309

Part III   Discussion of Results—Applications of the *Know Your Self* Curriculum In Prevention-Oriented Mental Health Practice and Higher Education

12   The *Know Your Self* Curriculum: An Effective Template for Mentoring Psychological Resilience and Culturally-Inclusive Community   335
   Implications for Prevention-Oriented Mental Health Practice   335

13   Person-Centered Psychospiritual Maturation: Strengthening Campus Cultures of Health, Social Justice, and Peace   355
   Implications for Engaged Learning in Higher Education   355

Index   373

PART I

—Conceptual Foundations—
Person-Centered Psychospiritual Maturation:
A Missing Ingredient in Higher Education

CHAPTER 1

Prologue to an Experiment in Higher Education: Mentoring Psychospiritual Maturation, Breaking Humanity's *Chain of Pain*

Over the past three decades, higher education has challenged itself to cultivate campus cultures of health, social justice, and peace. Since Ernest Boyer's seminal research on campus life (Boyer 1990), it has become evident that many students experience psychological distress, behavioral dysregulation, and lack of community: factors that undermine their well-being, academic success, and a positive campus culture (AAC&U 2002; Swaner 2005). But efforts to rectify these issues have had limited success (ACHA 2014).

As a professor of counseling and psychology, I will offer an explanation: higher education has not recognized student needs for *person-centered* learning that facilitates *psychospiritual maturation* during young adulthood. We expect students to undertake difficult programs of study and participate capably in culturally-inclusive campus communities without mentoring psychological resilience and interpersonal skills necessary to navigate this difficult terrain. Further, we often assume that students are the cause of their problems, rather than recognizing that their behaviors mirror societal issues.

This book describes a curriculum that I have developed, *Know Your Self*. The curriculum mentors a person-centered approach to psychospiritual maturation that helps students address these problematic issues. The book also presents research demonstrating the effectiveness of this curriculum. Student Life professionals will find this curriculum relevant to their co-curricular work with students. However, I will argue that psychospiritual development must become a core element of academic activity, taught by engaged faculty, if we hope to transform our campuses into model cultures of health, social justice, and peace.

This orientation to my work as a teacher begins each fall, when I meet with my new academic advisees as a group. The primary purpose of their studies, I explain, is to develop skills and knowledge essential for a meaningful career and fruitful life. As emerging adults, they have entered a stage of autonomy in which they must learn to think, feel, and act for themselves (Arnett 2000, 2015; Parks 1986, 2000). Building foundations for a productive career is an essential step toward their new autonomous identity.

Breaking Humanity's *Chain of Pain*: A Deeper Purpose for Higher Education

At the same time, I explain, there is a deeper purpose to their studies in higher education. Throughout history, human beings have been locked in a traumatic *chain of pain*: a tragic cycle, passed from one generation to another, in which hatred, violence, and destructive behavior—toward self and others—has disrupted families, communities, and the very structures of the society in which we live (Kass 2007b). This relentless nightmare is so pervasive and profound that people sometimes wonder whether humanity—and perhaps life itself—are fatally flawed. How can it be—during every historical period, in every major culture—that greed, self-serving elites, patriarchy, racism, heterosexism, socioeconomic stratification, the willingness to dominate others (even through brutal violence), and self-destructive behaviors fueled by alcohol, drugs, and despair—have played such a chilling role in human civilizations? Are we doomed to repeat our chain of pain ad infinitum, or is there a way to interrupt this pernicious process?

As an ethical foundation for students' career and personal development, we will investigate humanity's chain of pain, examining how it replicates itself. We will also explore how to break its tenacious grip on society and our personal lives. For what is the value of a successful career if it actually perpetuates humanity's chain of pain? In whatever career niche students establish, it is possible and vital to apply skillful means toward breaking this self-replicating cycle.

But it would be naïve to think we are poised to succeed. The chain of pain has replicative mechanisms that run deep, affecting every individual and social system. A multidimensional analysis of its replicative mechanisms is needed, utilizing knowledge from multiple disciplines. To develop an intellectual foundation for this work, we must examine five dimensions of self and society that are consistently dysregulated by the chain of pain (Kass 2015):

1. **Bio-Behavioral:** Neural and physiological pathways regulating metabolic processes through which people respond to challenges, stress, and perceived threat
2. **Cognitive-Sociocultural:** Cognitive schema and sociocultural identity narratives that condition perceptions of self and *other* and legitimize systemic social dominance hierarchies
3. **Social-Emotional:** Templates of attachment that shape the capacity for constructive interpersonal relationships, families, and community/organizational networks
4. **Existential-Spiritual:** Templates of attachment through which we experience and derive meaning from our relationship with the cosmos
5. **Integrative Worldview Formation:** The synthesizing lens through which we perceive and respond to life events and people

To understand the replicative effects across these five dimensions, we will utilize the social sciences, historical and political studies, literature and the arts, and bio-cultural evolutionary neuroscience. Further, we will use the tools of science (critical analysis, hypothesis formation, qualitative inquiry, and quantitative hypothesis testing) to assess efforts to break the effects.

At the same time, we must engage in an introspective self-inquiry process to understand the complex ways our personal behavior is enmeshed in this repetitive cycle, suffers from it, and perpetuates it. During this reparative learning, we will examine our lives and behavior across these same five dimensions. I call this engaged learning process *person-centered psychospiritual maturation*. It is the focus of my prevention-oriented research program on psychological and social well-being, and I invite students to collaborate with me in this important area of study.

Part I of this book presents a conceptual rationale for engaged learning in higher education that mentors person-centered psychospiritual maturation. Part II reports results from empirical testing of the *Know Your Self* curriculum: a quasi-experimental, mixed-methods study with statistical and qualitative data (Kass et al. 2015). The results include illustrative case studies in which students developed psychological resilience and inclusive community-building skills: essential elements for academic success, civic participation in a multicultural society, and institutional efforts to cultivate an inclusive campus culture of health, social justice, and peace. These results demonstrate that it is possible to mentor students in person-centered psychospiritual growth responsibly and effectively, without imposing or privileging a specific existential, philosophical, or religious belief system.

CARL ROGERS: CONCEPTUAL AND METHODOLOGICAL INFLUENCES

This project is a result of my formative professional work with Dr. Carl Rogers, from 1976–1981, on the Person-Centered Approach Project (Rogers 1980b; Rogers et al. 1978). His contributions to education and counseling are profound, explicating interpersonal conditions that facilitate learning and developmental growth (Kirschenbaum 2007).

Subsequently, person-centered theory received valuable criticism and contributions from other psychotherapeutic perspectives, including: (a) multicultural and feminist theory (Ballou et al. 2002; Brown and Ballou 1992; Sue and Sue 1981); (b) neuroscientific models of the stress response and empathic attunement that demonstrated the clinical importance of cognitive-behavioral methods and psychodynamic attachment theory (Ainsworth 1985; Beck 1976; Benson et al. 1969; Cannon and Rosenblueth 1937; Porges 2011; Schore 2001); (c) trauma and peace psychology (Herman 1997; Kelman 1997; Mattson 2003; Solomon and Siegel 2003; van der Kolk 1994); and, (d) contemplative psychology (Germer and Siegel 2012; Kabat-Zinn 1990; Kass 1991; Newberg and D'Aquili 1998; Pargament et al. 1992; Rama et al. 1976).

The multidimensional model of person-centered psychospiritual maturation presented in this book incorporates these critiques and contributions, contributing to ongoing refinements in person-centered theory (Bozarth 1998; Cain and Seeman 2002; Cooper et al. 2007; Joseph and Worsley 2005; Tudor and Worrall 2006) and reformulation of humanistic psychology's role in social transformation (Proctor et al. 2006; Serlin 2011). Locating person-centered psychospiritual maturation at the relational interface between self, cosmos, human micro-systems, and socio-cultural macro-systems, this model highlights rigid hierarchy and social stratification as destructive forces that magnify humanity's chain of pain

(Kass 2007b). Further, it presents psychospiritual growth *within culturally- and religiously- diverse community* as an antidote to these destructive forces. The ability to be in community with the *other*, managing life's existential, interpersonal, and intergroup tensions with resilience, empathic attunement to others, and civility is a central feature of person-centered psychospiritual maturation (Hoshmand and Kass 2003).

THE *KNOW YOUR SELF* CURRICULUM

This *person-specific* process of psychospiritual development is undertaken in learning communities with students from diverse cultural identities and belief systems (including secular humanism), exploring areas of learning and growth necessary for the well-being of self and society (Kass 2007b, 2015; Kass and Lennox 2005). Students engage in the following activities.

Psychospiritual Self-Inquiry: Through a blend of student-directed and faculty-structured learning, students engage in intellectual studies, critical analysis, and introspective self-reflection regarding their life histories, family systems, religious upbringing, sociocultural identities, social position in society's stratified hierarchies, and existential-spiritual belief systems. They explore how these personal and sociocultural factors impact their way of being in the world and identify root causes of their destructive behaviors toward self and others. This introspective process is concretized through written self-inquiry essays, in conjunction with classroom-based experiential learning. These activities catalyze a person-specific process of psychospiritual growth that modifies distorted perceptions that have shaped and legitimized destructive behaviors.

Contemplative Practice: Students develop a meditation practice that facilitates their consolidation of self-regulation skills and psychospiritual exploration into the deep structure of consciousness. Students learn to integrate three generic approaches: mental concentration, mindfulness, and receptive awareness to intuitive insights.

Contemplative practices originated in the world's spiritual traditions, and the curriculum explores them through multiple lenses. First, it employs a cultural studies approach to organized religion: critiquing exclusivist claims for privileged access to the Divine and selective use of religious texts by controlling social dominance hierarchies for sociopolitical agendas (Moore 2007). Second, it reviews neuroscience research examining correlates of contemplative experience with metabolic processes in the brain (Cahn and Polich 2006; D'Aquili and Newberg 1999; Davidson 1976; Kass and Trantham 2014; Lazar et al. 2000; Lutz et al. 2004). Third, it explores contemplative spiritual experiences through the transpersonal lens of the *Perennial Philosophy* (Huxley 1945; Nasr 1997; Schuon 1984; Teasdale 1999). Ralph Waldo Emerson articulated this robust, nonsectarian philosophy of the human spirit in the United States. It identifies a shared cosmological core in the world's spiritual traditions: a transcendent Ground of Being immanently present at the root of human consciousness. This Transcendentalist philosophy is unequivocally committed to social justice because every person is considered a spark of the Divine (Emerson 1992). This inclusive lens has roots in neo-Platonic philosophy that influenced the development of Christian, Jewish, and Muslim spirituality; contemplative methods and ethical *dharma* teachings of Buddhist and Hindu psychology; and spiritual panentheism among indigenous peoples (Armstrong 2006; O'Brien 1964; Smith 1991; Spretnak 1991). It is currently expressed through multifaith initiatives for cooperation and social justice (Angilella and Ziajka 1998; Conde-Frazier et al. 2004; Eck 2001; Kujawa-Holbrook 2014; Tutu 1994). As students explore the spiritual traditions through these secular humanist and transpersonal lenses, they develop an existential-spiritual worldview congruent with their life experiences and personal belief systems. The curriculum does not privilege either lens. Instead, it fosters development of an internal locus of existential meaning-making that includes the ability to respect the meaning-systems of diverse others.

Experiential Community-Building: Students learn to build inclusive community with peers from diverse cultural backgrounds and belief systems. These communities become an in vivo laboratory for refining interpersonal skills and cultural competencies essential to individual and social well-being. Community-building includes discussions about their self-inquiry work, interactive learning about self and other, and arts-based activities that promote self-expression and group cohesion. For example, during group singing, students develop a more empowered individual voice, while experiencing polyphonic harmonies that emerge when diverse voices sing together. While examining their interpersonal conflict styles, students learn to approach these tensions as potential catalysts for psychospiritual growth and develop restorative dialogue skills.

Learning Outcomes

During this multifaceted learning process, students identify specific ways in which humanity's chain of pain dysregulates the five dimensions of self and society. In addition, they learn how person-centered psycho-spiritual maturation can provide reparative and prevention-oriented growth, through engaged learning that initiates growth in these same five dimensions:

1. **Bio-Behavioral:** *Neural and physiological pathways regulating metabolic processes through which people respond to challenges, stress, and perceived threat*

Students learn to recognize our most primitive and ancient responses to the aspects of life that frighten us. As soon as we become fearful, we become *aggressive* (fight) or *avoidant* (flight). When we fear for our lives (or essential aspects of our identities), these two responses escalate into *vicious attack* or *profound self-numbing*. When people do not monitor their self-protective instincts, their stress reactions can erupt in ways destructive to self and others. For humanity to mature, every person, sociocultural identity group, and working unit of our social systems must learn to monitor and regulate these reactive tendencies. Periodically, "fighting" still serves a purpose: protection against bullying aggressors. But we must develop judicious and mature ways to solve the psychosocial problems that create bullies, because violence inevitably produces more violence. At the same time, the need to regulate our survival instincts does not imply the need to repress natural emotions such as anger and grief. They are important signals of distress that we must learn to respect in ourselves and others (see Social-Emotional Dimension). Further, we must recognize the danger of *avoidant* and *self-numbing* tendencies. Alcohol and drug dependence are obvious examples. But the status-conferring distractions of technological society present equally dangerous examples: addiction to screen time, gaming, and television that reinforce avoidance of developmental challenges and subvert emotionally-connective activities; enmeshment in a competitive consumer economy that dulls moral awareness of socioeconomic disparities and suffering. Thus, both avoidant and aggressive behaviors contribute to humanity's chain of pain. Self-monitoring and self-regulation of these stress-coping behaviors are essential steps in the process of person-centered psychospiritual maturation.

2. **Cognitive-Sociocultural:** *Cognitive schema and sociocultural identity narratives that condition perceptions of self and other and legitimize systemic social dominance hierarchies*

Students learn to recognize our most primitive and ancient form of social organization: group-based social dominance hierarchies (Sidanius and Kurzban 2013; Sidanius and Pratto 1999). Hierarchical networks evolved in mammals and primates as group-based survival strategies before humans evolved. We inherited them through bio-cultural mechanisms of the evolutionary process. Initially, this rigid form of social organization constituted an effective attachment function: enabling humans to build early communities and civilizations. However, as we evolved, developing psychological needs for individuation, positive social identity, and self-determination, social dominance hierarchies became corrosive: creating patriarchy, racism, social class, and other toxic forms of exclusivism that grant privilege to the few and oppress the many. For humanity to mature, every person, sociocultural identity group, and working unit of our social systems must recognize that that these rigid structures are corrosive to the maturation of human culture. Notable political documents (e.g., Universal Declaration of Human Rights, Constitution of the United States) provide beacons for this maturational direction. Nonetheless, during perceived threat, we instinctively regress to rigid hierarchy, seeking powerful leaders to organize the protective pyramid that has been humankind's traditional fortress, even when survival for those at the bottom becomes tenuous. When we regress to this pattern, cycles of violence and inequality are perpetuated. In this cognitive-sociocultural dimension, students learn that human systems become safer, stronger, and more successful when we transcend the corrosive effects of group-based social dominance hierarchies

3. **Social-Emotional:** *Templates of attachment that shape the capacity for constructive interpersonal relationships, families, and community/organizational networks*

Humanity's chain of pain subverts secure relational attachments essential to individual and social well-being. Even if we understand its corrosive effects intellectually, we still require emotional self-awareness, healing, and interpersonal skill-building to establish constructive personal relationships, communities, and social systems. This begins with emotional awareness. Expression of afflictive emotions (anger and grief) are natural signals of distress; they require constructive attention. Suppression creates psychological fragmentation that ultimately erupts destructively. When we learn to express and receive these strong emotions constructively, our relational skills and ability to resolve conflicts equitably increase. This is a necessary reparative step toward achieving the secure attachments and peaceful communities so vital to society.

4. **Existential-Spiritual:** *Templates of attachment through which we experience and derive meaning from our relationship with the cosmos*

Humanity's chain of pain has conditioned many to accept a cynical, hopeless, chaotic worldview. Its relentless presence convinces us that life is brutal, meaningless, and random. Further, it advertises itself as an inherent aspect of life, undermining our sense of ethical and moral responsibility. As they analyze the existential-spiritual dimension of self, students explore the impact of humanity's chain of pain on self and society, recognizing distorting perceptions it creates about life. Through psychospiritual self-inquiry, contemplative practice, and inclusive community-building, they reduce their socially-conditioned agitation by cultivating internal composure. In addition, realizing that humanity's chain of pain can be broken through psychospiritual maturation, they develop a more optimistic understanding of life's difficulties as an emergent "curriculum" for human maturation at the individual and systemic levels.

Scientists must recognize that we inadvertently reinforce a chaotic worldview by implying that evolution proceeds *only* through a non-deterministic process of random mutations. Current bio-cultural evolutionary theory reminds us that niche construction and trait selection pressures play an equally important role (Lende and Downey 2012). These mechanisms produce incremental steps in bio-cultural complexity through selection of increasingly sophisticated biochemical and socio-cultural forms of *attachment* (Fricchione 2011). This process suggests a *formative tendency* in bio-cultural evolution through which humans are developing increased capacities for self-awareness, individuation, collaborative social organization, and mature behavior (Rogers 1980b). These indications of a formative tendency suggest a cosmological coherence that could facilitate meaningful dialogue between a secular humanist worldview and a mature spiritual worldview that incorporates evolutionary science.

For example, as bio-cultural evolutionary neuroscience identified emergent human capacities, it became clear that the human cerebral cortex has developed a complex array of self-reflective capacities, employing cognitive, affective, somatic, and intuitive modes of knowing. As psychology assimilates contemplative practices from the spiritual traditions, we have realized that the individualized ego is the externally-oriented aspect of human consciousness, and that we have only begun to explore the interior dimensions of consciousness. Roadmaps of the psyche from every tradition suggest that contemplatives experience a transpersonal consciousness that links the individual ego with a Ground of Being. While this subjective experience cannot be confirmed objectively, growing evidence in the social sciences suggests that these contemplative experiences enhance psychological resilience and pro-social behavior (Allport and Ross 1967; Bergin et al. 1987; Hood 1995; Kass 1991; Paloutzian and Park 2013; Pargament 1997). This evidence offers another potential bridge between a secular humanist and mature spiritual worldview that views this transpersonal dimension as an enfolded, implicate dimension of existence (Bohm 1980; Kass 2007a).

This study demonstrates the potential for maturational growth in the existential-spiritual dimension of self in a responsible manner that does not impose a particular philosophical or religious belief system, helping students consolidate an internal locus of existential-meaning, psychological well-being, and pro-social capacities to build culturally-inclusive community. It also illustrates how growth in the existential-spiritual dimension of self can help students and society overcome the cynical, disruptive worldview perpetuated by humanity's chain of pain.

The Confidence in Life and Self that emerges during person-centered psychospiritual maturation can be described as *secure existential attachment* (Kass 2007b, 2015). In this internal state of optimistic composure, existence itself is not experienced as an adversary. This resilient worldview can be operative while people remain fully responsive to human suffering, and fully engaged in efforts to break humanity's chain of pain. This construct synthesizes Paul Tillich's important concept *ontological insecurity* (Tillich 1952) with John Bowlby's and Mary Ainsworth's formulation of *secure attachment* (Ainsworth 1985; Bowlby 1969 #1083). Further, it provides a meaningful extension of Erik Erikson's term, *integrity*, the mature stage of lifespan development (Erikson 1963).

5. **Integrative Worldview Formation:** *The synthesizing lens through which we perceive and respond to life events and people*

As the previous discussion suggests, the resilience necessary to break the chain of pain requires *confidence in life and self*. As growth in the bio-behavioral, cognitive-sociocultural, social-emotional, and existential-spiritual dimensions of self proceeds, integrative learning takes place that consolidates this worldview. The prefrontal cortex is the executive center of this integrative learning, through robust neuronal networks that link multiple areas of the cortical hemispheres with the limbic system and brain stem (Siegel 2007). During this integrative growth process, people develop *confidence in self* through experiential confirmation that they have the capacity to break personal links in their chain of pain. They develop *confidence in life* through confirmation that life challenges can be resolved most effectively when reframed as an emergent "curriculum" for the maturation of self and society. Rather than losing confidence in life, they can conceptualize particular triggering issues as indication of the need for maturational growth in those specific circumstances.

This summary of learning outcomes in five dimensions of self and society provides an operant definition of person-centered psychospiritual maturation, explaining its salience as an antidote to humanity's chain of pain and its relevance as a reparative and prevention-oriented learning process for young adults in the context of higher education.

My Professional Background

I have been engaged in this work for nearly four decades. In addition to developing, teaching, and evaluating the *Know Your Self* curriculum on my local campus, I gained a national perspective on campus issues while serving as a Center Associate (2000–2002) with the *Higher Education Center on Alcohol, Other Drug Abuse, and Violence Prevention*, funded by the U.S. Department of Education. In addition to providing training in environmental management, this position enabled me to review promising initiatives that were being developed by the National Association of Student Personnel Administrators (Keeling 2004), the Association of American Colleges and Universities (AAC&U 2007), and Bringing Theory to Practice (Harward 2012; Swaner 2005). However, my commitment to person-centered learning and psychospiritual maturation has deeper roots in three areas of my professional development.

From 1976–1981, I worked closely with Carl Rogers as a staff member of the Person-Centered Approach Project (Rogers 1980a; Rogers et al. 1978). Our staff facilitated person-centered community-building, applying Rogers' therapeutic methods of interpersonal attunement as a foundation for group cohesion and individual learning. This project helped me refine person-centered teaching skills and group facilitation expertise for inclusive community-building. In addition, Natalie Rogers, Maria Villas-Boas Bowen, and I incorporated the expressive arts and meditation into the community-building process (Kass 1985). These experiential learning methods are foundational in the *Know Your Self* curriculum.

From 1985–1991, I conducted research with Herbert Benson, as a Visiting Lecturer on Medicine in the Section on Behavioral Medicine, Beth Israel-New England Deaconess Hospitals, Harvard Medical School. I was the principal investigator developing and validating two research scales. The *Inventory of Positive Psychological Attitudes (IPPA)* measures a resilient worldview, Confidence in Life and Self (CLS) (Kass 1998; Kass et al. 1991a). The *Index of Core Spiritual Experiences (INSPIRIT)* quantifies subjective spiritual experiences commonly reported during meditation (Kass 1995; Kass et al. 1991b). We used these scales to investigate potential relationships between contemplative spirituality and well-being. Later, I combined them in the *Spirituality and Resilience Assessment Packet* (www.resilientworldview.org), which is used in clinical and psychoeducational programs (Kass 2000). My work in Benson's pioneering clinic, as I will describe, facilitated my incorporation of cognitive-behavioral, trauma-sensitive, contemplative, and mind-body learning methods into the *Know Your Self* curriculum.

From 1989–2007, I participated in the Boston Clergy and Religious Leaders Group for Interfaith Dialogue (Eck and Pierce 1998). This social justice initiative provided a forum for religious leaders and social activists to engage in interfaith dialogue, exploring challenges faced by marginalized communities. While organized religion has a long history of destructive impact, I remain committed to its potential value as a resource for healing society's fragmentation. This project offered many opportunities to develop skills facilitating interfaith dialogue. I was invited to join the steering committee in 1991, eventually becoming coordinator. We explored multiple aspects of systemic injustice, including social privilege, patriarchy, racism, and the complicity of our religious traditions in many forms of injustice. We also explored *spirituality* as a call to social justice and a resource for psychospiritual resilience when confronting humanity's chain of pain. This project deepened my interest in the Perennial Philosophy, and helped me formulate key elements of the curriculum.

These projects provided conceptual and methodological foundations for my work facilitating person-centered psychospiritual maturation in higher education. As the research data and case studies will show, this learning process helps students develop psychological resilience and culturally-inclusive community, promoting a campus culture of health, social justice, and peace. In the concluding chapter, I will reiterate the need for faculty to play a central role in these efforts. I will further propose that the *Know Your Self* curriculum become the foundation for a multidisciplinary academic concentration that helps students develop the knowledge and psychospiritual maturation necessary to break humanity's chain of pain. A concentration of this kind will provide training relevant to multiple academic and professional disciplines.

References

AAC&U. (2002). *Greater expectations: A new vision for learning as a nation goes to college*. Washington, DC: Association of American Colleges and Universities.

AAC&U. (2007). *College learning for the new global century: Report from the National Leadership Council for Liberal Education and America's Promise*. Washington, DC: American Association of Colleges and Universities.

ACHA. (2014). *American College Health Association: National college health assessment II, 2014 executive summary*. Hanover, MD: American College Health Association.

Ainsworth, M. D. (1985). Attachments across the life span. *Bulletin New York Academy of Medicine, 61*(9), 792–812.

Allport, G. W., & Ross, J. M. (1967). Personal religious orientation and prejudice. *Journal of Personality and Social Psychology, 5*(4), 432–443.

Angilella, J. T., & Ziajka, A. (Eds.). (1998). *Rediscovering justice: Awakening world faiths to address world issues*. San Francisco, CA: University of San Francisco, Association of Jesuit University Presses.

Armstrong, K. (2006). *The great transformation: The beginning of our religious traditions*. New York, NY: Anchor Books.

Arnett, J. J. (2000). Emerging adulthood: A theory of development from the late teens through the twenties. *American Psychologist, 55*(5), 469–480.

Arnett, J. J. (2015). *Emerging adulthood: The winding road from the late teens through the twenties* (2nd ed.). Oxford, UK: Oxford University Press.

Ballou, M., Matsumoto, A., & Wagner, M. (2002). Toward a feminist ecological theory of human nature. In M. Ballou & L. S. Brown (Eds.), *Rethinking mental health and disorders: Feminist perspectives*. New York, NY: Guilford Press.

Beck, A. (1976). *Cognitive therapy and emotional disorders*. New York, NY: International Universities Press.

Benson, H., Herd, J. A., Morse, W. H., & Kelleher, R. T. (1969). Behavioral induction of arterial hypertension and its reversal. *American Journal of Physiology, 217*(4), 30–34.

Bergin, A. E., Masters, K. S., & Richards, P. S. (1987). Religiousness and mental health reconsidered: A study of an intrinsically religious sample. *Journal of Counseling Psychology, 34,* 197–204.

Bohm, D. (1980). *Wholeness and the implicate order*. New York, NY: Routledge.

Bowlby, J. (1969). *Attachment and loss* (Vol. 1: Attachment). New York, NY: Basic Books.

Boyer, E. L. (1990). *Campus life: In search of community*. Princeton, NJ: The Carnegie Foundation for the Advancement of Teaching.

Bozarth, J. (1998). *Person-centered therapy*. Ross-on-Wye, UK: PCCS Books.

Brown, L., & Ballou, M. (Eds.). (1992). *Personality and psychopathology: Feminist reappraisals*. New York, NY: Guilford Press.

Cahn, B. R., & Polich, J. (2006). Meditation states and traits: EEG, ERP, and neuroimaging studies. *Psychological Bulletin, 132*(2), 180–211.

Cain, D. J., & Seeman, J. (Eds.). (2002). *Humanistic psychotherapies: Handbook of research and practice*. Washington, DC: American Psychological Association.

Cannon, W. B., & Rosenblueth, A. (1937). *Autonomic neuro-effector systems*. New York, NY: Macmillan.

Conde-Frazier, E., Kang, S. S., & Parrett, G. A. (2004). *A many colored kingdom: Multicultural dynamics for spiritual formation*. Grand Rapids, MI: Baker Academic.

Cooper, M., O'Hara, M., Schmid, P. F., & Wyatt, G. (2007). *The handbook of person-centered psychotherapy and counselling*. Houndsmill, UK: Palgrave.

D'Aquili, E., & Newberg, A. B. (1999). *The mystical experience: Probing the biology of religious experience*. Minneapolis, MN: Fortress Press.

Davidson, J. M. (1976). The physiology of meditation and mystical states of consciousness. *Perspectives in Biology and Medicine, 19*(Spring), 345–379.

Eck, D. L. (2001). *A new religious America: How a "Christian country" has become the most religiously diverse nation*. San Francisco, CA: HarperSanFrancisco.

Eck, D. L., & Pierce, E. J. (Eds.). (1998). *World religions in Boston: A guide to communities and resources* (3rd ed.). Cambridge, MA: The Pluralism Project, Harvard University.

Emerson, R. W. (1992). *Selected writings of Ralph Waldo Emerson*. New York, NY: Modern Library.
Erikson, E. (1963). *Childhood and society* (2nd ed.). New York, NY: W.W. Norton.
Fricchione, G. L. (2011). *Compassion and healing in medicine and society: On the nature and use of attachment solutions to separation challenges.* Baltimore, MD: Johns Hopkins University Press.
Germer, C. K., & Siegel, R. D. (Eds.). (2012). *Wisdom and compassion in psychotherapy: Deepening mindfulness in clinical practice.* New York, NY: Guilford.
Harward, D. W. (Ed.). (2012). *Civic provocations*. Washington, DC: Bringing Theory to Practice.
Herman, J. (1997). *Trauma and recovery*. New York, NY: Basic Books.
Hood, R. (Ed.). (1995). *Handbook of religious experience*. Birmingham, AL: Religious Education Press.
Hoshmand, L. T., & Kass, J. D. (2003). Conceptual and action frameworks for peace. *International Journal for Advancement of Counseling, 25*(4), 205–213.
Huxley, A. (1945). *The perennial philosophy*. New York, NY: Harper Brothers.
Joseph, S., & Worsley, R. (Eds.). (2005). *Person-centered psychopathology: A positive psychology of mental health.* Ross-on-Wye, UK: PCCS Books.
Kabat-Zinn, J. (1990). *Full catastrophe living*. New York, NY: Dell Publishing.
Kass, J. D. (1985). The use of person-centered expressive therapies in the health professions. *Brennpunkt, Schweizerische Gesellschaft für Gesprachspsychotherapie und Person-Zentrierte Beratung, 24,* 20–33.
Kass, J. D. (1991). Contributions of religious experience to psychological and physical well-being: Research evidence and an explanatory model. *The Caregiver (College of Chaplains), 8*(4), 4–11.
Kass, J. D. (1995). Contributions of religious experience to psychological and physical well-being: Research evidence and an explanatory model. In L. Vandecreek (Ed.), *Spiritual needs and pastoral services: Readings in research* (pp. 189–213). Decatur, GA: Journal of Pastoral Care Publications.
Kass, J. D. (1998). The Inventory of Positive Psychological Attitudes: Measuring attitudes which buffer stress and facilitate primary prevention. In C. Zalaquett & R. Wood (Eds.), *Evaluating stress: A book of resources* (Vol. 2, pp. 153–184). Lanham, MD: University Press of America.
Kass, J. D. (2000). *Manual for the Spirituality and Resilience Assessment Packet* (Version 4.3). Cambridge, MA: Institute for Contemplative Education, Greenhouse, Inc., A Human Development Resource Center. www.resilientworldview.org.
Kass, J. D. (2007a). God images as indwelling spirit and core foundation of self. In P. Hegy (Ed.), *What do we imagine God to be? The function of "God images" in our lives*. Lewiston, NY: The Edwin Mellen Press.

Kass, J. D. (2007b). Spiritual maturation: A developmental resource for resilience, well-being, and peace. *Journal of Pedagogy, Pluralism, and Practice, 12*(Summer), 56–64.

Kass, J. D. (2015). Person-centered spiritual maturation: A multidimensional model. *Journal of Humanistic Psychology, 55*(1), 53–76. doi:10.1177/0022167814525261.

Kass, J. D., & Lennox, S. (2005). Emerging models of spiritual development: A foundation for mature, moral, and health-promoting behavior. In W. R. Miller & H. Delaney (Eds.), *Judeo-Christian perspectives on psychology: Human nature, motivation, and change*. Washington, DC: American Psychological Association.

Kass, J. D., & Trantham, S. M. (2014). Perspectives from clinical neuroscience: Mindfulness and therapeutic use of the arts. In L. Rappaport (Ed.), *Mindfulness and the arts therapies: Theory and practice*. London, UK: Jessica Kingsley.

Kass, J. D., Baxter, J., & Lennox, S. (2015). Mentoring person-centered spiritual maturation: A quasi-experimental mixed methods study of a contemplative self-inquiry curriculum. *Journal of Humanistic Psychology, 55*(4), 474–503. doi:10.1177/0022167814547578.

Kass, J. D., Friedman, R., Leserman, J., Caudill, M., Zuttermeister, P., & Benson, H. (1991a). An inventory of positive psychological attitudes with potential relevance to health outcomes. *Behavioral Medicine, 17*(3), 121–129.

Kass, J. D., Friedman, R., Leserman, J., Zuttermeister, P., & Benson, H. (1991b). Health outcomes and a new measure of spiritual experience. *Journal for the Scientific Study of Religion, 30*(2), 203–211.

Keeling, R. P. (2004). *Learning reconsidered: A campus-wide focus on the student experience*. Washington, DC: American College Personnel Association (ACPA)—National Association of Student Personnel Administrators (NASPA).

Kelman, H. C. (1997). Social-psychological dimensions of international conflict. In I. W. Zartman & J. L. Rasmussen (Eds.), *Peacemaking in international conflict: Methods and techniques*. Washington, DC: United States Institute of Peace Press.

Kirschenbaum, H. (2007). *The life and work of Carl Rogers*. Ross-on-Wye, UK: PCCS Books.

Kujawa-Holbrook, S. A. (2014). *God beyond borders: Interreligious learning among faith communities*. Eugene, OR: Pickwick Publications.

Lazar, S. W., Bush, G., Gollub, R. L., Fricchione, G. L., Khalsa, G., & Benson, H. (2000). Functional brain mapping of the relaxation response and meditation. *NeuroReport, 11*(7), 1581–1585.

Lende, D. H., & Downey, G. (Eds.). (2012). *The encultured brain: An introduction to neuroanthropology*. Cambridge, MA: MIT Press.

Lutz, A., Greischar, L. L., Rawlings, N. B., Ricard, M., & Davidson, R. J. (2004). Long-term meditators self-induce high amplitude gamma synchrony during mental practice. *Neuroscience, 101*(46), 16369–16373.
Mattson, M. P. (Ed.). (2003). *Neurobiology of aggression: Understanding and preventing violence.* Totowa, NJ: Humana Press.
Moore, D. L. (2007). *Overcoming religious illiteracy: A cultural studies approach to the study of religion in secondary education.* New York, NY: Palgrave Macmillan.
Nasr, S. H. (1997). *Man and nature: The spiritual crisis of modern man.* Chicago, IL: KAZI Publications.
Newberg, A. B., & D'Aquili, E. G. (1998). The neuropsychology of spiritual experience. In H. G. Koenig (Ed.), *Handbook of religion and mental health.* San Diego, CA: Academic Press.
O'Brien, E. (Ed.). (1964). *The essential Plotinus.* Indianapolis, IN: Hackett Publishing.
Paloutzian, R. F., & Park, C. L. (Eds.). (2013). *Handbook of the psychology of religion and spirituality* (2nd ed.). New York, NY: Guilford Press.
Pargament, K. I. (1997). *The psychology of religion and coping: Theory, research, practice.* New York, NY: Guilford.
Pargament, K. I., Maton, K. I., & Hess, R. E. (Eds.). (1992). *Religion and prevention in mental health: Research, vision, and action.* Binghamton, NY: Haworth Press.
Parks, S. D. (1986). *The critical years: The young adult search for a faith to live by.* San Francisco, CA: Harper and Row.
Parks, S. D. (2000). *Big questions, worthy dreams: Mentoring young adults in their search for meaning, purpose, and faith.* San Francisco, CA: Jossey-Bass.
Porges, S. W. (2011). *The polyvagal theory: Neurophysiological foundations of emotions, attachment, communication, self-regulation.* New York, NY: W.W. Norton.
Proctor, G., Cooper, M., Sanders, P., & Malcolm, B. (2006). *Politicising the person-centered approach: An agenda for social change.* Ross-on-Wye, UK: PCCS Books.
Rama, S., Ballantine, R., & Ajaya, S. (1976). *Yoga and psychotherapy: The evolution of consciousness.* Honesdale, PA: Himalayan International Institute.
Rogers, C. R. (1980a). *Building person-centered communities: Implications for the future. A way of being* (3rd ed.). Boston, MA: Houghton-Mifflin.
Rogers, C. R. (1980b). *A way of being* (3rd ed.). Boston, MA: Houghton-Mifflin.
Rogers, C. R., Justyn, J., Kass, J. D., Miller, M., Rogers, N., Villas-Boas Bowen, M., et al. (1978). Evolving aspects of person-centered workshops. *Self and Society, 6*(2), 43–49.

Schore, A. (2001). Effects of secure attachment relationship on right brain development, affect regulation, and infant mental health. *Infant Mental Health Journal, 22*(1–2), 7–66.
Schuon, F. (1984). *The transcendent unity of religions*. Wheaton, IL: Theosophical Publishing.
Serlin, I. (2011). The history and future of humanistic psychology. *Journal of Humanistic Psychology, 51*(4), 428–431.
Sidanius, J., & Kurzban, R. (2013). Toward an evolutionarily informed political psychology. In L. Huddy, D. O. Sears, & J. S. Levy (Eds.), *Oxford handbook of political psychology* (2nd ed.). New York, NY: Oxford University Press.
Sidanius, J., & Pratto, F. (1999). *Social dominance: An intergroup theory of social hierarchy and oppression*. Cambridge, UK: Cambridge University Press.
Siegel, D. J. (2007). *The mindful brain: Reflection and attunement in the cultivation of well-being*. New York, NY: W.W. Norton.
Smith, H. (1991). *The world's religions: Our great wisdom traditions*. New York, NY: HarperSanFrancisco.
Solomon, M., & Siegel, D. J. (Eds.). (2003). *Healing trauma: Attachment, mind, body, and brain*. New York, NY: W.W. Norton.
Spretnak, C. (1991). *States of grace: The recovery of meaning in the postmodern age*. San Francisco, CA: HarperSanFrancisco.
Sue, D. W., & Sue, D. (1981). *Counseling the culturally different: Theory and practice*. New York, NY: John Wiley.
Swaner, L. E. (2005). *Linking engaged learning, student mental health and well-being, and civic development: A review of the literature, Bringing Theory to Practice*. Washington, DC: American Association of Colleges and Universities.
Teasdale, W. (1999). *The mystic heart: Discovering a universal spirituality in the world's religions*. Novato, CA: New World Library.
Tillich, P. (1952). *The courage to be*. New Haven, CT: Yale University Press.
Tudor, K., & Worrall, M. (2006). *Person-centered therapy*. London, UK: Routledge.
Tutu, D. M. (1994). *The rainbow people of God: The making of a peaceful revolution*. New York, NY: Image Books/Random House.
van der Kolk, B. A. (1994). The body keeps the score: Memory and the evolving psychobiology of post-traumatic stress disorder. *Harvard Review of Psychiatry, 1*(5), 253–265.

CHAPTER 2

Recognizing Student Needs for Psychospiritual Development: A Preliminary Case Study

This chapter presents a case study of a young adult in a psychospiritual crisis that nearly undermined her academic goals. This crisis, like many that I have observed as a professor of counseling and psychology, convinced me that students would benefit from a structured self-inquiry curriculum that mentored a person-centered process of psychospiritual development. This realization emerged from advising sessions with many students who were experiencing developmentally-appropriate quandaries without sufficient self-knowledge or appropriate mentoring. These quandaries, which often escalated into crises, affected their personal lives and academic success, sometimes constraining career aspirations. "Kate" was a student who exemplified these issues. I have chosen to describe her crisis because she was a reasonably well-adjusted young woman. Nonetheless, nothing in her previous education or upbringing had prepared her to cope with a psychospiritual crisis.

I met Kate during a small-group interview when she was a prospective student. She had submitted a strong application: positive recommendations and well-written essays with intellectual depth. I was surprised, therefore, at the interview, when her self-presentation was hesitant and distracted. Her motivation and program readiness were not apparent. Afterwards, when reviewing her excellent essays, I wanted to offer her benefit of the doubt. But interviews often provide more accurate data than carefully massaged essays. As I was on the verge of rejecting her application, the telephone rang. Our office administrator explained that an applicant hoped to speak with me. It was Kate.

Our subsequent conversation crystallized my recognition of the complex psychospiritual crises that undermine students. It also illustrates reflective listening skills I developed in my work with Carl Rogers that are essential during person-centered mentoring.

Entering my office, Kate said, in the same halting voice, "I didn't do as well as I can in the interview.... I'm hoping to talk with you a little more." Inviting her to sit down, I let her lead the conversation. "My self-confidence is really down these days. I don't know why. For years, I've wanted to be a counselor. I love working with children and teenagers. Everyone tells me I'm good at it." She paused. Then her voice quickened. "But I find myself doubting everything these days: whether I'm good enough, whether becoming a counselor is worth it, what life is supposed to be about."

She paused again, then looked at me somewhat sheepishly. "I don't know if talking about this is going to help me get into the program. But I feel that I have to talk it out honestly. There's no use making the wrong choice."

We spoke for nearly an hour. For most of the time, I used reflective listening to step inside her world, as she experienced it. Rather than peppering her with questions, advice, or observations, I communicated accurate and empathic understanding of her thoughts and feelings. As my statements indicated genuine respect for what she had to say, Kate explored increasingly deep layers of self. Rogers' research had demonstrated the important growth that occurs when individuals develop an internal locus of meaning-making. Focused attunement is an essential mentoring skill to help students cultivate their self-reflective capacities.

Kate covered considerable territory. She had been working at a hospital for the past year as a health educator, enjoying her work. She saw it as a stepping stone to becoming a counselor. According to her evaluations, she had been doing well. She had planned to work another year before applying to graduate school. But the hospital had gone through unexpected downsizing. To her dismay, she was fired. Losing this job unexpectedly sent this bright young woman into a tailspin. Despite knowing that other competent people had been laid off, she wondered if being fired was somehow her fault. Even in the interview, she couldn't stop thinking she might really be a fraud. I mentioned the positive recommendations we had received. "I've told myself the same things," she replied, "over and over again. But it doesn't help me bounce back." As we talked further, Kate began to understand why. Getting fired seemed to prove not only her lack of competence as a health educator, but lack of worth as a person.

This reaction did not seem unusual. Job loss, as we know, can be devastating. Getting fired had shaken Kate's belief in herself. Yet there was nothing obvious in her background to explain the intensity of her reaction. She came from a stable family. Her mother was an elementary school music teacher. Her father managed an electrical appliance store. Kate had been raised by loving, hard-working parents.

However, as she briefly described her family, we realized that her parents, too, derived most of their self-worth from their work. Her father had lost a job 10 years earlier, when Kate still lived at home. He, too, had become depressed. He drank himself to sleep every afternoon for three long weeks before her mother convinced him to look for another job.

"It makes me feel a little better to realize that the same thing happened to my dad," she said with some strength. Then she began to bite her lip, as though preventing herself from going further. In response, I took a risk. "So you've been drinking a bit too much also?" Her face began to tremble, as if trying to decide whether it was acceptable to be seen and known in this way. "Relax," I said. "Very few people avoid difficulties like the ones you are describing."

Her quick look of gratitude changed to immediate defiance. "No, I haven't drunk myself to sleep every afternoon." She paused. "But I guess my partying quotient has risen quite a bit."

She became quiet for a few moments, and then went on. "Talking about this makes me feel a little better, but not that much. I still feel so lost. One part of me knows that I want to be a counselor and that I have what it takes to become one. But a deeper part of me feels mushy and dark, as though I'm falling into an endless tunnel." She paused again, her face turning somber. "It's like there's a place inside me where all of life seems up for grabs, as though it may not have any real meaning. I was feeling that this morning, when I came over for the interview, and I know how it affected me when I answered your questions."

"As I listen to what you are saying," I replied, "it seems that it is less a question of whether *you* have worth or meaning than whether *life itself* has any worth or meaning."

"That's it exactly," she exclaimed. "It's like suddenly you are without your job and then, 'Who are you?' Nobody. And it makes you ask yourself, 'What is life about?' And sometimes there are no answers, and it can feel like a big nowhere."

I was impressed by Kate's ability for self-examination. She was articulate and insightful; it seemed her crisis would be temporary. Given the quality of her written materials, I now knew enough to support her application. "You know, we could stop here if you would like," I said, giving her a reassuring smile. "I have a better understanding of your situation. You do want to be a counselor. And you know your own thoughts and feelings well. You've convinced me...."

"But I haven't convinced myself!" she shot back. "That's not good enough. When I feel like this, I know that I am really looking for something in my life that I haven't been able to find. I didn't get it in college. All I got were a lot of lectures, a lot of them pretty boring and useless. I didn't get it in church. There were lots of sermons, but very few answers there. I didn't even get it in counseling. I tried it once, when my grades weren't so good. But the counselor couldn't get what my real questions were. She said that I would feel better when I developed solid study habits. Well, the study habits helped my grades. But they didn't answer the real questions."

Her voice became very quiet.

"I think that I have felt lost for a really long time. I feel like I'm a nobody... living in a big nowhere. And now I'm falling down that tunnel all over again." I nodded and sat with her quietly, understanding the depth of what she was saying. "It's like I need to find a place to stand, to feel something sturdy beneath my feet, to have the feeling that life makes sense, that I'm part of something bigger than just a job."

When she paused, I quietly said to her, "That's not a place that professors or clergy or counselors can find for you. In the long run, it's a place you have to find inside yourself."

"I *know* that," she said, in a tone that was slightly dismissive while at the same time plaintive. "But I want help learning to do that. It must be possible. And that's what I think other people need help learning about too."

"It seems to me that you are talking about a very deep part of yourself. You want to find your connection to the fabric of life."

"Well, is there a fabric?"

Finding trustworthy answers to this question does not happen in a single conversation. A person's lifetime relationship with the fabric of life is too complex. That is why many people avoid these questions, or settle for stock ideological answers. Furthermore, these questions can't be answered *for* someone. They require cultivation of an internal locus of meaning-making. Nonetheless, my conversation with Kate reached a satisfactory conclusion. I thought she would succeed in our program. She sensed that our program could embrace her interconnected needs for professional and personal development.

This interview challenged me to examine the complex mix of thorny personal problems, developmental challenges, and existential quandaries that are intricately embedded in students' academic lives. When educators avoid helping students learn how to address these issues, they become an unexamined source of chaos in their lives, and we reinforce humanity's chain of pain. Equally problematic, we waste the maturational potential of these issues. If educators privilege intellectual learning and subordinate psychospiritual growth, students become fragmented human beings whose capacity for mature behavior toward self and other is impaired.

When Kate entered our counselor education program, I became her academic advisor. In this role, I learned more about her needs for psychospiritual growth. Meeting periodically, we usually discussed her career goals, academic program, and internships. But, at key moments, when she felt "overwhelmed" or "stalled out," we resumed deeper dialogue. She learned that her professional work was negatively affected, not only by the stress of programmatic performance demands, but also by pressing social, emotional, financial, and existential challenges. Personal and professional aspects of self were inseparable: interwoven threads in the fabric of her life. Kate needed to learn to be resilient as she confronted them: mindful of their impact, cultivating internal composure, and seeking mentoring when she had difficulty maintaining equilibrium.

Our discussions never crossed the boundary into the personal domains of psychotherapy. But, as a faculty mentor, it was impossible to avoid discussion about the overlap between her professional and personal development. Once I knew that Kate had the intellectual capability and emotional intelligence to become a skilled professional, I considered these personal issues developmental challenges whose resolution would contribute to her professional growth.

Further, I challenged Kate to approach her issues from the same maturational perspective. Blending unconditional acceptance and challenge, I helped Kate grow personally in the service of her professional development. This mentoring helped her become a sturdy person who could think for herself, ask for help when needed, and face life's problems as maturational challenges. For faculty to embrace the deepest pedagogical, ethical, and maturational potentials of higher education, this mentoring is essential (Palmer 1983, 1998; Parks 2000; Walsh 2002).

By the time Kate graduated, I understood that many students required similar mentoring through a structured curriculum that introduced them to person-centered psychospiritual growth. As my research about this pedagogical approach evolved, I identified five dimensions of self and society that are dysregulated by humanity's chain of pain, and which can be repaired through person-centered psychospiritual learning. It will be useful to analyze the issues that undermined Kate through this conceptual model.

The Dimensions of Kate's Psychospiritual Crisis

Bio-Behavioral: Before our program, Kate had developed self-regulating capacities. She had completed college and become a constructive member of the work-force. However, when she lost her job, her coping mechanisms regressed to impulsive flight through excessive partying and drinking. This regression is driven by neurobehavioral mechanisms of the stress response. When young adults experience autonomic hyperarousal, a typical response is to self-soothe through alcohol's "relaxing" effects. However, alcohol's impact on the central nervous system dampens cognitive attention and rational decision-making, often triggering depressive episodes. Kate's flight pattern ("increased partying quotient") had become so automatic that she was not aware of it. Nor was she fully aware of its connection to the triggering loss of her job.

Cognitive-Sociocultural: Job loss ignited two mutually-reinforcing negative cognitive schema. The first schema was personal: Kate was convinced her work performance had been inadequate. The second schema was sociocultural: our society demeans people without a job, and Kate had internalized this corrosive attitude. These negative scripts may also have been reinforced by her socially-constructed identity as a female. Women's second-tier status in a patriarchal society erodes self-confidence. But Kate did not articulate this feminist theme in our conversation. Her shame and loss of confidence seemed more directly related to society's rigid negative judgments about unemployed people: a profound stigma. Ironically, the impact of this stigma distracted her during an interview for professional advancement.

Social-Emotional: Establishing relational connections with peers and authority figures is a complex process. Most people have experienced untrustworthy relationships that make them wary. While this vigilance has protective value, it can become socially isolating. Kate benefited from growing up with two loving parents. After her ineffective interview, she was not afraid to approach the authority figure; nor did she assume I would be unsympathetic. Still, during the initial interview, Kate had demonstrated diminished self-confidence. She could have discussed her job loss during the interview, describing her psychospiritual quandary, and I probably would have been impressed by her self-awareness and courage. Instead, Kate's flattened affect and vague cognitive style reflected a type of withdrawn, frozen behavior that is often characteristic of adult insecure relational attachment. Even when parents have instilled a secure foundation, stressful circumstances and job-related performance expectations can rattle this secure template, triggering insecure behaviors.

Existential-Spiritual: This element of our conversation was suffused with poignant urgency. Kate expressed existential uncertainty that had been part of her life experience for many years. Am I simply "a nobody... living in a big nowhere?" Is there "a fabric" to life? Such ontological insecurity is a quandary that many people hold within themselves, unexpressed and unexplored, for most of their lives. Many find, as Kate noted, that their existential concerns are not addressed adequately by teachers, mental health counselors, or religious leaders.

Kate's realization that her family relied on work as their deepest source of identity and meaning was significant. Work, of course, is a central source of identity, particularly in our society. Still, there are pivotal moments when life's deepest existential elements become figural: when job identity is lost, when mortality looms, when a loved one's suffering evokes despair, or when communities encounter collective trauma (natural catastrophe, oppression, violence). In these moments, we exist in the universe without our usual identity-props, confront the pervasive reality of suffering, and face the unnerving possibility that life has no deeper fabric.

Kate's articulation of existential uncertainty supports Paul Tillich's thesis that *ontological insecurity* is a root cause of humanity's psychological agitation and destructive behavior (Tillich 1952). Maimonides, the Jewish philosopher and spiritual teacher, proposed the same thesis in his classic 12th-century text *Guide of the Perplexed* (Maimonides

1963). Discussing behaviors harmful to self (e.g., excessive consumption of food and inebriants) and others (e.g., domination of one people over another), he located the ultimate cause of these behaviors in the existential alienation humans experience when we feel cut off from relationship with the Ground of Being. He explains this experience of acute *privation* as a consequence of *ignorance*: lack of awareness of our existential connection to the Ground of Being. Contemplatives from every tradition agree: the Kingdom of Heaven (Ground of Being) can be experienced within the psyche as the core dimension of being. But our awareness has been veiled by ignorance (Easwaran 2003; Merton 1996; Nasr 2007; Teresa-of-Avila 1979).

Gautama Buddha, one of humanity's great psychological researchers, explained that this subjectively-verifiable experience does not require belief in a metaphysical or religious system. It requires the determination and skill to plumb the depths of the psyche, moving mindfully through layers of distorting ego perceptions that keep us feeling cut off, until we discover this unified, connective ground (Bodhi 2005).

However, despite the profound, reparative implications of these ideas, the experience of ontological relatedness requires decades of character refinement and contemplative practice, as we will discuss. In the interim, while psychospiritual growth is rudimentary, and humanity's chain of pain maintains the veil of ignorance that clouds our perceptions, how do people prevent existential alienation from having corrosive impact? How do we respond to our anguish and humanity's suffering without succumbing to behaviors destructive to self and others?

Students address this crucial question in the *Know Your Self* curriculum. As I developed it, during early mentoring work with students like Kate, I gained insights about this quandary from Viktor Frankl's classic, *Man's Search for Meaning* (Frankl 1959). Filled with despair, responding to the suffering that he witnessed and endured in a Nazi concentration camp, Frankl realized that he was asking a common existential question, "*Why is life doing this to me?*" He concluded that this question was useless. It disempowered him. It assumed an adversarial rift between life and himself. But he realized *life* had no battle with him; humans were the cause of this evil. To empower himself and affirm his relationship with life, Frankl changed the question. He asked, "*What does life expect of me as I face this suffering?*" He allowed life to demand from him a response that did not degrade him to the level of the Nazis: a response that drew upon his human capacity to elevate each moment morally and spiritually, through small acts of resistance and compassion, even if his responses were severely limited by situational constraints.

Frankl described brief moments of solitude when he turned within for dialogue with *life*. In this mental sanctuary, he described an inner freedom that the Nazis could not destroy. Frankl acknowledged that he collapsed many times, unable to maintain this elevating stance, describing episodes of selfish, self-protective behavior. Nonetheless, he affirmed a personal relationship with *life* that helped him maintain connection with his moral and spiritual capacities and the wisdom of his inner self. Surviving the war, he developed a Logotherapeutic Approach that attended to *crises of meaning*, while reframing life's suffering and struggles as potential sources of meaning and growth. This stance does not imply that all suffering is deserved or inevitable. Nonetheless, Frankl considered suffering a potential source of empowerment and self-transcendent growth (Holland and Lewis 2001; Kass 1996a, b). This maturational perspective became an integral feature of the *Know Your Self* curriculum.

However, as I learned with Kate (and many other students), during the poignant urgency of existential uncertainty, an individual's relationship with the fabric of life must be discovered experientially, as a source of meaning and coherence within the specific circumstances of that person's life. As Kate expressed her existential quandaries, rather than responding with a lecture about Frankl, I used reflective listening to acknowledge and clarify them. My attuned listening communicated familiarity with this existential territory. As a result, when she asked, "Is there a fabric?" it was not necessary to provide a detailed reply. Rather, it was sufficient to explain that, while these questions must be answered personally, our counseling program would help her learn to address them, and that she would encounter students and faculty on the same path: cultivating psychospiritual self-understanding and life wisdom. As Kate progressed through our program, developing the internal composure to approach life's difficulties as maturational challenges, she began to experience life from a new perspective: as a trustworthy ally and teacher.

Through this person-centered pedagogy, an individual's understanding about the fabric of reality can shift profoundly. When existence is no longer perceived as an uncaring adversary, but as the fabric of our maturational development, we can feel securely attached to its dynamic process—even amidst turmoil, our inevitable mortality, and humanity's chain of pain. Eventually, I developed the term *secure existential attachment* to describe this existentially-relational aspect of human development (Kass 2007, 2015).

Integrative Formation of a Resilient Worldview: By graduation, Kate demonstrated increased Confidence in Life and Self. Her confidence was not naïve. She had confronted many developmental hurdles and multiple ways that humanity's chain of pain undermines positive growth. But Kate had a new vantage point for approaching future hurdles. Life was a coherent process: a teacher, an ally, not an incorrigible adversary, and she could meet these challenges constructively. Through increased Confidence in Life and Self, her ability to maintain internal composure in times of stress solidified considerably. Some of Kate's resilience, of course, was already evident in our initial conversation. The secure foundation she had received as a child was a significant resilience factor. However, as an emerging adult, Kate required sustained mentoring to consolidate these foundations into an autonomous adult identity.

Conclusions

Emerging adulthood is a period of heightened challenges to bio-behavioral, cognitive-sociocultural, social-emotional, and existential-spiritual dimensions of self. These challenges are magnified by students' personal links to humanity's chain of pain. When faculty acknowledge their needs for psychospiritual growth, we can mentor learning that is essential for necessary positive transformation in self and society. However, as the next chapter will explore, higher education has been slow to accept this prosocial responsibility.

References

Bodhi, B. (2005). *In the Buddha's words: An anthology of discourses from the Pali canon*. Somerville, MA: Wisdom Publications.
Easwaran, E. (Ed.). (2003). *God makes the rivers to flow: Sacred literature of the world*. Tomales, CA: Nilgiri Press.
Frankl, V. (1959). *Man's search for meaning*. New York, NY: Simon and Schuster.
Holland, J. C., & Lewis, S. (2001). *The human side of cancer: Living with hope, coping with uncertainty*. New York, NY: Harper Perennial.

Kass, J. D. (1996a). Coping with life-threatening illnesses using a logotherapeutic approach, 1: Health care team interventions. *International Forum for Logotherapy, 19*(Spring), 15–19.
Kass, J. D. (1996b). Coping with life-threatening illnesses using a logotherapeutic approach, 2: Clinical mental health counseling. *International Forum for Logotherapy, 20*(Summer), 10–14.
Kass, J. D. (2007). Spiritual maturation: A developmental resource for resilience, well-being, and peace. *Journal of Pedagogy, Pluralism, and Practice, 12*(Summer), 56–64.
Kass, J. D. (2015). Person-centered spiritual maturation: A multidimensional model. *Journal of Humanistic Psychology, 55*(1), 53–76. doi:10.1177/0022167814525261.
Maimonides, M. (1963). *Guide of the perplexed* (S. Pines, Trans.). Chicago, IL: University of Chicago Press.
Merton, T. (1996). *Contemplative prayer*. New York, NY: Image/Doubleday.
Nasr, S. H. (2007). *The garden of truth: The vision and promise of Sufism, Islam's mystical tradition*. New York, NY: HarperCollins.
Palmer, P. (1983). *To know as we are known: Education as a spiritual journey*. San Francisco, CA: HarperSanFrancisco.
Palmer, P. (1998). *The courage to teach*. San Francisco, CA: Jossey-Bass.
Parks, S. D. (2000). *Big questions, worthy dreams: Mentoring young adults in their search for meaning, purpose, and faith*. San Francisco, CA: Jossey-Bass.
Teresa-of-Avila, (1979). *The interior castle*. New York, NY: Paulist Press.
Tillich, P. (1952). *The courage to be*. New Haven, CT: Yale University Press.
Walsh, D. C. (2002). Transforming education: An overview. In V. H. Kazanjian & P. Laurence (Eds.), *Education as transformation: Religious pluralism, spirituality, and a new vision for higher education in America*. New York, NY: Peter Lang.

CHAPTER 3

Higher Education: Model for Constructive Change? Or Mirror of Humanity's *Chain of Pain*?

This chapter examines a critical issue in post-secondary education. We have achieved unparalleled success as an engine for technological innovation, professional career development, and the advancement of knowledge. However, since Ernest Boyer's investigation of the college experience (Boyer 1987) and subsequent report, *Campus Life: In Search of Community*, it has been evident that "the idyllic vision so routinely portrayed in college promotional materials often masks disturbing realities of student life" (Boyer 1990, p. 3). Boyer found that students were disengaged from intellectual work. Further, many experienced psychological and behavioral dysregulation that undermined academic success and a positive campus culture. This chapter reviews research documenting these persistent problems, suggesting that higher education has become a mirror of humanity's chain of pain. It then reviews efforts to rectify these issues through engaged teaching and learning, documenting limited success using current methods. Finally, it explains how a person-centered approach to engaged learning, which mentors psychospiritual maturation in students, may offer a more effective response to these issues.

HIGHER EDUCATION: AN UNSETTLING MIRROR

Boyer's observations have become familiar territory for faculty and student life professionals. Many students experience:

- lack of academic focus and engagement
- procrastination, perfectionism, and difficulty completing assignments
- impulsive urges to consume alcohol and recreational drugs at dangerous levels
- social anxiety and lack of interpersonal communication skills
- stress-induced psychological and medical symptoms
- negative body image that triggers cigarette smoking or disordered eating
- self-doubt, anxiety, and depression
- existential alienation

These issues include troubling sociocultural dimensions. Many students experience:

- micro-aggressions and shunning based on race, ethnicity, or religion
- social isolation related to homophobia and trans-gender prejudice
- bullying and other harmful interpersonal power dynamics
- sexual harassment, assault, and rape
- alcohol-related physical violence

These problems are evidence that humanity's pervasive suffering is manifest on our campuses. Faculty and student life staff often observe students suffering from psychological and behavioral dysregulation, cognitive distortions and sociocultural biases about self and others, insecure social and emotional attachment systems, and existential anomie.

From an educational perspective, these issues could be rich catalysts for psychospiritual development. However, when unexamined and unacknowledged, they have negative impact on student well-being and campus culture. Higher education's reluctance to offer academic venues for *person-centered psychospiritual learning* perpetuates the chain of pain. We have become a mirror of our troubled society, rather than a model for constructive change.

Boyer's Legacy: Engaged Teaching and Learning

Boyer was never alone in his call for engaged, socially-responsible, health-promoting pedagogy. Higher education has been critiqued from multiple perspectives: social justice and communitarian (Adams et al.

1997; Bellah et al. 1987; Fanon 1968; Freire 1970; Harding 1981; hooks 1981; Miller 1976; Slater 1971); epistemological and pedagogical (Belenky et al. 1986; Deloria Jr. 1973, 1979; Freire 1973; Gilligan 1982; Mezirow 1990; Palmer 1998); psychosocial and developmental (Chickering and Reisser 1993; Hardiman and Jackson 1997; Helms 1990; Rogers 1961, 1969) and existential-spiritual (Astin 2004; Astin et al. 2011; Chickering et al. 2006; Kazanjian and Lawrence 2000; Palmer 1983; Parks 1986, 2000). Boyer distilled these critiques, urging the reevaluation of higher education's goals and pedagogy as well as improvements to the quality of campus culture.

The first major initiative to improve campus culture was led by Student Life Offices at many colleges and universities. They focused on reducing alcohol consumption and antisocial behavior through environmental management and student-led programs. They instituted alcohol- and smoke-free dormitories, prodded bars to enforce underage drinking laws, increased campus security, provided safe transportation vans, and introduced zero-tolerance policies for sexual violence and substance-related aggression. They organized student groups to combat sexual violence, homophobia, and racial discrimination; and they introduced campus-based social-norm marketing to change student perceptions about binge-drinking. They challenged recalcitrant alumni whose financial contributions to fraternities supported toga party norms. They increased counseling center staffs, coordinating medical and psychological treatment for dual diagnoses of depression and substance abuse (DeJong and Langford 2002; DeJong et al. 1998; Gebhardt et al. 2000; Haines and Spear 1996; HEC 2002; Perkins et al. 1999; Ross 2004; Zimmerman 2004).

The second major initiative focused on pedagogical methods to engage students in academic work (AAC&U 2002, 2007, 2008, 2010, 2012a, b; Colby et al. 2003; Harward 2012b; Keeling 2004, 2006; Keeling et al. 2008; Kuh et al. 2010; McDonald 2002). Faculty and administrators reasoned that *engaged teaching and learning* (e.g., increased student-faculty interaction, service learning, coursework promoting social justice awareness, co-curricular group activities) would have a positive effect, albeit indirect, on the psychological and behavioral well-being of students and campus culture (Kuh 2003; Kuh et al. 2005a, b; Swaner 2005, 2007, 2012). George Kuh developed the National Survey for Student Engagement (NSSE), and identified 10 strategies that enhance academic learning and retention. They include: learning communities, writing-intensive courses, collaborative assignments, diversity/global learning, service learning, first-year seminars, and student-faculty research. Enhanced student advising was an additional factor (Kuh 2008; NSSE 2007, 2014).

These pedagogical methods consistently yield positive results in academic achievement. However, their hypothesized indirect positive effect on psychological and behavioral well-being is not supported by results from numerous multi-university research surveys, including:

- American College Health Association Surveys of Mental Health, Substance Use, and Violence (ACHA 2004, 2011, 2014; Carr 2005)
- Association of American Universities Campus Climate Survey on Sexual Assault and Sexual Misconduct (Cantor et al. 2015b)
- Columbia University's Center on Addiction and Substance Abuse (CASA 2007);
- Core Institute Alcohol and Drug Surveys (CORE-Institute 2010; Meilman and Presley 1997; Perkins et al. 1999; Presley and Meilman 1994)
- Harvard School of Public Health College Alcohol Surveys (Wechsler et al. 1998, 2000a, b, 2001a, b, 2002, 2004; Wechsler and Nelson 2008)
- Higher Education Research Institute, National Norms for Student Campus Life (Eagan et al. 2014; Pryor et al. 2010)
- National Survey of College Counseling Centers (Erdur-Baker et al. 2006; Gallagher 2014)
- University of Southern Maine's Center for Prevention of Hate Violence (Wessler and Moss 2001a, b)

These surveys reveal persistent patterns of alcohol abuse, depression, psychological stress, emotional isolation, disordered eating, sexual misconduct and violence, hate crimes against gays, interracial and interreligious tensions, and lack of genuine campus community, with attendant negative impact on academic achievement. In every survey, alcohol consumption is correlated with behavioral misconduct, indicating the toxic nature of the campus drinking culture (Kadison and DiGeronimo 2004; SPRC 2004; Wechsler and Wuerthrich 2002).

These problems are not limited to first-year students or undergraduates, as commonly assumed. While the highest rates occur in freshman year, these problems persist through senior year. Further, graduate students experience them, albeit at lower rates. Harvard University President Drew Gilpin Faust deserves praise for institutional transparency by reporting graduate student results from the Survey on Sexual Assault and Sexual Misconduct, conducted by the Association of American Universities. In 2014–2015, 1–3% of students reported nonconsensual sexual contact in each graduate school, including Business, Design, Divinity, Education, Government, Law, Medicine, and Public Health (Cantor et al. 2015a; Hyman 2015).

Data from the 2014 National College Health Assessment highlight the results from these multiple surveys. NCHA collected data from 79,266 students at 140 public and private institutions from each region in the United States, distributed evenly among baccalaureate, masters, and research institutions. Results indicated psychological and behavioral dysregulation, warranting educational and clinical concern, in academics, mental health, substance use, and interpersonal misconduct (ACHA 2014). Thus, despite sustained efforts, environmental management and current engaged learning approaches have produced little meaningful progress.

Research Specifically Investigating Engaged Teaching and Learning

Engaged learning practitioners may argue, justifiably, that large-scale surveys do not reflect their efforts accurately because many faculty have not adopted these methods (Swaner 2012). But studies examining high-involvement teaching have produced similar negative results.

Alexander Astin conducted an early study at UCLA's Higher Education Research Institute (HERI) (Astin 1993). Using his Input-Environment-Output (I-E-O) linear regression model, developed at the Cooperative Institutional Research Program (Astin 1978, 1991), high-involvement teaching was associated with positive academic outcomes, but not psychological or behavioral well-being. In fact, during this multi-year study, psychological well-being declined; drinking increased; and emotional well-being was diminished further when students lacked a sense of community.

Astin also found that faculty had only a secondary effect on students' psychosocial development, reflecting a problematic disengagement between students and faculty. Boyer had noted students experiencing faculty as remote and self-involved in their professional work: "about 50% said they feel 'like a number in a book.' About 40% said they do not feel a sense of community on campus; about 2/3 said they have no professor 'interested in their personal lives'" (Boyer 1990, p. 48). The HERI results extended Boyer's findings.

Ernest Pascarella and Patrick Terenzini reached similar conclusions. They found that higher education promotes cognitive learning (substantive growth in verbal skills, subject matter, critical thinking, reflective judgment thinking, and conceptual complexity) and principled reasoning about moral issues. Further, it promotes openness to diversity and recognition that racism remains a societal problem. But regarding psychosocial growth, their findings were far less positive. Although academic and social self-concept improved, growth was evident in only 3–5% of students. Further, this statistic disguised two opposing trends. While some students showed marked increases in positive self-concept, others showed marked decreases (10–18% in both directions, p. 575). This result suggests that *person-centered* learning could yield broader positive effects on psychosocial growth. But they found little evidence that higher education currently improves psychological and behavioral well-being (p. 580) (Pascarella and Terenzini 2005). Their data casts further doubt on the efficacy of *indirect* pedagogical strategies.

Evidence continues to mount that engaged learning strengthens academic achievement. In Proceedings of the National Academy of Sciences, Scott Freeman reported a meta-analysis of 225 studies in STEM disciplines. Active learning produced substantively better outcomes than traditional lecturing (Freeman et al. 2014). The strengths of current engaged learning methods cannot be disputed; but they do not improve the psychological well-being of students.

Bringing Theory to Practice (BTtoP) investigates links between engaged learning, civic engagement, and psychological well-being. Lynn Swaner has developed conceptual models for these links (Swaner 2005, 2007, 2012). This project is directed by Donald Harward, former President of Bates College, with funding from the Charles Engelhard Foundation and AAC&U. It has become a leading voice for education of the whole person (Harward 2007, 2012b). BTtoP has published two research projects. Most methods of engaged learning, unfortunately, did not improve student well-being. There was one exception: cohesive community.

The first study, a multi-campus project, examined student engagement measures (NSSE) with alcohol consumption, depression, and psychological stress (Swaner and Finley 2007):

Alcohol consumption remained high: 4.32 drinks per sitting (near the 5-drink binge level). Engaged learning was associated with less likelihood of binge-drinking, but correlations were small ($r = -0.019$ to -0.125). Frequency of drinking also remained high: 2.74 times per week. Paradoxically, engaged learning was associated with *higher* frequency of drinking, though these correlations were also small ($r = 0.015$ to 0.098).

Depression and psychological stress were in the anticipated negative direction for most NSSE benchmarks. But correlations for student/faculty interactions, active and collaborative learning, enriched educational environment, and civic engagement were negligible. Further, academic challenge was *positively* correlated with depression and psychological stress, though at low levels. The exception was a negative correlation with supportive campus environment.

The second BTtoP study assessed the impact of engaged learning in first-year students at Dickinson College (Staub and Finley 2007). Ashley Finley, co-investigator, guides evaluation procedures for BTtoP (Finley 2011; Finley and Swaner 2008). The research design was creative. A first-year seminar is attended by all entering students; faculty from every department address discipline-related subjects, emphasizing writing skills, information literacy, and research. Faculty have contact with students two to three times each week, serving as academic advisors until students choose a major. Dickinson added a *learning community* program in 2003, linking seminars with common themes. Students in each community were housed in a common residence.

Staub and Finley studied the impact of different first-year seminar models on student learning, civic engagement, and psychological well-being (alcohol use and mental health). The sample included 153 students in learning communities and 419 who were not. In the learning communities, seminars emphasized traditional classroom learning (52%); experiential learning (20%); service-learning with academic credit (14%); community-service without credit (14%).

Alcohol Use

Learning Community vs. Non-Learning Community: There were no differences in pre-test data. By November, learning community students reported significantly less quantity and frequency of alcohol use. The differences persisted through spring semester. Staub and Finley concluded that residential learning communities have a positive effect on quantity and frequency of alcohol use, compared to students who only attend a first-year seminar. Thus, although first-year seminars are considered a high-impact practice, only residential learning communities had a positive effect on alcohol consumption.

Types of seminars among learning community students: The greatest reduction in alcohol was associated with traditional- and service-learning formats. This result supported the value of first-year seminars, but *only* in conjunction with intensive learning communities.

Mental Health (Depression and Psychological Stress)

Learning Community vs. Non-Learning Community: These results were negative. Pre-test data showed no significant differences. By November, the learning communities reported *higher* depression levels (for reasons explicated below). At the end of spring semester, the differences were non-significant. But learning community students had experienced more psychological distress than peers who only attended a first-year seminar.

Types of seminars among learning community students: End-of-year analyses revealed the spike in depression was attributable to the service-learning track. This suggested that service learning has a mixed effect on psychological well-being. Focus groups provided an explanation: community service required additional time commitments, creating significant stress. Students affirmed the benefits of service-learning. However, as an add-on to academic work, community service increased stress and depression at a vulnerable point in the semester.

In summary, BTtoP findings suggest that most current approaches to engaged learning do not contribute to psychological well-being, with one exception: supportive community. Before returning to this positive outcome, I will review two additional areas of research.

RESEARCH ON *FLOURISHING* IN HIGHER EDUCATION

Positive psychology investigates learning that promotes human flourishing (Seligman 2002; Seligman and Csikszentmihalyi 2000). The Mental Health Continuum (MHC), developed by Corey Keyes, taps three dimensions of flourishing: emotional well-being (affect), positive psychological functioning (self-concept), and positive social functioning (attitudes about people and society). Scores range from "languishing" to "flourishing." Keyes demonstrates that increases in flourishing are not adequately reflected by reductions in psychological dysfunction (Keyes 2002, 2005, 2006a, b, 2007). Felicia Huppert and Joyce Whittington provide supporting evidence (Huppert and Whittington 2003). Similarly, increases on an Inventory of Positive Psychological Attitudes were better correlated with positive outcomes in chronic pain patients than reductions in depression and anxiety (Kass et al. 1991a).

Results from recent studies using the MHC in higher education have been mixed. Kathryn Low, studying 500 students at a liberal arts college, found flourishing positively associated with community service and negatively with depression. But flourishing and community service were not associated with lower levels of substance use (Low 2011).

John Fink conducted a comprehensive study in which results were negative (Fink 2015). Using the multi-campus National Study of Living-Learning Programs, he analyzed data from 2008 (N = 1,161) and 2009 (N = 1,459), with the MHC as outcome measure. Fink used the I-E-O design, with step-wise regression analysis, to identify intervening environmental variables. As a mode of replication, he analyzed each year separately. The results were unexpected. Engaged learning (Social and Academic Interactions; Individual Engagement with College Environments) did not contribute to flourishing. Sense of Belonging (community) was the primary contributor. Sense of Civic Engagement had a nominal positive effect, though likely attributable to social affiliation during the activities. Thus, with the exception of supportive community, engaged learning did not have a positive impact on psychological well-being.

RESEARCH ON *SPIRITUALITY* IN HIGHER EDUCATION

The psychology of religion and spirituality is a second area that investigates positive resources for individual and social well-being. As Kenneth Pargament explains, spirituality is considered an independent construct from participation in an organized religion, though many people derive their sense of life meaning through religious participation (Pargament 1997, 2007). Gordon Allport, in studies of racial prejudice, introduced a similar distinction. He contrasted *intrinsic* religious orientation (lived spiritual values and personal experiences of sacred presence) with *extrinsic* religious orientation (participation for utilitarian motives, e.g., social status and support) (Allport 1950; Allport and Ross 1967). As social scientists accepted this distinction, existential *quest* for spiritual meaning (Batson and Schoenrade 1991) became a recognized developmental concern, especially during emerging adulthood (Arnett 2015; Chickering et al. 2006; Parks 1986, 2000). Alexander Astin and James Keen described *equanimity* (feeling centered, at peace, able to find meaning in times of hardship) as a central goal of spiritual growth (Astin and Keen 2006).

Using HERI's multi-campus survey protocol, Alexander Astin, Helen Astin, and Jennifer Lindholm explored the relationship between spirituality and psychological well-being, analyzing data from 14,527 undergraduates (Astin et al. 2011). Using the I-E-O design, *equanimity* was positively associated with psychological well-being over a four-year period ($B = 0.28$). But high scores in equanimity increased in only 4% of the sample (19%–23%), indicating a need for intentional interventions to strengthen equanimity. This observational study demonstrated the potential significance of mentored, person-centered, psychospiritual growth.

Studies teaching meditation to college students also suggest promising possibilities (Baer et al. 2006; Deckro et al. 2002; Peer and McAuslan 2016; Shapiro et al. 2011). BTtoP has begun to recognize these results (Bergen-Cico and Bylander 2012). They identify meditation as a tool for self-regulation through mindfulness and elicitation of the relaxation response. Their conclusions provide further preliminary support for incorporating a person-centered approach to psychospiritual development in higher education.

Thus, current methods of engaged learning do not contribute to psychological well-being, with two exceptions: *community-building* and *cultivating equanimity through meditation*. These pedagogical methods are central features of the *Know Your Self* curriculum, adding explanatory support to the positive findings of the effectiveness study reported in this book. Person-centered psychospiritual development may be an important addition to engaged learning methods.

Conclusions

This literature review suggests two conclusions. First, campus culture remains a disheartening mirror of humanity's chain of pain. Second, while current engaged learning methods have positive impact on academic outcomes and civic involvement, they have minimal impact on psychological well-being. I will offer two explanations:

1. *Current approaches do not engage students directly in necessary person-centered psychospiritual learning.* Higher education does not provide direct pedagogical opportunities for students to examine their psychospiritual worldviews and behavior, or the impact of these factors on individual and social well-being. Nor do we engage students directly in developing pro-social community-building skills. We hypothesize that they develop psychospiritual and community-building competencies through enhanced academic learning and extracurricular activities. But this *indirect* strategy does not work.
2. *Current approaches focus on pathology in students rather than pathology in society.* The psychosocial problems students experience reflect the pervasive presence of humanity's chain of pain. Rather than treating students as problems who need to be managed, we could engage them collaboratively, as emerging adults, in efforts to break humanity's intergenerational chain of pain. Some students, of course, require behavioral management through institutional regulations, behavioral prescriptions, zero-tolerance policies, and psychological counseling. These modes of environmental management should not be abandoned. However, they are not sufficient. Students would benefit from—and most could participate effectively in—a structured educational approach to person-centered psychospiritual growth in service of self and society. Student learning illustrated in this book demonstrates the capacity of young adults to engage in these modes of psychospiritual self-inquiry. Moreover, students find this pedagogical orientation congruent with their highest social ideals and personal/professional development goals.

Shifting the diagnostic focus to society will explain forces undermining campus culture more adequately. In this book, I explicate five dimensions of self and society subverted by humanity's chain of pain, discussing specific ways in which young adults on our campuses show signs of dysregulation in each dimension of self. I close this chapter with a summary:

1. **Bio-Behavioral Dimension:** Many students lack effective stress-coping skills and emotional self-regulation tools necessary to manage the academic and social challenges they encounter. They have little familiarity with the neural and physiological pathways that regulate their metabolic processes and through which they respond to challenges, stress, and perceived threat. As a result, many become vulnerable to high-risk behaviors, like binge-drinking, drug abuse, promiscuous sex, or socially-isolating behaviors, such as extensive playing of computer games and compulsive studying. When adults judge these actions as foolish or foolhardy, we fail to recognize the secondary benefits they provide. They often assuage the complex emotions and confusing agitation that students experience.
2. **Cognitive-Sociocultural Dimension:** Many students have developed negative cognitive schema that distort their perceptions and understanding of self. Equally problematic, they have developed negative schema that distort their perceptions and understanding of campus peers with sociocultural identities different than their own (whether by race, ethnicity, gender, sexual orientation, social class, religion, nationality, geographical region, or physical abilities). During this period of emerging adulthood, the negative cognitive schema that students have internalized (from familial and systemic social forces) often prevent them from persisting at times of academic challenge and self-doubt (Levy et al. 2016), or lead them to hurt others (willfully or inadvertently) in ways more damaging than they may realize.
3. **Social-Emotional Dimension:** Faculty often forget that many students feel deeply isolated on campus. Many have been separated abruptly from best friends, families, mentors, and communities that provided support and recognition. This loss of meaningful attachments is a primary source of distress (McDermott et al. 2015). These losses do not apply simply to first-year undergraduates. Graduate studies represent yet another dislocation of place, friendships, and family bonds. We forget how long it takes to develop secure attachments. When we see students joking at the beginning of class or laughing boisterously in a cafeteria, we often project on them a sense of secure attachment that they do not actually feel. Many develop a veneer of independence that masks their genuine feelings from us and themselves. Through my efforts

to become an engaged, person-centered mentor, I have learned that students yearn for the secure attachment and genuine sense of community we imagine them to have. But, in actuality, few have developed the interpersonal skills and internal psychological resources necessary to build robust community and secure relational attachments.

4. **Existential-Spiritual Dimension:** Adults juggling career pressures, family demands, and financial burdens may not recall the existential anomie that can permeate young adulthood. Students often experience *ontological insecurity*, a term Paul Tillich developed to denote the lack of perceived coherence and existential meaning in modern society. This profound dislocation is a root cause of anxiety, depression, and psychophysiological dysregulation (Kass 1995; Tillich 1952). In young adults, it triggers agitated behavior: binge drinking to blackout, sexual victimization, social media bullying, intellectual competitiveness, social anxiety, social isolation, depression, eating disorders, and suicide. Young adults, Sharon Daloz Parks argues, long to discover a sense of connection to the foundational fabric of life. But our religious and educational systems fail to address their developmental needs for psychospiritual mentoring (Parks 2000). In response, students often ripple with symptoms of ontological insecurity.

5. **Integrative consolidation of a resilient worldview**: Ideally, young adults would be exposed to a well-structured curriculum that addresses their needs for maturational growth in these four crucial dimensions of self: bio-behavioral, cognitive-sociocultural, social-emotional, and existential-spiritual. The results from my research show that, as students learn to explore these domains, they can develop a more resilient worldview, characterized by *confidence in life and self*. This positive worldview does not minimize human suffering or injustice. Rather, psychospiritual growth can help young adults find a deeper coherence in life that inspires them to engage in pro-social and health-promoting behavior.

In closing, dysregulation in these five dimensions of self and society explain the toxic impact of humanity's chain of pain on our students. To interrupt its multidimensional effects requires an educational strategy of equal dimensionality. The case studies and research data reported in this book describe students engaged in a person-centered process of psychospiritual growth in the service of self and society. While the *Know Your Self* curriculum is not a panacea, it provides an educational introduction to transformative growth and inclusive community-building that is necessary to break this toxic, self-replicating cycle of pain.

REFERENCES

AAC&U. (2002). *Greater expectations: A new vision for learning as a nation goes to college.* Washington, DC: Association of American Colleges and Universities.

AAC&U. (2007). *College learning for the new global century: Report from the National Leadership Council for Liberal Education and America's Promise.* Washington, DC: American Association of Colleges and Universities.

AAC&U. (2008). Should colleges focus more on personal and social responsibility? In E. Dey (Ed.). Washington, DC: Association of American Colleges and Universities.

AAC&U. (2010). Engaging diverse viewpoints: What is the campus climate for perspective-taking? In E. Dey (Ed.). Washington, DC: Association of American Colleges and Universities.

AAC&U. (2012a). *The LEAP Vision for learning.* Washington, DC: American Association of Colleges and Universities.

AAC&U. (2012b). Promising practices for personal and social responsibility: Findings from a national research collaborative. In N. O'Neill (Ed.). Washington, DC: Association of American Colleges and Universities.

ACHA. (2004). *American College Health Association: National college health assessment, 2004 executive summary.* Baltimore, MD: American College Health Association.

ACHA. (2011). *American College Health Association: National college health assessment II, 2011 executive summary.* Hanover, MD: American College Health Association.

ACHA. (2014). *American College Health Association: National college health assessment II, 2014 executive summary.* Hanover, MD: American College Health Association.

Adams, M., Bell, L. A., & Griffin, P. (Eds.). (1997). *Teaching for diversity and social change: A sourcebook* (1st ed.). New York, NY: Routledge.

Allport, G. W. (1950). *The individual and his religion.* New York, NY: Macmillan.

Allport, G. W., & Ross, J. M. (1967). Personal religious orientation and prejudice. *Journal of Personality and Social Psychology, 5*(4), 432–443.

Arnett, J. J. (2015). *Emerging adulthood: The winding road from the late teens through the twenties* (2nd ed.). Oxford, UK: Oxford University Press.

Astin, A. W. (1978). *Four critical years: Effects of college on beliefs, attitudes, and knowledge*. San Francisco, CA: Jossey-Bass.
Astin, A. W. (1991). *Assessment for excellence: The philosophy and practice of assessment and evaluation in higher education*. New York, NY: Macmillan/Oryx.
Astin, A. W. (1993). *What matters in college: Four critical years revisited*. San Francisco, CA: Jossey-Bass.
Astin, A. W. (2004). Why spirituality deserves a central place in liberal education. *Liberal Education, 90*(2), 34–41.
Astin, A. W., Astin, H. S., & Lindholm, J. A. (2011). *Cultivating the spirit: How college can enhance students' inner lives*. San Francisco, CA: Jossey-Bass.
Astin, A. W., & Keen, J. P. (2006). Equanimity and spirituality. *Religion and Education, 33*(2), 1–8.
Baer, R.A., Smith, G.T., Hopkins, J., Krietemeyer, J., & Toney, L. (2006). Using self-report assessment methods to explore facets of mindfulness. *Assessment, 13*(1), 27–45.
Batson, C. D., & Schoenrade, P. (1991). Measuring religion as quest: Validity concerns. *J. Scientific Study of Religion, 30*, 416–429.
Belenky, M. F., Clinchy, B. M., Goldberger, N. R., & Tarule, J. M. (1986). *Women's ways of knowing: The development of self, voice, and mind*. New York, NY: Basic Books.
Bellah, R., Sullivan, W., & Tipton, S. (1987). *Habits of the heart: Individualism and commitment in American life*. New York, NY: Perennial Library.
Bergen-Cico, D., & Bylander, J. A. (2012). Reuniting the often neglected aims of liberal education: Student well-being and psychosocial development. In D. W. Harward (Ed.), *Transforming undergraduate education: Theory that compels and practices that succeed*. Lanham, MD: Rowman & Littlefield.
Boyer, E. L. (1987). *College: The undergraduate experience in America*. New York, NY: HarperCollins.
Boyer, E. L. (1990). *Campus life: In search of community*. Princeton, NJ: The Carnegie Foundation for the Advancement of Teaching.
Cantor, D., Fisher, B., Chibnall, S., Bruce, C., Townsend, R., Thomas, G., et al. (2015a). *AAU-Harvard University data from the campus climate survey on sexual assault and sexual misconduct*. Rockville, MD: Association of American Universities - Harvard University - Westat Research.
Cantor, D., Fisher, B., Chibnall, S., Townsend, R., Lee, H., Bruce, C., et al. (2015b). *AAU campus climate survey report on sexual assault and sexual misconduct*. Rockville, MD: Association of American Universities/Westat Research.
Carr, J. L. (2005). *American College Health Association campus violence white paper*. Baltimore, MD: American College Health Association.

CASA. (2007). *Wasting the best and the brightest: Substance abuse at America's colleges and universities.* New York, NY: Center on Addiction and Substance Abuse at Columbia University.

Chickering, A. W., Dalton, J. C., & Liesa, S. (2006). *Encouraging authenticity and spirituality in higher education.* San Francisco, CA: Jossey-Bass.

Chickering, A. W., & Reisser, L. (1993). *Education and identity* (2nd ed.). San Francisco, CA: Jossey-Bass.

Colby, A., Ehrlich, T., Beaumont, E., & Stephens, J. (2003). *Educating citizens: Preparing America's undergraduates for lives of moral and civic responsibility.* San Francisco, CA: Jossey-Bass.

CORE-Institute. (2010). *2006–2008 National Data: Core alcohol and drug survey, long form, executive summary.* Carbondale, IL: Southern Illinois University.

Deckro, G. R., Ballinger, K. M., Hyot, M., Wilcher, M., Dusek, J., Myers, P., et al. (2002). The evaluation of a mind/body intervention to reduce psychological distress and perceived stress in college students. *Journal of American College Health 50*(6), 281–287.

DeJong, W., & Langford, L. (2002). A typology for campus-based alcohol prevention: Moving toward environmental management strategies. *Journal of Studies on Alcohol, Supplement 14#*, 140–147.

DeJong, W., Vince-Whitman, C., Colthurst, T., Cretella, M., Gilbreath, M., Rosati, M., et al. (1998). *Environmental management: A comprehensive strategy for reducing alcohol and other drug use on college campuses.* Newton, MA: Higher Education Center for Alcohol, Drug Abuse, and Violence Prevention.

Deloria, V., Jr. (1973). *God is red.* New York, NY: Grosset & Dunlap.

Deloria, V., Jr. (1979). *The metaphysics of existence.* New York, NY: Harper & Row.

Eagan, K., Stolzenberg, E. B., Ramirez, J. J., Aragon, M. C., Suchard, M. R., & Hurtado, S. (2014). *The American freshman: National norms Fall 2014.* Los Angeles, CA: Higher Education Research Institute, UCLA.

Erdur-Baker, O., Aberson, C. L., Barrow, J. C., & Draper, M. R. (2006). Nature and severity of college students' psychological concerns: A comparison of clinical and nonclinical national samples. *Professional Psychology: Research and Practice, 37*(3), 317–323.

Fanon, F. (1968). *The wretched of the earth.* New York, NY: Grove Press.

Fink, J. E. (2015). Flourishing: Exploring predictors of mental health within the college environment. *Journal of American College Health, 62*(6), 380–388.

Finley, A. P. (2011). Connecting the dots: A methodological approach for assessing students' civic engagement and psychosocial well-being. *Liberal Education, 97*(2), 52–56.

Finley, A. P., & Swaner, L. E. (2008). *Bringing Theory to Practice (BTtoP) cost study: College and university expenditures in addressing patterns of student disengagement.* Washington, DC: Association of American Colleges and Universities.

Freeman, S., Eddy, S. L., McDonough, M., Smith, Michelle K., Okoroafor, N., Jordt, H., et al. (2014). Active learning increases student performance in science, engineering, and mathematics. *Proceedings of the National Academy of Sciences, 111*(23), 8410–8415.

Freire, P. (1970). *Pedagogy of the oppressed* (20th anniversary ed.). New York, NY: Continuum.

Freire, P. (1973). *Education for critical consciousness.* New York, NY: Seabury.

Gallagher, R. P. (2014). *National survey of college counseling centers – 2014.* Alexandria, VA: International Association of Counseling Services.

Gebhardt, T. L., Kaphingst, K., & DeJong, W. (2000). A campus-community coalition to control alcohol-related problems off campus: An environmental management case study. *Journal of American College Health, 48*(5), 211–216.

Gilligan, C. (1982). *In a different voice: Psychological theory and women's development.* Cambridge, MA: Harvard U. Press.

Haines, M., & Spear, S. F. (1996). Changing the perception of the norm: A strategy to decrease binge drinking among college students. *Journal of American College Health, 45*(3), 134–141.

Hardiman, R., & Jackson, B. W. (1997). Conceptual foundations for social justice courses. In M. Adams, L. A. Bell, & P. Griffin (Eds.), *Teaching for diversity and social justice.* New York, NY: Routledge.

Harding, V. (1981). *There is a river: The Black struggle for freedom in America.* New York, NY: Harcourt Brace.

Harward, D. W. (2007). Engaged learning and the core purposes of liberal education: Bringing theory to practice. *Liberal Education, 93*(1), 6–15.

Harward, D. W. (Ed.). (2012). *Transforming undergraduate education: Theory that compels and practices that succeed.* Lanham, MD: Rowman & Littlefield.

HEC. (2002). *Alcohol and other drug prevention on college campuses: Model programs.* Washington, DC: United States Department of Education, Office of Elementary and Secondary Education, Safe and Drug-Free School Programs & Higher Education Center for Alcohol and Other Drug Prevention.

Helms, J. E. (Ed.). (1990). *Black and white racial identity development.* Westport, CT: Greenwood Press.

hooks, b. (1981). *Ain't I a woman: Black women and feminism.* Boston, MA: South End Press.

Huppert, F. A., & Whittington, J. E. (2003). Evidence for the independence of positive and negative wellbeing: Implications for quality of life assessment. *British Journal of Health Psychology, 8,* 107–122.

Hyman, S. E. (2015). *Harvard task force report on the prevention of sexual assault.* Cambridge, MA: Harvard University.

Kadison, R., & DiGeronimo, T. F. (2004). *College of the overwhelmed: The campus mental health crisis and what to do about it.* San Francisco, CA: Jossey-Bass.

Kass, J. D. (1995). Contributions of religious experience to psychological and physical well-being: Research evidence and an explanatory model. In L. Vandecreek (Ed.), *Spiritual needs and pastoral services: Readings in research* (pp. 189–213). Decatur, GA: Journal of Pastoral Care Publications.

Kass, J. D., Friedman, R., Leserman, J., Caudill, M., Zuttermeister, P., & Benson, H. (1991). An inventory of positive psychological attitudes with potential relevance to health outcomes. *Behavioral Medicine, 17*(3), 121–129.

Kazanjian, V. H., & Lawrence, P. L. (Eds.). (2000). *Education as transformation: Religious pluralism, spirituality, and a new vision for higher education in America.* Boston, MA: Peter Lang.

Keeling, R. P. (2004). *Learning reconsidered: A campus-wide focus on the student experience.* Washington, DC: American College Personnel Association (ACPA) - National Association of Student Personnel Administrators (NASPA).

Keeling, R. P. (2006). *Learning reconsidered 2: Implementing a campus-wide focus on the student experience.* Washington, DC: American College Personnel Association (ACPA) - National Association of Student Personnel Administrators (NASPA).

Keeling, R. P., Wall, A. W., Underhile, R., & Dungie, G. W. (2008). *Assessment reconsidered: Institutional effectiveness for student success.* Washington, DC: National Association of Student Personnel Administrators (NASPA).

Keyes, C. L. M. (2002). The mental health continuum: From languishing to flourishing in life. *Journal of Health and Social Research, 43*(June), 207–222.

Keyes, C. L. M. (2005). Mental illness and/or mental health? Investigating axioms of the complete state model of health. *Journal of Consulting and Clinical Psychology, 73*(3), 539–548.

Keyes, C. L. M. (2006a). Mental health in adolescence: Is America's youth flourishing? *American Journal of Orthopsychiatry, 76,* 395–402.

Keyes, C. L. M. (2006b). The subjective well-being of America's youth: Toward a comprehensive assessment. *Adolescent Family Health, 4,* 3–17.

Keyes, C. L. M. (2007). Promoting and protecting mental health as flourishing. *American Psychologist, 62*(2), 95–108.

Kuh, G. D. (2003). *The National Survey of Student Engagement: Conceptual framework and overview of psychometric properties.* Bloomington, IN: Indiana University Center for Postsecondary Research and Planning.

Kuh, G. D. (2008). *High-impact educational practices: What they are, who has access to them, and why they matter.* Washington, DC: Association of American Colleges and Universities.

Kuh, G. D., Kinzie, J., Schuh, J. H., & Whitt, E. J. (2005a). *Assessing conditions to enhance educational effectiveness: The inventory for student engagement and success.* San Francisco, CA: John Wiley.

Kuh, G. D., Kinzie, J., Schuh, J. H., & Whitt, E. J. (2005b). *Student success in college: Creating conditions that matter.* San Francisco, CA: Jossey-Bass.
Kuh, G. D., Kinzie, J., Schuh, J. H., & Whitt, E. J. (2010). *Student success in college: Creating conditions that matter.* San Francisco, CA: Jossey-Bass.
Levy, D. J., Heissel, J. A., Richeson, J. A., & Adam, E. K. (2016). Psychological and behavioral responses to race-based social stress as pathways to disparities in educational outcomes. *American Psychologist, 71*(6), 455–473.
Low, K. G. (2011). Flourishing, substance use, and engagement in students entering college: A preliminary study. *Journal of American College Health, 59*(6), 555–561.
McDermott, R. C., Cheng, H.-L., Wright, C., Browning, B. R., Upton, A. W., & Sevig, T. D. (2015). Adult attachment dimensions and college student distress: The mediating role of hope. *The Counseling Psychologist, 43*(6), 822–852.
McDonald, W. M. (Ed.). (2002). *Creating campus community: In search of Ernest Boyer's legacy.* San Francisco, CA: Jossey-Bass.
Meilman, P. W., & Presley, C. A. (1997). Average weekly alcohol consumption: Drinking percentiles for American college students. *Journal of Amercian College Health, 45*(5), 201–205.
Mezirow, J. (Ed.). (1990). *Fostering critical reflection in adulthood: A guide to transformative and emancipatory learning.* San Francisco, CA: Jossey-Bass.
Miller, J. B. (1976). *Toward a new psychology of women.* New York, NY: Penguin.
NSSE. (2007). *National Survey of Student Engagement. Experiences that matter: Enhancing student learning and success, annual report 2007.* Bloomington, IN: Indiana University Center for Postsecondary Research.
NSSE. (2014). *National Survey of Student Engagement: Bringing the Institution into Focus, Annual Results 2014.* Bloomington, IN: Indiana University Center for Postsecondary Research.
Palmer, P. (1983). *To know as we are known: Education as a spiritual journey.* San Francisco, CA: HarperSanFrancisco.
Palmer, P. (1998). *The courage to teach.* San Francisco, CA: Jossey-Bass.
Pargament, K. I. (1997). *The psychology of religion and coping: Theory, research, practice.* New York, NY: Guilford.
Pargament, K. I. (2007). *Spiritually integrated psychotherapy: Understanding and addressing the sacred.* New York, NY: Guilford Press.
Parks, S. D. (1986). *The critical years: The young adult search for a faith to live by.* San Francisco, CA: Harper and Row.
Parks, S. D. (2000). *Big questions, worthy dreams: Mentoring young adults in their search for meaning, purpose, and faith.* San Francisco, CA: Jossey-Bass.
Pascarella, E. T., & Terenzini, P. T. (2005). *How college affects students: Volume 2 - A third decade of research.* San Francisco, CA: Jossey-Bass.

Peer, J. W., & McAuslan, P. (2016). Self-doubt during emerging adulthood: The conditional mediating influence of mindfulness. *Emerging Adulthood, 4*(3), 176–185.

Perkins, W., Meilman, P. W., Leichliter, J. S., Cashin, J. R., & Presley, C. A. (1999). Misperceptions of the norms for the frequency of alcohol and other drug use on college campuses. *Journal of American College Health, 47*(6), 253–259.

Presley, C. A., & Meilman, P. W. (1994). Development of the Core Institute alcohol and drug survey: Initial findings and future directions. *Journal of American College Health, 42*(6), 248–255.

Pryor, J. H., Hurtado, S., DeAngelo, L., Palucki-Blake, L., & Tran, S. (2010). *The American freshman: National norms 2010*. Los Angeles, CA: Higher Education Research Institute, UCLA.

Rogers, C. R. (1961). *On becoming a person: A therapist's view of psychotherapy*. Boston, MA: Houghton-Mifflin.

Rogers, C. R. (1969). *Freedom to learn: A view of what education might become*. Columbus, OH: Charles E. Merrill.

Ross, V. (2004). Depression, anxiety, and alcohol or other drug use among college students. *Prevention Updates* (pp. 1–7). Newton, MA: Higher Education Center for Alcohol and Other Drug Prevention, funded by the US Dept. of Education.

Seligman, M. E. P. (2002). Positive psychology, positive prevention, and positive therapy. In C. R. Snyder & S. J. Lopez (Eds.), *Handbook of positive psychology*. New York, NY: Oxford University Press.

Seligman, M. E. P., & Csikszentmihalyi, M. (2000). Positive psychology: An introduction. *American Psychologist, 55*(1), 5–14.

Shapiro, S. L., Brown, K. W., & Astin, J. (2011). Toward the integration of meditation into higher education: A review of research evidence. *Teachers College Record, 113*(3), 493–528.

Slater, P. E. (1971). *The pursuit of loneliness: American culture at the breaking point*. Boston, MA: Beacon Press.

SPRC. (2004). *Suicide Prevention Resource Center Report: Promoting Mental Health and Preventing Suicide in College and University Settings*. Newton, MA: Educational Development Center Inc.

Staub, S. D., & Finley, A. P. (2007). Assessing the impact of engaged learning initiatives for first-year students. *peerReview, 9*(3), 18–21.

Swaner, L. E. (2005). *Linking engaged learning, student mental health and well-being, and civic development: A review of the literature, Bringing Theory to Practice*. Washington, DC: American Association of Colleges and Universities.

Swaner, L. E. (2007). Linking engaged learning, student mental health and well-being, and civic development: A review of the literature (abridged version). *Liberal Education, 93*(1), 16–25.

Swaner, L. E. (2012). The theories, contexts, and multiple pedagogies of engaged learning. In D. W. Harward (Ed.), *Transforming undergraduate education: Theories that Compel and Practices that Succeed*. Lanham, MD: Rowman & Littlefield.

Swaner, L. E., & Finley, A. (2007). The scope of BTtoP research: Design and findings from the demonstration project. *peerReview, 9*(3), 22–29.

Tillich, P. (1952). *The courage to be*. New Haven, CT: Yale University Press.

Wechsler, H., Kelley, K., Seibring, M., Kuo, M., & Rigotti, N. (2001a). College smoking policies and smoking cessation programs: Results of a survey of college health center directors. *Journal of American College Health, 49*(March), 1–8.

Wechsler, H., Kelley, K., Weitzman, E. R., San Giovanni, J. P., & Seibring, M. (2000a). What colleges are doing about student binge drinking: A survey of college administrators. *Journal of American College Health, 48*(5), 219–227.

Wechsler, H., Lee, J. E., Kuo, M., & Lee, H. (2000b). College binge drinking in the 1990's: A continuing problem. *Journal of American College Health, 48*(5), 199–211.

Wechsler, H., Lee, J. E., & Rigotti, N. A. (2001b). Cigarette use by college students in smoke-free housing: Results of a national study. *American Journal of Preventive Medicine, 20*(3), 202–207.

Wechsler, H., Lee, J. E., Kuo, M., Seibring, M., Nelson, T. F., & Lee, H. (2002). Trends in college binge drinking during a period of increased prevention efforts: Findings from four Harvard School of Public Health College Alcohol Study surveys: 1993–2001. *Journal of American College Health, 50*(5), 203–217.

Wechsler, H., & Nelson, T. F. (2008). What we have learned from the Harvard School of Public Health College Alcohol Study: Focusing attention on college student alcohol consumption and the environmental conditions that promote it. *Journal of Studies on Alcohol and Drugs, 69*(4), 481–490.

Wechsler, H., Rigotti, N. A., Gledhill-Hoyt, J., & Lee, H. (1998). Increased levels of cigarette use among college students: A cause for national concern. *Journal of the American Medical Association, 280*(19), 1673–1678.

Wechsler, H., Seibring, M., Liu, I.-C., & Ahl, M. (2004). Colleges respond to student binge drinking: Reducing student demand or limiting access. *Journal of American College Health, 52*(4), 159–168.

Wechsler, H., & Wuerthrich, B. (2002). *Dying to drink: Confronting binge drinking on college campuses*. New York, NY: Rodale Press.

Wessler, S., & Moss, M. (2001a). Hate crimes on campus: The problem and efforts to confront it. Washington, DC: U.S. Department of Justice, Bureau of Justice Assistance, Publication # 187249.

Wessler, S., & Moss, M. (2001b). Report on hate violence: University of Southern Maine, Center for Prevention of Hate Violence. http://www.cphv.usm.maine.edu.

Zimmerman, R. (2004). *Campus and community coalitions in AOD prevention Prevention Updates.* Newton, MA: Higher Education Center for Alcohol and Other Drug Prevention funded by the U.S. Department of Education.

CHAPTER 4

My Professional Journey: Becoming a Person-Centered Mentor with a Psychospiritual and Social Justice Orientation

This chapter will describe three projects that have been formative in my professional development as a person-centered university teacher and mental health clinician. Specifically, the chapter will describe how these projects helped me develop the psychospiritual and social justice orientation that is foundational in my teaching and research. Through my work with Carl Rogers, I learned that person-centered educators must engage in complementary processes of professional and personal growth in order to facilitate similar integrative growth in students. This chapter will describe my complementary learning process.

Rogers was instrumental in developing conceptual and methodological foundations for a person-centered approach in counseling and education. He recognized that prevention-oriented learning and systemic social change were more likely to emerge through the educational system than through psychotherapy. Understanding that a healthy, just society required an educational system that provided socially-consequential maturational growth, he adapted his person-centered learning methods for educational institutions and community-building initiatives (Rogers 1967, 1969). I was fortunate to work closely with him from 1976–1981 as a staff member of the Person-Centered Approach Project (Rogers 1977a, 1980a; Rogers et al. 1978). The mentoring I received from him until his death in 1987 was formative, as it was for many clinicians and teachers who worked with him. His person-centered methods have become so deeply embedded in clinical and educational practice that most professionals are no longer familiar with the details of his research and work.

Rogers identified specific interpersonal conditions that clinicians and educators must create as a foundation for psychological healing and maturational student learning: empathic understanding, emotional congruence and unconditional positive regard (Rogers 1950, 1951a, b, 1952a, 1957, 1959b, 1961, 1962, 1963; Rogers and Dymond 1954). He developed a highly-attuned method of reflective listening that empowers individuals to develop an internal locus of evaluation. His ability to understand the life narratives and emotions of his clients (while not supporting their destructive behaviors), helped them develop compassionate self-acceptance, enabling them to take greater responsibility for their behavior (Rogers 1952b, 1959a, 1961, 1967, 1969, 1971, 1980b).

Although his early conceptual work did not refer explicitly to the constraints of social oppression and positionality, Rogers demonstrated lifelong commitment to social justice. As a young adult, contemplating a career as a Christian minister, he travelled to China, where he observed and wrote about the destructive impact of rigid social hierarchy and white colonialism. This experience was central in his decision to leave the ministry and his subsequent development of psychotherapeutic methods that empower clients, challenging the hierarchical relationship of traditional clinical practice (Cornelius-White 2012; Kass 2015; Kirschenbaum 2007) Rogers respected Paolo Freire's critique of oppressive power dynamics in society and education (Freire 1970). He acknowledged Freire's work as more overtly sociopolitical than his, while perceiving congruence in the politics of their perspectives (Rogers 1977a). His lifelong opposition to racial discrimination extended from post-World War II support for equal treatment of African American veterans to anti-apartheid work in South Africa (Kirschenbaum 2007; Rogers 1986). His support for feminism was evident throughout his professional collaboration with many women colleagues, including his daughter Natalie Rogers (Rogers 1980).

It is important to note that Rogers' reflective listening method can be misused when clinicians lack multicultural competencies and social justice perspectives. Important critiques have been written by Derald Wing Sue in *Counseling the Culturally Different* (Sue and Sue 1981) and by Laura Brown and Mary Ballou in their excellent textbook, *Personality and Psychopathology: Feminist Reappraisals* (Brown and Ballou 1992). Howard Kirschenbaum relates a parody of reflective listening, often shared in Rogers' clinical circle, demonstrating awareness that these methods can be applied superficially (Kirschenbaum 2007). Nonetheless, when sociopolitical awareness and multicultural competencies are incorporated, Rogers' relational methods provide a foundation for highly attuned psychotherapy.

Rogers' relational approach is deeply infused in current approaches to trauma treatment. But his influence is rarely acknowledged. Few current clinicians are aware of his post-World War II clinical work with veterans, which included sensitivity to issues now described as PTSD (Rogers 1944a, b; Rogers and Wallen 1946). Further, few clinicians know that his laboratory conducted relevant neuroscience research. William Thetford's work on frustration tolerance during client-centered therapy through measurement of changes in autonomic nervous system reactivity was a prescient antecedent (Rogers 1961; Thetford 1952).

In short, Rogers deserves more recognition than he currently receives for pioneering contributions to psychology and education. As a young professional, I was profoundly moved observing him work firsthand. Because I knew him personally, as a human being with a distinct personality and complex life history, it was electrifying to watch him shift into a state of client-centered mindfulness. Through disciplined attention and genuine compassion, he entered fully into *I-Thou* interactions with each person. His ego-concerns seemed to dissolve as he listened intently, responded with intellectual and emotional depth, and remained receptively present. Clients moved naturally into deep emotional content, experiencing transformative insights and growth through an engaged relational process with such an attuned personal presence. My work with Rogers was the first of three professional projects that helped me develop methodological and conceptual foundations for the *Know Your Self* curriculum.

Project 1: Facilitating Person-Centered Community with Carl Rogers

In the final period of his career, Rogers hypothesized that the same interpersonal conditions that mentor individual growth could facilitate healthy community development. From his sociopolitical perspective, healthy communities do not control members through social coercion or stratified hierarchies. They respect individual and cultural differences; support person-centered growth into new aspects of identity; and communicate through respectful dialogue, honest emotional expression, and empathic listening. During the Person-Centered Approach Project, our seven-person staff tested these ideas in temporary learning communities. Approximately 100 people participated in each community, living in dormitories on a college campus for 2 weeks (Kass 2015; Rogers 1977b, 1980a; Rogers et al. 1978).

Our primary task as staff was not to structure community activities. This task belonged to the community. Our primary task was to model empathic presence, emotional congruence and unconditional positive regard during the community-building process. Fulfilling this role, we observed participants experimenting with these behaviors. In the initial days of this non-hierarchical approach, the process was often difficult, provoking anxiety, frustration, and anger with the staff. We had to trust the person-centered learning process that Rogers had investigated so thoroughly. Gradually, we saw this self-directed group process create a dynamic tension that was deeply empowering. Participants expressed themselves congruently, providing natural community leadership. Listening empathically, they developed sensitivity to the needs of others, including the community itself. Practicing altruistic regard, even in the midst of heated argument, they strengthened frustration tolerance, developing new levels of cognitive and emotional flexibility. Through this learning process, they experienced the human capacity to build person-centered communities that are noncoercive, respectful, and compassionate.

Our staff also experienced new learning: robust community benefited from nonverbal modes of expression and contemplative silence. Natalie Rogers, Maria Villas-Boas Bowen, and I incorporated expressive arts, body-centered experiential work, and meditation into community-building. These alternative modes of self-exploration loosened psychophysiological armoring, released residues of emotional pain and untapped capacities for laughter and joy, and helped individuals attune to core dimensions of self (Kass 1981, 1985; Rogers 1984). While we lacked current neuroscientific understanding about the clinical dynamics of these methods (Fosha et al. 2009; Kass and Trantham 2014; Ogden et al. 2006; Schore 2003; Siegel 2007), the incorporation of somatic expressive therapies and meditation strengthened congruent behavior and self-awareness in these communities.

Further, we learned that our multimodal approach contributed to a spiritual element of awareness that emerged periodically within these communities. This emergent phenomenon helped Rogers extend his conceptual understanding of human flourishing. In his last book, *A Way of Being*, he quoted a community member's written narrative that illustrated emergent spiritual awareness (Rogers 1980c, pp. 196–197):

> I found it to be a profound spiritual experience. I felt the oneness of experience in the community. We breathed together, felt together, even spoke for one another. I felt the power of the "life force" that infuses each of us—whatever that is. I felt its presence without the usual barricades of "me-ness" or "you-ness"—it was like a meditative experience when I feel myself as a center of consciousness, very much a part of the broader, universal consciousness. And yet with that extraordinary sense of oneness, the separateness of each person present has never been more clearly preserved.

This narrative illustrates important themes: the profound sense of interpersonal *connection* that often developed within these communities; the power of rich emotional bonding to elicit spiritual awareness; and the deep existential meaning that the experience offered to this participant. For a brief period, she experienced the fabric of life as an underlying unity.

As our community-building project developed, Rogers grew increasingly interested in spirituality as an internal resource for meaning-making (C.R. Rogers, personal communication, June 13, 1980). In early research, he concluded that human beings have an innate psychological capacity for maturation: a self-actualizing tendency. In a new, more existential formulation, he now described "a formative tendency…within the universe" through which "a creative, not a disintegrative, process is at work," and through which "the human organism has been moving toward the more complete development of awareness" (Rogers 1980c, pp. 124–128). Seven years later, in a letter to me, as he continued to contemplate the transpersonal dimension of human experience, Rogers referred to his initial formulation of the self-actualizing tendency (Rogers 1959b), observing that it included, in a small but meaningful way, "the tendency toward transcendence" (C.R. Rogers, personal communication, January 5, 1987) (Kass 2015).

The spiritual dimension of the *connectivity* that developed in these communities had profound impact on me, intellectually and personally, particularly because it had not been a goal of our staff. To understand how we had created a "non-theological" environment where spiritual awareness emerged naturally, I spoke with participants, exploring their sense of spirituality from a phenomenological, person-centered perspective. First, I learned that the deep bonding that took place increased their internal locus of evaluation. Feeling accepted as themselves, they became more trusting of their feelings and intuitive perceptions. But paradoxically, as they felt increasingly in touch with their inner selves, they also felt increasingly in touch with something greater than themselves: an inner domain of knowing which felt wiser than their individual self (Kass 1991a). It was patently clear that these experiences of a spiritual essence within self were not pathological. They did not undermine these individuals' autonomy or capacity for critical thinking. Further, they provided a source of rich existential meaning and deepened their capacity for altruistic compassion (Kass 1991b).

Before my work with Rogers, I had begun to develop a meditation practice, primarily as a tool for stress-reduction. But it was impossible to mistake similarities between the spiritual goals of meditation and phenomenological descriptions of *connection* reported by these participants. The word *yoga*, after all, means "bonding." This similarity shifted my understanding, and I began to consider meditation as a process of relational attachment at a core level of being.

Motivated by these new ideas, I intensified my meditation practice. Having learned to quiet my discursive thoughts through mindful focus on the breath, I began consciously to soften my self-protective emotional armor, cultivating relational receptivity. But rather than achieving tranquil attachment, I encountered turbulent waters. Waves of emotion and memory began to surface, and I found myself reviewing traumatic life events that had shaped my psychological development. Gradually, as I understood the psychological importance of this unfolding process, I became comfortable with this unexpectedly turbulent aspect of meditation. I learned to let the emotions elicited by these memories ripple through me, rather than distancing myself from them. Paradoxically, each time that I allowed this integrative emotional process to take place, my mind would then become calm. I experienced an inner state of receptivity and intuitive insight where I understood that my core self was intimately connected to a Ground of Being. After meditation, I felt unusually awake, experiencing heightened sensory awareness and a felt sense of connection between myself and the world, in which I was at peace, at-one, with life. The unitive serenity I am describing was always temporary. Nonetheless, having passed through this tumultuous process, over a multiyear period, I found that tranquil reverie, intuitive insights, and a felt sense of relational attachment to the Ground of Being was more available during meditation. Further, in my interpersonal relationships, I experienced more ability to be congruent, to be reciprocally attuned, to give and receive love. This personal growth overflowed into my professional work. As a psychotherapist and educator, my capacity for interpersonal attunement deepened.

As I tried to understand these experiences intellectually, they gradually made sense from several theoretical perspectives. Through a Rogerian lens, I was becoming more fully present and aware, and increasingly receptive to growth catalyzed by the formative tendency (Rogers 1980c). Through a Jungian lens, by incorporating the shadow, an integrative process of individuation was occurring, leading to greater wholeness and contact with the inner self (Jung 1964). Through a Bio-energetic and Gestalt lens, I was releasing somatic memories, stored in segmented musculature that regulates emotional suppression and expression, thereby increasing my capacity for interpersonal contact and love (Perls 1973; Reich 1960). Through a yoga psychology lens, I was experiencing memories and mental conditioning (*samskaras*) stored in the segmentally-arranged *chakras* of the subtle body (mental-emotional dimension of self). As these agitating, growth-limiting constructs were released, I was experiencing richer levels of inner tranquility and connection with my essential mind or wise, core self (Hui-neng 1998; Kornfield 2000; Rama et al. 1976). Through the lens of contemplatives from Christianity, Judaism, and Islam, the illusory veil that separates self and the Divine had been pushed aside briefly when I opened my heart, and I became receptive to insights and wisdom from the Ground of Being (Angha 1998; Green 2003; Kisly 2004; Merton 1996; Prager 2003). Each conceptual model contributed meaningful insights.

During this time, I began to study Jewish contemplative practice. I was raised in a vibrant Conservative synagogue where I learned to chant extraordinary melodies through which prayer can elicit contemplative states. But a contemplative perspective had not been taught. I now found a rich vein of Jewish scholarship deeply engaged in renewing this contemplative orientation to meditative prayer (Aron 1969; Bokser 1978; Buber 1947; Green and Holtz 1993; Heschel 1951; Idel 1988a; Kaplan 1978; Schachter-Shalomi 1993; Scholem 1941).

These studies eventually led me to the work of Maimonides (Rabbi Moses ben Maimon), the twelfth-century philosopher, physician, and leader of the Jewish community in Egypt and the Mediterranean region. His classic text *Guide of the Perplexed* presents an elegant exposition on psychospiritual maturation from a Jewish perspective that is deeply congruent with the Perennial Philosophy (Maimonides 1963). In Chap. 5, I will present his model of contemplative mind as a useful framework for understanding similar models in the other traditions. Moreover, his work reflects the cross-cultural pollination characteristic of this period. Maimonides was influenced by Muslim philosophers who preserved and refined the foundational contributions of Aristotelian and neo-Platonic philosophy to Western thought; and, in turn, his work influenced the development of Christian theology (Burrell 1986; Goodman 1999; Pines 1963).

Maimonides was born in 1135 C.E., in Cordoba, at the end of Spain's Golden Age. The Muslim Umayyad dynasty had supported a thriving multicultural society of Muslims, Jews, and Christians (Menocal 2002). But when a fundamentalist dynasty took power, his family fled to North Africa. He eventually settled in Fustat, the Jewish suburb of Cairo, serving as a physician in the court of the Muslim leader, Salah al-Din Yussuf ibn Ayyub (Saladin). In the midst of these tumultuous and demanding activities, Maimonides wrote many important texts, including the *Mishneh Torah*, a distillation of the ethics and rules which govern traditional Jewish life (Birnbaum 1967). Building on this text, *Guide of the Perplexed* explains the philosophical purpose of Jewish life: the psychospiritual maturation of individuals and society (Bokser 1950; Buijs 1998; Davidson 2005; Goodman 1976; Halbertal 2014; Harris 2007; Hartman 1976; Heschel 1982; Kelner 2006; Kraemer 2008; Zeitlin 1935). Maimonides is best known for his rationalism. He was a leading voice for incorporating science into Jewish cosmology. But he also wrote from a contemplative viewpoint (Blumenthal 1984; Burrell 1986; Faur 1999; Goodman 1999; Hartman 1976; Heschel 1996); and Abraham Abulafia, a pre-eminent Jewish mystic, considered Maimonides an important influence (Idel 1988b).

Though some scholars consider these perspectives antagonistic, Maimonides integrated rational and contemplative viewpoints in a thoughtful and subtle manner. Throughout his work, he deconstructed Biblical anthropomorphic images of God, insisted that prophetic vision was a subjective experience shaped by specific historical-cultural circumstances, and described these contemplative experiences as an inherent human capacity with meaningful authority that depends on the individual's level of maturation (Kass 2013, 2017; Kass and Lennox 2005).

My references to Maimonides will not privilege the Jewish tradition. Rather, his ideas will serve as an example of the articulate voices in every spiritual tradition that demonstrate a shared corpus of maturational goals and contemplative practices. I have found value in rooting myself in the spiritual tradition of my ethnic culture, while also expanding my philosophical orientation, contemplative practices, and understanding of my birth tradition, through a more inclusive, universalizing lens. This lens has been a central feature in my own person-centered process of psychospiritual development, and I recognize Carl Rogers' strong influence on my commitment to developing an internal locus of existential meaning-making.

In summary, my work on the Person-Centered Approach Project had unexpected impact on my psychospiritual development. In addition, it helped me develop facilitation skills for person-centered community-building, a key component of the *Know Your Self* curriculum. Finally, it propelled me into an unanticipated area of research. I now hoped to investigate spiritual awareness as a potential resource for psychological and social well-being. Specifically, I hoped to investigate meditation as an experience of attachment to a core dimension of self.

Project 2: Quantitative Research with Herbert Benson on Spirituality and Resilience

During my work with Rogers, I joined the graduate faculty at Lesley University in Cambridge, Massachusetts. Many of my colleagues were early adopters of clinical methods that employ a person-centered approach, social justice perspectives, expressive therapies, mind-body integration, and contemplative practice. While training mental health counselors through this holistic, integrative lens, I began a research program on psychological and social well-being.

With Rogers' professional support, I was invited by Herbert Benson, Chief of Behavioral Medicine at Beth Israel Hospital, Harvard Medical School, to collaborate on a research project investigating relationships between contemplative spirituality, psychological well-being, and physical health. This project (1985–1991) strengthened my skills in mind-body clinical practice.

Early in his career as a cardiologist, Benson had investigated the effects of stress on the heart (Benson et al. 1969). He worked in the Thorndike Laboratory where Walter Cannon, 50 years before, had identified an instinctive "fight-flight" response to real or perceived danger (Cannon 1929). This protective response is triggered by the sympathetic nervous system, the arousal-inducing circuits in the autonomic nervous system. It produces elevations in heart rate, blood pressure, oxygen consumption, and blood sugar levels, while inhibiting digestion (Cannon and Rosenblueth 1937). Cannon also recognized that the constancy of modern stress prevented restoration of homeostasis, creating vulnerability to disease (Cannon 1936). Hans Selye completed this model, observing that chronic activation of the stress response produced organismic exhaustion, including suppression of the immune system (Selye 1956).

Benson's research demonstrated that meditation can restore homeostasis through a hypo-metabolic process that lowers heart rate, blood pressure, and metabolism. He called this health-promoting restorative process the *Relaxation Response* (Beary et al. 1974; Benson 1975; Benson et al. 1974a, b; Wallace et al. 1971). In addition to success treating high blood pressure, his team found eliciting the relaxation response through meditation prepared patients for cardiac surgery (Leserman et al. 1989). Extending this research to the immune system (Borysenko 1984), his team developed treatments for other stress-related illnesses (Borysenko 1989; Esch et al. 2003). These included gastrointestinal dysregulation, stress headaches, and sleep disorders (Hellman et al. 1990); infertility (Domar et al. 1990), premenstrual syndrome (Goodale et al. 1990); and pediatric migraines (Fentress et al. 1986). In addition, they found that meditation improved workplace health and performance (Peters et al. 1977) and exercise physiology (Benson et al. 1978), and could be incorporated into psychotherapy (Kutz et al. 1985).

Jon Kabat-Zinn, Founding Director of the Mind-Body Stress Reduction Program at the University of Massachusetts Medical Center, extended the research on meditation substantively by investigating the self-regulatory benefits of *mindfulness* (Kabat-Zinn 1990). His team demonstrated that mindfulness meditation was effective managing chronic pain (Kabat-Zinn 1982; Kabat-Zinn and Chapman-Waldrop 1988; Kabat-Zinn et al. 1985, 1986), psoriasis (Kabat-Zinn et al. 1998); and anxiety (Miller et al. 1995). With Richard Davidson, he then determined that mindfulness meditation increased anterior left-hemisphere activity (associated with positive affect) and immune function (Davidson et al. 2003). Through Kabat-Zinn's pioneering work in Buddhist psychology, mindfulness has become a central feature of stress reduction programs in medical settings (Santorelli 2000); mental health practice (Germer 2009; Germer and Siegel 2012; Germer et al. 2005); substance abuse treatment (Marlatt and Kristeller 1999; Peltz 2013); trauma treatment (Follette et al. 2015; Ogden 2009); chaplaincy programs (Giles and Miller 2012); and consciousness studies (Lutz et al. 2004; Varela and Shear 1999).

Subsequent research illuminated the sociocultural dimensions of stress. Economic disparities and social stratification are primary causes of chronic stress (Evans and Kim 2007; Sapolsky 2005a). Robert Sapolsky highlights strong associations between systemic racism, poverty, and illness (Sapolsky 2005b). His focus on sociocultural stress has contributed to current understanding that racial trauma, social stigma, and minority stress are correlated with vulnerability to physical illness, substance abuse, and psychopathology (Bryant-Davis 2008; Bryant-Davis and Ocampo 2005; Chou et al. 2012; Daniel 2000; Hatzenbuehler and McLaughlin 2014; McLaughlin et al. 2007).

Bessel van der Kolk and Stephen Porges have further explicated the psychophysiological mechanisms of traumatic stress (Porges 1995; van der Kolk 2014; van der Kolk et al. 1996). These mechanisms trigger a "freeze" response (confusion, emotional numbing, or dissociation) in conjunction with fight-flight hyperarousal (van der Kolk 1987, 1988). As a result, individuals become emotionally and behaviorally dysregulated, increasing likelihood to harm self or others. Traumatic stress also undermines the ability of the central nervous system to restore homeostasis, reinforcing hyperarousal, through reduced levels of cortisol, a hormone with receptors in the hypothalamus that regulates the stress response (Sapolsky 1996, 2003; Yehuda et al. 1990a, b).

Thus, trauma victims exhibit a paradoxical mixture of high SNS-adrenaline and low HPA-cortisol levels (Mason et al. 2001; McGirr et al. 2010; Yehuda et al. 1991). However, this combination is familiar in animal studies (Kass and Trantham 2014). Dangerously aggressive animals exhibit this pattern (Koolhaas et al. 1991). While most aggressive behavior in animals involves posturing (e.g., vocalization, chest-beating) meant to avoid actual fighting, animals with low cortisol attack without warning, viciously striking to kill (Haller and Kruk 2003). These studies suggest potentially similar effects in humans. Exposure to traumatic violence may create a predisposition for vicious attack, while numbing empathic concern for the suffering of victims (Kass and Trantham 2014). In my clinical work, I now distinguish between the stress response (fight/flight) and a magnified trauma response that includes the potential for hyperaggression and dissociative, protective numbing.

The Benson-Henry Institute for Mind-Body Medicine at Massachusetts General Hospital (BHI), where I am a Visiting Scholar, is now directed by Gregory Fricchione (Fricchione 2011; Stern et al. 2004; Ting and Fricchione 2006). With other colleagues at Mass General, the Institute continues to investigate the physiological mechanisms of meditation. These teams have found that meditation reduces the output of constitutive nitric oxide, a chemical regulating norepinephrine in the central nervous system (Stefano et al. 2001); increases heart rate variability (Peng et al. 2004, 1999); activates limbic and prefrontal structures regulating attention and arousal (Lazar et al. 2000); increases cortical thickness in brain regions regulating attention, interoception, and sensory processing (Lazar et al. 2005); and has positive effects on gene expression that regulates immune responses, inflammation, thinning of the brain cortex during aging, and pathological mechanisms of oxidative stress (Dusek et al. 2008).

This discussion has intentionally given shared credit to Benson and Kabat-Zinn in their pioneering introduction of meditation and cognitive-behavioral approaches to stress reactivity in behavioral medicine. Learning to recognize and interrupt psychophysiological symptoms of stress is now a central feature of all mind-body psychotherapies. But as their work proceeded, a bifurcation occurred in how they taught meditation. Benson's team taught *mental concentration methods* that elicit the relaxation response (interrupting agitated thoughts and emotions through diaphragmatic breathing; release of muscular tension; visualization techniques; prayer/mantra). Kabat-Zinn's team taught attentional methods that promote *mindfulness* (witnessing thoughts, emotions, and somatic processes nonreactively and without judgment). These meditative methods are not antagonistic, though it sometimes seems that they are presented this way. In my professional work, it is invaluable to integrate aspects of each method, whether working with trauma survivors or mentoring person-centered learning with students.

Judith Herman's model for trauma treatment explains this necessity (Herman 1997). In the first stage, when intrusive memories and somatic flashbacks overwhelm clients, the primary clinical task is to create safety by teaching the client to contain or interrupt intrusive thoughts and feelings. Following education about the psychophysiological symptoms of PTSD, learning to elicit the relaxation response is a first step toward creating safety: it is empowering for patients to learn they can control their thoughts and feelings. When clients begin to develop self-regulation skills, it is then useful to create structured experiences where they learn to witness their intrusive thoughts and emotions mindfully. Pat Ogden describes developing a *window of tolerance*, where self-regulatory mechanisms prevent escalation into agitated fight-flight or dissociative freeze responses (Ogden et al. 2006). In the second stage (remembrance and mourning), patients learn to speak about their traumatic experiences, allowing themselves to experience the emotions they have suppressed (Fosha et al. 2009). This stage of healing requires a combination of relaxed internal composure and mindful self-awareness in order to allow emotional expression while creating a coherent self-narrative about these experiences. At the end of therapeutic sessions, it is useful to return to a centering mode of deep relaxation that helps patients transition back to their daily lives. I suspect that most skilled clinicians integrate elicitation of the relaxation response and mindfulness in their treatment protocols. When training clinicians, I teach students how to integrate Rogers' attuned person-centered listening methods with cognitive-behavioral methods that include elicitation of the relaxation response and mindfulness.

Rogers, I will note, was interested in my exploration of Benson's meditation-based paradigm for therapeutic treatment, despite its methodological differences from his person-centered relational approach to psychotherapy. At that time, Benson's treatment program was directed by Joan Borysenko, a skilled clinician with background in psychoneuroimmunology (Borysenko 1989). It was clear that Borysenko facilitated the interpersonal conditions that were central to Rogers' work. But Rogers was interested in another aspect: a connection I proposed between Benson's research on the relaxation response and an investigation conducted by one of Rogers' students at the University of Chicago's Counseling Center. As previously mentioned, William Thetford investigated frustration tolerance, measuring changes in autonomic arousal during client-centered counseling. Experimental and control groups completed a stress-inducing cognitive test. Their autonomic reactivity was measured by monitoring galvanic skin resonance, respiration, and heart rate, establishing baselines for each group. Both groups were tested again after the experimental group received multi-session client-centered counseling. This group returned to baseline significantly faster than the control group, and significantly faster than pre-counseling. Further, the experimental group exhibited significantly less cardiac excitation during post-therapy monitoring (Thetford 1952). Thetford did not measure heart-rate variability, the current preferred indicator of autonomic arousal (Porges 1972). But his results demonstrated that the relational experience of client-centered counseling reduced autonomic reactivity in a manner similar to meditation. Rogers found this connection intriguing (C.R. Rogers, personal communication, June 28, 1985). For me, it offered evidence that meditation and relational attachment were related phenomena. This connection contributed to my emerging focus on meditation as an experience of attachment to a core dimension of self.

Thus, in my research with Benson's team, I did not investigate meditation from a cognitive-behavioral perspective that viewed this ancient practice as a tool for self-regulation. Rather, I investigated meditation from the Perennial Philosophy's psychospiritual perspective: as a method for transpersonal relational attachment (Kass 1995). This perspective was figural in the development of the INSPIRIT measurement scale I developed for this research project.

Benson had always acknowledged the spiritual roots of meditation (Benson 1975). However, while introducing it to the medical community as a tool for autonomic self-regulation, he de-emphasized the spiritual concepts. His work was now sufficiently well-established for him to explore spirituality empirically and explicitly. We received a grant from Laurance Rockefeller to investigate contemplative spiritual experience as a potential resource for psychological and physical health. In the first phase of our project, I led a team that developed an Inventory of Positive Psychological Attitudes (IPPA), measuring a resilient worldview (Kass et al. 1991a). In the second phase, I led a team that developed an Index of Core Spiritual Experience (INSPIRIT), measuring spiritual experiences commonly reported by novice and advanced meditators (Kass et al. 1991b). These measures are described in detail in Chap. 6.

The INSPIRIT is responsive to diverse religious and philosophical belief systems. The instructions state, "The following questions concern your spiritual or religious beliefs and experiences. There are no right or wrong answers. People have many different images and definitions of the 'Higher Power' that we often call 'God.' Please use your image and definition of God when answering the following questions." Each item also includes a potential response that indicates no belief in God. This approach was appropriate in Benson's clinic. First, his patients came from a range of religious backgrounds, predominantly Catholic, Protestant, and Jewish. Second, many were secular humanists. Whether religious or secular, they often wanted to practice meditation in a manner consistent with their cultural background and belief system. Thus, secular patients learned to meditate through mental focus on the breath and repetition of a religiously-neutral word like *one* or *peace*. Religiously-oriented patients were invited to repeat a word or phrase from a self-selected prayer.

Meditation, of course, is different than supplicatory prayer, which maintains discursive thought. Meditation engages people in contemplation. By practicing mental concentration and mindfulness, they quiet the discursive mind, cultivating an internal frame of awareness. As they develop this skill, people often experience an internal state of peace and calm. Deepening this practice, they often report feelings of equanimity and joy. Further, they may report a sense of connection to a transpersonal dimension of being. The INSPIRIT is a self-report scale that taps these experiences, including relational attachment to a transcendent dimension of life.

We did not conceptualize contemplative spirituality as a cure for the serious medical illnesses of patients in Benson's program. However, we knew that many suffered, as a result of their illnesses, from anxiety, depression, and increased frequency of stress-triggered medical symptoms. We hypothesized that contemplative spirituality could be a resource for resilience.

Our results confirmed this hypothesis. Using multiple regression analysis to control for baseline scores, the INSPIRIT was associated with improvement in a resilient worldview, Confidence in Life and Self, as measured by the IPPA. We also found negative correlations between the INSPIRIT and frequency of stress-related medical symptoms (Kass 1995; Kass et al. 1991b).

We also investigated whether *belief in God* had the same resilience-building effects, by including a separate question about belief. Interestingly, there were no correlations. But there was a statistical explanation for this result: minimal variance. Virtually all patients had indicated Belief in God. Knowing that many of these patients were secular humanists, we concluded that this question did not produce reliable results. However, there *had* been significant variance on the INSPIRIT, indicating reliable data about contemplative experiences. We concluded that contemplative spirituality, in which individuals had internal experiences of equanimity and relational connection to the Ground of Being, had more resilience-building vitality than a stated belief in God (Kass et al. 1991b). In summary, this research provided quantitative confirmation for observations that I had made following my work with Rogers. Contemplative spirituality and personally-experienced relational attachment to a transcendent dimension of life can promote psychological resilience.

After completing my work with Benson, I became cognizant of an additional implication of our results. INSPIRIT scores had not changed significantly during the 10-week intervention (Kass 1995; Kass et al. 1991b). Patients who benefited from contemplative spiritual experience had high scores on the INSPIRIT at the outset. This result did not contradict Benson's thesis that meditative elicitation of the relaxation response increases psychophysiological self-regulation. However, it suggested that the additional benefit conferred by contemplative spirituality had been cultivated prior to the treatment program. This result suggested to me that psychospiritual growth is most effective as a preventive resource for resilience, cultivated prior to life crises.

This significant reformulation shifted the orientation of my research program from treatment to prevention and led me to develop the *Know Your Self* curriculum for university students: a person-centered approach to psychospiritual growth that could prepare them to cope more effectively with developmental challenges, life crises, and humanity's chain of pain.

Project 3: Interfaith Dialogue for Social Justice and Multicultural Community

Despite the significance of the two previous projects, they lacked sufficient focus on pressing social justice issues. It has been clear to me for many years that we must recognize the toxic reality of systemic white male privilege and historical racial trauma as crucial steps toward ending humanity's chain of pain (particularly as it manifests in the United States). As a new generation of African American social activists spotlight persistent violence and discrimination against black men in our criminal justice system, they offer a grim indictment of our country's shockingly insufficient progress in breaking this cycle of racial trauma (Alexander

2010; Coates 2015; Comas-Diaz 2016; Hardy 2013; Lowery 2016; Powell 2012; Stevenson 2014).

In 1989, as part of my personal and professional commitment to address these social issues, I joined the Boston Clergy and Religious Leaders Group for Interfaith Dialogue. It is a troubling irony that organized religion often plays a chilling role in humanity's chain of pain, contradicting the spiritual teachings at their core. While progressive religious denominations have been prominent in the battle for social justice, fundamentalism and exclusivism in each tradition foment prejudice, divisive "tribal" loyalties, and violence (Marty 2000). From my perspective, interfaith dialogue is necessary to overcome fundamentalist doctrines and exclusivist claims of privileged access to the Ground of Being. These distorted and toxic perspectives create legitimizing narratives for racism and other forms of social injustice.

The Boston Clergy and Religious Leaders Group met for nearly 20 years (1989–2007), strengthening interfaith community in the Greater Boston area (Eck and Pierce 1998, p. 131). Our meetings drew 50–75 leaders from diverse religious, racial, and ethnic groups. Each monthly meeting had a scheduled presentation in which leaders from these groups described specific problems faced by their communities. Leaders of the Black Ministerial Alliance and Ten Point Coalition discussed the urgent need for workforce development, police-community tensions, socioeconomically-engineered segregation, and efforts to rectify these issues. Muslim leaders deplored the 9/11 terrorist attacks, explained Islam as a religion of peace, and reported subsequent hate crimes against their mosques and communities. Leaders from Cooperative Metropolitan Ministries discussed successes and difficulties of urban-suburban congregational partnerships. Social service professionals described clinical work with war-displaced immigrant populations. Clergy from social justice ministries described projects to reduce homelessness, poverty, sex trafficking, violence against women, and LGBT discrimination. Social activists discussed relevant international issues: corporate globalization, climate change, war refugees, and displaced ethnic groups. Leaders from the Greater Boston Interfaith Organization discussed city and state political initiatives. In addition, we discussed structural and historical elements of racism, sexism, and poverty, noting their traumatic intersecting effects.

In 1991, I was invited to join the Steering Committee of this group, ultimately serving as Coordinator. In this role, I helped facilitate our interfaith dialogues, and I now apply these skills when teaching the *Know Your Self* curriculum. Several principles became clear to me. First, in order to build inclusive community, we could not avoid challenging conversations about race, gender, ethnicity, sexual orientation, social stratification, and religiously-sanctioned violence. Second, it was vital to create an atmosphere of civility that fostered honest, respectful discussion. This was particularly necessary because the content of our discussions was fraught with traumatic pain: legacies of violence and oppression among the religious, racial, and cultural groups represented by our participants. These meetings repeatedly confronted our interfaith group with the enormity of the challenge in the Greater Boston area.

These perspectives on systemic social injustice are figural in the *Know Your Self* curriculum. It incorporates material about the social dynamics of power and oppression (Pinderhughes 1989), social dominance theory (Sidanius and Pratto 1999), social identity development (Hardiman and Jackson 1997; Helms 1990), white privilege (Gallardo 2014; Irving 2014; Rothenberg 2002), targeting of black males through gendered prejudice (Sidanius and Kurzban 2013), the case for reparations (Coates 2014), lack of constructive dialogue about race (Tatum 2007), the necessity for social justice advocacy (Adams et al. 1997; Aldarondo 2007); and the African American church as a resource for community-based resilience, resistance, and transcendence (Billingsley 1992; Curry et al. 1990; Freedman 1993; Moore 1992; Thurman 1976, 1977, 1986).

Serving as Coordinator of our interfaith group and teaching the *Know Your Self* curriculum has also challenged me to examine the complexities of my own sociocultural identity. As described, Jewish spirituality is central to my identity. Further, I am deeply aware of the 2000-year history of diaspora and genocide that my ancestors endured as well as the struggles of my relatives as Eastern European refugees and immigrants seeking acceptance in this country. I have also experienced anti-Semitism in my own life, during childhood, college, and adulthood. However, at the same time, I have had to examine my culture-based stress reactivity, recognizing when it distorts my perceptions. Further, I have confronted the social privilege I have acquired in this country as Jewish people were accepted as white (Brodkin 2002) and the racism that people of color have experienced from Jews. When Rabbi Everett Gendler asked Reverend Dr. Martin Luther King, Jr. why the alliance between African and Jewish Americans was breaking down, Dr. King began by thanking

Rabbi Abraham Joshua Heschel for marching with him at Selma, affirming firm support from the Jewish community in the struggle for civil rights. But he went on to explain that black people living in urban ghettoes also knew Jewish people as mercantile landlords and shopkeepers who were no different than other white people (Washington 1986). As I discuss these issues with students, I acknowledge the complexity of valuing my Jewish identity, while recognizing that Jewish people are not exempt from racism.

In our Division of Counseling and Psychology at Lesley University, we have learned the value of speaking personally, among ourselves and with students, about complex contradictions that are often part of our sociocultural identities. Practicing cultural humility and empathic self-reflection, we identify personal events that shaped our own implicit biases (Gallardo 2014).

For example, I grew up in a middle class suburb with liberal values. My family and neighborhood supported the civil rights movement. I was a high school student when three civil rights activists (Michael Schwerner, Andrew Goodman, and James Chaney) were murdered in Mississippi. Schwerner's mother was a science teacher in my school. Our community mourned these devastating murders with anger and grief. But I thought the problem was "down there" in the South. I did not recognize the racism in the structural organization of our multi-story high school. Advanced classes, in which I was tracked, were taught on the top floor. Trade classes were taught in the basement. Stark differences in racial demography on these floors, reinforced by a seemingly merit-based tracking system, were transparent. But this evidence of systemic racism was invisible to students on the third floor, despite our liberal ideals. While I honor the progressive political vision of our country's constitution, it is essential to recognize that I benefit from a social system that was built upon slavery and racism.

In summary, my work with the Boston Clergy and Religious Leaders Group for Interfaith Dialogue and professional development with faculty colleagues in the Division of Counseling and Psychology helped me develop self-awareness and teaching tools for incorporating a social justice orientation into the *Know Your Self* curriculum. Narratives in Chaps. 7, 8, and 11 offer examples of students engaged in this learning as they explore their social identity development, approach cultural differences as catalysts for psychospiritual growth, and overcome biases.

Conclusion

The three projects I have described in this chapter were central in my development of the psychospiritual and social justice orientation that shapes my work as a mental health clinician, professor of counseling and psychology, and person-centered educator. These professional and personal learning experiences were equally central in my development of the *Know Your Self* curriculum, and the multidimensional model of person-centered psychospiritual maturation that I present in the next chapter. Throughout the curriculum, students learn to approach their lives as potential sources of psychospiritual maturation. This chapter has described professional and personal events in my life that have helped me develop this positively-oriented perspective.

References

Adams, M., Bell, L. A., & Griffin, P. (Eds.). (1997). *Teaching for diversity and social change: A sourcebook* (1st ed.). New York, NY: Routledge.

Aldarondo, E. (Ed.). (2007). *Advancing social justice through clinical practice.* New York, NY: Routledge, Taylor & Francis.

Alexander, M. (2010). *The new Jim Crow: Mass incarceration in the age of color-blindness.* New York, NY: The New Press.

Angha, N. (1998). *Sufism: The journey of the lovers.* San Rafael, CA: International Association of Sufism.

Aron, M. (1969). *Ideas and ideals of the Hassidim.* Secaucus, NJ: Citadel Press.

Beary, J. F., Benson, H., & Klemchuck, P. (1974). A simple physiologic technique which elicits the hypometabolic changes of the relaxation response. *Psychosomatic Medicine, 36,* 115–120.

Benson, H. (1975). *The relaxation response.* New York, NY: Morrow.

Benson, H., Dryer, T., & Hartley, L. H. (1978). Decreased [Vdot]O2 consumption during exercise with elicitation of the relaxation response. *Journal of Human Stress, 4*(2), 38–42.

Benson, H., Herd, J. A., Morse, W. H., & Kelleher, R. T. (1969). Behavioral induction of arterial hypertension and its reversal. *American Journal of Physiology, 217*(4), 30–34.

Benson, H., Marzetta, B. R., & Rosner, B. A. (1974a). Decreased blood pressure associated with the regular elicitation of the relaxation response. In R. S. Eliot (Ed.), *Contemporary problems in cardiology* (Vol. 1). Mt. Kisco, NY: Futura Publications.

Benson, H., Rosner, B. A., Marzetta, B. R., & Klemchuk, H. M. (1974b). Decreased blood-pressure in pharmacologically treated hypertensive patients who regularly elicited the relaxation response. *Lancet, 1*(7852), 289–291.

Billingsley, A. (1992). *Climbing Jacob's ladder: Enduring legacies of African-American families.* New York, NY: Simon and Schuster.
Birnbaum, P. (Ed.). (1967). *Maimonides' Mishneh Torah: Selections.* New York, NY: Hebrew Publishing Company.
Blumenthal, D. R. (1984). Maimonides' intellectualist mysticism and the superiority of the prophesy of Moses. In D. R. Blumenthal (Ed.), *Approaches to Judaism in medieval times.* Chico, CA: Scholars Press (Program in Jewish Studies, Brown University).
Bokser, B. Z. (1950). *The legacy of Maimonides.* New York, NY: Hebrew Publishing Co.
Bokser, B. Z. (Ed.). (1978). *Abraham Isaac Kook: Selected writings.* Mahwah, NJ: Paulist Press.
Borysenko, J. (1984). Stress, coping, and the immune system. In J. D. Matarazzo, S. M. Weiss, J. A. Herd, N. E. Miller, & S. M. Weiss (Eds.), *Behavioral health: A handbook of health enhancement and disease prevention.* New York, NY: Wiley.
Borysenko, J. (1989). *Minding the body, mending the mind.* Boston, MA: Addison-Wesley.
Brodkin, K. (2002). How Jews became white folks. In P. S. Rothenberg (Ed.), *White privilege: Essential readings on the other side of racism.* New York, NY: Worth Publishers.
Brown, L., & Ballou, M. (Eds.). (1992). *Personality and psychopathology: Feminist reappraisals.* New York, NY: Guilford Press.
Bryant-Davis, T. (2008). *Thriving in the wake of trauma: A multicultural guide.* Lanham, MD: AltaMira Press.
Bryant-Davis, T., & Ocampo, C. (2005). The trauma of racism: Implications for counseling, research, and education. *The Counseling Psychologist, 33*(4), 574–578.
Buber, M. (1947). *Tales of the Hasidim: Early masters.* New York, NY: Schocken Books.
Buijs, J. A. (Ed.). (1998). *Maimonides: A collection of critical essays.* Notre Dame, IN: University of Notre Dame Press.
Burrell, D. B. (1986). *Knowing the unknowable God: Ibn-Sina, Maimonides, Aquinas.* Notre Dame, IN: University of Notre Dame Press.
Cannon, W. B. (1929). *Bodily changes in pain, hunger, fear, and rage: An account of recent researches into the function of emotional excitement* (2nd ed.). New York, NY: Appleton.
Cannon, W. B. (1936). The role of emotions in disease. *Annals of Internal Medicine, 9*(11), 1453–1465.
Cannon, W. B., & Rosenblueth, A. (1937). *Autonomic neuro-effector systems.* New York, NY: Macmillan.

Chou, T., Asnaani, A., & Hofmann, S. G. (2012). Perception of racial discrimination and psychopathology across three U.S. ethnic minority groups. *Cultural Diversity and Ethnic Minority Psychology, 18*(1), 74–81.

Coates, T. N. (2014). The case for reparations. *The Atlantic*, June, 54–71.

Coates, T. N. (2015). *Between the world and me.* New York, NY: Spiegel & Grau.

Comas-Diaz, L. (2016). Racial trauma recovery: A race-informed therapeutic approach to racial wounds. In A. Alvarez, C. Liang, & H. Neville (Eds.), *The cost of racism for people of color: Contextualizing experiences of discrimination.* Washington, DC: American Psychological Association.

Cornelius-White, J. H. D. (Ed.). (2012). *Carl Rogers: The China diary.* Ross-on-Wye, UK: PCCS Books.

Curry, S. J., Wagner, E. H., & Grothaus, L. C. (1990). Intrinsic and extrinsic motivation interventions with a self-help smoking cessation program. *Journal of Clinical and Consulting Psychology, 59*, 318–324.

Daniel, J. H. (2000). The courage to hear: African American women's memories of racial trauma. In L. Jackson & B. Greene (Eds.), *Psychotherapy with African American women: Innovations in psychodynamic perspective and practice.* New York, NY: Guilford Press.

Davidson, H. A. (2005). *Moses Maimonides: The man and his works.* New York, NY: Oxford University Press.

Davidson, R. J., Kabat-Zinn, J., Schumacher, J., Rosenkranz, M., Muller, D., Santorelli, S., ... Sheridan, J. F. (2003). Alterations in brain and immune function produced by mindfulness meditation. *Psychosomatic Medicine, 65*(4), 564–570.

Domar, A., Seibel, M. M., & Benson, H. (1990). The mind/body program for infertility: A new behavioral treatment approach for women with infertility. *Fertility and Sterility, 53*(2), 246–249.

Dusek, J. A., Otu, H. H., Wohlheuter, A. L., Bhasin, M., Zerbini, L. F., Joseph, M.G., ... Liberman, T. A. (2008). Genomic counter-stress changes induced by the relaxation response. *PLOS ONE, 3*(7), e2576.

Eck, D. L., & Pierce, E. J. (Eds.). (1998). *World religions in Boston: A guide to communities and resources* (3rd ed.). Cambridge, MA: The Pluralism Project, Harvard University.

Esch, T., Fricchione, G. L., & Stefano, G. B. (2003). The therapeutic use of the relaxation response in stress-related diseases. *Medical Science Monitor, 9*(2), 23–34.

Evans, G. W., & Kim, P. (2007). Childhood poverty and health: cumulative risk exposure and stress dysregulation. *Psychological Science, 18*, 953–957.

Faur, J. (1999). *Homo mysticus: A guide to Maimonides' guide for the perplexed.* Syracuse, NY: Syracuse University Press.

Fentress, D. W., Masek, B. J., Mehegan, J. E., & Benson, H. (1986). Biofeedback and relaxation response training in the treatment of pediatric migraine. *Developmental Medicine and Child Neurology, 28*(2), 139–146.

Follette, V. M., Briere, J., Rozelle, D., Hopper, J. A., & Rome, D. I. (Eds.). (2015). *Mindfulness-oriented interventions for trauma: Integrating contemplative practices.* New York, NY: Guildford Press.

Fosha, D., Siegel, D. J., & Solomon, M. (Eds.). (2009). *The healing power of emotion: Affective neuroscience, development, and clinical practice.* New York, NY: W.W. Norton.

Freedman, S. (1993). *Upon this rock: The miracles of a black church.* New York, NY: Harper Collins.

Freire, P. (1970). *Pedagogy of the oppressed* (20th anniversary ed.). New York, NY: Continuum.

Fricchione, G. L. (2011). *Compassion and healing in medicine and society: On the nature and use of attachment solutions to separation challenges.* Baltimore, MD: Johns Hopkins University Press.

Gallardo, M. E. (Ed.). (2014). *Developing cultural humility: Embracing race, privilege, and power.* Los Angeles, CA: SAGE.

Germer, C. K. (2009). *The mindful path to self-compassion: Freeing yourself from destructive thoughts and emotions.* New York, NY: Guilford Press.

Germer, C. K., & Siegel, R. D. (Eds.). (2012). *Wisdom and compassion in psychotherapy: Deepening mindfulness in clinical practice.* New York, NY: Guilford.

Germer, C. K., Siegel, R. D., & Fulton, P. R. (2005). *Mindfulness and psychotherapy.* New York, NY: Guilford.

Giles, C. A., & Miller, W. B. (Eds.). (2012). *The arts of contemplative care: Pioneering voices in Buddhist chaplaincy and pastoral work.* Somerville, MA: Wisdom Publications.

Goodale, I. L., Domar, A. D., & Benson, H. (1990). Alleviation of premenstrual syndrome symptoms with the relaxation response. *Obstetrics and Gynecology, 75*(4), 649–655.

Goodman, L. E. (1976). *Rambam: Readings in the philosophy of Moses Maimonides.* New York, NY: Viking Press.

Goodman, L. E. (1999). *Jewish and Islamic philosophy: Crosspollinations in the classic age.* New Brunswick, NJ: Rutgers University Press.

Green, A. (2003). *Seek my face: A Jewish mystical theology.* Woodstock, VT: Jewish Lights Publishing.

Green, A., & Holtz, B. W. (Eds.). (1993). *Your word is fire: The hasidic masters on contemplative prayer.* Woodstock, VT: Jewish Lights Publishing.

Halbertal, M. (2014). *Maimonides: Life and thought.* Princeton, NJ: Princeton University Press.

Haller, J., & Kruk, M. R. (2003). Neuroendocrine stress responses and aggression. In M. P. Mattson (Ed.), *Neurobiology of aggression: Understanding and preventing violence*. Totowa, NJ: Humana Press.

Hardiman, R., & Jackson, B. W. (1997). Conceptual foundations for social justice courses. In M. Adams, L. A. Bell, & P. Griffin (Eds.), *Teaching for diversity and social justice*. New York, NY: Routledge.

Hardy, K. V. (2013). Healing the hidden wounds of racial trauma. *Reclaiming Children and Youth, 22*(1), 24–28.

Harris, J. M. (Ed.). (2007). *Maimonides after 800 years: Essays on Maimonides and his influence*. Cambridge, MA: Harvard University Press.

Hartman, D. (1976). *Maimonides: Torah and philosophic quest*. Philadelphia, PA: Jewish Publication Society of America.

Hatzenbuehler, M. L., & McLaughlin, K. A. (2014). Structural stigma and hypothalamic-pituitary-adrenocortical axis reactivity in lesbian, gay, and bisexual young adults. *Annals of Behavioral Medicine, 47*(1), 39–47.

Hellman, C. C., Budd, M., Borysenko, J., McClelland, D., & Benson, H. (1990). A study of the effectiveness of two group behavioral medicine interventions for patients with psychosomatic complaints. *Behavioral Medicine, 16*(4), 165–173.

Helms, J. E. (Ed.). (1990). *Black and white racial identity development*. Westport, CT: Greenwood Press.

Herman, J. (1997). *Trauma and recovery*. New York, NY: Basic Books.

Heschel, A. J. (1951). *Man is not alone*. New York, NY: Farrar, Strauss, Giroux.

Heschel, A. J. (1982). *Maimonides: A biography*. New York, NY: Farrar, Strauss, Giroux.

Heschel, A. J. (1996). *Prophetic inspiration after the prophets: Maimonides and other medieval authorities*. Hoboken, NJ: Ktav Publishing House Inc.

Hui-neng. (1998). *The sutra of Hui-Neng: Grand master of Zen* (T. Cleary, Trans.). Boston, MA: Shambhala Publications.

Idel, M. (1988a). *Kabbalah: New perspectives*. New Haven, CT: Yale University Press.

Idel, M. (1988b). *Studies in ecstatic kabbalah*. Albany, NY: SUNY Press.

Irving, D. (2014). *Waking up white: Finding myself in the story of race*. Cambridge, MA: Elephant Room Press.

Jung, C. G. (1964). Approaching the unconscious. In C. G. Jung (Ed.), *Man and his symbols*. New York, NY: Doubleday and Co.

Kabat-Zinn, J. (1982). An outpatient program in behavioral medicine for chronic pain patients based on the practice of mindfulness meditation. *General Hospital Psychiatry, 4*(1), 33–47.

Kabat-Zinn, J. (1990). *Full catastrophe living*. New York, NY: Dell Publishing.

Kabat-Zinn, J., & Chapman-Waldrop, A. (1988). Compliance with an outpatient stress reduction program: Rates and predictors of program completion. *Journal of Behavioral Medicine, 11*(4), 333–352.

Kabat-Zinn, J., Lipworth, L., & Burney, R. (1985). The clinical use of mindfulness meditation for the self-regulation of chronic pain. *Journal of Behavioral Medicine, 8*(2), 163–190.

Kabat-Zinn, J., Lipworth, L., Burney, R., & Sellers, W. (1986). Four-year follow-up of a meditation-based program for the self-regulation of chronic pain: Treatment outcomes and compliance. *The Clinical Journal of Pain, 2*(3), 159–174.

Kabat-Zinn, J., Wheeler, E., Light, T., Skillings, A., Scharf, M. J., Cropley, T.G., ... Bernhard, J. D. (1998). Influence of a mindfulness meditation-based stress reduction intervention on rates of skin clearing in patients with moderate to severe psoriasis undergoing phototherapy (UVB) and photochemotherapy (PUVA). *Psychosomatic Medicine, 60*(5), 625–632.

Kaplan, A. (1978). *Meditation and the Bible*. New York, NY: Samuel Weiser.

Kass, J. D. (1981). *Mantalk*. Cambridge, MA: Greenhouse, Center for Personal and Social Change.

Kass, J. D. (1985). The use of person-centered expressive therapies in the health professions. *Brennpunkt, Schweizerische Gesellschaft für Gesprachspsychotherapie und Person-Zentrierte Beratung, 24,* 20–33.

Kass, J. D. (1991a). Contributions of religious experience to psychological and physical well-being: Research evidence and an explanatory model. *The Caregiver (College of Chaplains), 8*(4), 4–11.

Kass, J. D. (1991b). Integrating spirituality into personality theory and counseling practice. American Counseling Association, 1991 Annual Meetings. Reno, Nevada.

Kass, J. D. (1995). Contributions of religious experience to psychological and physical well-being: Research evidence and an explanatory model. In L. Vandecreek (Ed.), *Spiritual needs and pastoral services: Readings in research* (pp. 189–213). Decatur, GA: Journal of Pastoral Care Publications.

Kass, J. D. (2013). Revisiting Maimonide's Guide of the Perplexed: How yoga psychology can clarify our understanding of Jewish practice. 15th International Conference for Jewish Renewal (ALEPH). Rindge, NH.

Kass, J. D. (2015). Person-centered spiritual maturation: A multidimensional model. *Journal of Humanistic Psychology, 55*(1), 53–76. doi:10.1177/0022167814525261.

Kass, J. D. (2017). Maimonides' Guide of the Perplexed: A Jewish model of psychospiritual maturation that integrates scientific and contemplative perspectives. Manuscript in preparation.

Kass, J. D., & Lennox, S. (2005). Emerging models of spiritual development: A foundation for mature, moral, and health-promoting behavior. In W. R.

Miller & H. Delaney (Eds.), *Judeo-Christian perspectives on psychology: Human nature, motivation, and change*. Washington, DC: American Psychological Association.

Kass, J. D., & Trantham, S. M. (2014). Perspectives from clinical neuroscience: Mindfulness and therapeutic use of the arts. In L. Rappaport (Ed.), *Mindfulness and the arts therapies: Theory and practice*. London, UK: Jessica Kingsley.

Kass, J. D., Friedman, R., Leserman, J., Caudill, M., Zuttermeister, P., & Benson, H. (1991a). An inventory of positive psychological attitudes with potential relevance to health outcomes. *Behavioral Medicine, 17*(3), 121–129.

Kass, J. D., Friedman, R., Leserman, J., Zuttermeister, P., & Benson, H. (1991b). Health outcomes and a new measure of spiritual experience. *Journal for the Scientific Study of Religion, 30*(2), 203–211.

Kelner, M. (2006). *Maimonides' confrontation with mysticism*. Portland, OR: Littman Library of Jewish Civilization.

Kirschenbaum, H. (2007). *The life and work of Carl Rogers*. Ross-on-Wye, UK: PCCS Books.

Kisly, L. (2004). *The prayer of fire: Experiencing the Lord's Prayer*. Brewster, MA: Paraclete Press.

Koolhaas, J. M., Korte, S. M., De Boer, S. F., Van Der Vegt, B. J., Van Reenen, V., & Hopster, H. (1991). Coping styles in animals: Current status in behavior and stress physiology. *Neuroscience and Behavioral Reviews, 23*(7), 925–935.

Kornfield, J. (2000). *After the ecstasy, the laundry: How the heart grows wise on the spiritual path*. New York, NY: Bantam Books.

Kraemer, J. L. (2008). *Maimonides: The life and world of one of civilization's greatest minds*. New York, NY: Doubleday.

Kutz, I., Borysenko, J., & Benson, H. (1985). Meditation and psychotherapy: A rationale for the integration of dynamic psychotherapy, the relaxation response, and mindfulness meditation. *American Journal of Psychiatry, 142*(1), 1–8.

Lazar, S. W., Bush, G., Gollub, R. L., Fricchione, G. L., Khalsa, G., & Benson, H. (2000). Functional brain mapping of the relaxation response and meditation. *NeuroReport, 11*(7), 1581–1585.

Lazar, S. W., Kerr, C. E., Wasserman, R. H., Gray, J. R., Greve, D. N., Treadway, M. T., ... Fischl, B. (2005). Meditation is associated with increased cortical thickness. *NeuroReport, 16*(17), 1893–1897.

Leserman, J., Stuart, E., Mamish, M. E., & Benson, H. (1989). The efficacy of the relaxation response in preparing for cardiac surgery. *Behavioral Medicine, 15*(3), 111–117.

Lowery, W. (2016). *They can't kill us all: Ferguson, Baltimore, and a new era in America's racial justice movement*. New York, NY: Little, Brown and Company.

Lutz, A., Greischar, L. L., Rawlings, N. B., Ricard, M., & Davidson, R. J. (2004). Long-term meditators self-induce high amplitude gamma synchrony during mental practice. *Neuroscience, 101*(46), 16369–16373.
Maimonides, M. (1963). *Guide of the perplexed* (S. Pines, Trans.). Chicago, IL: University of Chicago Press.
Marlatt, G. A., & Kristeller, J. L. (1999). Mindfulness and meditation. In W. R. Miller (Ed.), *Integrating spirituality into treatment*. Washington, DC: American Psychological Association.
Marty, M. E. (2000). Fundamentalism as a precursor to violence. In J. H. Ehrenkranz (Ed.), *Religion and violence, religion and peace*. Fairfield, CT: Sacred Heart University Press.
Mason, J. W., Wang, S., Yehuda, R., Riney, S., Charney, D. S., & Southwick, S. M. (2001). Psychogenic lowering of urinary cortisol levels linked to increased emotional numbing and a shame-depressive syndrome in combat-related post-traumatic stress disorder. *Psychosomatic Medicine, 63*(3), 387–401.
McGirr, A., Diaconu, G., Berlim, M. T., Pruessner, J. C., Sable, R., Cabot, S., et al. (2010). Dysregulation of the sympathetic nervous system, hypothalmic-pituitary-adrenal axis and executive function in individuals at risk for suicide. *Journal of Psychiatry and Neuroscience, 35*(6), 399–408.
McLaughlin, K. A., Hilt, L. M., & Nolen-Hoeksema, S. (2007). Racial/ethnic differences in internalizing and externalizing symptoms in adolescents. *Journal of Abnormal Child Psychology, 35*(5), 801–816.
Menocal, M. R. (2002). *Ornament of the world: How Muslims, Jews, and Christians created a culture of tolerance in medieval Spain*. Boston, MA: Little, Brown and Company.
Merton, T. (1996). *Contemplative prayer*. New York, NY: Image/Doubleday.
Miller, J. J., Fletcher, K., & Kabat-Zinn, J. (1995). Three-year follow-up and clinical implications of a mindfulness meditation-based stress reduction intervention in the treatment of anxiety disorders. *General Hospital Psychiatry, 17*(3), 192–200.
Moore, T. (1992). The African-American church: A source of empowerment, mutual help, and social change. In K. Pargament, K. Maton, & R. Hess (Eds.), *Religion and prevention in mental health* (pp. 166–175). Binghamton, NY: Haworth Press.
Ogden, P. (2009). Emotion, mindfulness, and movement: Expanding the regulatory boundaries of the window of affect tolerance. In D. Fosha, D. J. Siegel, & M. F. Solomon (Eds.), *The healing power of emotion*. New York, NY: W.W. Norton.
Ogden, P., Minton, K., & Pain, C. (2006). *Trauma and the body: A sensorimotor approach to psychotherapy*. New York, NY: W.W. Norton.
Peltz, L. (2013). *The mindful path to addiction recovery: A practical guide to regaining control over your life*. Boston, MA: Shambhala Publications.

Peng, C. K., Mietus, J. E., Liu, Y., Khalsa, G., Douglas, P. S., Benson, H., et al. (1999). Exaggerated heart rate oscillations during two meditation techniques. *International Journal of Cardiology, 70,* 101–107.

Peng, C. K., Henry, I. C., Mietus, J. E., Hausdorff, J. M., Khalsa, G., Benson, H., et al. (2004). Heart rate dynamics during three forms of meditation. *International Journal of Cardiology, 95*(1), 19–27.

Perls, F. (1973). *The Gestalt approach and eye witness to therapy.* New York, NY: Science and Behavior Books.

Peters, R. K., Benson, H., & Porter, D. (1977). Daily relaxation response breaks in a working population. *American Journal of Public Health, 67*(10), 946–953.

Pinderhughes, E. (1989). *Understanding race, ethnicity, and power: The key to efficacy in clinical practice.* New York, NY: Free Press.

Pines, S. (1963). Philosophic sources of the guide of the perplexed. In S. Pines (Ed.), *Guide of the perplexed by Moses Maimonides.* Chicago, IL: University of Chicago Press.

Porges, S. W. (1972). Heart rate variability and deceleration as indexes of reaction time. *Journal of Experimental Psychology, 92,* 103–110.

Porges, S. W. (1995). Orienting in a defensive world: Mammalian modifications of our evolutionary heritage. *Psychophysiology, 32*(4), 301–318.

Powell, J. A. (2012). *Racing to justice: Transforming our conceptions of self and others to build an inclusive society.* Bloomington, IN: Indiana University Press.

Prager, M. (2003). *The path of blessing: Experiencing the energy and abundance of the Divine.* Woodstock, VT: Jewish Lights.

Rama, S., Ballantine, R., & Ajaya, S. (1976). *Yoga and psychotherapy: The evolution of consciousness.* Honesdale, PA: Himalayan International Institute.

Reich, W. (1960). Therapy: Breakthrough into the vegetative realm. In W. Reich (Ed.), *Wilhelm Reich: Selected writings.* New York, NY: Farrar, Straus, and Giroux.

Rogers, C. R. (1944a). *Adjustment after combat: A study of returned combat gunners and their utilization in the flexible gunnery training program (restricted publication).* Forty Myers, FL: Army Air Forces Instructors School Flexible Gunnery.

Rogers, C. R. (1944b). Psychological adjustments of discharged service personnel. *Psychological Bulletin, 41,* 689–696.

Rogers, C. R. (1950). A basic orientation for counseling. *Pastoral Psychology, 1*(1), 26–34.

Rogers, C. R. (1951a). *Client-centered therapy: Its current practices, implications, and theory.* Boston, MA: Houghton Mifflin.

Rogers, C. R. (1951b). Through the eyes of a client. *Pastoral Psychology, 2*(16), 32–40.

Rogers, C. R. (1952a). "Client-centered" psychotherapy. *Scientific American, 87*(5), 66–74.

Rogers, C. R. (1952b). Dealing with interpersonal conflict. *Pastoral Psychology*, *3*(28), 14–20.

Rogers, C. R. (1957). The necessary and sufficient conditions of therapeutic personality change. *Journal of Consulting Psychology*, *21*, 95–103.

Rogers, C. R. (1959a). Significant learning: In therapy and in education. *Educational Leadership*, *16*, 232–242.

Rogers, C. R. (1959b). A theory of therapy, personality, and interpersonal relationships, as developed in the client-centered framework. In S. Koch (Ed.), *Psychology: A study of a science* (Vol. III). Formulations of the person and the social context. New York, NY: McGraw-Hill.

Rogers, C. R. (1961). *On becoming a person: A therapist's view of psychotherapy*. Boston, MA: Houghton-Mifflin.

Rogers, C. R. (1962). Toward becoming a fully functioning person. In A. W. Combs (Ed.), *Perceiving, behaving, becoming: A new focus for education* (Vol. 1962 Yearbook). Washington, DC: Association for Supervision and Curriculum Development, National Educational Association.

Rogers, C. R. (1963). The concept of the fully functioning person. *Psychotherapy: Theory, Research, and Practice*, *1*(1), 17–26.

Rogers, C. R. (1967). The interpersonal relationship in the facilitation of learning. In R. Leeper (Ed.), *Humanizing education: The person in process* (Vol. 1967 Yearbook). Washington, DC: Association for Supervision and Curriculum Development, National Education Association.

Rogers, C. R. (1969). *Freedom to learn: A view of what education might become*. Columbus, OH: Charles E. Merrill.

Rogers, C. R. (1971). Can schools grow persons? *Educational Leadership*, *28*, 215–217.

Rogers, C. R. (1977a). *On personal power: Inner strength and its revolutionary impact*. New York, NY: Delacorte Press.

Rogers, C. R. (1977b). A person-centered workshop: Its planning and fruition In C. R. Rogers, *On personal power*. New York, NY: Delacorte Press.

Rogers, C. R. (1980a). Building person-centered communities: Implications for the future. In C. R. Rogers, *A way of being* (3rd ed.). Boston: MA: Houghton-Mifflin.

Rogers, C. R. (1980b). Can learning encompass both ideas and feelings? In C. R. Rogers, *A way of being*. Boston, MA: Houghton-Mifflin.

Rogers, C. R. (1980c). *A way of being* (3rd ed.). Boston, MA: Houghton-Mifflin.

Rogers, C. R. (1986). The dilemmas of a South African white. *Person-Centered Review*, *1*, 15–35.

Rogers, C. R., & Dymond, R. (1954). *Psychotherapy and personality change*. Chicago, IL: University of Chicago Press.

Rogers, C. R., Justyn, J., Kass, J. D., Miller, M., Rogers, N., Villas-Boas Bowen, M., et al. (1978). Evolving aspects of person-centered workshops. *Self and Society*, *6*(2), 43–49.

Rogers, C. R., & Wallen, J. L. (1946). *Counseling with returned servicemen.* New York, NY: McGraw-Hill.
Rogers, N. (1980). *Emerging woman: A decade of mid-life transitions.* Point Reyes, CA: Personal Press.
Rogers, N. (1984). *The creative connection: A person-centered approach to expressive therapy* (1st edition. (Pre-Publication Manuscript)).
Rothenberg, P. S. (Ed.). (2002). *White privilege: Essential readings on the other side of racism.* New York, NY: Worth Publishers.
Santorelli, S. (2000). *Heal thy self: Lessons on mindfulness in medicine.* New York, NY: Harmony Publishing.
Sapolsky, R. M. (1996). Stress, glucocorticoids, and damage to the nervous system: The current state of confusion. *Stress, 1*(1), 1–19.
Sapolsky, R. M. (2003). Stress and plasticity in the limbic system. *Neurochemical Research, 28*(11), 1735–1742.
Sapolsky, R. M. (2005a). The influence of social hierarchy on primate health. *Science, 308,* 648–652.
Sapolsky, R. M. (2005b). Sick of poverty. *Scientific American, 293*(6), 92–99.
Schachter-Shalomi, Z. (1993). *Paradigm shift: From the Jewish renewal teachings of Reb Zalman Schacter-Shalomi.* Northvale, NJ: Jason Aronson Inc.
Scholem, G. G. (1941). *Major trends in Jewish mysticism.* New York, NY: Schocken Books.
Schore, A. (2003). *Affect regulation and the repair of the self.* New York, NY: W.W. Norton.
Selye, H. (1956). *The stress of life.* New York, NY: McGraw-Hill.
Sidanius, J., & Kurzban, R. (2013). Toward an evolutionarily informed political psychology. In L. Huddy, D. O. Sears, & J. S. Levy (Eds.), *Oxford handbook of political psychology* (2nd ed.). New York, NY: Oxford University Press.
Sidanius, J., & Pratto, F. (1999). *Social dominance: An intergroup theory of social hierarchy and oppression.* Cambridge, UK: Cambridge University Press.
Siegel, D. J. (2007). *The mindful brain: Reflection and attunement in the cultivation of well-being.* New York, NY: W.W. Norton.
Stefano, G. B., Fricchione, G. L., Slingsby, B., & Benson, H. (2001). The placebo effect and relaxation response: Neural processes and their coupling to constitutive nitric oxide. *Brain Research Reviews, 35*(1), 1–19.
Stern, T. A., Fricchione, G. L., Cassem, N. H., Jellinek, M. S., & Rosenbaum, J. F. (2004). *Handbook of general hospital psychiatry* (5th ed.). Philadelphia, PA: Mosby/Elsevier.
Stevenson, B. (2014). *Just mercy: A story of justice and redemption.* New York, NY: Spiegel & Grau.
Sue, D. W., & Sue, D. (1981). *Counseling the culturally different: Theory and practice.* New York, NY: John Wiley.

Tatum, B. D. (2007). *Can we talk about race?* Boston, MA: Beacon Press.
Thetford, W. N. (1952). An objective measure of frustration tolerance in evaluating psychotherapy. In W. Wolff (Ed.), *Success in psychotherapy*. New York, NY: Grune and Stratton.
Thurman, H. (1976). *Jesus and the disinherited*. Boston, MA: Beacon Press.
Thurman, H. (1977). *Disciplines of the spirit*. Richmond, IN: Friends United Press.
Thurman, H. (1986). *The search for common ground*. Richmond, IN: Friends United Press.
Ting, W., & Fricchione, G. L. (2006). *The heart-mind connection*. New York, NY: McGraw-Hill.
van der Kolk, B. A. (1987). *Psychological trauma*. Washington, DC: American Psychiatric Association.
van der Kolk, B. A. (1988). The trauma spectrum: The interaction of biological and social events in the genesis of the trauma response. *Journal of Traumatic Stress, 1*(3), 273–290.
van der Kolk, B. A. (2014). *The body keeps the score: Brain, mind, and body in the healing of trauma*. New York, NY: Viking.
van der Kolk, B. A., McFarlane, A. C., & Weisaeth, L. (Eds.). (1996). *Traumatic stress: The effects of overwhelming experience on mind, body, and society*. New York, NY: Guilford Press.
Varela, F., & Shear, J. (Eds.). (1999). *The view from within: First-person approaches to the study of consciousness*. New York, NY: Imprint Academic.
Wallace, R. K., Benson, H., & Wilson, A. F. (1971). A wakeful hypometabolic physiologic state. *American Journal of Physiology, 221*, 795–799.
Washington, J. M. (Ed.). (1986). *A testament of hope: The essential writings and speeches of Martin Luther King, Jr.* New York, NY: HarperCollins.
Yehuda, R., Giller, E. L., Southwick, S. M., Lowy, M. T., & Mason, J. W. (1991). Hypothalamic-pituitary-adrenal dysfunction in post-traumatic stress disorder. *Biological Psychiatry, 30*, 1031–1048.
Yehuda, R., Southwick, S. M., Mason, J. W., & Giller, E. L. (1990a). Interactions of the hypothalamic-pituitary-adrenal axis and the catecholaminergic system in post-traumatic stress disorder. In E. L. Giller (Ed.), *Biological assessment and treatment of PTSD*. Washington, DC: American Psychological Association.
Yehuda, R., Southwick, S. M., Nussbaum, G., Wahby, V., Giller, E. L. J., & Mason, J. W. (1990b). Low urinary cortisol secretion in patients with post-traumatic stress disorder. *Journal of Nervous and Mental Disease, 178*(6), 366–369.
Zeitlin, S. (1935). *Maimonides: A biography*. New York, NY: Bloch Publishing Co.

CHAPTER 5

Person-Centered Psychospiritual Maturation: A Multidimensional Model

This conceptual chapter presents a multidimensional model of person-centered psychospiritual maturation. It describes five dimensions of self that can be dysregulated by humanity's chain of pain and presents person-centered psychospiritual maturation as an antidote to these dysregulating effects. The chapter further examines the human capacity for person-centered psychospiritual maturation as an emergent phenomenon of bio-cultural evolution.

In previous chapters, I began to identify a complex dynamic through which the chain of pain replicates itself. During stress, individuals and social systems regress to primitive survival responses that affect bio-behavioral, cognitive-sociocultural, social-emotional, and existential-spiritual functioning. These responses are ineffective, and ultimately destructive, when coping with society's increasingly complex forms of stress, which include high-performance work demands, stratified social systems, chronic poverty, broken relationships and trauma-ridden families, social isolation, racial and gender inequality, and conflictual intergroup relations across race, ethnicity, class, and religion.

Managing complex forms of stress, while insuring well-being for all, requires mature psychospiritual coping skills at individual, micro- and macro-system levels. The skills are obvious. Our spiritual traditions have advocated them consistently: love neighbor as self, behave justly and ethically, resolve problems peacefully through justice, empathy, and altruism, know and respect *every* human being (including self) as a sacred manifestation of the life-force, live lovingly and joyfully, approach mortality with composure by cultivating psychospiritual growth, and focus your life energy through engaged devotion to aspects of existence you consider sacred and vital to the well-being of self and society. But these skills are difficult to sustain. Overwhelmed by stress, we regress to primitive stress-coping across multiple dimensions of self.

Over the course of bio-cultural evolution, humans have gradually acquired the capacity for mature psychospiritual coping skills. Our brain/body is wired to utilize them. But evolution is economical. It has conserved a range of coping mechanisms because primitive modes retain value. When confronting vicious aggression or natural catastrophes, they activate individual and group responses that can be protective. But modern society's complex stressors cannot be solved by these primitive modes. They require utilization of mature stress-coping skills.

While the spiritual traditions espouse mature coping, their organizational behavior often contradicts these goals. Psychology has developed maturational learning strategies that support the ethical core of the spiritual traditions and incorporate their contemplative practices. As I learned to integrate these methods, my research suggested that psychospiritual maturation requires growth in five dimensions of self: bio-behavioral, cognitive-sociocultural, social-emotional, existential-spiritual, and integrative worldview-formation (Kass 2015; Kass and Lennox 2005). Each dimension includes a continuum of primitive and mature coping modes. This discussion begins with a biocultural evolutionary perspective that explains how a continuum of primitive and mature coping modes developed in each dimension.

Psychospiritual Maturation: An Emergent Evolutionary Phenomenon

Current bio-cultural evolutionary theory recognizes that humanity has introduced culture into the evolutionary process. The cultural niches we develop (e.g., social systems, technology, higher-order linguistic, cognitive, and aesthetic worldview construction, and intergenerational knowledge transmission) create selection pressures for traits that favor survival and advancement of our genetic pool. While the Darwinian formulation (*survival of the fittest*) remains operant, *most fit* can no longer be understood reductively as *most powerful*. Power remains a potent reality in human culture, and societies require defensive capabilities to repel attacks by violent aggressors. But history demonstrates that obsession with power and domination undermines a society through internal pressures. Leaders with these obsessions do not cooperate effectively. Their self-serving actions and in-fighting erode stability and prevent necessary collaboration. Such actions also oppress people on lower rungs of social hierarchies, undermining society's ethical principles and creating tensions that erode civil behavior. At our complex stage of bio-cultural evolution, selection pressures for *most fit* require traits that are *most mature*.

Carl Rogers pointed to a maturation-oriented directionality in bio-cultural evolution. He described "a formative tendency…within the universe…a trend toward increased order and interrelated complexity." As part of this trend, "the human organism has been moving toward the more complete development of awareness," which enables us to respond more adequately to complex sources of stress (Rogers 1980, pp. 124–128).

Gregory Fricchione proposes a mechanism for this directionality using attachment theory (Fricchione, 2011). To flourish, people require secure attachments (Ainsworth et al. 1978; Bowlby 1969). They wither if *separation challenges* (e.g., relational ruptures, individuation, insecure attachment) are not resolved through new *attachment solutions*. This *separation challenge-attachment solution dialectic* is a primary catalyst for psychosocial growth. But Fricchione proposes that this dialectic precedes humanity, as an underlying trait selection pressure. While many selection pressures emerge from local environmental conditions, this dynamic is generic. He analyzes phase transitions in which life evolved from simple inorganic molecules into complex molecules with autocatalytic capacities, and then traces phase transitions through which protocells evolved into complex organisms. Each transition produced organisms with higher-order structural and functional complexities, offering survival advantages. He designates this synthesis of structures and functions as a series of evolutionary *attachment solutions*. He designates structural and functional limitations in predecessors as *separation challenges* that created selection pressures for advancement. Explicating the primary mechanism of evolution (non-deterministic random mutation) through this separation challenge-attachment solution dialectic, he identifies selection pressures that constitute a maturation-directed formative tendency in bio-cultural evolution (Fricchione 2011).

Social justice activists express justifiable distrust of evolutionary theory because it has been misused to justify white superiority (Smedley and Smedley 2005). Cultural anthropology offers ample evidence against these racist claims (Carneiro 2003; Diamond 1997). Further, neuroanthropology has developed a complex model of the encultured brain as an interactive feedback loop between cultural *niche construction*, social learning pathways in the developing brain, and phylogenetic evolution (Lende and Downey 2012; Li 2003; MacKinnon and Fuentes 2012). This model explains group-based social dominance hierarchies as modifiable aspects of cultural niche construction, and is consistent with current social justice advocacy theory (Adams et al. 2016; Aldarondo 2007; Motulsky et al. 2014; Sidanius et al. 2004). Similarly, religious leaders distrust evolutionary neuroscientific perspectives that reduce religious experience to biochemical mechanisms. But neuroscientific studies of meditation have moved the field in the opposite direction: providing respectful explanatory insights about the neurological correlates of spiritual experience (D'Aquili and Newberg 1999; Kass 1995; Siegel 2007) and its positive impact on psychological and social well-being (Kass 2007b). Thus, evolutionary psychology and neuroscience need not be construed as antagonistic to a socially-progressive model of psychospiritual maturation.

Paul MacLean's phylogenetic model of brain development provides a foundation for understanding humanity's evolution toward mature coping capacities. He divides the brain into three sections that emerged incrementally during evolution of reptiles (brain stem), mammals (limbic system), and primates (cerebral cortex) (MacLean 1990). The brain stem ("reptilian") regulates primary metabolic systems, including attention, awareness, and primitive coping mechanisms (fight-flight-freeze). Reptiles are social isolates and employ individualistic survival mechanisms. But evolution subsequently developed the limbic system ("mammalian brain") that enables social bonding and emotional attachment. Mammals create social groups that provide survival advantages through cooperation. These groups contain dominance hierarchies: the organizational template for human systems (Sidanius and Kurzban 2013). Mature systems are egalitarian and collaborative. But during real or perceived threat, they regress into rigid, tribal hierarchies (Shapiro 2010). The cerebral cortex ("primate/human brain"), with capacities for self-reflection, can assess and modulate brain stem and limbic reactions. These executive functions integrate cognitive, affective, intuitive, and somatically-based mental processes. When operant, they facilitate accurate, mature responses to modern society's complex sources of stress (Kass and Trantham 2014; Lambert and Kinsley 2005). MacLean's triune model provides further evidence for a formative tendency in evolution, highlighting dynamic tension between primitive and mature modes of stress coping. It offers a foundation for examining the five dimensions of psychospiritual maturation and understanding the dynamics underlying humanity's chain of pain.

1. **Bio-Behavioral:** *Neural and physiological pathways regulating metabolic processes through which people respond to challenges, stress, and perceived threat.*

Cultivating pro-social behavior and reducing destructive tendencies are figural goals in every spiritual tradition. From a person-centered perspective, this maturational learning does not begin with imposed behavioral prescriptions. Rather, it begins when mentors invite students to explore behaviors harmful to self and others that they would like to improve.

These explorations reveal that their destructive behavior is triggered by perceived threat, afflictive emotions (anger, fear, grief), and impulsive reactivity. Mindfulness, a learned behavior that enhances self-regulation, is a first step toward reducing reactivity. In mindfulness practice, feelings are not suppressed. Afflictive emotions are signals of distress that require empathic attention. Through mindfulness, students can examine afflictive emotions without regression to destructive behavior and strengthen internal composure that promotes mature responses (Armstrong 2011; Borysenko 1989; Germer 2009; Germer and Siegel 2012; Kabat-Zinn et al. 1985; Kass 1995; Kass and Trantham 2014; Siegel 2007).

Mindfulness is an important feature of person-centered psychospiritual maturation. During self-inquiry about behaviors harmful to self and others, mindfulness helps students examine cognitive dysregulation, agitated emotions, unhealthy substance use, eating habits, or sexual behavior, explicit or implicit bias against cultural *others*, group-based social dominance orientation, hostile interpersonal behavior during conflict, escalation of anger into violence, and compulsive materialism (for self-soothing or self-aggrandizement).

Mindfulness was first adopted as a clinical method by the field of behavioral medicine, as a tool for affect regulation and self-observation during sitting meditation (Benson et al. 1974; Borysenko 1989; Kabat-Zinn et al. 1985). It was adopted in substance abuse treatment when researchers recognized that prescriptive abstinence ("Just Say No") had limited efficacy (CSR 1995; Leshner 1995; Marlatt and Marques 1977; Tobler and Stratton 1995). Behavioral change in addiction required a complex process of contemplation, preparation, and action (DiClemente 2006; Prochaska et al. 1992). As the therapeutic value of affect regulation and self-observation became clear, mindfulness became a common practice in psychotherapy (Germer et al. 2005; Kass and Trantham 2014; Kutz et al. 1985; Linehan 1993; Ogden et al. 2006; Shapiro 1980). All of these clinicians recognized that destructive behaviors are triggered by deeply-ingrained autonomic stress-coping mechanisms. The adaptive value of these protective mechanisms makes them difficult to override (Sarafino 2008).

Meditation is a subtle process (Goleman 1988). It elicits a *relaxation response* that provides effective counter-conditioning to the stress response (Benson 1975), diminishing ANS hyperarousal through reduced activity in the hypothalamic-pituitary-adrenal axis (HPA) (Sapolsky et al. 2000). Deep breathing, a central method, increases heart-rate variability, a bio-marker for ANS homeostasis and reductions in psychophysiological disorders (Gevirtz 2011), through the mediating effects of the parasympathetic ventral vagal complex (Porges 2007). Practicing mindfulness during meditation has further benefits. It reduces amygdala activity and density, increases left hemisphere prefrontal cortex activity and insula density, and increases hemispheric synchrony (Creswell et al. 2007; Davidson et al. 2003; Holzel et al. 2011; Holzel et al. 2010; Lutz et al. 2004). These changes are associated with nuanced awareness of sensations and thoughts, accurate stress appraisal, and heightened cognitive attention. In summary, meditation that integrates elicitation of the relaxation response and mindfulness interrupts the stress response, reduces behavioral reactivity to afflictive thoughts and emotions, and contributes to mental clarity (Coffey et al. 2010; Kass 2015) .

Polyvagal Theory, developed by Stephen Porges, provides an additional bio-behavioral perspective on the evolving capacity for mature coping (Porges 2011), and offers a more precise explanation for meditation's clinical value (Kass and Trantham 2014). Early explanations of the stress response focused on activation of the sympathetic nervous system (SNS) (Benson 1975; Cannon 1929; Kabat-Zinn 1990).

Porges focused on the parasympathetic vagus nerve. The vagus plays an important role regulating the heart. Heart muscle contracts naturally, governed by the sinoatrial node. But its intrinsic rate (100–120 bpm) is not healthy over long periods (Opthof 2000). During calm functioning and restorative rest, the vagus nerve inhibits heart rate (60–80 bpm), becoming a protective "vagal brake" (Porges et al. 1996). During mobilization, the vagus relaxes the brake, increasing metabolism. If threat is perceived, it relinquishes control to the SNS, triggering fight-flight. But if dangerous threat is not perceived, the vagal brake can mobilize necessary coping energy without SNS activation (Porges 1995). Sapolsky further explains that HPA stress hormone secretion is not needed to cope with psychological stress (Sapolsky 2004) (p. 399). For most modern varieties of stress, the PNS can activate sufficient energy for resilient coping.

This insight is important for four reasons. SNS activation requires high metabolic output (Porges 1995). Chronic SNS hyperarousal degrades metabolic functioning in cardiovascular, gastrointestinal, and immune systems (Sapolsky 2004). Unregulated SNS hyperarousal has negative psychological effects that include anxiety, depression, hostility, and substance use (Lambert and Kinsley 2005). SNS activation disengages the brain's social engagement system, reducing interpersonal communication, emotional support, and cooperation (Porges 1995).

Thus, the beneficial role of meditation in resilient coping becomes increasingly clear. When people retain internal composure during life challenges, they can mobilize metabolic energy and utilize social support more effectively to meet challenges calmly, constructively, and cooperatively. Further, when SNS activation is necessary, internal composure enables the vagal brake to inhibit fight-flight as quickly as possible, aiding cardiovascular recovery (Porges 1998).

Polyvagal Theory also explicates the health effects of diaphragmatic breathing. The lungs and heart are *linked* through shared circuits of the vagus nerve. During inhalation, heart rate increases slightly. During exhalation, heart rate decreases slightly. The difference is called heart rate variability (HRV). As diaphragmatic breathing deepens, HRV increases. This has physiological and psychological significance. High HRV (vagal tone) indicates cardiovascular health (Porges 1998, 2007) and predicts psychological well-being across the lifespan (Kass and Trantham 2014). Vagal tone is strongly associated with psychological resilience and health.

Polyvagal Theory also contributes to recognition of a maturational direction in bio-cultural evolution. The resilience-conferring functions of the vagus nerve are not present in reptiles. They evolved in mammals and were refined during primate/human development. Mammals have two vagal circuits. The dorsal vagal complex (DVC) is the primitive reptilian circuit. It lacks a myelinated sheathing: its signal speed is slow, limiting gradations in regulatory capacity. The DVC circuit is attached to all major organs. But in usual circumstances, it only regulates organs in the abdominal cavity. Organs above the diaphragm are regulated by the more evolved mammalian circuit: the ventral vagal complex (VVC), in the brainstem's nucleus ambiguus (NA). As it evolved, the VVC migrated away from the DVC, developing myelinated sheathing. Its signal is fast, enabling significant gradations in regulatory capacities. The VVC is the connective link between lungs and heart. It regulates the vagal brake and subtle gradations in responsivity to environmental stimuli. The NA also contains cranial nerves that regulate facial expression and hearing: key modes of social engagement. Thus, the human social engagement system is linked with heart-lung connections. Consequently, a smiling face can calm agitation in another person, empathic words can resolve escalating arguments, and silent attunement between parent and infant can build secure attachment (Porges 1995, 1998, 2001). In short, this "smart" vagus, central to resilient coping, reflects the maturational direction of bio-cultural evolution.

Porges employs these insights to identify three tiers of stress-coping. Mature coping is regulated by the VVC. Fight-flight arousal is controlled by the SNS. During traumatic events beyond the individual's control, when fight-flight is not effective, the DVC protectively reduces metabolism (e.g., fainting) and awareness (e.g., numbing, dissociation) (Porges 2011; van der Kolk 2014). But SNS activation persists, manifesting as emotionally-agitated freeze responses or unpredictable vicious aggression (Kass and Trantham 2014).

In conclusion, this discussion highlights humanity's evolutionary development of mature stress-coping mechanisms and clarifies a central dynamic in humanity's chain of pain. When stressful events magnify specific links, coping regresses to primitive mechanisms. They become increasingly destructive to self and others, further escalating the chain of pain. This cycle is figural in its replication. Psychospiritual maturation helps students become mindful of stress-coping mechanisms, strengthening their capacity for mature bio-behavioral self-regulation.

2. Cognitive-Sociocultural: *Cognitive schema and sociocultural identity narratives that condition perceptions of self and other and legitimize systemic social dominance hierarchies.*

Humanity's chain of pain, however, infects additional dimensions of self. Maturational models that focus predominantly on stress reactivity obscure social aspects of human experience. The most traumatic manifestation of unregulated stress reactivity is violent intergroup conflict (Fisher et al. 2013; Kelman 1997), magnified frequently by demonization of the religious *other* (Ehrenkranz and Coppola 2000). Further, cognitive schema that trigger the most injurious social behaviors are deeply rooted in prejudice: humanity's reliance on oppressive group-based social dominance hierarchies as the organizing mode in human systems (Fox and Prilleltensky 1997; Kinder 2013; Miller 1976; Pinderhughes 1989; Sidanius and Kurzban 2013; Sidanius and Pratto 1999). Systemic inequalities corrode the psychological, economic, and physical well-being of self and society (Friedli 2009; Sapolsky 2004, 2005b; Sterling 2004). As Robert Sapolsky notes wryly, "It is a testimony to the power of humans, after inventing material technology and the unequal distribution of its spoils, to corrosively subordinate its have-nots" (p. 652) (Sapolsky 2005a). Further, stress-coping mechanisms utilized by individuals and groups are shaped by positionality on society's pyramid of power. Top-tier people often use socially-sanctioned power to reduce stress at the expense of low-tier people. Low-tier people often express powerlessness through self-destructive stress-coping. But intersectionality can blend top-tier and low-tier aspects of social identity (e.g., race/gender) triggering a volatile mix of self-destructive and top-down coping behaviors in families and systems (Kass 1991b, 2007b, 2015).

Thus, social dominance hierarchies are a driving force in humanity's chain of pain. When people and groups interact through positions of power and subordination, they develop distorted schema about self and others (Koenig and Eagly 2014; Pratto et al. 2006; Sidanius and Pratto 1999). These distortions are magnified because each tier triggers the stress response (Sapolsky 2004, 2005a; Zink et al. 2008). This hyperarousal increases mistrust and behavioral reactivity (Critcher and Zayas 2014; Mooijman et al. 2015), reduces accurate appraisal and social engagement (Gable and Poole 2015; Porges 1995), and magnifies the intergenerational transmission of trauma through dysfunctional systems (Bloom and Farragher 2013; Felitti et al. 1998; Henry and Wang 1998; Schore 2003; Verona and Sachs-Ericsson 2005). Further, during perceived threat of external danger, groups experience a collective stress response: regressing to rigid hierarchical structures, accepting subordinate roles to assure protection, and affirming within-group "tribal" identity (Fisher et al. 2013; Kelman 1997; Marsella 2009; Shapiro 2010, 2016; Sidanius and Pratto, 1999; Staw et al. 1981). Intergroup tensions are further magnified when legitimized through religiously-sanctioned prejudice and selective use of sacred texts to demonize the *other* (Allport 1950, 1954, 1966; Moore 2007).

Students are often challenged by this aspect of psychospiritual maturation. They enter this learning process enmeshed in humanity's chain of pain, including their social identity, position in the pyramid of power, and introjected schemas about self and *other*. Recognizing distorted cognitive schemas and sociocultural narratives is difficult because they have inherited them from respected authorities. Further, recognition uncovers embarrassing personal attitudes, behaviors, and past actions (Adams et al. 1997; Gallardo 2014). Thus, students benefit from mindfulness skills that help them explore their uncomfortable emotions without regressing defensively into primitive stress-coping. It is also helpful to recognize that destructive attitudes and behaviors are not caused by personal defects. They have systemic, historical, and bio-cultural evolutionary roots which make them a collective human concern. This framework helps students develop *empathic self-reflection* skills, helping them explore ways they perpetuate these attitudes and behaviors without diluting self-interrogation necessary to break these patterns.

Empathic self-reflection is an extension of Rogers' therapeutic concepts (Kass 1991b, 2005). As students develop their capacities for empathy, congruence, and unconditional positive regard, they develop compassionate attitudes toward self and *other*. As they experience being empathically received by others, their capacity to reciprocate grows proportionally. Further, their self-structures grow less rigid, enabling them to acknowledge attitudes, feelings, and past actions dissonant with their ideal selves (Rogers 1959, 1961).

A bio-cultural evolutionary perspective on social dominance hierarchies offers further evidence that humanity is evolving toward more mature behavior. Anthropological evidence demonstrates that humans inherited this social system template from primate ancestors with highly-structured, kin-favoring systems (MacKinnon and Fuentes 2012; Sapolsky 2004, 2005a; Sidanius and Pratto 1999). There is no evidence of a dominance-favoring gene. These ancestors required stable social networks for well-being. They utilized the survival benefits of their social-bonding mammalian brains to develop complex cultural rules governing intragroup and intergroup behavior. Their group organization patterns were transmitted culturally, as humans gradually evolved a separate cultural niche (MacKinnon and Fuentes 2012).

Adapting to the need for complex communication, the human brain then evolved direct connections from the cortex to brainstem nuclei that regulate orofacial motor control (Downey and Lende 2012). Cooperative hunting was an early application, creating decisive survival advantages, ecological dominance, and a broad cultural niche for sociocultural development (Day et al. 2003; Fuentes et al. 2010). Sedentary agricultural societies evolved with economic surplus and role specialization (Diamond 1997; Downey and Lende 2012), including male warriors who competed to control material resources and human capital. They accumulated sufficient power to maintain elaborate social dominance hierarchies, existent in early empires of every racial/cultural group. Thus, social dominance hierarchies were a natural product of bio-cultural evolution. Research suggests they originated in males, but not a particular racial or ethnic group (Sidanius and Kurzban 2013).

There is strong evidence that humans subsequently developed a differential preference for own-group social dominance or an egalitarian orientation. Variance on a measure of *social dominance orientation* is correlated with political ideologies that reject or promote egalitarianism (Pratto et al. 1994). There is some evidence that a genetic factor heightens preference for social dominance: people who carry only the S allele of the serotonin transporter gene (5-HTTLPR). This genetic variation may have evolved bio-culturally as status-based protection against pathogens transmitted by farm animals. The S allele is associated with harm avoidance, fear conditioning, increased negative emotion, heightened anxiety, and magnified amygdala response to negative stimuli. Thus, this genetic preference for social dominance reflects exaggerated fear responses and low stress tolerance (Chiao 2010; Chiao and Blizinsky 2010). Additional research shows that preference for own-group social dominance is negatively correlated with neural activity in brain regions associated with affective components of empathy (left anterior insula and anterior cingulate cortex): people with high scores on *social dominance orientation* showed less response when perceiving the pain of others (Chiao et al. 2009). Thus, people with a genetic predilection for social dominance are more likely to be fearful of, and less empathic toward, cultural *others*. These genetic tendencies may make it more difficult to develop inclusive attitudes. But they do not *determine* behavior. They magnify tension all humans experience between primitive and mature coping mechanisms.

In summary, during early human development, social dominance hierarchies provided substantive, though unequally distributed, survival benefits. These hierarchical human systems can be regarded as an attachment-solution to limitations in the cultural niche inhabited by hunter-gatherer tribes. However, as human needs for individuation, identity-formation, and equality became figural, group-based social dominance hierarchies became regressive. By stratifying, segregating, and subordinating people, they have become an urgent separation-challenge. In the cognitive-sociocultural dimension of self, students develop critical analysis skills that help them understand the toxic impact of social dominance hierarchies; and empathic self-reflection skills to recognize nondefensively their perpetuation of these patterns. This aspect of person-centered psychospiritual maturation is an important step in the transformation of self and society.

3. **Social-Emotional:** *Templates of* attachment *that shape the capacity for constructive interpersonal relationships, families, and community/ organizational networks.*

Although critical analysis and sociocultural awareness are essential to psychospiritual maturation, social-emotional development is also necessary. Humanity's chain of pain destroys relational networks vital to individual and social well-being. Further, it subverts development of social engagement skills necessary to rebuild broken networks. By undermining the human need for secure relational attachment, it reinforces insecure attachment, producing psychologically-wounded people with anxious, avoidant, or disorganized attachment systems (Ainsworth 1985; Bowlby 1969; Main 1995; van Ijzendoorn and Sagi-Schwartz 2008). Psychospiritual maturation requires social-emotional recovery from these toxic effects. This recovery can be educative, facilitated by in vivo learning communities where culturally-diverse individuals experience trustworthy relationship and inclusion. These learning communities demonstrate that positive relationality is possible, providing a laboratory where students can explore and refine attachment behaviors. The communities also provide an empathic holding environment where students can explore and heal emotional and somatic residues of suffering they have experienced (Fosha et al. 2009; Ogden et al. 2006; Rothschild 2000). When this learning is absent, psychologically-wounded people maintain high levels of psychophysiological agitation, highly-defended self-structures, and insecure attachment templates that subvert growth of constructive relational skills. These deficits heighten likelihood that they will perpetuate the chain of pain through behavior destructive to self and others.

Research shows that secure relational attachment is crucial to well-being, strengthening self-regulation skills in children and adults (Mikulincer and Shaver 2008; Schore 2001; Siegel 2012). Securely attached adults appraise stressful events as less threatening and have more positive expectations about their ability to cope (Shaver and Mikulincer 2002). They employ a mature "secure base script" organized around three strategies for affect regulation: acknowledging and displaying distress, focused problem-solving, and seeking social support (Waters et al. 1998). Securely attached adults, when angry, recognize internal arousal, seek to repair ruptured relationships, and express anger without hostility (Mikulincer 1998). Secure attachment also reinforces healthy responses to traumatic events (Schore 2003; Solomon and Siegel 2003): adults retain narrative access to painful memories and reexperience negative emotions without becoming overwhelmed (Hesse 2008; Shaver and Mikulincer 2002).

Insecure attachment produces hyper- and hypo-aroused responses to stress (Schore 2009; Shaver and Mikulincer 2002). Anxiously attached adults maintain a narcissistic focus on personal distress, dwell on negative thoughts, and use emotion-focused coping, amplifying threat perception. Avoidantly attached adults distance themselves cognitively and emotionally from stressors and do not acknowledge emotions. They often exhibit dissociated anger: without being aware of this feeling, they exhibit physiological distress, hostility, and perceive others as hostile (Mikulincer and Florian 1998). Disorganized attachment, a result of trauma, impairs empathic attunement (Siegel 2012) and neurobehavioral self-regulation (Schore 2002). It reinforces cyclic predisposition to hostility and violence (Lyons-Ruth and Jacobvitz 2008; Schore 2003).

Secure attachment mediates genetic tendencies for impulsive stress reactivity and alcohol dependence. As noted, the S allele of the serotonin transporter gene (5-HTTLPR) is associated with magnification of fear conditioning, negative emotion, and amygdala reactivity to negative stimuli (Chiao 2010; Chiao and Blizinsky 2010). In rhesus monkeys, the S allele is associated with impulsive behavior: excessive consumption of alcohol in "happy hour" conditions and increased aggression. However, these behaviors are evident only when they have been raised without secure mother-child attachment (Suomi 2003).

Secure attachment also contributes to positive intergroup bonds. When secure attachment is reinforced in dominant group adults, negative reactions to outgroups diminish (Mikulincer and Shaver 2001) . But it is important that intergroup contact is not limited to superficial harmony that minimizes systemic bias (Saguy et al. 2011). Gordon Allport's work on prejudice reduction suggests the need for egalitarian interpersonal environments in which people from diverse sociocultural groups can develop rich empathic bonds. The efficacy of this approach has been well-established (Allport 1954; Pettigrew and Tropp 1998; Pettigrew et al. 2011; Sidanius et al. 2008). Intergroup contact theory provides a clear rationale for inclusive community building in person-centered psychospiritual maturation.

Attachment theory provides additional insight into negative effects of social dominance hierarchies. Positions of power have an adverse effect on social-emotional leadership behavior, subverting establishment of secure bonds between authority figures and subordinates (Mikulincer and Shaver 2011). Authority figures are emotionally distant from subordinates (Smith and Trope 2006) and objectify them as a means to attain personal goals (Gruenfeld et al. 2008). Authority figures are less willing to understand subordinate's perspectives or relate empathically (Galinsky et al. 2006). Further, power over others increases the harshness of punishment behaviors (Mooijman et al. 2015). These relational dynamics further explain how social dominance perpetuates humanity's chain of pain.

The emergent human capacity for secure relational attachment provides further support for a maturation-oriented direction in bio-cultural evolution. While a separation challenge-attachment solution dialectic can be observed throughout evolution (Fricchione 2011), it is very apparent in the shift from socially-isolated reptiles to socially-attached mammals. It is even more evident in the emergence of humans from their primate ancestors, where increased needs for attachment are associated with structural and hormonal changes in female reproductive physiology and formation of stable pair-bonds with specialized gender roles (Fisher 1982). These pair-bonds were initially transactional, reflecting the hierarchical structures of early human societies. However, as human culture evolved, people developed the capacity for a complex developmental process of psychological separation and attachment: symbiotic bonding and emotional attunement during infancy, self-differentiation and identity formation in childhood and adolescence, separation from the nuclear family in young adulthood, relationship formation during emergent adulthood (with attendant ruptures and repair), and raising children with their urgent needs for attuned attachment (Erikson 1963; Mahler et al. 1975). This complex developmental process, in which people experience the benefits and challenges of maintaining secure attachments, has produced the capacity for mature, reciprocal love. Thus, in early human societies, transactional pair-bonds with specialized gender roles reflected more advanced forms of attachment than our primate ancestors. But as humans developed the capacity for mature relational love, based in reciprocal attunement and individual identity formation, old modes of transactional pair-bonding with rigid gender roles became regressive. While mature love is elusive in current society, this capacity highlights the continuum of attachment behaviors that have emerged in the social-emotional dimension of self during humanity's bio-cultural evolutionary development and provides further evidence of a *formative tendency* (Rogers 1980). Experiential growth in this dimension of self is a central aspect of person-centered psychospiritual maturation.

4. Existential-Spiritual: *Templates of attachment through which we experience and derive meaning from our relationship with the cosmos.*

Despite the healing effects of social-emotional growth, people cannot escape the harsh existential reality that Buddha encountered in his youth as he recognized that human life leads inevitably to old age, sickness, and death (Hanh 1991). The existential-spiritual dimension of self requires exploratory growth during person-centered psychospiritual maturation.

Paul Tillich coined the term *ontological insecurity* to describe the alienating fear that life is meaningless and incoherent (Tillich 1952). He considered this existential anxiety a root cause of psychological dysfunction and stress-related illnesses (Kass 1991a; Tillich 1984). Viktor Frankl reached similar conclusions, observing the human need for existential meaning and purpose (Frankl 1959, 1965). Aaron Antonovsky's research on *sense of coherence* as a stress modulator provided initial support for these hypotheses (Antonovsky 1979, 1987). Subsequent empirical research on the stress-buffering effects of *life purpose* provided further confirmation (Crumbaugh 1968; Crumbaugh and Maholick 1964; Kass 1998; Kass et al. 1991a; Kobasa et al. 1982; Reker and Peacock 1981; Reker et al. 1987).

Frankl and Tillich identified an aspect of spirituality crucial to perceptions of existential coherence: subjectively-experienced relationship with the Ground of Being (whether this term is understood through a religious or secular humanist lens). As discussed in Chap. 2, Frankl found that existential despair cannot be dispelled if *life* is considered an adversary. When he approached *life* as an ally and moral guide, this connection helped him cope with profound suffering (Kass 1996a, b). For Tillich, the Ground of Being is the transcendent dimension of life and the immanent core of self. His solution for ontological insecurity is subjectively-experienced relationship with the Ground of Being (Kass 1995). These ideas are consistent with Gordon Allport's distinction between *intrinsic religious orientation* (personal life guided by spiritual values and experiences of the divine) and *extrinsic religious orientation* (utilitarian religiosity, e.g., group membership, status) (Allport 1950, 1954, 1966; Allport and Ross 1967). Research on intrinsic religious orientation consistently finds psychological and health benefits (Bergin 1983; Bergin et al. 1987; Hood 1995; Kass et al. 1991b; Koenig McCullough and Larson 2001; Paloutzian and Park 2013; Pargament 1997).

Subjectively-experienced relationship with the Ground of Being is a central feature of the Perennial Philosophy: the shared maturational goals, existential insights, and contemplative practices of the world's spiritual traditions (Emerson 1992; Huxley 1945; James 1902/1986; Nasr 2007; Schuon 1984; Stace 1960a, b; Teasdale 1999), discussed in Chap. 1. The Perennial Philosophy is the inclusive framework through which the *Know Your Self* curriculum presents these traditions.

However, the terminology and imagery through which the spiritual traditions express relationality with the Ground of Being is problematic. The Ground of Being is often described by anthropomorphic God-images that can be both confusing and psychologically damaging. As discussed in Chap. 4, *The Guide of the Perplexed*, a twelfth-century text by Maimonides, provides a model of psychospiritual maturation consistent with the Perennial Philosophy. He teaches that anthropomorphic God-images should not be taken literally: the Ground of Being does not have human attributes. Sacred texts that use these terms were received through the minds of the prophets during contemplative illumination. These sages lived during specific periods in the history of their people. The God images they employed were attuned to the developmental level of these communities (Kass and Lennox 2005; Maimonides 1963). Diane Moore extends this perspective in her cultural studies approach to religious literacy. The specific texts and God-images that religious leaders select from sacred literature to govern community behavior reflects their particular sociocultural times, political agendas, and maturity (Moore 2007). These choices are vulnerable to distorting influences.

Similarly, within families, God images often provide diagnostic insight about impaired attachment systems (Granqvist and Kirkpatrick 2008; Hegy 2007; Kirkpatrick 2005; Rizzuto 1979). Some children develop positive images, representing secure attachment or compensation for relational deficits. But many introject shame-inducing God images that mirror family impairments or social dominance hierarchies. For example, God images are often gender- or racially-dissonant, conditionally loving, judgmental, and punitive (Clinebell 1984; Doehring 1993; McDonald et al. 2005; Spretnak 1982), reinforcing insecure attachment templates that undermine self-concept and adult behavior. In these cases, ascribed relationship with the Ground of Being can have negative effects.

During psychospiritual maturation, these images can undergo transformation (Fowler 1996; Rizzuto 1979). For example, childhood representations of God as trustworthy protector are often rejected after traumatic life events. When this shattered attachment is healed through psychospiritual mentoring, or spiritually-integrated counseling (Jordan 1986; Koenig and Pritchett 1998; Miller 1999; Pargament 2007; Richards and Bergin 1997), a more mature God-representation can emerge (e.g., inner guiding spirit; core dimension of self actively present amidst suffering) (Kass 2007a). Thus, psychospiritual self-inquiry and critical analysis are often necessary before the Ground of Being is perceived as a healthy source of secure attachment. Case studies in this book offer illustrative examples.

To cultivate subjectively-experienced relationship with the Ground of Being, the spiritual traditions teach contemplative modes of knowing (Kass 1995, 2015; Kass et al. 1991b; Kass and Lennox 2005). Meditation offers more than behavioral self-regulation: it can transform existential awareness. Ontological insecurity, from Maimonides' perspective, reflects a rupture in the spectrum of awareness that produces elemental *ignorance* (Kass and Lennox 2005; Maimonides 1963). This term is used consistently in the Perennial Philosophy to explain perceived existential alienation (Easwaran 2007; Nasr 2007). Meditation bridges this rupture, creating an *internal perceptual orientation* that opens a doorway to deeper dimensions of consciousness (Kass 1991a). Meditators learn that discursive thought is an externally-oriented, surface phenomenon of the psyche, produced by a limiting form of *ego consciousness* (Goleman 1988; Kass 1991a).

From an evolutionary perspective, development of an externally-oriented *ego* (which scans the environment, differentiates between objects, and regulates approach-avoidance behaviors) had distinct survival benefits. Antonio Damasio locates its origin in the *proto-self*: the ancient brain-stem area in vertebrates that registers attraction and aversion (Damasio 2010). The differentiating ego emerges in human infancy because it offers important survival benefits (and because ontogeny recapitulates phylogeny). The value of *differentiating awareness* is clear in most human activities, reaching an apex in the scientific method: differentiation of phenomena to determine causal relationships that help humans understand and manipulate the natural environment. However, as climate change shows, excessive manipulation can be dangerous. Similarly, excessive reliance on the externally-oriented ego suppresses awareness of the internal psychospiritual dimensions of self. When externally-oriented and internally-oriented aspects of the psyche become fragmented, people do not recognize unconscious stress reactivity, lose touch with emotions, fail to heal psychological trauma, and rupture access to insights and wisdom that are available from core dimensions of self. While ego consciousness provides important survival advantages, its fragmenting, isolative effects have become an urgent separation-challenge.

The capacity for psychospiritual self-awareness that has emerged in the human brain may offer evolution's attachment-solution. Our advanced prefrontal cortex enables sophisticated integration of right/left hemisphere and sub-cortical processes which confer somatic, affective, cognitive, and intuitive modes of knowing that can correct the distorting impact of restrictive ego consciousness (Siegel 2007). Providing access to subconscious, unexamined dimensions of self, psychospiritual awareness bridges fragmented ruptures in the psyche, creating pathways that restore emotional self-awareness, regulate primitive stress-reactivity, correct distorted cognitive schema, repair insecure attachment templates, and heal ontological insecurity (Jung 1933, 1959, 1964; Kass 1991a,

2015; Kass and Lennox 2005). The capacity for self-reflective awareness that enables integration emerges during adolescence/young adulthood. It constitutes the brain's emergent capacity for *connective awareness* (Kass 2007b), an attachment-solution to the separation-challenge created by *differentiating awareness*.

To explain the process of psychospiritual integration, contemplative schools within the spiritual traditions developed multidimensional models of the psyche. Maimonides' *Guide of the Perplexed* provides a useful example (Goodman, 1999; Hartman 1976; Maimonides 1963). His conceptual model, elegantly consistent with the Perennial Philosophy, has discernible parallels to contemplative roadmaps of the psyche in Buddhism, Hinduism, Islam, and Christianity (Bodhi 2005; Easwaran 1987; Nasr 2002; Teresa-of-Avila 1979).

In Maimonides' model, the psyche has four levels (Kass 2013; Kass and Lennox 2005). The first level, called the *moral faculty*, is ego consciousness: the discursive mind of daily life (sense perceptions, emotional reactions, cognitions, rumination about past, present and future, and moral decision-making). The purpose of daily life, he teaches, is the refinement of moral behavior: learning to walk in God's way (in Islam, the straight path; in Buddhism and Hinduism, *dharma*; in Christianity, imitating Jesus' actions). Because the ego has the freedom to engage in selfish, unethical behavior, Maimonides calls it the *moral faculty*, where templates of daily action are defined. During psychospiritual growth, the ego practices self-restraint and ethical awareness.

The second level of the psyche, called the *rational faculty*, is an advanced ego function: self-reflective critical analysis. The rational faculty identifies distorted cognitions and emotions which undermine moral behavior and accurate understanding about self, others, and the world. Maimonides shocked rabbinic peers by affirming the scientific principles of rational analysis developed by the Greek philosophers (and preserved by Islamic philosophy). Science offered methods through which religion could mature. Using critical analysis, Maimonides deconstructed anthropomorphic God images and the literal meaning of sacred Jewish texts, explicating them with intellectual and spiritual interpretations of their underlying meaning. In Islam, too, spiritual hermeneutics (*ta'wil*) became a figural aspect of psychospiritual development (Nasr 2007).

The *rational faculty* has the reflective capacity to observe the mind. This function prepares the individual to confront a primary danger during meditative contemplation. If the mind is filled with anger and grief, the individual's capacity for accurate contemplative insights is subverted (Kass 2013; Kass and Lennox 2005). In Hindu yoga psychology, these cognitive-emotional distortions are called *samskaras*: mental conditioning that produces inaccurate understanding and destructive actions (Aranya 1983; Jung 1996; Rama et al. 1976). In Buddhist yoga psychology, they are called *sankharas*: inaccurate mental formations (Bodhi 2005). In Judaism, Maimonides calls them *polluting moral qualities* that require *purification of the heart* (Maimonides 1963). In Christianity, St. John of the Cross describes them as *spiritual vices* or *imperfections* (Kavanaugh 1987). In Islam, they are called *nafs*: knots of evil tendencies that surround the spiritual *heart*, preventing unitive knowledge (*marifah*) (Nasr 2007).

The third level of the psyche is called the *imaginative faculty* in Maimonides' model. It is an intuitive mode of knowing. When the *moral faculty* has developed self-restraint, and the *rational faculty* has dispelled distorted cognitions and emotions, the psyche can enter an innerdirected contemplative state, in which the prophets received direction, insights, symbolic images, and visions. However, every person has potential access to this state of inner-knowing at a lesser degree of intensity through dreams and contemplative prayer (Maimonides 1963).

Maimonides' focus on receiving guidance through symbolic imagery may seem contrary to Buddhist practice, which often instructs meditators to disregard mental formations (Bodhi 2005). However, the Dalai Lama's descriptions of traditional Tibetan practice offer a broader perspective. The Buddha's awakened mind, he teaches, is available to the receptive contemplative as a source of guidance. He also describes visualization practices that facilitate quietude and receptivity, as well as visionary experiences of Buddhist contemplatives (Gyatso and Chodron 2014). In *Secret of the Golden Flower*, a fourteenth-century Chinese Taoist/ Buddhist text, Master Lu Tung-pin instructs students to differentiate distorting images arising from ego consciousness and wisdom images arising from the *Tao* (Wilhelm 1962).

Thus, the receptive *imaginal* dimension of human consciousness is a recognized mental faculty in the spiritual traditions. Henry Corbin, a scholar of Islamic mysticism, distinguishes *imaginal* from *imaginary*. The *imaginal* dimension of contemplative awareness confers access to personally-meaningful symbolic images and maturational insights (Cheetham 2012; Corbin 1969, 1980). Jung's investigations of archetypal dream symbolism provide additional support for the maturational significance of this intuitive dimension of consciousness (Jung 1959, 1964).

The fourth level of the psyche, in Maimonides' model, transcends individualized ego consciousness. It is the point of contact between the ego and the Ground of Being (Goodman 1999). Maimonides called it the *Active Intellect*, using Aristotelian terminology. The *Active Intellect* can be compared to Jung's *transcendent function* (Jung 1964) and Rogers' *formative tendency* (Rogers 1980): a coherent transpersonal energy that catalyzes maturational growth. When contemplatives experience the Ground of Being directly, they discover their elemental formlessness and the primordial unity of existence. Buddhism describes it as emptiness, suchness, or radiant light (Conze 2001). Christianity designates it as Christ-consciousness, the interior Kingdom of Heaven (Merton 1996; Pennington 1980; Teresa-of-Avila 1964, 1979). Hinduism calls it *Brahman*, the unitive Self (Easwaran 1987). Islam describes it as the foundation of all being, expressing its infinitude symbolically through the 99 names of Allah (Nasr 2002). Describing the prophets that he considered most advanced (in the Jewish tradition), Maimonides taught that Abraham, Moses, and Miriam could apprehend the unitive, formless Divine ceaselessly while serving actively as community leaders. For Maimonides, the ability to participate in daily responsibilities, while securely anchored in contemplative illumination, is the height of psychospiritual maturation (Kass 2013; Kass and Lennox 2005).

Since William James's classic study, the transformative but essentially subjective nature of religious experience remains contentious (James 1902/1986; Wulff 1997). Critics insist these experiences are socially-constructed (Katz 1978; Proudfoot 1985), irrational defense mechanisms (Ellis 1986; May and Yalom 1989), mental conditioning reinforced by religious fundamentalism and cults (Deikman 1994), symptoms of neurological dysfunction (Persinger 1987), and vulnerable to distortion during traumatic political violence (Ehrenkranz and Coppola 2000). These criticisms are unquestionably accurate in some cases. However, human meaning-making takes place at the interface between objective and subjective experience. Charlene Spretnak argues that post-modern constructivism does not preclude the possibility that human consciousness and the phenomenal world emerge from a substrate of unitive being (Spretnak 1991). Quantum physics suggests similar possibilities (Bell 2008; Bohm 1980; Bohm and Hiley 1993; Tegmark 2015). Unitive spiritual experiences may not be caused *by* psychological distortions. Rather, as reported by advanced contemplatives, they occur when conditioned, distorted, or restrictive forms of perception have been transcended (Easwaran 2007; Green 2003; Kornfield 1979; Merton 1996; Nasr 2007; Pennington 1980; Dass 1979; Shaku 1906).

While few individuals become established in this unitive state, temporary experiences of numinous inspiration fill the research literature on mysticism (Hood 1995; Hood et al. 1979), reporting transformative learning and expanded awareness of self. Transcending the isolative boundaries of ego consciousness, meditators experience themselves securely attached to a unitive Ground of Being (de Castro 2017; Kass 2007b; Stace 1960a; Tillich 1952). When consolidated through sustained contemplative practice, a shift in self-structure occurs, in which anchored awareness is incorporated into daily living (Maimonides 1963; Merton 1998). Thus, meditation may confer mature stress coping through the internal composure of *secure existential attachment* (Kass and Trantham 2014).

Neuroscience research identifies brain processes correlated with the unitive experiences and intuitive modes of knowing during meditation, suggesting that these subjective experiences are an innate, naturally-occurring human capacity (Cahn and Polich 2006; Newberg and D'Aquili 1998). Three complementary explanatory models have emerged:

1. Meditation deepens an internally-focused perceptual orientation by diminishing body, spatial, and temporal awareness through deafferentation of the left superior parietal lobe (D'Aquili and Newberg 1999; Taylor 2009).
2. Meditation creates a state of heightened attention to internal experience by inducing hemispheric synchrony in high-amplitude gamma waves (Lutz et al. 2004).
3. Meditation reduces activity in the default mode network, interrupting self-referential awareness (Holzel et al. 2011; Pagnoni et al. 2008). In addition, it reduces functional connections among a wide range of other cortical areas, eliciting experiences of non-attachment and ego transcendence (Lehmann et al. 2012).

Reduced activity in the default mode network is a particularly meaningful explanatory model. First, sleep research demonstrates that the frontal cortex decouples from the default mode network during delta sleep. This restorative mode of deep sleep (dreamless) produces restful dissolution of self-awareness (Horovitz et al. 2009). Second, in the *Upanishads*, deep sleep is described as the state of quiescent consciousness that precedes unitive awareness (Easwaran 1987; Prabhavananda 1947). In an early application of neurophenomenology (Varela and Shear 1999) at the Menninger Foundation, an advanced yogi generated delta rhythms during meditation, subsequently describing unitive awareness in this interior perceptual state (Green et al. 1971; Rama et al. 1976).

In their pioneering research, Elmer and Alyce Green developed a neuroscientific model of meditation explaining experiences of intuitive inspiration (Green 1984a; Green and Green 1977; Green 1984b). They measured electrical activity in the cortex (analogue EEG), integrating data from sleep research to refine their model. Beta activity (13–26 cps) is predominant in waking consciousness, when externally-focused perceptions maintain environmental scanning, vigilant arousal, and varied levels of anxiety. When meditators draw attention inward, practicing focused concentration on the breath, alpha activity (8–12 cps) becomes dominant, associated with alert peaceful calm and the ability to witness thoughts and emotions non-reactively. After more extensive practice, theta activity (4–8 cps) increases. This rhythm is associated with hypnagogic imagery in Stage I sleep. Meditators, alternatively, maintain an attentive state of nonactive, mental receptivity. In this contemplative theta state, meditators experience creative insight, intuition, and problem-solving, often through symbolic imagery. This neurological process is now understood to include integration of right hemisphere, left hemisphere, and subcortical processes (Jung-Beeman et al. 2004; Salvi et al. 2016; Siegel 2007). Although meditative elicitation of the delta state by an advanced yogi has only been documented once (Green et al. 1971), elicitation of theta states has been replicated frequently (Cahn and Polich 2006). Thus, there is compelling evidence that meditation can elicit intuitive states of consciousness that offer creative insights into problems of daily life.

Elicitation of theta states also provides a neuroscientific model for the intuitive learning that occurs during Jung's psychotherapeutic process, *active imagination*, in which individuals cultivate a receptive mode of inwardly-focused contemplation (Chodorow 1997; Hannah 1981).

Active imagination catalyzes the imaginal dimension of self in which symbols of transformation are generated by the *transcendent function* (Chodorow 1997; Hannah 1981; Jung 1964; Shamdasani 2009). This internal dimension of consciousness provides an integrative meeting place for right-brain intuitive processes and left-brain cognitive processes (Schore 2009; Siegel 2007). Mary Watkins integrated these methods into *imaginal dialogue* work, where individuals embody archetypal parts of self, including the guidance of a wise, inner self (Birnbaum and Birnbaum 2004; Watkins 1984, 1986). Similar methods can be found in psychosynthesis (Assagioli 2000), Gestalt therapy (Perls 1973), and Internal Family Systems (Schwartz 1995).

From Jung's perspective, exclusive focus on unitive awareness can be counterproductive, subverting maturation of ego processes necessary to healthy functioning (Jung 1931, 1933, 1959, 1964; Shamdasani 1996). His therapeutic orientation adds depth to Maimonides' model of the psyche, identifying the *personal* and *collective unconscious* as distinct regions where sequestered mental formations create cognitive distortions and emotional reactivity that require exploration and healing. Jung's research preceded recent advances in interpersonal neurobiology and sociocultural theory, which clarify his model. The *personal unconscious* sequesters cognitions, emotions, and somatically-frozen traumatic memories acquired through personal experience. They include anger, grief, rage, and terror that individuals must suppress to survive in their social systems and life circumstances. The *collective unconscious* contains cognitions, emotions, and templates of behavior that have been encoded in the encultured human brain during four million years of biocultural evolutionary development: primitive survival mechanisms, sexual desire, gendered behavior, social dominance orientation, and instinctive fear of the *other*.

Jung recognized that the highly combustible material in the personal and collective unconscious cannot be healed through an overly simplistic quest for unitive awareness and inner peace. Nor can it be healed simply through efforts to resolve systemic inequalities through legislation, as rationalist political philosophy suggests (Fisher et al. 2013; Jung 1957; Shapiro 2010; Sidanius and Kurzban 2013). We must also address the fragmentation of our psyches, as individuals and society, through psychospiritual development (Jung 1964; Singer 1990; von Franz 1964; Whitmont 1969).

Recognizing the maturational need to examine and heal this combustible material, I developed an approach to contemplative practice in the *Know Your Self* curriculum that includes emotional processing of material sequestered in the personal and collective unconscious. Without therapeutic understanding and resolution of these mental formations, they persist, fomenting destructive behavior toward self and others. To overcome attachment to the destructive desires these mental formations create, we must explore them concretely, disentangling ourselves from the afflictive emotions that persist within us as toxic residue from humanity's chain of pain.

Case studies in subsequent chapters will illustrate this approach to contemplative practice, where psychospiritual exploration includes material from the personal and collective unconscious. This work often takes place in the imaginal dimension of awareness, as material becomes available for processing through mindfulness and elicitation of the relaxation response. These explorations include guidance from the archetypal inner mentor: the maturation-oriented core dimension of self. The case study material illustrates the educative, autonomous qualities of this core self, which led Jung to differentiate it completely from ego consciousness.

In the spiritual traditions, psychospiritual maturation is often described as eradication of the ego. But this language does not accurately describe the integrative learning process that this case study material describes. Nor is it congruent with the robust behavior of advanced contemplatives, whose active engagement in teaching, community-building, and social transformation indicates that their externally-oriented ego functions remain strong. But their external actions are no longer limited by self-protective ego consciousness. Nor do they appear burdened by unexamined mental formations sequestered in the unconscious. Their psychospiritual maturation is better described as a state of wholeness: *an expansion of self-awareness beyond the restrictions and limiting isolation of ego consciousness.* Behaviorally, there is a fullness to their actions. Grounded in the physical world, while securely attached to the transcendent dimension of life, they exhibit robust, fearless, tranquil energy: a manifestation of their *secure existential attachment* (Kass 2007b, 2015).

From a bio-cultural evolutionary perspective, the human capacity for connective awareness and secure existential attachment emerged after the far earlier development of an externally-oriented ego that utilizes differentiating awareness for survival. Thus, in the existential-spiritual dimension of self, a perceptual continuum developed between *differentiating* and *connective* modes of awareness. As in the other dimensions of self, the evolutionary formative tendency preserves both modes of awareness, because each serves survival functions. However, in the progressive movement of humanity toward mature individual and social behavior, cultivation of the capacity for connective awareness becomes increasingly important. This learning is a figural aspect of person-centered psychospiritual maturation.

5. Integrative Worldview Formation: *The synthesizing lens through which we perceive and respond to life events and people.*

During psychospiritual development, the bio-behavioral, cognitive-sociocultural, social-emotional, and existential-spiritual dimensions of self undergo synergistic learning. Through this integrative growth, individuals develop a resilient worldview that helps them confront life's developmental, interpersonal, intergroup, and existential challenges with internal composure and the ability to derive maturational growth (Kass and Trantham 2014).

This resilient worldview can be characterized as Confidence in Life and Self (CLS) (Kass 1998). In response to daily frustrations and stress, CLS helps people maintain inner calm, make constructive, empowering decisions, develop cognitive flexibility, and maintain secure relational attachments in the midst of interpersonal tension. In response to life's existential calamities and humanity's chain of pain, CLS helps individuals develop and discern life purpose and meaning; balance empowering action with calm acceptance; and maintain secure existential attachment. Thus, CLS helps them respond to challenges with maturity, rather than destructive reactivity. In this way, CLS becomes a functional expression of person-centered psychospiritual maturation.

Research in neuroscience offers insight into the consolidation of a resilient worldview. Neurologically, the ventromedial prefrontal cortex plays a central role. This region integrates left hemisphere, right hemisphere, limbic, and brain stem processes into coherent narratives about self, others, and life (Kass and Trantham 2014; Schore 2012; Siegel 2007). This integrative process produces interactive learning in bio-behavioral, cognitive-sociocultural, social-emotional, and existential-spiritual dimensions of self, helping people break personal links in their chain of pain. Consequently, they develop *confidence in self*. Through the same integrative process, they learn that life challenges can be solved best when reframed as an emergent curriculum for maturation of self and society. Rather than losing confidence in life when the chain of pain is resurgent, they conceptualize these crises as evidence that maturational growth is required. This reframing generates *confidence in life*. Through both forms of learning, individuals acquire the resilient worldview Confidence in Life and Self as a perceptual lens for responding constructively to stress-inducing life events and people.

Research in positive psychology by Barbara Fredrickson demonstrates that a resilient worldview has significant health-promoting and pro-social effects (Fredrickson 1998). During heightened stress, resilient attitudes promote cardiovascular recovery from autonomic mobilization (Fredrickson and Levenson 1998). People maintain a greater degree of life satisfaction, continue to experience love for—and support from—others, remain mindfully attentive to what is new and different in their daily experience, maintain their capacity for self-affirmation and joy, and remain confident that their lives have meaning and purpose (Tugade and Fredrickson 2004; Waugh et al. 2008). Positivity broadens thought-action repertoires and creates an upward spiral of well-being (Fredrickson 2001; Fredrickson and Cohn 2008; Fredrickson and Joiner 2002). The pro-social value of resilient attitudes are equally evident (Diener 2000; Fredrickson 1998): they reduce own-race bias in face recognition (Johnson and Fredrickson 2005), promote self-other overlap (Waugh and Fredrickson 2006), and strengthen nonmaterialist strategies for happiness (Diener and Seligman 2004). Fredrickson has also demonstrated that resilient attitudes are durable over time when reinforced by meditation (Cohn and Fredrickson 2010). This research supports growing evidence that psychospiritual development has a beneficial effect on resilience (Southwick et al. 2005).

In summary, the prefrontal cortex synthesizes interactive learning in bio-behavioral, cognitive-sociocultural, social-emotional, and existential-spiritual dimensions of self. This learning manifests as a resilient worldview, Confidence in Life and Self. This worldview helps people face life's harsh realities with internal composure and secure existential attachment (Kass 2007b; Kass and Trantham 2014). Confidence in Life and Self, as this discussion suggests, is a concrete manifestation of person-centered psychospiritual maturation.

CONCLUSIONS

This chapter has provided an operant definition of person-centered psychospiritual maturation by exploring research on major essential dimensions of self, explained the salience of this maturational process as an antidote to humanity's chain of pain, and clarified its relevance as a reparative and prevention-oriented learning process for emerging adults in higher education. Further, it has presented neuroscientific and biocultural evolutionary perspectives that establish an exploratory bridge between the sciences and spiritual traditions that could help them work together more effectively to break humanity's chain of pain.

REFERENCES

Adams, M., Bell, L. A., & Griffin, P. (Eds.). (1997). *Teaching for diversity and social change: A sourcebook* (1st ed.). New York, NY: Routledge.

Adams, M., Bell, L. A., Goodman, D. J., & Joshi, K. Y. (Eds.). (2016). *Teaching for diversity and social change* (3rd ed.). New York, NY: Routledge.

Ainsworth, M. D. (1985). Attachments across the life span. *Bulletin NY Acad Med*, 61(9), 792–812.

Ainsworth, M. D., Blehar, M., Waters, E., & Wall, S. (1978). *Patterns of attachment: Assessed in the strange situation and at home.* Hillsdale, NJ: Lawrence Erlbaum.

Aldarondo, E. (Ed.). (2007). Advancing social justice through clinical practice. New York, NY: Routledge, Taylor & Francis.

Allport, G. W. (1950). *The individual and his religion.* New York, NY: Macmillan.

Allport, G. W. (1954). *The nature of prejudice* (2nd ed.). Reading, MA: Addison-Wesley.

Allport, G. W. (1966). The religious context of prejudice. *Journal for the Scientific Study of Religion*, 5, 447–457.

Allport, G. W., & Ross, J. M. (1967). Personal religious orientation and prejudice. *Journal of Personality and Social Psychology*, 5(4), 432–443.

Antonovsky, A. (1979). *Health, stress, and coping.* San Francisco, CA: Jossey-Bass.

Antonovsky, A. (1987). *Unraveling the mystery of health.* San Francisco, CA: Jossey-Bass.

Aranya, S. H. (1983). *Yoga philosophy of Patanjali.* Albany, NY: SUNY Press.

Armstrong, K. (2011). Religion is about how you behave: The essential virtue is compassion. In A. Sharma (Ed.), *The world's religions.* Minneapolis, MN: Fortress Press.

Assagioli, R. (2000). *Psychosynthesis: A collection of basic writings*. Amherst, MA: The Synthesis Center.
Bell, J. S. (2008). *Speakable and unspeakable in quantum physics*. New York, NY: Cambridge University Press.
Benson, H. (1975). *The relaxation response*. New York, NY: Morrow.
Benson, H., Rosner, B. A., Marzetta, B. R., & Klemchuk, H. M. (1974). Decreased blood-pressure in pharmacologically treated hypertensive patients who regularly elicited the relaxation response. *Lancet, 1*(7852), 289–291.
Bergin, A. E. (1983). Religiosity and mental health: A critical reevaluation and meta-analysis. *Professional Psychology: Research and Practice, 14,* 170–184.
Bergin, A. E., Masters, K. S., & Richards, P. S. (1987). Religiousness and mental health reconsidered: A study of an intrinsically religious sample. *Journal of Counseling Psychology, 34,* 197–204.
Birnbaum, L., & Birnbaum, A. (2004). In search of inner wisdom: Guided mindfulness meditation in the context of suicide. *The Scientific World Journal, 4,* 216–227.
Bloom, S. L., & Farragher, B. (2013). *Restoring sanctuary: A new operating system for trauma-informed systems of care*. New York, NY: Oxford University Press.
Bodhi, B. (2005). *In the Buddha's words: An anthology of discourses from the Pali canon*. Somerville, MA: Wisdom Publications.
Bohm, D. (1980). *Wholeness and the implicate order*. New York, NY: Routledge.
Bohm, D., & Hiley, B. J. (1993). *The undivided universe*. New York, NY: Routledge.
Borysenko, J. (1989). *Minding the body, mending the mind*. Boston, MA: Addison-Wesley.
Bowlby, J. (1969). *Attachment and loss, volume 1: Attachment*. New York, NY: Basic Books.
Cahn, B. R., & Polich, J. (2006). Meditation states and traits: EEG, ERP, and neuroimaging studies. *Psychological Bulletin, 132*(2), 180–211.
Cannon, W. B. (1929). *Bodily changes in pain, hunger, fear, and rage: An account of recent researches into the function of emotional excitement* (2nd ed.). New York, NY: Appleton.
Carneiro, R. L. (2003). *Evolutionism in cultural anthropology: A critical history*. Boulder, CO: Westview Press.
Cheetham, T. (2012). *All the world an icon: Henry Corbin and the angelic function of beings*. Berkeley, CA: North Atlantic Books.
Chiao, J. Y. (2010). Neural basis of social status hierarchy across species. *Current Opinion in Neurobiology, 20,* 1–7.
Chiao, J. Y., & Blizinsky, K. D. (2010). Culture-gene coevolution of individualism-collectivism and the serotonin transporter gene (5-HTTLPR). *Proceeding of Biological Sciences, 277,* 529–537.

Chiao, J. Y., Mathur, V. A., Harada, T., & Lipke, T. (2009). Neural basis of preference for human social hierarchy versus egalitarianism. *Annals of the New York Academy of Science: Values, Empathy, and Fairness across Social Barriers, 1167*, 174–181.

Chodorow, J. (Ed.). (1997). *Jung: On active imagination.* Princeton, NJ: Princeton University Press.

Clinebell, H. (1984). *Pastoral care and counseling: Resources for the ministry of healing and growth.* Nashville, TN: Abingdon Press.

Coffey, K. A., Hartman, M., & Fredrickson, B. L. (2010). Deconstructing mindfulness and constructing mental health: Understanding mindfulness and its mechanisms of action. *Mindfulness, 1*(4), 235–253.

Cohn, M. A., & Fredrickson, B. L. (2010). In search of durable positive psychology interventions: Predictors and consequences of long-term positive behavior change. *Journal of Positive Psychology, 5*(5), 355–366.

Conze, E. T. (2001). *Buddhist wisdom: The diamond sutra and the heart sutra.* New York, NY: Vintage Spiritual Classics.

Corbin, H. (1969). *Alone with the alone: Creative imagination in the Sufism of Ibn 'Arabi.* Princeton, NJ: Princeton University Press.

Corbin, H. (1980). *Avicenna and the visionary recital.* Dallas, TX: Spring Publications.

Creswell, J. D., Baldwin, M. W., Eisenberger, N., & Lieberman, M. (2007). Neural correlates of dispositional mindfulness during affect labeling. *Psychosomatic Medicine, 69*(6), 560–565.

Critcher, C. R., & Zayas, V. (2014). The involuntary excluder effect: Those included by an excluder are seen as exclusive themselves. *Journal of Personality and Social Psychology, 107*(3), 454–474.

Crumbaugh, J. C. (1968). Crossvalidation of the purpose-in-life test based on Frankl's concepts. *Journal of Individual Psychology, 24,* 74–81.

Crumbaugh, J. C., & Maholick, L. T. (1964). An experimental study in existentialism: The psychometric approach to Frankl's concepts of noogenic neurosis. *Journal of Clinical Psychology, 20,* 200–207.

CSR. (1995). *Study of implementation and effectiveness of CSAP high risk youth demonstration grants: Third annual report.* Rockville, MD: Center for Substance Abuse Prevention, Substance Abuse and Mental Health Services Administration.

Damasio, A. (2010). *Self comes to mind: Constructing the conscious brain.* New York, NY: Vintage Books.

D'Aquili, E., & Newberg, A. B. (1999). *The mystical experience: Probing the biology of religious experience.* Minneapolis, MN: Fortress Press.

Davidson, R. J., Kabat-Zinn, J., Schumacher, J., Rosenkranz, M., Muller, D., Santorelli, S., et al. (2003). Alterations in brain and immune function produced by mindfulness meditation. *Psychosomatic Medicine, 65*(4), 564–570.

Day, R. D., Laland, K. N., & Odling-Smee, J. (2003). Rethinking adaptation: The niche-construction perspective. *Perspectives in Biology and Medicine, 46*(1), 80–95.

de Castro, J. M. (2017). A model of enlightened/mystical/awakened experience. *Psychology of Religion and Spirituality, 9*(1), 34–45.

Deikman, A. J. (1994). *The wrong way home: Uncovering the patterns of cult behavior in American society.* Boston, MA: Beacon Press.

Diamond, J. (1997). *Guns, germs, and steel: The fates of human societies.* New York, NY: W.W. Norton.

DiClemente, C. C. (2006). *Addiction and change: How addictions develop and addicted people recover.* New York, NY: Guilford Press.

Diener, E. (2000). Subjective well-being: The science of happiness and a proposal for a national index. *American Psychologist, 55*(1), 34–43.

Diener, E., & Seligman, M. E. P. (2004). Beyond money: Toward an economy of well-being. *Psychological Sciences in the Public Interest, 5*(1), 1–31.

Doehring, C. (1993). *Internal desecration: Traumatization and representations of God.* Lanham, MD: University Press of America.

Downey, G., & Lende, D. H. (2012). Evolution and the brain. In D. H. Lende & G. Downey (Eds.), *The encultured brain: An introduction to neuroanthropology.* Cambridge, MA: MIT Press.

Easwaran, E. (1987). *The Upanishads.* Tomales, CA: Nilgiri Press.

Easwaran, E. (Ed.). (2007). *The Dhammapada.* Tomales, CA: Nilgiri Press.

Ehrenkranz, J. H., & Coppola, D. L. (Eds.). (2000). *Religion and violence, religion and peace.* Fairfield, CT: Sacred Heart University Press.

Ellis, A. (1986). *The case against religion: A psychotherapist's view and the case against religiosity.* Austin, TX: American Atheist Press.

Emerson, R. W. (1992). *Selected writings of Ralph Waldo Emerson.* New York, NY: Modern Library.

Erikson, E. (1963). *Childhood and society* (2nd ed.). New York, NY: W.W. Norton.

Felitti, V. J., Anda, R. F., Nordenberg, D., Williamson, D. F., Spitz, A. M., Edwards, V., et al. (1998). Relationship of childhood abuse and household dysfunction to many of the leading causes of death in adults. *American Journal of Preventive Medicine, 14*(4), 245–258.

Fisher, H. E. (1982). *The sex contract: The evolution of human behavior.* New York, NY: William Morrow and Company.

Fisher, R. J., Kelman, H. C., & Nan, S. A. (2013). Conflict analysis and resolution. In L. Huddy, D. O. Sears, & J. S. Levy (Eds.), *Oxford handbook of political psychology* (2nd ed.). New York, NY: Oxford University Press.

Fosha, D., Siegel, D. J., & Solomon, M. (Eds.). (2009). *The healing power of emotion: Affective neuroscience, development, and clinical practice.* New York, NY: W.W. Norton.

Fowler, J. (1996). *Faithful change: The personal and public challenges of postmodern life.* Nashville, TN: Abingdon Press.
Fox, D., & Prilleltensky, I. (Eds.). (1997). *Critical psychology.* Thousand Oaks, CA: Sage.
Frankl, V. (1959). *Man's search for meaning.* New York, NY: Simon and Schuster.
Frankl, V. (1965). *The doctor and the soul: From psychotherapy to logotherapy.* New York, NY: Alfred A. Knopf.
Fredrickson, B. L. (1998). What good are positive emotions? *Review of General Psychology, 2*(3), 300–319.
Fredrickson, B. L. (2001). The role of positive emotions in positive psychology: The broaden-and-build theory of positive emotions. *American Psychologist, 56*(3), 218–226.
Fredrickson, B. L., & Cohn, M. A. (2008). Positive emotions. In M. Lewis, J. M. Haviland-Jones, & L. F. Barrett (Eds.), *Handbook of emotions* (3rd ed., pp. 777–796). New York, NY: Guilford Press.
Fredrickson, B. L., & Joiner, T. (2002). Positive emotions trigger upward spirals toward emotional well-being. *Psychological Science, 13*(2), 172–175.
Fredrickson, B. L., & Levenson, R. W. (1998). Positive emotions speed recovery from the cardiovascular sequelae of negative emotions. *Cognition and Emotion, 12*(2), 191–220.
Fricchione, G. L. (2011). *Compassion and healing in medicine and society: On the nature and use of attachment solutions to separation challenges.* Baltimore, MD: Johns Hopkins University Press.
Friedli, L. (2009). *Mental health, resilience, and inequalities.* Copenhagen, Denmark: World Health Organization.
Fuentes, A., Wyczalkowski, M. A., & MacKinnon, K. C. (2010). Niche construction through cooperation: A nonlinear dynamics contribution to modeling facets of evolutionary history in the genus Homo. *Current Anthropology, 51*(3), 435–444.
Gable, P. A., & Poole, B. D. (2015). Anger perceptually and conceptually narrows cognitive scope. *Journal of Personality and Social Psychology, 109*(1), 163–174.
Galinsky, A. D., Magee, J. C., Inesi, M. E., & Gruenewald, T. L. (2006). Power and perspectives not taken. *Psychological Science, 17,* 1068–1074.
Gallardo, M. E. (Ed.). (2014). *Developing cultural humility: Embracing race, privilege, and power.* Los Angeles, CA: Sage.
Germer, C. K. (2009). *The mindful path to self-compassion: Freeing yourself from destructive thoughts and emotions.* New York, NY: Guilford Press.
Germer, C. K., & Siegel, R. D. (Eds.). (2012). *Wisdom and compassion in psychotherapy: Deepening mindfulness in clinical practice.* New York, NY: Guilford.
Germer, C. K., Siegel, R. D., & Fulton, P. R. (2005). *Mindfulness and psychotherapy.* New York, NY: Guilford.

Gevirtz, R. (2011). Autonomic nervous system markers for psychophyiological, anxiety, and physical disorders. In E. Gordon & S. H. Koslow (Eds.), *Integrative neuroscience and personalized medicine*. New York, NY: Oxford University Press.
Goleman, D. (1988). *The meditative mind: The varieties of meditative experience*. Los Angeles, CA: Jeremy P. Tarcher Inc.
Goodman, L. E. (1999). *Jewish and Islamic philosophy: Crosspollinations in the classic age*. New Brunswick, NJ: Rutgers University Press.
Granqvist, P., & Kirkpatrick, L. A. (2008). Attachment and religious representations and behavior. In J. Cassidy & P. R. Shaver (Eds.), *Handbook of attachment: Theory, research, and clinical applications*. New York, NY: Guilford Press.
Green, A. (2003). *Seek my face: A Jewish mystical theology*. Woodstock, VT: Jewish Lights Publishing.
Green, A. M. (1984a). Psychophysiology and health: Personal and transpersonal. In S. Grof (Ed.), *Ancient wisdom and modern science*. Albany, NY: SUNY Press.
Green, E. E. (1984b). Science and psychophysiology: Psychophysics and mythology. In S. Grof (Ed.), *Ancient wisdom and modern science*. Albany, NY: SUNY Press.
Green, A. M., & Green, E. E. (1977). *Beyond biofeedback*. New York, NY: Delacorte Press.
Green, E. E., Green, A. M., & Walters, D. (1971). *Bio-feedback for mind-body self regulation: Healing and creativity*. Topeka, KS: Menninger Foundation.
Gruenfeld, D. H., Inesi, M. E., Magee, J. C., & Galinsky, A. D. (2008). Power and the objectification of social targets. *Journal of Personality and Social Psychology, 95*, 1450–1466.
Gyatso, T., & Chodron, T. (2014). *Buddhism: One teacher, many traditions*. Somerville, MA: Wisdom Publications.
Hanh, T. N. (1991). *Old path white clouds: Walking in the footsteps of the Buddha*. Berkeley, CA: Parallax Books.
Hannah, B. (1981). *Encounters with the soul: Active imagination as developed by C.G. Jung*. Boston, MA: Sigo Press.
Hartman, D. (1976). *Maimonides: Torah and philosophic quest*. Philadelphia, PA: Jewish Publication Society of America.
Hegy, P. (Ed.). (2007). *What do we imagine God to be? The function of "God images" in our lives*. Lewiston, NY: The Edwin Mellen Press Ltd.
Henry, J. P., & Wang, S. (1998). Effects of early stress on adult affiliative behavior. *Psychoneuroendocrinology, 23*(8), 863–875.
Hesse, E. (2008). The adult attachment interview: Protocol, methods of analysis, and empirical studies. In J. Cassidy & P. R. Shaver (Eds.), *Handbook*

of attachment: Theory, research, and clinical applications. New York, NY: Guilford Press.

Holzel, B. K., Carmody, J., Evans, K. C., Hoge, E. A., Dusek, J. A., Morgan, L., . . . Lazar, S. W. (2010). Stress reduction correlates with structural changes in the amygdala. *Social Cognitive and Affective Neuroscience, 5*(1), 11–17. doi:10.1093/scan/nsp034.

Holzel, B. K., Lazar, S. W., Gard, T., Schuman-Olivier, Z., Vago, D. R., & Ott, U. (2011). How does mindfulness meditation work? Proposing mechanisms of action from a conceptual and neural perspective. *Perspectives on Psychological Science, 6*(6), 537–559.

Hood, R. (Ed.). (1995). *Handbook of religious experience.* Birmingham, AL: Religious Education Press.

Hood, R., Hall, J., Watson, P. J., & Biderman, M. (1979). Personality correlates of the report of mystical experiences. *Psychological Reports, 43*(3), 804–806.

Horovitz, S. G., Braun, A. R., Carr, W. S., Picchioni, D., Balkin, T. J., Fukunaga, M., et al. (2009). Decoupling of the brain's default mode network during deep sleep. *Proceedings of the National Academy of Science, 106*(27), 11376–11381.

Huxley, A. (1945). *The perennial philosophy.* New York, NY: Harper Brothers.

James, W. (1902/1986). *Varieties of religious experience.* New York, NY: Penguin.

Johnson, K. J., & Fredrickson, B. L. (2005). We all look the same to me: Positive emotions eliminate own-race bias in face recognition. *Psychological Science, 16*(11), 875–881.

Jordan, M. (1986). *Taking on the gods.* Nashville, TN: Abingdon Press.

Jung, C. G. (1931). Commentary. In R. Wilhelm (Ed.), *The secret of the golden flower: A Chinese book of life.* New York, NY: Harcourt Brace.

Jung, C. G. (1933). *Modern man in search of a soul.* New York, NY: Harcourt Brace.

Jung, C. G. (1957). *The undiscovered self.* New York, NY: Mentor Books.

Jung, C. G. (1959). *The archetypes and the collective unconscious.* Princeton, NJ: Princeton University Press.

Jung, C. G. (1964). Approaching the unconscious. In C. G. Jung (Ed.), *Man and his symbols.* New York, NY: Doubleday and Co.

Jung, C. G. (1996). In S. Shamdasani (Ed.), *The psychology of kundalini yoga.* Princeton, NJ: Princeton University Press.

Jung-Beeman, M., Bowden, E. M., Haberman, J., Frymiare, J. L., Arambel-Liu, S., Greenblatt, R., et al. (2004). Neural activity when people solve verbal problems with insight. *PLoS Biology, 2*(4), 0500–0510.

Kabat-Zinn, J. (1990). *Full catastrophe living.* New York, NY: Dell Publishing.

Kabat-Zinn, J., Lipworth, L., & Burney, R. (1985). The clinical use of mindfulness meditation for the self-regulation of chronic pain. *Journal of Behavioral Medicine, 8*(2), 163–190.

Kass, J. D. (1991a). Contributions of religious experience to psychological and physical well-being: Research evidence and an explanatory model. *The Caregiver (College of Chaplains), 8*(4), 4–11.

Kass, J. D. (1991b). Integrating spirituality into personality theory and counseling practice. *American Counseling Association, 1991 Annual Meetings.* Reno, Nevada.

Kass, J. D. (1995). Contributions of religious experience to psychological and physical well-being: Research evidencde and an explanatory model. In L. Vandecreek (Ed.), *Spiritual needs and pastoral services: Readings in research* (pp. 189–213). Decatur, GA: Journal of Pastoral Care Publications.

Kass, J. D. (1996a). Coping with life-threatening illnesses using a logotherapeutic approach, 1: Health care team interventions. *International Forum for Logotherapy, 19*(Spring), 15–19.

Kass, J. D. (1996b). Coping with life-threatening illnesses using a logotherapeutic approach, 2: Clinical mental health counseling. *International Forum for Logotherapy, 20*(Spring), 10–14.

Kass, J. D. (1998). The inventory of positive psychological attitudes: Measuring attitudes which buffer stress and facilitate primary prevention. In C. Zalaquett & R. Wood (Eds.), *Evaluating stress: A book of resources* (Vol. 2, pp. 153–184). Lanham, MD: University Press of America.

Kass, J. D. (2005). Know your self: A curriculum for mentoring students in the development of health promoting behaviors. Effective Interventions for Student Mental Health on Campus, Collaboration and Community, Annual Meeting of the National Association of Student Personnel Administrators (NASPA). Newport, RI.

Kass, J. D. (2007a). God images as indwelling spirit and core foundation of self. In P. Hegy (Ed.), *What do we imagine God to be? The function of "God images" in our lives.* Lewiston, NY: The Edwin Mellen Press Ltd.

Kass, J. D. (2007b). Spiritual maturation: A developmental resource for resilience, well-being, and peace. *Journal of Pedagogy, Pluralism, and Practice, 12*(Summer), 56–64.

Kass, J. D. (2013). Revisiting Maimonide's Guide of the Perplexed: How yoga psychology can clarify our understanding of Jewish practice. 15th International Conference for Jewish Renewal (ALEPH). Rindge, NH.

Kass, J. D. (2015). Person-centered spiritual maturation: A multidimensional model. *Journal of Humanistic Psychology, 55*(1), 53–76. doi:10.1177/0022167814525261.

Kass, J. D., & Lennox, S. (2005). Emerging models of spiritual development: A foundation for mature, moral, and health-promoting behavior. In W. R. Miller & H. Delaney (Eds.), *Judeo-Christian perspectives on psychology: Human nature, motivation, and change.* Washington, DC: American Psychological Association.

Kass, J. D., & Trantham, S. M. (2014). Perspectives from clinical neuroscience: Mindfulness and therapeutic use of the arts. In L. Rappaport (Ed.), *Mindfulness and the arts therapies: Theory and practice*. London, UK: Jessica Kingsley.
Kass, J. D., Friedman, R., Leserman, J., Caudill, M., Zuttermeister, P., & Benson, H. (1991a). An inventory of positive psychological attitudes with potential relevance to health outcomes. *Behavioral Medicine, 17*(3), 121–129.
Kass, J. D., Friedman, R., Leserman, J., Zuttermeister, P., & Benson, H. (1991b). Health outcomes and a new measure of spiritual experience. *Journal for the Scientific Study of Religion, 30*(2), 203–211.
Katz, S. T. (1978). Language, epistemology, and mysticism. In S. Katz (Ed.), *Mysticism and philosophical analysis*. New York, NY: Oxford University Press.
Kavanaugh, K. (Ed.). (1987). *John of the cross: Selected writings*. New York, NY: Paulist Press.
Kelman, H. C. (1997). Social-psychological dimensions of international conflict. In I. W. Zartman & J. L. Rasmussen (Eds.), *Peacemaking in international conflict: Methods and techniques*. Washington, DC: United States Institute of Peace Press.
Kinder, D. R. (2013). Prejudice and politics. In L. Huddy, D. O. Sears, & J. S. Levy (Eds.), *Oxford handbook of political psychology*. New York, NY: Oxford University Press.
Kirkpatrick, L. A. (2005). *Attachment, evolution, and the psychology of religion*. New York, NY: Guilford Press.
Kobasa, S., Maddi, S., & Kahn, S. (1982). Hardiness and health: A prospective study. *Journal of Personality and Social Psychology, 42*(1), 168–177.
Koenig, A. M., & Eagly, A. H. (2014). Evidence for the social role theory of stereotype content: Observations of groups' roles shape stereotypes. *Journal of Personality and Social Psychology, 107*(3), 371–392.
Koenig, H. G., & Pritchett, J. (1998). Religion and psychotherapy. In H. G. Koenig (Ed.), *Handbook of religion and mental health*. San Diego, CA: Academic Press.
Koenig, H. G., McCullough, M. E., & Larson, D. L. (2001). *Handbook of religion and health*. New York, NY: Oxford University Press.
Kornfield, J. (1979). Intensive insight meditation: A phenomenological study. *Journal of Transpersonal Psychology, 2*(1), 41–58.
Kutz, I., Borysenko, J., & Benson, H. (1985). Meditation and psychotherapy: A rationale for the integration of dynamic psychotherapy, the relaxation response, and mindfulness meditation. *American Journal of Psychiatry, 142*(1), 1–8.
Lambert, K., & Kinsley, C. H. (2005). *Clinical neuroscience: The neurobiological foundations of mental health*. New York, NY: Worth Publishers.

Lehmann, D., Faber, P. L., Tei, S., Pascual-Marqui, R. D., Milz, P., & Kochi, K. (2012). Reduced functional connectivity between cortical sources in five meditation traditions detected with lagged coherence using EEG tomography. *NeuroImage, 60*(2), 1574–1586.

Lende, D. H., & Downey, G. (2012). The encultured brain: Development, case studies, and methods. In D. H. Lende & G. Downey (Eds.), *The encultured brain: An introduction to neuroanthropology*. Cambridge, MA: MIT Press.

Leshner, A. (1995). *Director's report #1 to the National Advisory Council on drug abuse*. Rockville, MD: National Institute of Drug Abuse.

Li, S. C. (2003). Biocultural orchestration of developmental plasticity across levels: The interplay of biology and culture in shaping the mind and behavior across the life span. *Psychological Bulletin, 129*(2), 171–194.

Linehan, M. M. (1993). *Cognitive-behavioral treatment of borderline personality disorder*. New York, NY: Guilford Press.

Lutz, A., Greischar, L. L., Rawlings, N. B., Ricard, M., & Davidson, R. J. (2004). Long-term meditators self-induce high amplitude gamma synchrony during mental practice. *Neuroscience, 101*(46), 16369–16373.

Lyons-Ruth, K., & Jacobvitz, D. (2008). Attachment disorganization: Genetic factors, parenting contexts, and developmental transformation from infancy to adulthood. In J. Cassidy & P. R. Shaver (Eds.), *Handbook of attachment: Theory, research, and clinical appplications*. New York, NY: Guilford Press.

MacKinnon, K. C., & Fuentes, A. (2012). Primate social cognition, human evolution, and niche construction: A core context for neuroanthropology. In D. H. Lende & G. Downey (Eds.), *The encultured brain: An introduction to neuroanthropology*. Cambridge, MA: MIT Press.

MacLean, P. D. (1990). *The triune brain in evolution*. New York, NY: Plenum Press.

Mahler, M., Pine, E., & Bergman, A. (1975). *The psychological birth of the human infant*. New York, NY: Basic Books.

Maimonides, M. (1963). *Guide of the perplexed* (S. Pines, Trans.). Chicago, IL: University of Chicago Press.

Main, M. M. (1995). Attachment: Overview, with implications for clinical work. In S. Goldberg, R. Muir, & J. Kerr (Eds.), *Attachment theory: Social, developmental, and clinical perspectives* (pp. 407–474). Hillsdale, NJ: Analytic Press.

Marlatt, G. A., & Marques, J. K. (1977). Meditation, self control, and alcohol use. In R. B. Stuart (Ed.), *Behavioral self-management: Strategies, techniques, and outcomes*. New York, NY: Brunner/Mazel.

Marsella, A. J. (2009). Diversity in a global era: The context and consequences of differences. *Counseling Psychology Quarterly, 22*(1), 119–135.

May, R., & Yalom, I. (1989). Existential psychotherapy. In R. J. Corsini & D. Wedding (Eds.), *Current psychotherapies* (4th ed.). Itasca, IL: F. E. Peacock.

McDonald, A., Beck, R., Allison, S., & Norsworthy, L. (2005). Attachment to God and parents: Testing correspondence vs. compensation hypotheses. *Journal of Psychology and Christianity, 24*(1), 21–28.

Merton, T. (1996). *Contemplative prayer.* New York, NY: Image/Doubleday.

Merton, T. (1998). *Contemplation in a world of action.* Notre Dame, IN: University of Notre Dame Press.

Mikulincer, M. (1998). Adult attachment style and individual differences in functional versus dysfunctional experiences of anger. *Journal of Personality and Social Psychology, 75,* 420–435.

Mikulincer, M., & Florian, V. (1998). The relationship beween adult attachment styles and emotional and cognitive reactions to stressful events. In J. A. Simpson & W. S. Rhodes (Eds.), *Attachment theory and close relationships.* New York, NY: Guilford Press.

Mikulincer, M., & Shaver, P. R. (2001). Attachment theory and intergroup bias: Evidence that priming the secure base schema attenuates negative reactions to outgroups. *Journal of Personality and Social Psychology, 81*(1), 97–115.

Mikulincer, M., & Shaver, P. R. (2008). Adult attachment and affect regulation. In J. Cassidy & P. R. Shaver (Eds.), *Handbook of attachment: Theory, research, and clinical applications* (2nd ed.). New York, NY: Guilford Press.

Mikulincer, M., & Shaver, P. R. (2011). Attachment, anger, and aggression. In P. R. Shaver & M. Mikulincer (Eds.), *Human aggression and violence: Causes, manifestations, and consequences.* Washington, DC: American Psychological Association.

Miller, J. B. (1976). *Toward a new psychology of women.* New York, NY: Penguin.

Miller, W. R. (Ed.). (1999). *Integrating spirituality into treatment.* Washington, DC: American Psychological Association.

Mooijman, M., van Dijk, W. W., Ellemers, N., & van Dijk, E. (2015). Why leaders punish: A power perspective. *Journal of Personality and Social Psychology, 109*(1), 75–89.

Moore, D. L. (2007). *Overcoming religious illiteracy: A cultural studies approach to the study of religion in secondary education.* New York, NY: Palgrave Macmillan.

Motulsky, S. L., Gere, S. H., Saleem, R., & Trantham, S. M. (2014). Teaching social justice in counseling psychology. *The Counseling Psychologist, 42*(8), 1058–1083.

Nasr, S. H. (2002). *The heart of Islam: Enduring values for humanity.* San Francisco, CA: Harper San Francisco.

Nasr, S. H. (2007). *The garden of truth: The vision and promise of Sufism, Islam's mystical tradition.* New York, NY: HarperCollins.

Newberg, A. B., & D'Aquili, E. G. (1998). The neuropsychology of spiritual experience. In H. G. Koenig (Ed.), *Handbook of religion and mental health.* San Diego, CA: Academic Press.

Ogden, P., Minton, K., & Pain, C. (2006). *Trauma and the body: A sensorimotor approach to psychotherapy.* New York, NY: W.W. Norton.
Opthof, T. (2000). The normal range and determinants of the intrinsic heart rate in man. *Cardiovascular Research, 45*(1), 177–184.
Pagnoni, G., Cekic, M., & Guo, Y. (2008). Thinking about not-thinking: Neural correlates of conceptual processing during Zen meditation. *PLOS ONE, 3*(9), e3083. doi:3010.1371/journal.pone.0003083.
Paloutzian, R. F., & Park, C. L. (Eds.). (2013). *Handbook of the psychology of religion and spirituality* (2nd ed.). New York, NY: Guilford.
Pargament, K. I. (1997). *The psychology of religion and coping: Theory, research, practice.* New York, NY: Guilford.
Pargament, K. I. (2007). *Spiritually integrated psychotherapy: Understanding and addressing the sacred.* New York, NY: Guilford.
Pennington, M. B. (1980). *Centering prayer: Renewing an ancient Christian prayer form.* New York, NY: Image Books.
Perls, F. (1973). *The gestalt approach and eye witness to therapy.* New York, NY: Science and Behavior Books.
Persinger, M. A. (1987). *Neuropsychological bases of God beliefs.* New York, NY: Praeger.
Pettigrew, T. F., & Tropp, L. R. (1998). A meta-analytic test of intergroup contact theory. *Journal of Personality and Social Psychology, 90*(5), 751–783.
Pettigrew, T. F., Tropp, L. R., Wagner, U., & Christ, O. (2011). Recent advances in intergoup contact theory. *International Journal of Intercultural Relations, 35,* 271–280.
Pinderhughes, E. (1989). *Understanding race, ethnicity, and power: The key to efficacy in clinical practice.* New York, NY: Free Press.
Porges, S. W. (1995). Orienting in a defensive world: Mammalian modifications of our evolutionary heritage. *Psychophysiology, 32*(4), 301–318.
Porges, S. W. (1998). Love: An emergent property of the mammalian autonomic nervous system. *Psychoneuroendocrinology, 7*(8), 837–861.
Porges, S. W. (2001). The polyvagal theory: Phylogenetic substrates of a social nervous system. *International Journal of Psychophysiology, 42*(2), 123–146.
Porges, S. W. (2007). The polyvagal perspective. *Biological Psychology, 74*(2), 116–143.
Porges, S. W. (2011). *The polyvagal theory: Neurophysiological foundations of emotions, attachment, communication, self-regulation.* New York, NY: W.W. Norton.
Porges, S. W., Doussard-Roosevelt, J. A., Portales, A. L., & Greenspan, S. I. (1996). Infant regulation of the vagal "brake" predicts child behavior problems: A psychobiological model of social behavior. *Developmental Psychobiology, 29*(8), 697–712.

Prabhavananda, S. (1947). Mandukya Upanishad. In S. Prabhavananda & F. Manchester (Eds.), *The Upanishads: Breath of the immortal.* Hollywood, CA: Vedanta Press.
Pratto, F., Sidanius, J., Stallworth, L. M., & Malle, B. F. (1994). Social dominance orientation: A personality variable predicting social and political attitudes. *Journal of Personality and Social Psychology, 67*(4), 741–763.
Pratto, F., Jim, S., & Levin, S. (2006). Social dominance theory and the dynamics of intergroup relations: Taking stock and looking forward. *European Review of Social Psychology, 17*(8), 271–320.
Prochaska, J. O., DiClemente, C. C., & Norcross, J. C. (1992). In search of how people change: Applications to addictive behaviors. *American Psychologist, 47*(9), 1102–1114.
Proudfoot, W. (1985). *Religious experience.* Berkeley, CA: University of California Press.
Ram Dass. (1979). *Miracle of love: Stories about Neem Karoli Baba.* New York, NY: Dutton.
Rama, S., Ballantine, R., & Ajaya, S. (1976). *Yoga and psychotherapy: The evolution of consciousness.* Honesdale, PA: Himalayan International Institute.
Reker, G. T., & Peacock, E. J. (1981). The life attitude profile (LAP): A multidimensional instrument for assessing attitudes toward life. *Canadian Journal of Behavioural Science, 13*, 264–273.
Reker, G. T., Peacock, E. J., & Wong, P. T. (1987). Meaning and purpose in life and well-being: A life-span perspective. *Journal of Gerontology, 42*(1), 44–49.
Richards, P. S., & Bergin, A. E. (1997). *A spiritual strategy for counseling and psychotherapy.* Washington, DC: American Psychological Association.
Rizzuto, A. M. (1979). *The birth of the living God: A psychoanalytic study.* Chicago, IL: University of Chicago Press.
Rogers, C. R. (1959). A theory of therapy, personality, and interpersonal relationships, as developed in the client-centered framework. In S. Koch (Ed.), *Psychology: A study of a science (Vol. III. Formulations of the person and the social context).* New York, NY: McGraw-Hill.
Rogers, C. R. (1961). *On becoming a person: A therapist's view of psychotherapy.* Boston, MA: Houghton-Mifflin.
Rogers, C. R. (1980). *A way of being* (3rd ed.). Boston, MA: Houghton-Mifflin.
Rothschild, B. (2000). *The body remembers: The psychophysiology of trauma and trauma treatment.* New York, NY: W.W. Norton.
Saguy, T., Tausch, N., Dovidio, J. F., Pratto, F., & Singh, P. (2011). Tension and harmony in intergroup relations. In P. R. Shaver & M. Mikulincer (Eds.), *Human aggression and violence: Causes, manifestations, and consequences.* Washington, D.C.: American Psychological Association.
Salvi, C., Bricolo, E., Kounios, J., Bowden, E. M., & Jung-Beeman, M. (2016). Insight solutions are correct more often than analytic solutions. *Thinking & Reasoning, 22*(4), 443–460.

Sapolsky, R. M. (2004). Social status and health in humans and other animals. *Annual Review of Anthropology, 33,* 393–418.
Sapolsky, R. M. (2005a). The influence of social hierarchy on primate health. *Science, 308,* 648–652.
Sapolsky, R. M. (2005b). Sick of poverty. *Scientific American, 293*(6), 92–99.
Sapolsky, R. M., Romero, L. M., & Munck, A. M. (2000). How do glucocorticoids influence stress responses? Integrating permissive, suppressive, stimulatory, and preparative actions. *Endocrine Review, 21*(1), 55–89.
Sarafino, E. P. (2008). *Health psychology* (6th ed.). New York, NY: John Wiley.
Schore, A. (2001). Effects of secure attachment relationship on right brain development, affect regulation, and infant mental health. *Infant Mental Health Journal, 22*(1–2), 7–66.
Schore, A. (2002). Dysregulation of the right brain: A fundamental mechanism of traumatic attachment and the psychopathogenesis of posttraumatic stress disorder. *Australian and New Zealand Journal of Psychiatry, 36*(1), 9–30.
Schore, A. (2003). Early relational trauma, disorganized attachment, and the development of a predisposition to violence. In M. F. Solomon & D. J. Siegel (Eds.), *Healing trauma: Attachment, mind, body, and brain.* New York, NY: W.W. Norton.
Schore, A. (2009). Right-brain affect regulation: An essential mechanism of development, trauma, dissociation, and psychotherapy. In D. Fosha, D. J. Siegel, & M. F. Solomon (Eds.), *The healing power of emotion: Affective neuroscience, development, and clinical practice.* New York, NY: W.W. Norton.
Schore, A. (2012). *The science of the art of psychotherapy.* New York, NY: W.W. Norton.
Schuon, F. (1984). *The transcendent unity of religions.* Wheaton, IL: Theosophical Publishing.
Schwartz, R. C. (1995). *Internal family systems.* New York, NY: Guilford.
Shaku, S. (1906). *Zen for Americans: The sutra of forty-two chapters.* New York, NY: Barnes & Noble Books.
Shamdasani, S. (Ed.). (1996). *C.G. Jung: The psychology of kundalini yoga.* Princeton, NJ: Princeton University Press.
Shamdasani, S. (Ed.). (2009). *The red book by C.G. Jung.* New York, NY: W.W. Norton.
Shapiro, D. H. (1980). *Meditation: Self-regulation strategy and altered state of consciousness.* New York, NY: Aldine.
Shapiro, D. L. (2010). Relational identity theory: A systematic approach for transforming the emotional dimension of conflict. *American Psychologist, 65*(7), 634–645.
Shapiro, D. L. (2016). *Negotiating the non-negotiable.* New York, NY: Viking Press.

Shaver, P. R., & Mikulincer, M. (2002). Attachment-related psychodynamics. *Attachment and Human Development,* 4(2), 133–161.
Sidanius, J., & Kurzban, R. (2013). Toward an evolutionarily informed political psychology. In L. Huddy, D. O. Sears, & J. S. Levy (Eds.), *Oxford handbook of political psychology* (2nd ed.). New York, NY: Oxford University Press.
Sidanius, J., & Pratto, F. (1999). *Social dominance: An intergroup theory of social hierarchy and oppression.* Cambridge, UK: Cambridge University Press.
Sidanius, J., Pratto, F., van Laar, C., & Levin, S. (2004). Social dominance theory: Its agenda and method. *Political Psychology,* 25(6), 845–880.
Sidanius, J., Levin, S., van Laar, C., & Sears, D. O. (2008). *The diversity challenge: Social identity and intergroup relations on the college campus.* New York, NY: Russell Sage Foundation.
Siegel, D. J. (2007). *The mindful brain: Reflection and attunement in the cultivation of well-being.* New York, NY: W.W. Norton.
Siegel, D. J. (2012). *The developing mind: How relationships and the brain interact to shape who we are* (2nd ed.). New York, NY: Guilford.
Singer, J. (1990). *Seeing through the visible world: Jung, gnosis, and chaos.* New York, NY: Harper Collins.
Smedley, A., & Smedley, B. D. (2005). Race as biology is fiction, racism as a social problem is real: Anthropological and historical perspectives on the social construction of race. *American Psychologist,* 60(1), 16–26.
Smith, P. K., & Trope, Y. (2006). You focus on the forest when you're in charge of the trees: Power priming and abstract information processing. *Journal of Personality and Social Psychology,* 90, 578–596.
Solomon, M., & Siegel, D. J. (Eds.). (2003). *Healing trauma: Attachment, mind, body, and brain.* New York, NY: W.W. Norton.
Southwick, S. M., Vythilingam, M., & Charney, D. S. (2005). The psychobiology of depression and resilience to stress: Implications for prevention and treatment. *Annual Review of Clinical Psychology,* 1(1), 255–291.
Spretnak, C. (Ed.). (1982). *The politics of women's spirituality.* New York, NY: Anchor Books.
Spretnak, C. (1991). *States of grace: The recovery of meaning in the postmodern age.* San Francisco, CA: HarperSanFrancisco.
Stace, W. T. (1960a). *Mysticism and philosophy.* New York, NY: J.B. Lippincott.
Stace, W. T. (1960b). *The teachings of the mystics.* New York, NY: New American Library.
Staw, B. M., Sandelands, L. E., & Dutton, J. E. (1981). Threat rigidity effects in organizational behavior: A multilevel analysis. *Administrative Science Quarterly,* 26(4), 501–524.
Sterling, P. (2004). Principles of allostasis: Optimal design, predictive regulation, pathophysiology, and rational therapeutics. In J. Schulkin (Ed.), *Allostasis,*

homeostasis, and the costs of adaptation. New York, NY: Cambridge University Press.
Suomi, S. J. (2003). Gene-environment interactions and the neurobiology of social conflict. *Annals of the New York Academy of Science, 1008*, 132–139.
Taylor, J. B. (2009). *My stroke of insight: A brain scientist's personal journey.* New York, NY: Plume/Penguin Group.
Teasdale, W. (1999). *The mystic heart: Discovering a universal spirituality in the world's religions.* Novato, CA: New World Library.
Tegmark, M. (2015). Consciousness as a state of matter. *Chaos, Solitons & Fractals 76*, 238–270.
Teresa-of-Avila, (1964). *The way of perfection.* Garden City, NY: Image Books.
Teresa-of-Avila., (1979). *The interior castle.* New York, NY: Paulist Press.
Tillich, P. (1952). *The courage to be.* New Haven, CT: Yale University Press.
Tillich, P. (1984). *The meaning of health: Essays in existentialism, psychoanalysis, and religion.* Chicago, IL: Exploration Press.
Tobler, N. S., & Stratton, H. (1995). Effectiveness of school-based prevention programs: A meta-analysis of the research. Society for Prevention Research, Annual Meeting. Rochester, NY.
Tugade, M. M., & Fredrickson, B. L. (2004). Resilient individuals use positive emotions to bounce back from negative emotional experiences. *Journal of Personality and Social Psychology, 86*(2), 320–333.
van der Kolk, B. A. (2014). *The body keeps the score: Brain, mind, and body in the healing of trauma.* New York, NY: Viking.
van Ijzendoorn, M. H., & Sagi-Schwartz, A. (2008). Cross-cultural patterns of attachment: Universal and contextual dimensions. In J. Cassidy & P. R. Shaver (Eds.), *Handbook of attachment: Theory, research, and clinical applications.* New York, NY: Guilford Press.
Varela, F., & Shear, J. (Eds.). (1999). *The view from within: First-person approaches to the study of consciousness.* New York, NY: Imprint Academic.
Verona, E., & Sachs-Ericsson, (2005). The intergenerational transmission of externalizing behaviors in adult participants: The mediating role of childhood abuse. *Journal of Consulting and Clinical Psychology, 73*(6), 1135–1145.
von Franz, M. L. (1964). The process of individuation. In C. G. Jung (Ed.), *Man and his symbols.* New York, NY: Doubleday & Company.
Waters, H. S., Rodrigues, L. M., & Ridgeway, D. (1998). Cognitive underpinnings of narrative attachment assessment. *Journal of Experimental Child Psychology, 71*, 211–234.
Watkins, M. (1984). *Waking dreams.* Dallas, TX: Spring Publications.
Watkins, M. (1986). *Invisible guests: The development of imaginal dialogues.* Boston, MA: Sigo Press.

Waugh, C. E., & Fredrickson, B. L. (2006). Nice to know you: Positive emotions, self-other overlap, and complex understanding in the formation of a new relationship. *Journal of Positive Psychology, 1*(2), 93–106.

Waugh, C. E., Wager, T. D., Fredrickson, B. L., Noll, D. C., & Taylor, S. F. (2008). The neural correlates of trait resilience when anticipating and recovering from threat. *Social Cognitive and Affective Neuroscience, 3*(4), 322–332.

Whitmont, E. C. (1969). *The symbolic quest: Basic concepts of analytical psychology.* New York, NY: Harper Colophon.

Wilhelm, R. (1962). *The secret of the golden flower: A Chinese book of life.* New York, NY: Harcourt, Brace & World.

Wulff, D. M. (1997). *Psychology of religion.* New York, NY: John Wiley.

Zink, C. F., Tong, J., Chen, Q., Bassett, D. S., & Stein, J. L. (2008). Know your place: Neural processing of social hierarchy in humans. *Neuron, 58,* 273–283.

PART II

—Research Project—
Mentoring Psychological Resilience and Inclusive Community Through Person-Centered Psychospiritual Maturation

CHAPTER 6

The *Know Your Self* Curriculum: Overview and Research Results

Part II of this book examines the *Know Your Self* curriculum as a process of engaged learning that mentors person-centered psychospiritual maturation and inclusive community-building. This chapter will summarize results from an effectiveness study of the curriculum. The study employed a quasi-experimental, mixed methods design. This approach produced a highly granular qualitative analysis of individual and group psychospiritual development among participants in the *Know Your Self* curriculum (experimental group), with triangulated statistical comparisons of learning outcomes between experimental and control groups. This chapter will report statistical results from the quantitative component of the study and numerical summaries of results from the qualitative component. These data provide an evidence-based introduction to the case studies that will be presented in subsequent chapters. This chapter will conclude with an introduction to these individual and group case studies.

Overview

Know Your Self has been taught since 1987 as the experiential learning component of a graduate-level counseling course examining spirituality as a resource for psychological and social well-being. It is also attended electively by adult undergraduates and graduate students in education. It was developed to address student needs for person-centered psychospiritual growth in the service of their personal, professional, and civic development (Kass 1998a, 2001, 2012). The class met weekly (seminar-format, 45 contact hours). The curriculum presents personally-meaningful spirituality and participation in organized religion as independent constructs with potential overlap (Batson and Schoenrade 1991; Pargament et al. 1995). Students with diverse belief systems, including secular humanism, examine psychospiritual development as a resource for psychological and social well-being in a multicultural society. *Know Your Self* introduces them experientially to person-centered psychospiritual growth, illustrating its role building inclusive communities.

Learning Agreement for Course Participation

The person-centered nature of this learning is discussed in the syllabus and first class. We review experiential methods, content areas for psychospiritual self-inquiry, the potential to experience emotional turmoil, and necessary commitment of energy and time. Differences between a mentored introduction to this learning process and psychotherapy are explained: the class is educational, teaching students *how* to engage in person-centered psychospiritual maturation. They will choose areas in which they are comfortable exploring, retaining control over the depth of these explorations. If students want individual consultation about current readiness to participate in this curriculum, they can schedule a meeting with the instructor prior to the second class.

Students appreciate the clarity of this informed consent. Periodically, a student has decided not to take the class. During the class, some have required referral to the university counseling center. In these instances, the curriculum played a preventive role by identifying psychological issues that require professional attention. No students have experienced a serious crisis as a result of class participation. They consistently express appreciation for the personal and experiential nature of the self-inquiry process, emphasizing their self-perceived needs for maturational development as part of their higher education experience.

Research Design

The study employed a quasi-experimental design, with a non-equivalent control group (Creswell 2005). Because statistical analysis is effective for hypothesis testing and qualitative analysis for identifying complex learning processes, we conducted a mixed methods study, concurrently collecting quantitative data from the experimental and control groups (pre-post intervention), while gathering written qualitative data (self-inquiry essays) from the experimental group throughout the intervention (Creswell 1994). The quantitative and qualitative data were analyzed independently and for convergent triangulation (Creswell and Clark 2011).

Sample

Experimental group: seven cohorts of students who participated in the *Know Your Self* curriculum ($N = 127$). These were graduate and adult undergraduates studying counseling and education. Most were young adults (age 23–35 = 63%), with ages ranging from 23 to 59 (Median = 30). Mean educational level was 17.1 years (SD = 1.6). Students were largely female (89%) and white (97%): typical demographics at my university. In their written narratives, 9% self-reported as gay or lesbian. Birth religions were Roman Catholic (46%), Protestant (34%), Jewish (12%), Muslim (3%), Greek Orthodox (1%), other (2%), and none (3%).

Control group: six cohorts of graduate and adult undergraduate students attending a course on Theories of Holistic Counseling and Psychotherapy (N = 138). The demographic characteristics of the control and experimental groups were similar. Using t-tests for continuous variables and chi-square tests for categorical variables, we found no significant differences for *age* ($t[216] = 1.56$; $p = 0.12$); *educational level* ($t[218] = -1.53$; $p = 0.13$); *gender* ($\chi^2[1] = 1.16$; $p = 0.28$); *race* ($\chi^2[3] = 1.34$; $p = 0.72$); or *religion* ($\chi^2[9] = 8.39$; $p = 0.50$).

There was an additional methodological consideration for choosing this control group. Because the effectiveness of *engaged learning* has been well established, it is no longer useful to employ traditional lecture courses as control groups. To investigate the efficacy of *new* engaged learning strategies, they should be compared to well-established methods (Freeman et al. 2014). The Theories of Holistic Counseling course that served as control group employed well-established engaged learning methods: intensive faculty-student interaction, small group discussions, intensive writing assignments that require original thinking, detailed feedback on writing assignments. Furthermore, this theories course examined concepts and methods of psychospiritual development. The *Know Your Self* curriculum employed these same well-established engaged learning methods. However, in addition, psychospiritual development was practiced experientially and personally. Thus, this study specifically evaluated the effectiveness of *an experiential, person-centered approach* to psychospiritual development.

QUALITATIVE ANALYTIC PROCEDURES

We employed Grounded Theory, an empirical approach to narrative data analysis (Glaser and Strauss 1967; Strauss 1987). This inductive procedure codes narrative descriptions of phenomena and organizes them into categories. When conceptual saturation is reached, categories are organized into constructs for higher-order theoretical and numerical analysis. Grounded Theory is particularly useful for studying dynamics of change (Chamberlain 1999; Strauss and Corbin 1998), employing a phenomenological perspective that examines the lived experience of participants (Hoshmand 1989; Polkinghorne 1983). Students' self-inquiry essays provided written documentation for close textual analysis of learning processes (Polkinghorne 1988). Each student generated 40–60 pages of written narrative.

To refine coding procedures, the research team reviewed their coding for the narratives of 35 participants. There was a high-degree of interrater reliability (86%). Differences in coding were resolved and consolidated into a consistent model. Subsequently, the narratives from the entire experimental group were coded and reviewed at least three times. When coding was complete, a memo was written about each student, summarizing the learning process. These memos became the basis for individual case studies, a process of "vertical" analysis that examined the lived experience of person-centered psychospiritual maturation.

We also conducted cross-sectional ("horizontal") analyses to identify and categorize behavioral change goals, structural components of the learning process, and learning outcomes in the experimental group. During initial coding and category development, we did not impose the five-dimension model of person-centered psychospiritual maturation. Later, during higher-order analysis, its applicability became evident. Then, to assess student learning, we quantified their learning in each of the five dimensions.

Quantitative Measures for Statistical Comparison of Experimental and Control Groups

Inventory of Positive Psychological Attitudes (IPPA) (Kass 1998b; Kass et al. 1991a). This scale measures a resilient worldview, Confidence in Life and Self. It is a 32-item strengths-based instrument, sensitive to cultural differences, that has been used in positive psychology research and psychoeducational programs (Hales 2009; Kass 1998b; Simmons and Lehmann 2012). Respondents self-assess their attitudes and behaviors when under stress, using Likert scales with opposing statements. The IPPA has two sub-scales: Self-Confidence during Stress (SCDS) and Life Purpose and Satisfaction (LPS). Together, they constitute the unified construct Confidence in Life and Self (CLS). Internal reliability and concurrent validity have been robust (Cronbach's α coefficients: $SCDS = 0.86$; $LPS = 0.91$; $CLS = 0.93$) (Kass et al. 1991a). In this study, Cronbach's α coefficients were: $SCDS = 0.87$; $LPS = 0.88$; $CLS = 0.92$.

The IPPA offers advantages over other positively-oriented measures of psychological well-being. First, resilient attitudes are most vulnerable during stress. The IPPA taps these attitudes specifically *during* perceived stress. Second, self-efficacy measures often reveal a cultural bias toward autonomy. The SCDS sub-scale does not focus strictly on individual self-efficacy; it also taps confidence that help will be received from others. Third, life satisfaction scales usually measure global positive affect, producing insufficient information about sources of life meaning. The LPS sub-scale taps specific dimensions of life meaning (personal/existential) during stress, generating a detailed profile. Thus, the IPPA generates a robust portrait of resilient attitudes about self and life during perceived stress.

Index of Core Spiritual Experience (INSPIRIT) (Kass 1995; Kass et al. 1991b). This seven-item self-report scale measures key elements of contemplative experience and practice. It is responsive to diverse belief systems (theist, transpersonal non-theist, secular humanist), with instructions stating "people have many different definitions and images of the *Higher Power* that people often call *God*. Please use *your definition and image*...." Each item also has a potential response that indicates no belief in God. As a unified scale, the INSPIRIT taps a figural aspect of secure existential attachment: perceived relationship with the Ground of Being.

Questions measure behavioral commitment (How often do you engage in spiritual practices?), affective attitudes (How close do you feel to God/Higher Power?), and subjective experience (Have you experienced a spiritual dimension/presence in your life?)

Two INSPIRIT items can be analyzed independently. Q6 measures perceived internal locus of connection with the Ground of Being. A Likert scale taps agreement with the statement: *God dwells within you*. Q7 is a checklist of 12 experiences commonly reported by novice and advanced meditators, ranging from inner peace to the felt presence of a transcendent spiritual presence. VandeCreek et al. (1995) recommend independent use of this checklist to measure frequency of these experiences.

The primary focus of the INSPIRIT is phenomenological, distinguishing it from measures of participation in organized religion and belief in God. It is has been used in many studies of spirituality and meditation (Easterling et al. 2000; Lin et al. 2009; McBride et al. 1998; Okozi and Foley 2008; VandeCreek et al. 1995; Watkins van Asselt and Baldo Senstock 2009), and is referenced in textbooks on the psychology of religion and spirituality (Hill and Hood 1999; Kelley 1995; Paloutzian and Park 2013). The internal reliability and concurrent validity of the INSPIRIT have been robust (Cronbach's $\alpha = 0.90$) (Kass et al. 1991b)). In this study, Cronbach's $\alpha = 0.79$.

STATISTICAL PROCEDURES

We calculated changes on IPPA and INSPIRIT scores (pre-post intervention) in the experimental and control groups. To determine the appropriate test for group comparisons, we examined the distributions of the change scores using the Kolmogorov-Smirnov and Shapiro-Wilk tests (Park 2008). The familiar Student's t-test and Analysis of Variance require standard distributions (Creswell 2005). The scores for this sample did not fit a standard distribution (skew/outliers). Consequently, the Mann-Whitney U-test was more appropriate. This less familiar, but highly reliable, nonparametric test provides a control for variations from a standard distribution (Aron et al. 2012; Ferguson and Takane 1989).

Statistical differences between experimental and control groups were highly significant. However, statistical significance cannot be equated with practical importance. Consequently, we calculated the effect size of these differences. We used Rosenthal's derivation of the Pearson correlation coefficient for the Mann-Whitney U test ($r = Z/\sqrt{N}$) (Cohen 1988; Field 2009; Rosenthal 1991). To assess practical importance, we used Cohen's heuristic: small effect, $r = 0.1$; medium effect, $r = 0.3$; large effect, $r = 0.5$ (Cohen 1988). Rosenthal and Cohen explain r as the difference in success rates between groups. Thus, $r = 0.1$ represents 10% greater improvement in the experimental group. In the behavioral sciences, this effect size is meaningful and typical (Cohen 1988; Rosenthal 1991).

QUALITATIVE RESULTS—EXPERIMENTAL GROUP

We conducted cross-sectional analyses (horizontal) and individual case study analyses (vertical) to produce a granular understanding of behavioral change goals, structural components of the learning process, and learning outcomes in the experimental group. The horizontal and vertical findings were integrated through higher-order conceptual analysis, ultimately yielding the five dimensions of person-centered psychospiritual maturation. The results were quantified to assess the extent of learning in the group. Individual case studies were subsequently written to illustrate successful learning in each of the identified behavioral change goals. Finally, a group case study was developed to illustrate pro-social, culturally inclusive community building.

1. Behavioral Change Goals

The cross-sectional analysis identified 13 areas where experimental group members sought behavioral change. They clustered around four central themes:

(a) **Social-Emotional Impairment of Academic Performance**: (1) procrastination—difficulty completing assignments, (2) pressure to overachieve/somatic symptoms of stress
(b) **Health-Compromising Attitudes and Behaviors**: (1) unhealthy diet, (2) cigarette smoking, (3) alcohol dependence, (4) negative body image/depression, (5) low self-confidence
(c) **Impaired Relational Skills**: (1) sexual promiscuity, (2) fear of intimate relationships, (3) social anxiety

(d) **Existential Struggles and Spiritual Alienation**: (1) existential coping with a chronic illness, (2) alienation from God and religion/quest for spirituality, (3) lack of faith in life.

While these behavioral change goals were quite diverse, they reflected many behavioral and developmental issues that are problematic and not adequately addressed in higher education (ACHA 2004, 2011; Boyer 1990; CASA 2007). Thus, these behavioral change goals had content validity for assessing the curriculum. Case studies were subsequently developed to illustrate individual psychospiritual growth in the four thematic areas.

2. **Structural Components of Curriculum**

The cross-sectional analysis identified four key components:

(a) **Students Engage in a Written Self-Inquiry Project.** This intensive writing project began with a person-centered assignment: students selected a personal behavior or attitude that harms self or others, which they wanted to modify. This self-selected goal created motivation and focus for subsequent learning. Students then wrote three- to five-page self-inquiry essays between class meetings. These essays blended their responses to structured self-inquiry assignments with nondirective journal writing about their in-class experiential learning. The essays explored their behavioral change goals, psychospiritual identity development, interpersonal group learning, meditation experiences, and self-assessment of learning as the class ended. The essays helped students consolidate their learning and develop an internal locus of evaluation. This writing project became the foundation of their self-inquiry work, generating synergy among the four components of the curriculum.

(b) **Students Explore Their Psychospiritual Development.** After selecting a behavioral change goal, they began their self-inquiry projects by writing psychospiritual autobiographies. Structured assignments examined intersecting factors shaping their thoughts, emotions, and behavior. They explored figural aspects of their religious, sociocultural, and personal identities, academic and/or other current stressors, somatic, emotional, and cognitive responses to these stressors, conflict resolution styles, the underlying existential worldview governing their stress response, and sociocultural factors and family histories that shape their narratives about self, others, and life. For many students, this autobiography was a first opportunity to systematically develop cogent narratives about their lives, and to examine harmful aspects of their attitudes and behavior using emergent skills that blended critical analysis and empathic self-reflection.

(c) **Students Engage in Contemplative Self-Inquiry through Meditation**. The curriculum taught students to integrate two generic methods, *mental concentration* (one-pointed attention on an object of contemplation: breath, image, personally-meaningful word or prayer), and *mindfulness* (non-judgmental witnessing of current experience). The complementary use of these methods in Western and Eastern spiritual traditions was discussed, incorporating neuroscientific research about meditation, including its health and pro-social benefits (Cahn and Polich 2006; Ekman et al. 2005; Goleman 1988; Kass and Trantham 2014; Poloma and Gallup 1991; Wallace 2002; Wallace and Shapiro 2006). Initially, meditation was taught as a tool for self-regulation. Later, it was used to explore the deep structure of contemplative mind. Students gradually learned to use meditation in four ways: (1) to monitor stress reactivity and interrupt destructive behavior through mindfulness and elicitation of the relaxation response, (2) to become aware of cognitive/emotional schema and psychological wounds that distort perceptions of self, others, and life, (3) to cultivate a tranquil mind that is receptive to integrative insights, intuitive wisdom, and psychospiritual healing of psychological wounds, (4) to gain temporary access to core spiritual experiences of unitive awareness and altruistic love (Kass 1995, 2015; Kass and Trantham 2014). For many students, this meditative work was a first opportunity to experience stress-modulating internal composure and the deep structure of contemplative mind.

(d) **Students Engage Interactively Building Inclusive, Person-Centered Community**. The community-building component introduced students to socially-collaborative participation in person-centered psychospiritual development. Through active experiential participation, they learned that personal individuation and inclusive group-building can be complementary. As students gradually allowed themselves to be known, understood, and accepted by others, their individuation manifested through increasingly creative, courageous, and self-acceptant behavior. In short, they developed an increasingly internalized locus of evaluation. Analogously, as they came to know, understand, and accept their peers at levels of increasing depth, inclusive group cohesion manifested as increased attachment and attunement to their peers. In short, students developed an increased capacity for unconditional altruistic love and compassion. This learning process was gradual and often challenging: it required mindful cultivation of trust and safety, both by students and the faculty member, learning to approach differences and interpersonal tensions constructively, using self-reflective and contemplative skills to gain perspective on tension-producing interpersonal issues, and increasing their capacity for respectful restorative dialogue as a tool for building group cohesion without sacrificing personal individuation.

This community-building process included an intentional blend of structured group activities and nondirective interpersonal group dynamics. Reflective discussion helped students become mindfully aware of their personal reactions to the community-building process, learning they could discuss their reactions collaboratively, in the service of deeper self-understanding and group cohesion. Structured activities included sharing material from their written self-inquiry essays and psychospiritual autobiographies, intellectual discussion about spiritual traditions they were exploring, including assigned reading and discussion about traditions they had learned to consider *other*; experiential work with somatic/expressive modalities that cultivate mindfulness, emotional balance, psychological resilience, and interpersonal contact (e.g., improvisational movement, hatha yoga, listening to sacred music from diverse traditions, circle dancing, singing, drawing); and group meditation.

3. Learning Outcomes (with Numerical Quantification)

The initial inductive coding procedures identified numerous categories of learning. During higher-order analysis, the five dimensions of person-centered psychospiritual maturation provided a meaningful template to organize these categories thematically. Cross-sectional analysis demonstrated substantive learning in each dimension. However, it was not uniform. We quantified our observations to assess these differences.

(a) *Bio-behavioral Dimension*: 68% demonstrated improvement in their behavioral change goals (self-regulation skills that promote individual and social well-being).
(b) *Cognitive-Sociocultural Dimension*: 51% demonstrated improved understanding of the impact of humanity's *chain of pain* on their lives. This cognitive learning altered sociocultural identity narratives about self and *other*, improving health-promoting and pro-social attitudes.
(c) *Social-Emotional Dimension*: 55% showed evidence of repair to insecure attachment templates inherited from their personal chain of pain. Repair contributed to secure attachment, strengthening their compassionate attunement to self and others.
(d) *Existential-Spiritual Dimension*: 48% reported meditation experiences that expanded self-structure (changes in self-experience from cut off/alone to connection with self, others, and life). Narratives included increased expression of secure existential attachment and altruistic love.
(e) *Integrative Worldview Formation*: 57% demonstrated growth in a resilient worldview Confidence in Life and Self. Growth was reflected in students' increased ability to address their life challenges constructively, with sufficient internal composure to derive maturational learning.

Thus, across these five dimensions, maturational learning ranged from 48 to 68%.

To clarify the results, we quantified them by participant: 93% demonstrated growth in at least one dimension; 7% did not demonstrate any growth. Thus, maturational learning was wide-spread. Most participants were in an early stage of psychospiritual maturation. Consequently, we developed a criterion-based rubric: *growth in three to five dimensions = substantive introductory maturational learning*. We found that 60% met this criterion, 33% demonstrated limited learning (growth in one or two dimensions), and 7% showed negligible learning.

In summary, a robust proportion demonstrated substantive learning. While this learning was not uniform, cautious interpretation suggests the *Know Your Self* curriculum provided a meaningful introduction to person-centered psychospiritual maturation. Specifically, a large proportion demonstrated substantive growth in the resilient worldview, Confidence in Life and Self, and notable increases in secure existential attachment.

STATISTICAL RESULTS: COMPARISON OF EXPERIMENTAL AND CONTROL GROUPS

To confirm the qualitative findings, we compared the experimental group to learning outcomes in an appropriate control group. We used the Inventory of Positive Psychological Attitudes to evaluate changes in the resilient worldview, Confidence in Life and Self; and the Index of Core Spiritual Experience to evaluate changes in secure existential attachment. Statistical comparison of pre-post intervention data corroborated the qualitative results.

RESILIENT WORLDVIEW—INVENTORY OF POSITIVE PSYCHOLOGICAL ATTITUDES (IPPA)

We hypothesized that the experimental group would improve more than the control group on the IPPA scales: *Confidence in Life and Self* (CLS), *Life Purpose and Satisfaction* (LPS), and *Self-Confidence During Stress* (SCDS). We used the Mann-Whitney U-test to compare the groups. As Table 6.1 indicates, mean rank values for the control group were lower than the experimental group; these differences were highly significant for CLS, LPS, and SCDS.

To assess the practical significance of these differences, we measured their effect size. As Table 6.1 indicates, they ranged from $r = 0.21$ to 0.15. Improvements were 21% higher in LPS, 15% higher in SCDS, and 19% higher in overall CLS. These substantive but moderate improvements are meaningful in the behavioral sciences (see Methods). As discussed, the qualitative analysis observed substantive, introductory growth in a resilient worldview. Thus, these statistical results provided convergent corroboration for the effectiveness of the curriculum.

Table 6.1 Statistical Comparisons with Effect Size, Control and Experimental Groups: Growth in Resilient Worldview (IPPA); Growth in Secure Existential Attachment (INSPIRIT) (Adapted from {Kass et al. 2015})

	N	Mean Rank	Mann-Whitney U	Z	p (2-tail)	Effect size
IPPA						
Δ CLS						
Con	108	96.9				
Ex	109	120.99				
Total	217		4579	−2.827	0.005	−0.19
Δ LPS						
Con	108	95.7				
Ex	109	122.17				
Total	217		4450	−3.107	0.002	−0.21
Δ SCDS						
Con	108	99.66				
Ex	109	118.25				
Total	217		4877.5	−2.182	0.029	−0.15
INSPIRIT						
Δ INSPIR						
Con	108	99.89				
Ex	111	119.83				
Total	219		4902.5	−2.357	0.018	−0.16
Δ Q6						
Con	108	100.52				
Ex	110	118.32				
Total	218		4970	−2.55	0.011	−0.17
Δ Q7						
Con	109	99.44				
Ex	112	122.25				
Total	221		4843.5	−2.658	0.008	−0.18

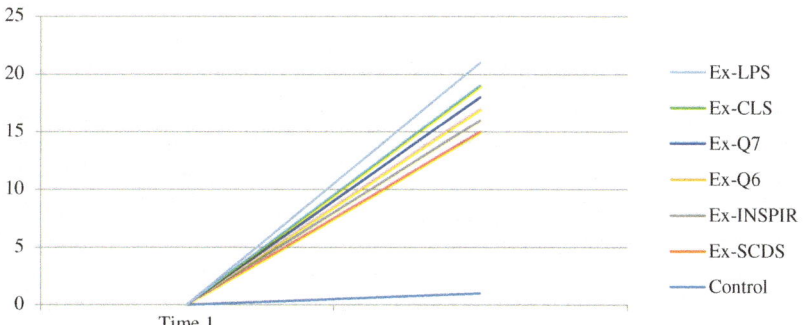

Secure Existential Attachment—Index of Core Spiritual Experience (INSPIRIT)

We hypothesized that the experimental group would improve more than the control group on *INSPIRIT* (indicator of secure existential attachment), including the two questions that can be scored independently: *Q6* (perceived internal locus of connection—God/Higher Power dwells within); and *Q7* (personally meaningful meditative experiences). We used the Mann-Whitney U-test to compare groups. As Table 6.1 shows, mean rank values were lower for the control group than the experimental group; the differences were highly significant for INSPIRIT, Q6, and Q7.

As Table 6.1 indicates, these effect sizes ranged from $r = 0.18$ to 0.16. Increases were 18% higher for the experimental group on (Q7); 17% higher on Q6; and 16% higher on INSPIRIT. These meaningful moderate effects were consistent with the qualitative analysis, which observed substantive introductory movement toward secure existential attachment. Thus, these results offered further convergent corroboration for the effectiveness of the curriculum.

Using VandeCreek's recommendations (VandeCreek et al. 1995), we identified specific meditation experiences (Q7) where the experimental group showed notable increases. Two categories showed robust growth: (a) inner peace and joy; (b) presence of God/Higher Power. The difference between these experiential categories often reflects the meditator's existential belief system: secular humanist vs. religious. The substantive increases in both types of meditative experience offered indirect confirmation that the curriculum supported both belief systems, helping students consolidate a personally-congruent existential worldview.

Discussion of Research Results

The results from this study highlight the value of a mixed methods research design. Statistical comparison of the experimental and control groups provided valuable confirmation that the *Know Your Self* curriculum helped students develop two indicators of person-centered psychospiritual maturation: the resilient worldview, *Confidence in Life and Self*, and growth in *Secure Existential Attachment*. The control group selected for this study was particularly apt: demographically, it was similar to the experimental group; the two courses had overlapping intellectual content; both employed well-established strategies for engaged learning. There was one key difference: while the control group examined psychospiritual maturation conceptually, the experimental group engaged in a sustained, experiential introduction to this learning process. Thus, the substantive differences in learning outcomes between the two groups can be attributed to the curriculum. The moderate effect sizes were predictable and reasonable. Person-centered psychospiritual maturation is incremental. A one-semester, introductory class should not be expected to produce more than moderate results. However, these results suggest it is reasonable to hypothesize greater effects from more extended periods of learning.

At the same time, despite the value of statistical comparisons, these results would be somewhat opaque without valuable information gained through qualitative analysis of written narratives by students in the experimental group. As subsequent chapters will show, the case study material generated by cross-sectional analyses (group learning) and vertical analyses (individual learning) explicate person-centered psychospiritual maturation phenomenologically. Further, these granular descriptions offer additional conceptual and methodological insights about this maturational process that are not evident in the statistical data.

LIMITATIONS OF STUDY

While these positive results were robust, there were methodological limitations. First, the sample lacked sufficient racial and ethnic diversity. Although the group and individual case studies illustrate students of color benefiting from the curriculum and reflect student growth in multicultural competencies, additional studies with greater demographic diversity are needed. Second, these students were engaged in academic disciplines where self-reflection is expected. This selection bias does not negate the study's positive outcomes because experimental and control groups came from these same disciplines. As the curriculum is disseminated, students from other disciplines may experience less comfort with reflective self-inquiry. Evaluation will be needed, including potential curricular refinements.

Additional Corroborative Data

After completing data collection for the effectiveness study, the project continued to gather written data from new students. Self-inquiry work from six additional cohorts ($N = 99$) with similar demographic features was analyzed using the same Grounded Theory methods. These students participated in an intensive weekend format (45 contact hours). Their narratives provided additional material for the group case study of inclusive community-building. This corroborative material has been incorporated in the four group case study chapters.

Introduction to Case Study Material (Chapters 7–11)

The case study material presented in subsequent chapters illustrates the learning process of these students. Using selections from their self-inquiry work, these chapters provide granular portraits of person-centered psychospiritual development and inclusive community-building. While teaching the curriculum, I became increasingly aware of the intense academic stress that every student experienced. Challenging course workloads, service-learning or part-time work, internal performance demands, perfectionism, and intrusive inner critics magnified their anxiety, contributing to behavioral impairment ranging from mental and physical exhaustion to avoidant procrastination. In response, the curriculum focuses the first stage of their self-inquiry work on coping with academic stress. This focus helped students bond around a shared issue, initiating a supportive community-building process (illustrated in Chaps. 7, 8, and 9), and introduced students to reflective self-inquiry on a topic that felt comparatively safe to explore in the classroom. This introductory focus on academic stress prepared them to engage in deeper forms of individual self-inquiry (illustrated in Chap. 10).

Analysis of the community-building process identified three modules of self-inquiry work. These were not linear in progression. Rather, they overlapped, generating synergistic learning and growth. Each module is reported in a separate chapter:

1. Chapter 7: Establishing foundations for person-centered learning and inclusive community-building. During this module, students explored their responses to academic stress, meeting each other as vulnerable human beings who can benefit from supportive,

inclusive community. Through interactive experiential work and introductory meditation practices, they learned to cultivate mindfulness and the relaxation response. This learning strengthened their capacity for psychophysiological self-regulation and reflective self-inquiry, helping them reduce destructive reactivity to academic stress.
2. Chapter 8: Approaching sociocultural differences and interpersonal conflict as catalysts for psychospiritual growth. During this module, students learned to approach conflict as an inevitable—and potentially growth-producing—aspect of human experience. They explored their sociocultural identities, the impact of group-based social dominance hierarchies on their own psychospiritual development, and their current behavioral responses to interpersonal conflict, learning that these conflicts, when approached proactively with internal composurecan help them achieve healthy psychospiritual growth.
3. Chapter 9: Introduction to the deep structure of contemplative mind: from self-regulation to psychospiritual exploration. In this module, students developed an internal locus of existential meaning-making. Through psychospiritual self-inquiry, they identified the existential worldview that fuels their destructive responses to academic stress. Then they made positive changes in this worldview through meditative explorations in the deep structure of contemplative mind. These explorations helped them develop new insights about their attitudes and behaviors, while experiencing connection to a wise, core dimension of self.

In summary, Chaps. 7, 8, and 9 provide a detailed explanation of the structural components and learning modules of the curriculum, describing specific steps in the self-inquiry process and specific ways that inclusive community-building is mentored. This material also provides a useful introduction to the individual case studies that follow.

Chapter 10 presents individual case studies that illustrate person-centered psychospiritual learning in representative students. After identifying personally-salient behavioral change goals, each student in the experimental group wrote a psychospiritual autobiography, explored their stress-reactivity, and developed a meditation practice that helped them build self-regulation skills and develop a positive existential worldview. The case studies illustrate this learning process, providing granular descriptions of person-specific individual growth. Each case study follows a consistent organizational structure:

1. Introduction to Student (with Self-Selected Behavioral Change Goal)
2. Psychospiritual Autobiography (Distillation of Student's Work)
3. Contemplative Self-Inquiry during Meditation (Distillation of Student's Work)
4. Self-Evaluation of Learning (Distillation of Student's Observations)

This chapter concludes with an analysis of student learning in the five dimensions of person-centered psychospiritual maturation: bio-behavioral, cognitive-sociocultural, social-emotional, existential-spiritual, and integrative formation of a resilient worldview.

Chapter 11 completes the group case study, examining *learning-in-community* as a catalytic, pro-social, culturally inclusive holding environment for psychospiritual growth. In the previous chapter, the depth of each student's individual learning process is emphasized. This chapter clarifies the bi-directional interactive effects of individual self-inquiry and community-building. The importance of the learning community is described for student growth in each dimension of psychospiritual maturation. Thus, this chapter presents final evidence for the effectiveness of the *Know Your Self* curriculum, and concludes the presentation of data and results from this research project.

References

ACHA. (2004). *American College Health Association: National college health assessment, 2004 executive summary.* Baltimore, MD: American College Health Association.
ACHA. (2011). *American College Health Association: National college health assessment II, 2011 executive summary.* Hanover, MD: American College Health Association.
Aron, A., Aron, E. N., & Coups, E. (2012). *Statistics for psychology* (6th ed.). Englewoood Cliffs, NJ: Pearson Prentice Hall.
Batson, C. D., & Schoenrade, P. (1991). Measuring religion as quest: Validity concerns. *Journal for the Scientific Study of Religion, 30,* 416–429.

Boyer, E. L. (1990). *Campus life: In search of community.* Princeton, NJ: The Carnegie Foundation for the Advancement of Teaching.

Cahn, B. R., & Polich, J. (2006). Meditation states and traits: EEG, ERP, and neuroimaging studies. *Psychological Bulletin, 132*(2), 180–211.

CASA. (2007). *Wasting the best and the brightest: Substance abuse at America's colleges and universities.* New York, NY: Center on Addiction and Substance Abuse at Columbia University.

Chamberlain, K. (1999). Using Grounded Theory in health psychology: Practices, premises, and potential. In M. Murray & K. Chamberlain (Eds.), *Qualitative health psychology: Theories and methods* (pp. 183–201). London, UK: Sage Publications.

Cohen, J. (1988). *Statistical power analysis for the behavioral sciences.* Hillsdale, NJ: Lawrence Erlbaum.

Creswell, J. W. (1994). *Research design: Qualitative and quantitative approaches.* Thousand Oaks, CA: Sage Publications.

Creswell, J. W. (2005). *Educational research: Planning, conducting, and evaluating quantitative and qualitative research* (2nd ed.). Upper Saddle River, NJ: Pearson Prentice Hall.

Creswell, J. W., & Plano Clark, V. L. (2011). *Designing and conducting mixed methods research* (2nd ed.). Thousand Oaks, CA: Sage Publications.

Easterling, L. W., Gamino, L. A., Sewell, K. W., & Stirman, L. S. (2000). Spiritual experience, church attendance, and bereavement. *Journal of Pastoral Care, 7*(2), 436–451.

Ekman, P., Davidson, R. J., Ricard, M., & Wallace, B. A. (2005). Buddhist and psychological perspectives on emotions and well-being. *Current Directions in Psychological Science, 14*(2), 59–63.

Ferguson, G. A., & Takane, Y. (1989). *Statistical analysis in psychology and education.* New York, NY: McGraw Hill.

Field, A. (2009). *Discovering statistics through SPSS* (3rd ed.). London, UK: Sage Publications.

Freeman, S., Eddy, S. L., McDonough, M., Smith, Michelle K., Okoroafor, N., Jordt, H., et al. (2014). Active learning increases student performance in science, engineering, and mathematics. *Proceedings of the National Academy of Sciences, 111*(23), 8410–8415.

Glaser, B. G., & Strauss, A. L. (1967). *The discovery of Grounded Theory: Strategies for qualitative research.* Chicago, IL: Aldine Publishers.

Goleman, D. (1988). *The meditative mind: The varieties of meditative experience.* Los Angeles, CA: Jeremy P. Tarcher Inc.

Hales, D. (2009). *An invitation to health* (14th ed.). Belmont, CA: Wadsworth Cengage Learning.

Hill, P. C., & Hood, R. (Eds.). (1999). *Measures of religious experience.* Birmingham, AL: Religious Education Press.

Hoshmand, L. T. (1989). Alternate research paradigms. *The Counseling Psychologist*, 17(1), 3–79.

Kass, J. D. (1995). Contributions of religious experience to psychological and physical well-being: Research evidence and an explanatory model. In L. Vandecreek (Ed.), *Spiritual needs and pastoral services: Readings in research* (pp. 189–213). Decatur, GA: Journal of Pastoral Care Publications.

Kass, J. D. (1998a). A curriculum for transformative learning in higher education: Cultivating personally-meaningful spirituality as a resource for self-knowledge and well-being. National Conference on Education as Transformation: Religious Pluralism, Spirituality, and Higher Education. Wellesley College, Wellesley, MA.

Kass, J. D. (1998b). The Inventory of Positive Psychological Attitudes: Measuring attitudes which buffer stress and facilitate primary prevention. In C. Zalaquett & R. Wood (Eds.), *Evaluating stress: A book of resources* (Vol. 2, pp. 153–184). Lanham, MD: University Press of America.

Kass, J. D. (2001). Mentoring students in the development of leadership skills, health-promoting behavior, and pro-social behavior: A rationale for teaching contemplative practices. Lesley University Colloquium on Contemplative Practice. Cambridge, MA.

Kass, J. D. (2012). Mentoring social-emotional learning in higher education: A contemplative self-inquiry curriculum. International Symposia for Contemplative Studies. Denver, CO.

Kass, J. D. (2015). Person-centered spiritual maturation: A multidimensional model. *Journal of Humanistic Psychology*, 55(1), 53–76. doi:10.1177/0022167814525261.

Kass, J. D., & Trantham, S. M. (2014). Perspectives from clinical neuroscience: Mindfulness and therapeutic use of the arts. In L. Rappaport (Ed.), *Mindfulness and the arts therapies: Theory and practice*. London, UK: Jessica Kingsley.

Kass, J. D., Baxter, J., & Lennox, S. (2015). Mentoring person-centered spiritual maturation: A quasi-experimental mixed methods study of a contemplative self-inquiry curriculum. *Journal of Humanistic Psychology*, 55(4), 474–503. doi:10.1177/0022167814547578.

Kass, J. D., Friedman, R., Leserman, J., Caudill, M., Zuttermeister, P., & Benson, H. (1991a). An inventory of positive psychological attitudes with potential relevance to health outcomes. *Behavioral Medicine*, 17(3), 121–129.

Kass, J. D., Friedman, R., Leserman, J., Zuttermeister, P., & Benson, H. (1991b). Health outcomes and a new measure of spiritual experience. *Journal for the Scientific Study of Religion*, 30(2), 203–211.

Kelley, E. W. (1995). *Spirituality and religion in counseling and psychotherapy*. Alexandria, VA: American Counseling Association.

Lin, K., Marx, C., Caboclo, L., Centeno, R., Sakamoto, A., & Yacubian, E. (2009). Sign of the Cross (Signum Crucis): Observation of an Uncommon Ictal Manifestation of Mesial Temporal Lobe Epilepsy. *Epilepsy and Behavior*, *14*, 400–403.

McBride, J. L., Arthur, G., Brooks, R., & Pilkington, L. (1998). The relationship between a patient's spirituality and health experiences. *Family Medicine*, *30*(2), 122–126.

Okozi, I. F., & Foley, P. F. (2008). Validation of a spirituality measure with a Muslim sample. *Counseling and Spirituality*, *27*(2), 81–99.

Paloutzian, R. F., & Park, C. L. (Eds.). (2013). *Handbook of the psychology of religion and spirituality* (2nd ed.). New York, NY: Guilford Press.

Pargament, K. I., Sullivan, M. S., Balzer, W. K., Van Haitsma, K. S., & Raymark, P. H. (1995). The many meanings of religiousness: A policy capturing approach. *Journal of Personality*, *63*, 953–983.

Park, H. M. (2008). Univariate analysis and normality testing (Working Paper). Bloomington, IN: Indiana University Information Technology Services (UITS), Center for Statistical and Mathematical Computing. http://www.indiana.edu/~statmath/stat/all/normality/index.html.

Polkinghorne, D. E. (1983). *Methodology for the human sciences: Systems of inquiry*. Albany, NY: SUNY Press.

Polkinghorne, D. E. (1988). *Narrative knowing and the human sciences*. Albany, NY: SUNY Press.

Poloma, M. M., & Gallup, G. H. (1991). *Varieties of prayer: A survey report*. Philadelphia, PA: Trinity Press International.

Rosenthal, R. (1991). *Meta-analytic procedures for social research*. Newbury Park, CA: Sage Publications.

Simmons, C. A., & Lehmann, P. (2012). *Tools for Strength Based Assessment and Evaluation*. New York, NY: Springer Publishing.

Strauss, A. L. (1987). *Qualitative analysis for social scientists*. New York, NY: Cambridge University Press.

Strauss, A. L., & Corbin, J. (1998). *Basics of qualitative research: Techniques and procedures for developing Grounded Theory* (2nd ed.). Thousand Oaks, CA: Sage Publications.

VandeCreek, L., Ayres, S., & Bassham, M. (1995). Using INSPIRIT to conduct spiritual assessments. *Journal of Pastoral Care*, *49*(1), 83–89.

Wallace, B. A. (2002). The spectrum of Buddhist practice in the West. In C. S. Prebish & M. Baumann (Eds.), *Westward dharma: Buddhism beyond Asia*. Berkeley, CA: University of California Press.

Wallace, B. A., & Shapiro, S. L. (2006). Mental balance and well-being: Building bridges between Buddhism and Western psychology. *American Psychologist*, *61*(7), 690–701.

van Watkins Asselt, K., & Baldo Senstock, T. B. (2009). Influence of counselor spirituality and training on treatment focus and self-perceived confidence. *Journal of Counseling and Development*, *87*(4), 412–419.

CHAPTER 7

Establishing Foundations for Person-Centered Learning and Inclusive Community-Building: Group Case Study #1

This chapter presents the first learning module of the *Know Your Self* curriculum, which establishes foundations for participation in person-centered learning and inclusive community-building. Students begin their self-inquiry projects exploring a subject they share in common: academic stress. As this chapter will show, their exploration of this issue catalyzes important learning, helping students develop skills in mindfulness, reflective self-inquiry, and behavioral self-regulation. Exploring academic stress also creates opportunities for students to meet each other as vulnerable human beings. Collaborative investigation of their stress reactivity reveals important similarities, despite their significant sociocultural differences. These similarities and vulnerabilities become a foundation for building an inclusive, person-centered community.

Before the first class, students review the syllabus and introductory materials that explain this self-inquiry project and the goals of person-centered psychospiritual learning. To reinforce this informed consent procedure, we discuss these issues and their readiness to undertake *person-centered* learning in the first class. Person-centered psychospiritual maturation is presented as an educational process that helps students learn to live more wisely and compassionately, both as individuals and members of a multicultural, democratic society. From an academic perspective, person-centered learning facilitates *personal growth in the service of professional development and constructive civic engagement.* From a humanistic, social justice perspective, it helps students develop awareness and skills for breaking humanity's chain of pain.

We also review grading. Traditional academic activities (conceptual papers) receive letter grades. Person-centered learning activities (self-inquiry essays, experiential learning) are graded pass-fail. Students can elect not to participate in particular experiential activities, but are expected to participate in most. Conscientious person-centered learning earns a passing grade.

Then I briefly review my professional work as an educator, clinician, and social science researcher interested in psychospiritual maturation as a resource for psychological and social well-being, highlighting my commitment to higher education as a venue for building inclusive communities where people with diverse sociocultural identities and existential belief systems can learn to work and live harmoniously. I also discuss the Perennial Philosophy as an affirmation of the shared maturational goals and contemplative practices at the heart of each spiritual tradition.

Afterwards, students introduce themselves. In preparation, they have written a self-inquiry essay exploring their motivations for taking this class. They have also begun to read about a spiritual tradition that currently holds interest for them. The following selections from their essays illustrate the broad range of their motivations, backgrounds, and spiritual interests:

- JoAnne, a white American female, who works full-time during graduate studies, wrote:

The questions regarding academic stress discussed in the [introductory] readings were relevant for me. I believe this course will help me manage my academic and life stress. I find this challenging, as I have worked full-time throughout my graduate school program.

I am a practicing Christian, originally from South Florida. I grew up in a school system where Christian and Jewish holidays were equally observed. But I had no true educated reference point for Judaism. I am using the class readings to learn more about it.

I had not heard of the Perennial Philosophy or known it was the highest common factor of all religions. Your inclusion of Maya Angelou and Dr. Martin Luther King, Jr. to illustrate the connection between the Perennial Philosophy and society was illuminating.

- Ernest, a white American male, who will later introduce himself as gay, wrote:

  To me, spiritual wellness represents a process of meaning-making that orients and guides us in our own lived experience. Referencing the course syllabus, I identify myself as being in the preliminary stage of spiritual exploration. I have developed a deep curiosity about my personal spiritual development. I am looking forward to learning through self-inquiry and exploration within an academically structured environment.

  As someone who grew up without any religious affiliation, I generally connect with broader principles and concepts when exploring my emerging spirituality. I enjoyed the way Diana Eck's (1998) *A New "We": The Bridges that Bring Us Together* described how universal ideas are found "at the heart" of many spiritual traditions.

- Eugene, an African American male, who has faced many sociocultural barriers, wrote:

  Throughout my life, my belief in a higher power has helped keep me grounded and given me direction. I believe that a human being is more than a mind and physical being, but also has a spiritual component. In a general sense, God has called us to do good works and spread the good news of His Gospel to the oppressed and those in need. I hope this [self-inquiry project] will help me [clarify] the plans and purposes that He has for my life.

  My Christian tradition includes worshipping God with other like-minded believers. I enjoy the music, which is inspirational, encouraging participation of all the congregants for an uplifting worship experience. I have a special bond and sense of brotherhood and belonging with my fellow ushers.

- Jazmin, a first generation Latina American, wrote:

  I grew up in a Roman Catholic household, under the strong influence of my mother. Though Catholicism has noble and respectable aspects (i.e., "love your enemies"), other aspects of the religion (i.e., damnation to hell, tallying up one's sins) really brainwashed me and tainted my view on life. This is connected to attending Catholic school and my mother highlighting the more punitive aspects of the religion. One of my reasons for taking this class is to learn how to live a [healthy] spiritual life.

- Robert, a white American male, raised Jewish, wrote:

  I continue to not identify myself with a particular religion, or even as religious. But I am continuously pursuing enlightenment and connection to divinity in all things in my own way. There are pieces of Buddhism and Hinduism that I draw from when I consider the shape of my spirituality. The Hindu belief that the world's purpose is "to provide a training ground for the human spirit" resonates deeply with me (Smith 1991).

- Christina, a South Asian female, and recent immigrant, wrote:

  [As a counselor in training], I understand it is important to accept value systems and beliefs contrary to mine. Every individual has some essence of spirituality, whether a religious doctrine, moral code, or set of values. I hope this course will help me develop an understanding of other people's spirituality, whether similar or contradictory to mine. A big [motivation] to join this program was to support society by building community and bridging gaps.

  My identity has been shaped by Christianity and my parents' strong commitment to its ideals. The educational institutions I attended were religiously affiliated. I was immersed in environments that stressed religious principles as a way of life.

  My parents, like the rest of my country of birth, place utmost importance in the values of their spiritual tradition. I was raised to believe that the Christian "God" was the only true God. I struggled with this concept. I concluded that all spiritual pathways lead to the same truth, God, spirit (whatever one wants to call it). The concept of pluralism was introduced by Eck (1998), where she suggests that by actively participating in dialogue amongst the diverse religions, there will be recognition of common themes.

As students introduce themselves, presenting material from these essays, they recognize the diversity of their cultural identities, interests, and motivations. We note differences in religious background, existential belief system, gender, race, and ethnicity. Our differences, I suggest, can contribute to the richness of the inclusive learning community we will build. But we are likely to encounter situations when our differences challenge us, provoking disagreement or conflict. If we learn to approach them mindfully and respectfully, rather than reactively, in the service of psychospiritual growth, they can help us learn to break humanity's chain of pain.

After setting ground rules for respectful dialogue and confidentiality, conversation deepens. Students respond positively to an educationally-oriented approach to psychospiritual development that embraces an inclusive, social justice perspective. They express keen interest in a pedagogy that integrates personal, professional, and civic development. Often, this discussion elicits optimism that society can mature. But this hopefulness often evokes pessimism in others. They note the long road society must traverse to overcome the sexism, racism, heterosexism, systemic oppression, and violence endemic in our society. Each student cohort addresses these issues in his or her own ways, both in our discussions and written self-inquiry essays.

- Angeline, a white American female, who is raising children during her studies, wrote:

    This year has [evoked] fear about my children's future in this violent culture. I suffered sadness and disillusionment with the many shootings, the government's inability to change gun laws, and rising violence surrounding us. I have spent sleepless nights worrying. It is hard for me to trust that there is good and safety in the world.

- Daniela, a Latina American, who has experienced the financial, psychosocial, and academic challenges faced by urban youth in higher education, wrote:

    There are few colleges and universities with programs to prepare students [of color] for the reality they face. The theory of go to college, get a degree, and get a job is leaving our population of low-income, first-generation college students... [disadvantaged and] financially broke! I am one of "those" people. This is a crisis.

These sobering rebuttals highlight crucial maturational and social justice challenges.

Students also discuss their yearning for personally-meaningful spirituality that can help them become healthy and whole.

- Camila, a first generation Latina American, wrote:

    During adolescence and early twenties, I did not feel comfortable with the word *God*. The concern for religious growth in my family always felt more like "pressure to believe" to save my soul, than an attempt to introduce spirituality into my life. I did not feel the freedom to decide for myself what it all meant. I need to find a spirituality that I can tangibly practice on a daily basis.

- Paul, a white American male, raised Protestant, now immersed in Buddhism, wrote:

Western psychology is primarily concerned with understanding the workings of the mind. Matters of the spirit—or heart—have been left to religion. Yet much of the world's traditional wisdom holds that psyche is indistinguishable from spirit. The distinction between heart and mind is peculiar to modern Western understanding. In the Buddhist traditions, for example, the word *citta* refers to both heart and mind.

- Melinda, a white American female, who has considered herself an agnostic, wrote:

Studying the connection between mind and body for health and healing, I have begun to learn about the spiritual traditions that accompany these practices. I've been introduced to concepts from Buddhism and Hinduism (universal consciousness, karma, dharma) that have brought comfort and peace. I did not realize studying the mind and body would lead me down a spiritual path. This has been surprising, as I have identified as agnostic. However, I have begun to realize that I have been searching for meaning and purpose from outside myself, and maybe what I need to do is search within.

Other students express the need for personal spirituality more tentatively. They feel loyal to the religious tradition of their family and culture, while hinting at tensions and unexamined needs for individuation.

- Felipe, a Latino American, who emigrated from Mexico, wrote:

The Catholic tradition helped me develop a relationship with God. In my country, *El Nacimiento* is a popular custom. On Christmas night, every family places a figure of baby Jesus in the nacimientos to commemorate the birth of the Lord. I learned to respect God from my mother. I still attend some ceremonies.... [But] I have had obstacles in my life and think my spirituality has been missing or hiding.

This individuation process, as many students express, is deeply personal. Whether it involves returning to their cultural heritage, or breaking away, it is shaped by complex aspects of their life experiences and identity.

- Alice, an Asian American female, wrote:

  Spirituality was always present in my home. But it was overshadowed by other pressing life developments. In junior high, my mental focus was on grappling with social anxiety, puberty, and my budding realization that I was gay. My sexual orientation was part of my identity I struggled to accept. It got all my attention for most of my high school years. This left little time to examine spiritual beliefs, especially when I was feeling ostracized by my Christian peers. I am finally ready to explore my spirituality.

  I feel drawn to learn more about Taoism, a spiritual practice that has been part of my family's culture for generations. I am still on my journey to discover my spiritual beliefs, but find myself aligning with much that I learned about Taoism from my parents. I am starting to explore what this means for me, and feel closer to my family and culture.

- James, a white American male, linked his history of drug problems with existential alienation that his religious upbringing did not help him address:

  In my teens, I stopped going to church and joined peers experimenting with alcohol, marijuana, and other drugs. I turned to drugs for several reasons. I was insecure about friendships and eagerly joined in when invited to smoke pot. I was bored with school and home. My traditional Baptist upbringing provided no answers when I began asking deep questions about the meaning of life. Jesus and his heavenly father didn't have anything to do with my reality.

- Kaitlin, a white American female, wanted to develop a meditation practice as a resource for resilience and existential meaning. But her history of sexual trauma concerned her:

  Religion has been a big part of my life. I attended Catholic school during elementary and middle school. But I haven't been spiritually in tune with myself for a long time.

  I struggled to feel safe and secure at home. Instead, I found safety at school and in the church. The adults who cared for me and showed me kindness were from the church.

  When my family moved and I began attending public school I no longer had access to the church, and my faith faded. As I struggled to make sense of the abuse I was experiencing in secret, I felt abandoned by everyone and everything that had been responsible for protecting me, including God.

One part of the course that I am nervous about is meditation. I have attempted to meditate before and it has not gone well. I have a hard time being present, and much of my adult life has been spent on not being present. Finding ways to bring myself out of my body has kept me safe until this point. Therefore, I have never learned to operate on a level of genuine presence without feeling extremely anxious. I am now ready to recognize that anxiousness as an opportunity for growth.

As I read the texts, I find this course will be even more relevant than I originally thought. I hadn't anticipated talking about addiction, which has been a prevalent theme in my life, and I have been reading *Addiction and Grace* with great interest. I also had not made the connection between my lack of spirituality and my chronic illness, but as I read *Minding the Body, Mending the Mind*, I identify with the people who are described as struggling to accept change as an opportunity for growth.

Finding the texts to be eerily relevant, I wonder if at the core of things that need fixing in my life, my lack of spirituality has been a bigger problem than I thought. After years of feeling out of touch with myself, I am ready to start exploring my spirituality and grateful to have the opportunity to do so in a supportive community setting.

These poignant discussions help students begin to develop a sense of community, amidst the diversity of their identities and life experiences. I also acknowledge that some students may feel outside their comfort zones, as they meet peers from different backgrounds. If they feel too uncomfortable, I remind them that they can consult with me privately, while emphasizing that such discomfort can be the prelude to important psychospiritual growth.

In the next session, I begin to introduce the experiential work we will do, by teaching them a simple song with an inclusive community-building theme. We begin with the chorus:

Sisters and brothers from every land,
We're a human quilt with many strands.
Don't you think the time has come
To learn to live in peace?

Singing, of course, generates performance anxiety for many people. For this reason, I explain, we can approach group singing as a mindfulness practice, in which we practice being aware of our physical and mental reactions to stressful events. We begin with diaphragmatic breathing, physical stretches, and relaxing the throat. Then, forming a circle, we sing the chorus numerous times, until words and melody are familiar. We then pause briefly "to process" this experiential work, with students sharing their internal responses. This processing reinforces mindfulness: a practice that is new for many students, and I have learned not to rush. Gradually, students share their visceral and emotional responses. They include anxiety about singing, relaxation during the physical stretching, relief that they are not being judged, and genuine enjoyment.

This activity becomes more complex when I explain that this song can be sung as a two-part round. We divide into sub-groups in separate parts of the room. I suggest that students in each separate circle make eye contact while they sing, helping keep the melody steady. After numerous repetitions, the intriguing harmony created by this simple two-part round begins to emerge. Students are typically delighted with the result.

Then a new complexity is added. Like a Venn diagram with overlapping circles, I ask the two subgroups to overlap. Again, I suggest they make eye contact with subgroup members to keep the melody steady in this more complex configuration. While the proximity of the subgroups creates additional stress, requiring greater mental focus to maintain their melodic identity, the rich tonality of the harmonic structure also increases. When we process this experience, students note that, while the subgroups fully maintained their autonomy, the interlocking structure of the whole group deepened the music's haunting beauty.

Finally, the subgroups form one large circle with alternating members from each group. Again, I suggest they make eye contact with members of their subgroup to maintain their melodic identity. But I warn them that, after a few repetitions, I will suggest that they close their eyes (if comfortable), in order to hear and experience the harmony fully.

When we process this experience, students express the pleasure they derived from our harmonic singing, highlighting the importance of the safe, nonjudgmental atmosphere that is being created. Then we review the steps in this activity: the challenge of learning a new song, strength and support gained from being part of a subgroup, and pleasure they experience when the two subgroups became a unified circle. Students observe that this activity includes three tiers of experience: each person has an individual identity as an autonomous singer, a social identity as part of a subgroup, and a larger unifying identity as part of the whole. They also become mindful of internal shuttling between these three aspects of identity: their individual voice, the separate voice of their subgroup, and the unified voice of the harmonic whole.

Afterwards, I explain that this mindfulness activity also illustrates a distilled version of social identity development. Each individual has the capacity to express her own individual voice. But if we don't feel confident, or if the situation is not sufficiently safe, it helps to identify with a subgroup that shares the same melodic strand. Initially, this can produce tensions between the subgroups, as each stabilizes its own identity. Then, as individuals become grounded in the melody of his or her subgroup, he or she becomes able to interact harmonically with other subgroups. At the same time, subgroups become aware that each carries a melodic strand that contributes to the beauty and strength of the music we are creating. As we learn to join with other groups and allow them to join with us, the harmony becomes richer and more refined, until we can allow ourselves to become a unified whole. Our shuttling between these three aspects of identity—individual self, social subgroup, unified whole—never ends. But it becomes a comfortable experience, in which we can savor the complexity of our multiple identities.

At the same time, this exercise explicates the Perennial Philosophy. Each spiritual tradition has its own unique qualities and integrity. Drawing from the particular historical period and culture of its founding teachers, each tradition expressed maturational goals for humanity and developed practices for becoming psychospiritually mature. These practices included the discipline of behavioral self-restraint, the cultivation of positive personality characteristics, community-building to support social well-being, and contemplative practices that help people experience unitive identity with a larger, transcendent spirit of life. Sadly, these organized groups often become rigid social dominance hierarchies that contribute to humanity's chain of pain. But, as we recognize the Perennial Philosophy at their core, a multicultural society can affirm the integrity of each tradition while helping members from all traditions participate in building a just society that affirms their multiple identities as separate individuals, members of meaningful subgroups, and members of a unified, interdependent human community, while also affirming a yet deeper unifying connection to a transcendent Ground of Being.

Finally, I sing the verses of this song, which I wrote to express key elements of the Perennial Philosophy:

A peaceful mind is the place to start,
Know Your Self, and heal your heart,
Hurt breeds hate; love brings peace—
Break the chain of pain.

Love is the source that gives us life,
Justice and compassion can end all strife.
Love each other as your self—
We are one.

The pain we've suffered can cloud our love,
It can teach us to hate ourselves and others.
But you're a child of the spirit, you're worthy of love—
Break the chain of pain.

Every river flows to the sea,
Find your source, and you'll be free.
It lives in you, and it lives in me—
We are one.

These verses, I explain, express concepts central to the *Know Your Self* curriculum: healing the individual mind and heart, becoming an agent of social justice and compassion, transcending the traumatizing history that has divided humanity into subgroups, and deepening our capacity for the unitive experience of contemplative mind. I invite students to discuss themes that resonate with them. This discussion creates a reflective, conceptual conclusion to the session. I remind students that if they return for our next class meeting, this constitutes their informed agreement to participate in our process of person-centered, engaged learning.

In the next session, students begin the self-inquiry project at the core of the *Know Your Self* curriculum. We begin with a focus on academic stress: an issue that confronts all students on a daily basis. It provides a clear focus for them to begin investigating their stress coping skills, as prelude for deeper areas of psychospiritual growth.

As prelude, I explain that we will begin this investigation through *anonymous sharing*. For example, in our first exercise, I will ask them to name an aspect of academic work they find stressful. They will write it on a piece of paper, placing it in a basket at the center of our circle. I will redistribute them to the group, with students choosing papers not their own. Students then read these papers out loud, as though the statements are their own. Individuals are not identified with the stressor they wrote. This procedure does not dilute the intensity of the sharing process and creates a valuable sense of safety. It is powerful for students to hear their ideas read aloud, and it provides them with an opportunity to learn if their ideas are "outliers," a central anxiety for many students during classroom discussions. Equally important, no student remains silent or without voice, and each voice is equally significant. In summary, this procedure reduces competition and increases a spirit of collaboration. As the data shows, students appreciate anonymous sharing and benefit significantly.

During the first exercise, they identify key areas of academic stress. Qualitative analysis identified five primary areas:

1. **Overwhelmed by Quantity of Assignments: Anxiety, Defeat, Anger**

    - Can't keep up with all the reading and assignments from multiple classes.
    - Feel inferior when I can't complete it all.
    - Trying to balance working full time and going to school full time. Pulling frequent all-nighters and feel behind in all my classes.
    - Feeling so overwhelmed that I stop trying.
    - Assignments stop feeling rewarding or significant.

2. **Difficulty with Self-Regulation**

    - I have two modes: all out sprint and passed out on the couch.
    - Not having enough time for assignments between job, service learning, and friends.
    - Difficulty structuring time to get the assignments done.
    - Organizational difficulties. I don't keep up to date and have to cram assignments. I end up cancelling plans with friends and losing sleep.
    - For final papers and exams, I put my life on hold for weeks.
    - Difficulty with procrastination: getting started on assignments, meeting deadlines. Most assignments are begun less than 24 hours before the deadline, creating constant anxiety.

3. **Perfectionism**

    - Compulsion to complete assignments perfectly. Difficulty with self-imposed standards.
    - If I don't get an A, I am a failure.
    - I never feel that my work is good enough.

4. **High Levels of Anxiety**

    - When I can't complete all the assignments, I get anxious and feel inferior.
    - I feel overwhelmed and start to doubt myself. Maybe I'm not good enough, smart enough. Maybe I don't know what I am doing.
    - Somatic symptoms: chest pain, shoulder pain, back pain, indigestion, headaches, sleep disturbance, nightmares.
    - I feel very stressed when I don't understand the content being discussed in class. When I have a class where I feel lost or don't understand what is being taught or discussed, I begin to dislike the class and create negative feelings around attending it.

5. **Social Anxiety**

    - I get stressed about social aspects, like initiating conversations with classmates. I feel self-conscious and fear people are talking to me out of obligation/to be polite.
    - Being in class with others whom I don't know.
    - I get stressed when I have to speak or present in front of a large group of people.
    - I can't verbally share in class as quickly as others. This makes me doubt my abilities. I worry that the professor and other students think I am unengaged or not trying.
    - Feel inadequate amongst my peers.
    - I struggle to convey my competence or understanding of my course material.
    - I get very nervous when I answer questions or share in class. I worry that I will answer incorrectly and sound stupid. I leave class with sore muscles: neck, shoulders, and back.
    - I am stressed by speaking in class. Will I sound foolish? Arrogant? Am I boring people? Have I offended someone? Sometimes I don't speak. Then I feel bad for not contributing.

These lists deserve careful review by faculty and student life professionals. They provide more granular information than traditional survey data. Categories 2–5 reflect students' honest and vulnerable recognition that they lack mature stress coping skills. Still, the anger expressed in Category 1 must be taken seriously. From the student perspective, most faculty behave as if "their" course is the center of a student's life, disregarding the multiple course responsibilities expected of students, time-demands of service learning and internships, financial needs to earn supplementary income, and social needs to maintain a personal life with friends and family.

During discussions following this anonymous sharing, students regularly become tearful. It is a profound relief for them to learn they are not alone with these issues, as they often assume. Learning they are not outliers, inferior, or defective in their responses to academic stress is an important prelude to developing more effective stress-coping skills and positive self-concept. These realizations are particularly empowering for students from subordinated social groups, disconfirming internalized oppression that conditions them to view themselves as inferior or outliers. It is valuable for students from both dominant and subordinate social groups to bond over shared self-perceptions of inadequacy and shame. This shared experience is foundational in the formation of inclusive, person-centered community.

When I began using anonymous sharing, to confirm its value, I conducted numerous "anonymous sharing" exercises about the process. Here are representative student responses:

- After hearing what everyone wrote, I feel validated and relieved.
- It's good to know I am not the only one who feels isolated because of academic work.
- The group conversation has been incredibly validating and meaningful. It reduces stress to connect with other people, and know we aren't alone with our feelings and reactions.
- I loved this experience! It provided a release for many unspoken thoughts.
- I identified with what other people had to say. It was comforting knowing that I'm not the only one that feels inferior.

In the next exercise, students begin to build mindfulness skills necessary for effective stress coping. They envision a situation where they experienced academic stress, and identify four modes of reactivity: physical, emotional, mental, and behavioral. Here are common themes:

- Physical: My mouth begins to feel dry.
  Emotional: I become anxious and defensive.
  Mental: I judge myself harshly.
  Behavioral: I isolate myself.

- Physical: Clenched, stiff neck and shoulders; shallow breathing.
  Emotional: Emotional extremes, unable to regulate (anger/sadness/irritability).
  Mental: Think in black & white; catastrophize.
  Behavioral: Get impatient/annoyed with those I love.

- Physical: My stomach feels uneasy.
  Emotional: I feel overwhelmed.
  Mental: I can't think clearly and get flustered.
  Behavioral: I keep busy. I focus on others rather than myself.

- Physical: I get very tired and sleep a great deal.
  Emotional: I avoid tasks that need to get done.
  Mental: "You're never going to get everything done. Why bother trying?"
  Behavioral: I neglect exercise, eat more, and smoke pot.

- Physical: All-day panic attack. Inability to focus/transition from task to task.
  Emotional: I disassociate; get fearful I am doing everything wrong.
  Mental: I go blank; my internal dialogue is fragmented.
  Behavioral: I run around trying to get things done. Behavior is chaotic.

Students are relieved to discover the "almost boring repetition of themes," as one student observed. Their dysregulated, vulnerable reactions to stress are markedly similar. Two common themes are particularly important in this process of destigmatization: the notable prevalence of a toxic inner critic and abrasive interpersonal behavior.

The class ends with conceptual discussion and psychoeducation about their self-inquiry work. We examine their reactions to academic stress through a neurobiological lens as expressions of the human stress response. It is useful to normalize these reactions further by understanding their fight, flight, and freeze behaviors as part of an innate, protective response. We explore conceptual material on the neuroscience of stress and resilient coping (as discussed in Chap. 5). This provides a conceptual handle for students to understand how reactivity to stress and perceived threat contributes to the chain of pain on individual and systemic levels. It also explains the cultivation of mindfulness as a foundation for breaking the chain of pain by helping them cope with stress and perceived threat less reactively. Students begin to understand polyvagal theory and their capacity for resilient coping.

In the next session, we begin to build resilient coping skills that integrate mindfulness with elicitation of the relaxation response. While meditation is the standard method, this practice is elusive for many students. Developmentally, they require preparatory experiential work that is more dynamic. I developed a peacock feather exercise that has been very effective. These light feathers, approximately 30 inches long, have an iridescent circular shape near the top. Students will eventually will learn to focus their attention on this circular shape. Initially, they are invited to balance the feather on a fingertip. This activity, which is fun and challenging, galvanizes their energy. Because the long feather sways easily, they must place full attention on this activity to assure that it does not fall. As it sways, the feather requires each student to move carefully, maintaining their fingertip under the feather's center of gravity. Laughter is infectious. But the sound level diminishes quickly as students become fully engaged.

After several minutes, I ask them to become aware of physical qualities that help them keep the feather balanced. They call out individual words that describe these qualities. When we pause to discuss these qualities, we distill them into five terms: *flexibility...strength... balance...focus... attunement*. Returning to the activity, I invite them to practice these five qualities as they move with the feather. Highlighting the importance of focus, I suggest that they place their attention on the circular shape at the top of the feather. The effect is immediate, helping them become more attuned to the feather's movements.

Then I suggest that they travel across the room and back, keeping the feather balanced while at the same time activating the intention to travel directionally. Infectious laughter returns, as students practice moving with their feather, avoiding bumping into each other, slowly learning to reach their destination, while acceding to the non-linear path that the feather requires. But this laughter feels different, no longer driven by performance anxiety. Deeply mindful and attuned, the students are having genuine fun. Then I ask them to note their ability to intuit the feather's movements, and their ability to use these intuitive insights to help them reach their destination.

As they continue, I describe this activity as a metaphor for life. Each of them is traveling through life, trying to reach specified destinations. If they treat the feather as an impediment that prevents them from taking a direct route, the feather will fall. But if they maintain flexibility, strength, balance, focus, and attunement, they can reach their destination by following the non-linear path the feather creates. Further, by cultivating attunement and intuitive insight, the non-linear path they are following becomes increasingly clear to them. To live fully, deeply, and effectively requires a subtle balance of effort and surrender.

Finally, I suggest an additional idea: while the destinations we pursue are important, it is equally important to experience the deep pleasure we can derive from these qualities of being. If they learn to respond to life's challenges as they are responding to their peacock feather, they can discover an internal locus of joyful vitality. Life, I suggest, is a dynamic process that can teach them to cultivate flexibility, strength, balance, focus, and attunement. Further, it can teach them to cultivate their capacity for intuitive insight. This discussion has shifted, I point out, from describing physical qualities necessary for balancing a feather to psychospiritual qualities necessary for cultivating a fulfilling life.

The following narratives highlight life coping skills students develop during this exercise:

- The exercise let me focus in the moment. All other distractions in my mind got set aside. After, I felt more relaxed, lighthearted, and energized. Being in the moment is a struggle for me, and this exercise brought a calm to my mind that I can now recognize and look for in future exercises or daily activities.

- I learned better ways to relate to life. Meditation has been a challenge for me, and this provided a tangible way to focus the mind and eliminate the chatter.

- Focusing was the key. If I began to pay attention to others around me and compare myself, I would struggle. When I focused on what I was doing, I was able to succeed.

- When I focused on the beauty of the feather, balancing it was a graceful act which I found soothing. But as soon as I began to focus on a destination, I became anxious. Instead of appreciating the feather, I began to see it as something getting in the way.

- All too often I think about the future or dwell in the past. Spending too much time in these areas is not productive and takes me out of the moment. The biggest takeaway: mindfulness is also about allowing myself to have fun and enjoy an activity.

- I appreciate how natural it was to become mindful focusing on the feather. I wasn't thinking about how my body felt or my worries. I loved the life metaphors that could be drawn from the activity. I have not had so much fun in months.

- My relationship with my feather felt symbolic of my relationship with my life, and it definitely evolved. At first, I was so focused on keeping it up. I could not "go with its flow." Then I discovered I could push its boundaries a little, but also learned I needed to give it the freedom to move where it wanted, or it would fall. By the end, I was just enjoying the "dance" of being with the feather.

- The peacock feather was an inspiring teacher. I liked the metaphor of balance, especially when we were trying to balance the feather and balance ourselves emotionally. I found myself feeling grateful...for the experience, for the insights everyone had to offer, and for the abundance of humor and kindness we are showing one another.

In summary, these narratives reflect the atmosphere of warmth and loving-kindness that begins to emerge in these learning communities through interactive work, the consolidation of important life-coping skills, and a new degree of readiness to practice meditation.

In the next part of the exercise, we build additional foundations for resilient coping that further prepare students for a meditation practice. As they examined their reactions to academic stress, students had noted the presence of a toxic inner critic. Because the critic is triggered by the stress response, mental health counselors have learned to recognize the protective role it is trying to play. We often teach clients to dialogue with this intrapsychic subpersonality, helping them acknowledge its protective efforts while blunting its punitive nature.

But the punitive nature of the inner critic is difficult to modify. It expresses negative self-concepts that have been deeply introjected: the painful inheritance from each individual's personal links to humanity's chain of pain. As Jung explains, every person must eventually confront this shadow aspect of self, or be controlled and undermined by its toxic messages.

As an archetypal mental formation, the inner critic creates persistent problems during early stages of meditation. It generates agitating mental activity that impedes mindful immersion in the present, and contemplative explorations into deeper dimensions of self. In addition to its harsh self-commentaries, the inner critic ruminates obsessively about the future and past. In its vigilant, overprotective zeal, it tries to predict, control, or fix perceived dangers and deficits. Like a tornado drawing energy from the atmosphere, the inner critic draws energy from the ego's fundamental state of ontological insecurity.

These considerations inform the second part of the peacock feather exercise, in which students confront the inner critic. They begin by naming its typical messages. Then they divide into pairs for focused work. One student identifies a negative message that feels comfortable to explore in class and then resumes balancing the peacock feather. The partner role plays the inner critic, trying to make the feather fall by vigorously repeating the negative message. I explain that we will do this exercise lightheartedly: our goal is to disempower the inner critic. Students will then switch roles, sharing the "burden" of serving as someone's inner critic, in the service of that person's growth. The exercise is humorous: picture eight students walking around a classroom, trying to keep their feathers balanced, while eight others shadow them, expressing messages of the inner critic in loud voices.

But the impact of the exercise is not superficial. In follow-up discussions, I ask what it was like to play the inner critic. Invariably, they say it was not pleasant. Some express concern that they may have hurt their partner. But their partners speak up quickly to refute this fear. It was helpful, they explain, to hear the voice of the inner critic expressed out loud. During the exercise, they began to realize these critical remarks were ridiculously exaggerated. As partners kept repeating them, the criticisms seemed laughable. Their partners agree. One said, "Someone really trying to help you would never say something like that, something that undermines you, and is patently untrue." Another student said, "Isn't it ridiculous that we do this to ourselves?" Others agreed. Then one added, "But we didn't make these messages up. As I listened to my inner critic, I knew exactly where it came from."

The following anonymous sharing narratives reflect central learning themes:

- Hearing messages from my inner critic filled me with sadness. I was surprised that others also felt sadness. One person said it angered her that society can make us feel this way.

- My inner critic is not based on truths, it's rooted in *fear*.

- What I say to myself I would never feel was true if I said it to someone else.

- I deserve an Olympic medal for the amount of thoughts that come into my head. There is literally not a minute that goes by that I am free from the discursive thinking that goes on in my mind. I often hear thoughts or messages that say I am unworthy of anyone's time, love, and friendship. These are extreme cases. I am more intruded on by thoughts of feeling incompetent—incapable of accomplishing the things I want most.

- This activity helped me to see how my thoughts affect my behavior. When stuck in my negative thoughts, I am less focused, more likely to fail. Self-fulfilling prophecy.

- I learned that other people have inner critics as mean as mine.

- I learned that I give a lot of power to my inner critic and felt a sense of normalization that many other people did as well.

- Hearing the mean things I say to myself from another person diminishes them.

- Hearing my negative internal tape out loud helped me gain distance and perspective.

- I noticed how difficult it was to ignore my inner critic. But when I did, I experienced a moment of peace that felt like freedom.

- I was amazed at how easy it was to laugh at my inner critic in this exercise. Laughing was a great release of all that bottled up energy.

As these statements indicate, mindful observation of the inner critic in a collaborative, interactive learning atmosphere helps students disempower these toxic, introjected messages. The two segments of the peacock feather exercise complement each other, helping students develop important self-regulation skills, while preparing them for the challenges of meditation.

Students are then introduced to meditation as a resource for mindful self-awareness, elicitation of the relaxation response, emotional balance, and behavioral self-regulation. They are taught two classic forms of meditation (see Chaps. 4 and 5). First, they practice mental concentration on an object of contemplation, initially the rhythmic flow of the breath. Later, they will use visualization methods and an anchoring phrase as objects of focus. Second, they practice mindfulness: focused awareness of the present moment in a nonjudgmental, nonreactive, witnessing frame of mind, during sitting meditation and outdoor walking meditation. These traditional forms are introduced as complementary, not antagonistic. Students gradually discover the benefits and challenges of each method. As they develop their own person-centered approach to meditation, they learn when and how each method is useful to them as a mode of self-regulation and introspective self-inquiry. Readings and discussion about the neurobiology of meditation, stress, trauma, and resilient coping supplement their experiential work, providing useful conceptual frameworks.

We use anonymous sharing after each meditation session. This normalizes the broad range of difficulties they experience, helping students develop patience and self-acceptance:

- I went back and forth. First a clear mind focused on peace—witnessing the in and out of the breath. [But] then thoughts about random things "to do" crept in.

- It was very difficult to stay seated and still for that long—just something my body isn't used to doing with my muscles.

- At one point my thoughts were so scrambled: a conversation I did not want to be part of was going on in my head. Sometimes I was able to excuse myself from the conversation, and other times I felt like I was eavesdropping at inappropriate times. "Why the heck are you thinking that? What the hell is wrong with you?"

- At times I found this to be peaceful, but for the most part I struggled to stay focused. My energy kept going to thoughts about my body hurting in the position that I was in. I am working on not letting my mind take over like this, but today was not the day.

Anonymous sharing also facilitates non-competitive sharing of positive experiences:

- I felt my thoughts come and go but was able to bring myself back to the breath easily and felt as if I was very kind to myself. The inner critic must have been asleep.

- It was difficult to concentrate at first. But I relaxed each part of my body, one area at a time. As I focused inside, I was able to picture a beach and the waves….so relaxing… This was my first meditation experience and it was very powerful for me.

- It was amazing to feel so connected to my body. I assumed there would be physical intensity associated with sitting in one position for 10 minutes, but it turned out to be a great experience to acknowledge that discomfort, accept it, and not criticize myself for it.

- At first I was able to calm my mind. But after a few minutes, my knees began to ache. I thought about changing positions, but decided to see if I could mentally overcome it. It took me a minute or so, but I was able to focus on the peacock feather and clear my mind. Surprisingly, the pain disappeared when I did not think about it.

- Powerfully centering. Even when thoughts came in, it was easy to gently embrace them and then let them go as they are, not changing them or covering over the thought content.

- My breath remained the center of my focus. It gave me a stillness I haven't found elsewhere recently.

- Going for a meditation walk around Lesley's campus was a moment of learning: I never looked at how gorgeous fall is. I always viewed it as a prelude to winter. I took the time to see the changing leaves and I felt the crisp air. I'll never take another fall for granted.

- I felt my body sink into the floor. My legs, arms, and head were heavy. I felt myself surrender to the experience. It was like I could not move, analyze, or question. All I could do was *be* in my body. I allowed myself the honor of being connected and aware. It was truly humbling.

- I was distracted by thoughts when I began. I attempted to focus on my breathing but found that my mind remained filled with thoughts. The thoughts were so compelling that at times I forgot that I was supposed to be trying to clear them from my mind. I began to make more of an effort to ignore the words. When I finally let go of the thoughts, I became distinctly aware, for the first time, of the change in perception that occurs during meditation. I became acutely aware of the stillness inside of me.

Anonymous sharing also provides students with a way to share effective methods:

- My mind was jutting from corner to corner until I located my center, in between my eyebrows, and my breathing became more rhythmic and calm.

- When my mind started up with anxious thoughts, I tried to focus back to my breath. I was able to put critical thoughts to the side and soften them. My mantra was *shhhh*.

- I could not silence the thoughts so I decided to let them speak and would come back to my breath after each one. I let myself feel the negative emotions without becoming them. I feel better knowing that I let the thoughts have a voice and have put aside my concerns for right now about attaining "clarity."

- I can't say I quieted my mind completely. But I was gentle with myself when my thoughts wandered, and that helped my body relax. I was so relaxed that I nodded off a bit, which I will accept as a good thing. I gave myself permission to relax and to be still.

- The image of waves crashing on a beach became a visual focus. Most of the time, my mind was somewhere else, but each time I returned to the beach, the more I was sure that I want to train myself to be able to stay present on that shore without dissociating.

Quite often, the anonymous sharing process includes an element of humor that fuses the immense frustrations and elevated states of mind that meditation can produce:

- Busy, busy, busy, busy, busy mind. Wait, is that how you spell busy? Or is it b-u-s-y? No, no, no ... it's busy. See, it was like that. Thoughts like that, except I thought them probably three times faster than you just read them. And then I was anxious and agitated. Jared! Why are you making us do this?! And then I laughed to myself because, at home, I get annoyed with the kitchen timer I use to meditate. I usually assume that it's broken because it is forgetting to beep and tell me that the 20 minutes are over and I can stop meditating now. NOW? Now? Is it over yet? Jared?! Then the music really was over and my brain got tired, and I laughed a little more to myself. And then I find my breath, and it is enough, and I rest in that sweet place for what doesn't feel long enough.

It is impossible to overstate the value of anonymous sharing as a collaborative method for deepening meditation practice. Anonymity lightens and normalizes this challenging learning process, highlighting the wisdom that emerges from the group when every voice is heard and affirmed. There is no need for the professor to dispense further commentary or "wise" advice.

As students continue to practice meditation, in conjunction with their self-inquiry work, the inner critic's subverting effects gradually diminish, and their psychophysiological self-regulation skills solidify. This learning helps them respond to academic stress more resiliently: they approach these challenges with self-awareness and internal composure, rather than through fight, flight, or freeze reactivity. These constructive results are evident in the individual case studies (Chap. 10) and the concluding group case study (Chap. 11).

Recognizing the self-regulatory benefits of this combined approach, students continue to investigate the impact and origins of their inner critic. They begin to see its roots in personal and systemic aspects of humanity's chain of pain. These insights solidify as structured self-inquiry assignments help them write a psychospiritual autobiography. This project includes creating a timeline of their psychospiritual development that identifies critical life experiences, family influences, religious education, and sociocultural identity factors that supported and undermined their growth. As group cohesion increases, students share material from their psychospiritual autobiographies in class. Anonymous sharing provides a first step in building cohesion and trust:

- I have learned that the inner critic is a *part* of me, not necessarily me, and that it has *origins* whether they be familial, cultural, existential, or from some protective standpoint. The class has helped me gain an understanding of the potential origins of the inner critic. It's been beneficial to name it in the way we have and to externalize it. It's also been great to do the anonymous sharing and hearing what others deal with.

- If I attempt to block out my critic, it will only perpetuate unfulfilling aspects of my life. If I acknowledge the critic, I can move forward with awareness and self-compassion.

- These exercises help me see my life in a different light. I have realized that the negative influences were actually bigger than I thought. I have spent such a long time avoiding them (as no big deal)…maybe to help me compartmentalize them?

- As a child, I received the message from my parents that I was a disappointment and nothing I did was good enough.

- I grew up in a house of blame. When things went wrong, you pointed a finger outward to the person who "caused it." This didn't stop with tangible occurrences. If you were angry or sad, it was someone's fault for making you feel that way. I not only learned to blame others for my negative emotions, but I internalized the blame that I received.

- My parents got divorced when I was 2 years old. I spent my life between two worlds, trying to please and be loved by two very different people with different values about what is good, expected, important, and worthy. I am trying to become more integrated as me, not who others will love and think is valuable, seeking my own sense of self-worth. A challenge has been being accepted for a major part of who I am: GAY. Dealing with my mother's tears over it.

- An angry father who often lost his temper and hurt me physically and emotionally. A mother who could not protect me or show me how to walk away from angry men. Being told don't think too highly of yourself or people won't like you.

- My inner critic has deep roots in my history with my biological parents [and their struggles] to survive in this society. I grew up believing there was something about me that made them give me up…stay away…never return. No one ever told me that, but it was the only way I could makes sense of it…until I began to understand the vice-grip that addiction and sexual pain has had on my family.

- The messages were passed to me from others. They too had messages passed to them. The critic needs me to believe self-defeating thoughts in order to stay powerful. It will do anything to convince me to believe it to survive. But the chain can break here.

The purpose of these autobiographical explorations, as students realize, is not to cast blame. Rather, by learning to investigate their chain of pain through empathic self-reflection, they develop a more compassionate understanding of its intergenerational replication: people are driven to destructive behavior through reactive desperation and distorted inflation of their self-protective impulses. In this state of fearful hyperarousal, people lose touch with their moral compass and ability to respond to life's challenges maturely: with internal composure, empathic self-understanding, and compassionate concern for others. This understanding of humanity's chain of pain does not absolve responsibility for those who perpetuate it. But it explains how to break it: determination to overcome the internal and systemic factors that provoke reactive and destructive aspects of our self-protective impulses. If our educational systems helped society understand this dynamic, person-centered psychospiritual development in culturally-inclusive learning communities could provide pathways to reduce these internal and systemic factors.

In summary, as students grapple with these deeply personal and systemically-relevant issues, they build foundations to engage in person-centered psychospiritual growth and inclusive community-building. Using the practical focus of their reactivity to academic stress, students develop essential skills: mindfulness, reflective self-inquiry, and behavioral self-regulation. Equally important, they meet each other as vulnerable human beings in search of support and community, despite significant differences in religious backgrounds, existential belief systems, and sociocultural identities.

References

Eck, D. L. (1998). A new "We": The bridges that bring us together. In, J. T. Angilella & A. Ziajka (Eds.), *Rediscovering justice: Awakening world faiths to address world issues.* San Francisco, CA: University of San Francisco, Association of Jesuit University Presses.

Smith, H. (1991). *The world's religions: Our great wisdom traditions.* New York, NY: HarperSanFrancisco.

CHAPTER 8

Approaching Sociocultural Differences and Interpersonal Conflict as Catalysts for Psychospiritual Growth: Group Case Study #2

This chapter presents the second learning module of the *Know Your Self* curriculum, in which students realize that if they approach sociocultural differences and interpersonal conflict proactively with internal composure, rather than responding through habitual modes of stress reactivity, these issues can become sources of psychospiritual growth and new relational skills. The chapter describes six ways that this learning is taught and mentored. First, the curriculum introduces these issues through psychoeducation about group-based stress reactivity to perceived threats. Second, it creates structured opportunities for students to discuss differences in their sociocultural identities. Third, students learn to examine how group-based social dominance hierarchies have affected their psychospiritual development. Fourth, students develop greater religious literacy by reading about a tradition they consider *other*. Fifth, students examine their conflict engagement styles, exploring their interpersonal behavior under stress. Sixth, students experience naturally occurring *in vivo* conflicts in their learning community which help them develop restorative dialogue skills and constructive solutions to conflict. As noted (Chap. 6), the learning modules in this curriculum overlap; they are not sequential. Thus, this module is integrated into the student learning experience throughout the curriculum.

Psychoeducation: Group-Based Stress Reactivity

Psychoeducation begins in the first class when sociocultural differences and interpersonal tensions are framed as natural aspects of human relations. When approached as catalysts for thoughtful social engagement and inclusive attachment-solutions, rather than as triggers for competitive battle or isolative separation, they can generate psychospiritual growth. As prelude to deeper discussions, we acknowledge sociocultural differences among group members.

Psychoeducation continues through readings and discussion. Utilizing material discussed in Chap. 5, students recognize similar dynamics in interpersonal and intergroup conflict. Both arise from perceived threats to identity, survival, or dignity (the right to be treated with justice and respect). Both include differentials in social power that undermine constructive negotiation as equals. Both are preceded by a sequence of events where at least one party feels increasingly disregarded, disempowered, aggrieved, or victimized. Both trigger instinctive, protective aspects of the stress and trauma responses (fight-flight or vicious attack-protective numbing). In both cases, this psychophysiological hyperarousal further amplifies perceptions of threat, escalating reactivity. Further, it inhibits neural pathways that promote social engagement, decreasing the potential to de-escalate tensions through dialogue. Finally, both types of conflict could be prevented if individuals and groups engaged in constructive dialogue about tensions before they erupted into hostile aggression or sullen withdrawal. Thus, a key element in breaking the chain of pain is shared commitment to the survival, identity, and dignity of *every* individual and social group. To actualize this commitment, people in dominant and subordinate groups must engage in psychospiritual growth that prepares them to participate in mutually-empowering dialogue.

Student Explorations of Sociocultural Differences

After students have learned to engage interactively (Chap. 7), the curriculum introduces experiential work that helps them discuss their ethnic and racial differences. Listening to music from diverse cultures (and using this music as background for movement-based stress-reduction), helps elicit the relaxation response and mindfulness skills prior to these discussions. We often listen, for example, to music of the Roma (Gypsies). Describing their 1500 year diaspora from India to Europe, persecution by the Nazis, and current marginalization in Europe, I explain how their music became a foundation for their resilience and survival as a distinct ethnic group.

Then I introduce a beach ball decorated with a map of global Earth. As we pass the globe around the group, each student identifies the country of origin of their great-grandparents. The geographic range is large. Many great-grandparents lived outside the United States, in countries from every continent and many island nations. Other great-grandparents were born in the United States, in every geographic region.

As the conversation deepens, many students share personal memories about grandparents and great-grandparents, revealing deep connections to their ancestors. Their touching memories personalize the discussion, and students see each other even more fully as human beings with shared life experiences. Afterwards, if they feel comfortable, students share family secrets: narratives often withheld from public discourse. Regularly, some students share Roma ancestry. Often, they have never heard Roma music. Other secrets have included ancestors who were Caribbean pirates, Irish freedom fighters, Mayflower colonists, frontier settlers who battled American Indians, Jews who passed as WASP, African Americans who passed as white, plantation slaves, Anglo or Spanish enslavers, Europeans forced to enlist in the Nazi army, and Muslim nobility from Persia and North Africa. Their willingness to share complex historical aspects of their racial, ethnic, and religious identities is an affirmation of their growing trust in each other. Discussions have never devolved into attacks on members of "oppressor" groups. Students consistently acknowledge the raw poignancy of our tragic, shared history. Using anonymous sharing, they express pride and strength they derive from their cultural backgrounds, while naming ways their cultural groups have suffered from, and perpetuated, the chain of pain:

- I feel proud of my grandparents' resilience in surviving the Depression and flourishing afterwards with large, healthy, happy families. I'm proud of every family member who fought in a war, especially my grandfather, and carried on with his life after that. I'm not sure I'll ever truly understand how someone could do that.

- When my family immigrated, my parents were picked on for not speaking English. Sometimes it is difficult to feel connected either to our home country or the U.S. because we have been made to feel not American enough here in the U.S. and not cultural enough in our country of origin when we visit.

- My heart aches knowing that my ancestors who came over on the Mayflower brutally tried to wipe out my Native American ancestors. Even when there was peace in the union of my great grandparents, other relatives continued the chain of pain. I also feel for my paternal great-grandmother and her loss of religious identity, because of the suffering her Jewish ancestors experienced, and the pain involved in hiding that history.

- I am American. Soy salvadoreña y colombiana. I am Salvadorian and Colombian. El Salvador is a small country, but its heart and people are resilient, beautiful, and hard-working. Colombia is a big country with warmth, dance, and joy. Both countries have shed blood for years. My family is Roman Catholic. God saved my mother from the tanks in El Salvador. She felt and still feels Him to this day.

- I feel strength and pride knowing people in my family overcame hardship to get where they ended up in America. I also know my ancestors are part of the chain of pain, simply by being White. Even if they faced struggles making it, there remains a privilege that perpetuates this chain of pain.

- The background of my family is working class. I have Italian, Irish, and English roots, which instilled a strong sense of community. I don't know many personal stories. But I know my Irish and Italian immigrants encountered strife early on, with each other and with those from an English background.

- Overcoming challenges that come from immigrating, learning a new language, and starting from nothing has given me lots of strength because I made it through those very difficult times. But I have been treated like an outsider since coming to the U.S. I was teased by my American peers for my Russian accent and for being different. People have treated me as less than, though many times I think it has been unintentional. For example, when I share that I'm from a different country, many ask, "Are you an illegal alien?"

- The Irish are an enduring people, [with a] history of stubbornness and survival. My family is full of women who raised their children alone. That gives me confidence in moments of self-doubt. [But my mixed background] creates a dichotomy. My English ancestors were oppressive to my Irish and Native American ancestors, placing part of my identity in the perpetrator category, while other parts suffered greatly. The fact that these cultures all exist in me gives me hope.

These discussions demonstrate the difficulties of immigration, and why desperate people seek sanctuary in the United States. They highlight for students the impact of social class, ethnicity, race, gender, and white privilege on the challenges people encounter and the successes they achieve. They also explicate the pain of social marginalization, the reality that all groups have a history of engaging in these behaviors, and multiple ways that group-based social dominance hierarchies continue to fracture the fabric of our society.

IMPACT OF GROUP-BASED SOCIAL DOMINANCE HIERARCHIES ON PSYCHOSPIRITUAL DEVELOPMENT

During their written autobiographical work, students explore how their psychospiritual development has been affected by formative aspects of their sociocultural identity (gender, race, ethnicity, sexual orientation, social class, physical ability, religious upbringing, and family power dynamics). Three figural themes emerge consistently:

1. *Legitimizing messages of in-group superiority in religious upbringing*

    - My church ignored other cultures and ethnic groups. We were a self-contained unit. As a child, I was convinced that ours was the right way, the only way. Other religions and people were not worth bothering with.

    - Nearly everyone was white and upper middle class. There was no cultural diversity. Social class mattered. Clothes mattered. The size of your house mattered. The priests lived in a mansion and drove Cadillacs. Social class and rank was embedded in the hierarchy of the church. I felt more shame about not being wealthy than being a sinner.

    - The valued members in my church were the best dressed families who sat in front. The fact that poorer families were ignored, and the richest members were the most valued, definitely shaped my young opinions about who mattered in this world and who did not.

    - As a child and teen, I was a devoted Catholic. I went to church often. I prepared the offerings for the altar and cleaned the church as well. My family was very proud of me when I was chosen to do a reading in church on the day of my First Holy Communion. [But] I was not exposed to people of different ethnic or religious backgrounds. I was taught my religion and ethnicity were superior.

- I have struggled most with the belief that there is only one true God. How can so many people be wrong especially when I see so many attractive qualities about other religions?

2. *Negative impact of white male heterosexual privilege:*

- My white, Anglo-Saxon, Protestant background has a lot to do with my concept of God. I always thought of Him as male and white. I could identify more easily with a white God than one of Color because I felt like we had more in common. I have just recently begun to question my assumptions and try to figure out why I need a white male God.

- [It has been]... difficult to relate to God as a male and to trust in him when some of the male role models in my life [have] not been very trustworthy. Women have had to give up power and control to men all their lives. To also have to do that with God makes this whole religious aspect of life seem way out of balance.

- I was raised in a Roman Catholic, Italian/Irish/German household. We attended church every Sunday as a "model" family. I connected strongly to the Lenten "Stations of the Cross" services. The pain and suffering of Christ touched me deeply. But where was "I" in the scheme of religious practice? When I looked at the altar, I saw only men and boys allowed as active participants in the sacraments. I balked. I was not interested in being a passive recipient in the life of the spirit. When I left home, I rebelled—allowing a darker side to develop, in my search for spirit through alcohol, drugs, and sex.

- I identify my sexual orientation as having the most impact on my spiritual development. I am a gay man who has grown up in a culture that hates homosexuals. I knew from a young age that I was different. I learned as years went by to hate myself for my different orientation. As I reached out for spiritual understanding, I learned that if you are gay you are a sinner and will burn in hell forever. My greatest fear was that maybe this is true. Maybe I am not living the way that God wants me to. Everyone hates homosexuals so much, they can't all be wrong. I knew not a soul, through my childhood and adolescence, who spoke kindly of homosexuality.

So I created a deep shell around me and created two personalities: a false personality to put on the mask that would allow me to survive in the world and my true sexual identity that remained in hiding. I learned to stuff it deep down for many years. I used drugs and alcohol to dilute my strong emotions. I was trying to kill a part of myself that I hated. And God was not my friend. He hated me just as I hated myself.

3. *Negative impact of rigid family hierarchy on current behavior*

- Around the age of 12, I stopped talking to my mother because "it didn't matter anymore." Nothing I would say or do would make a difference. I was expected to do what she wanted or said—and stop talking back. I became silent and rebelled with anger directed inwardly by using drugs and acting promiscuously. The "silent treatment" behavior and negative attitude has stayed with me.

- My parents would continuously fight. My mom would run to her room crying and lock herself in her room. My dad would run after her, and when she refused to let him in, he would bury himself in his work. I would sit and listen to them fight behind closed doors, my muscles would tighten, I would get teary eyed, and I would get extremely angry at them, and I would scream silently, "Shut up. Stop fighting. You are always fighting."

  As a result, I would scream and lash out and be completely controlling of my little sister… I despised being near my family. I hated sitting at the dinner table. I would usually sit turned away from the table… Eventually, I would set off my father's temper. He would scream at me and punish me, usually sending me to my room. Perhaps I wanted to make him angry. Perhaps I wanted a way out. Lashing out at others is definitively how I react under stressful conditions.

- When my church said I was born in sin, I knew it was wrong. When my church taught that God is present only in our religion, I knew it was wrong. When my mother punished me for learning a prayer from another religion, I knew she was wrong. When I first felt the ecstatic joy that came with the discovery of my sexuality, I praised and thanked God. Then I was taught that these feelings were bad. Sinful. *I knew they were wrong.*

These explorations highlighted toxic intersections between the ascribed moral authority of the spiritual traditions and their flawed social dominance hierarchies. As students from different religious backgrounds shared similarly toxic experiences, they recognized destructive hypocrisy as a shared human problem.

Critical analysis continues with readings and discussions based on material in Chap. 5. This material includes social science perspectives on the competing functions of the spiritual traditions as sources of *inclusive* secure existential attachment and *exclusive* group social identity, bio-cultural evolutionary perspectives on the role of social dominance hierarchies in human culture, and the neuroscience of the stress and trauma responses in the collective behavior of social identity groups.

STRENGTHENING RELIGIOUS LITERACY: LEARNING ABOUT THE *OTHER*

Students are assigned to investigate a spiritual tradition that has a history of conflict with their birth religion or that they learned to consider *other*. Their papers begin with an exploration of attitudes they were taught, or currently hold, about the tradition. Using assigned readings, they explore the tradition's history, beliefs, and customs, philosophy of social justice, and selections from its sacred literature that locate it within the Perennial Philosophy. They are asked to identify areas of personal resonance. Additionally, they are invited to think critically, articulating concerns and questions for further exploration.

Students consistently identify three traditions as *other*: Judaism, Christianity, and Islam. The following passages illustrate their efforts to approach each tradition with cultural humility, while maintaining critical awareness of problematic dimensions that perpetuate intragroup subordination and/or intergroup conflict:

- A Caucasian American Catholic female wrote:

  > I am from South Florida, where there is a large concentration of Jewish people. My most distinct memory about Judaism came from my world history teacher in high school. I'll never forget his impact on my thinking what it means to be persecuted for your faith. He showed a movie about the Holocaust. I was not prepared for the horror and gravity of what I saw. Most of my class had tears rolling down our faces. Before he showed us the movie, he went around the class and put us all on one side or the other of the room. I had no idea what he was doing. He told us he had just segregated us based upon who would be killed and who would be spared. I still remember being sick to my stomach as I was put on the living side. This is when I understood just how much impact religion can have if you are considered to be in the "other" category.

[But prior to this class] I have had a very loose understanding of Jewish faith and culture. I had friends and neighbors who were Jewish. But it was inappropriate in my family to ask people questions about their faith. I have been to a synagogue only once. I can't even recall why. I distinctly remember not understanding anything that was going on.

- A Latina American Catholic wrote:

   Since I was a child in my native country, the Dominican Republic, I heard a lot of stuff about the Protestant religion. Things like, "Don't listen to people from this church. They are crazy. They do not have a real occupation in life." Such statements were normal from Catholic adults in my community, including my adult family members. But there is also a religion that Dominicans in general think is totally different than the rest: Judaism.

   During the 1930s the dictator Rafael Trujillo opened the doors of the country to accept Jewish refugees. He thought that bringing white skin Jews to the Dominican country, where the majority of people have dark skin, would mix the two races. But most Dominicans did not understand this new culture and religion. The situation got so bad that it was almost a sin to get together with a Jewish person.

   When the Jewish community built its own cemetery, the situation got even worse. From my great-grandparents to my parents it was normal to hear "not to get close to the Jews because they do not believe in God and as proof of that, they do not want to be buried with people who are believers of Jesus' words. Therefore they have built their own cemetery." That is what was told to the children and adolescents, including myself.

- A Caucasian American Jewish female wrote:

   Studying Christianity, I have confronted previously-held, partially-veiled prejudices. I gained an appreciation for the richness and beauty of the teachings of Jesus, and a better understanding of the historical context of Christian Anti-Semitism. It is unlikely that I would have revised some of my negative and incomplete beliefs about Catholicism without the research and sustained reflection this paper provided.

   I have noticed a palpable decrease in my discomfort among Christians. As I mentioned in class, I had a wonderful conversation about Catholicism with the administrative assistant at work. I wouldn't have felt comfortable talking about our beliefs prior to this class.

- A Latina American wrote:

  It might seem strange for me to explore Christianity as the religion I consider "other," when Roman Catholicism has been the path guiding my family for more than 100 years. It was the doctrine fed to my mother and father, from Baptism, First Communions, and Confirmations into early adulthood. My father's parents wanted him to become a priest. This was favorable and prestigious in Catholic families. My father and mother ran away from that kind of life, ruled by the God of that church. That is why I grew up thinking Catholicism was trying to force God on me. God was "the guy" who made my uncle hide that he was a homosexual from our family until the day he died.

  I was comforted to read Huston Smith's book. It offered a pure form of Jesus' teachings and the foundation of Christianity. Jesus was a profound teacher. He lived what he taught at its purest form. I would have loved to sit in his presence.

- A Caucasian American gay male wrote:

  The tradition from which I have felt most apart is Christianity. I was raised agnostic and felt like an outsider in my extended family, as well as with friends, all of whom attended church. Growing older, I didn't have a place in a Christian church because I identify as gay. I have continued to assume that Christianity is anti-LGBT. My lack of knowledge and feelings of "otherness" led me to explore Christianity for this assignment.

  I learned an incredible amount by reading about Christianity. I could identify with many foundational values. I also learned a lot about the life of Jesus. He disliked barriers that disconnect people. He believed that by categorizing behaviors as "clean or unclean," we prevent ourselves from being truly compassionate to our fellow man. Although religion in today's world has been misused to alienate people, including the LGBT community, the original teachings of Jesus urge us to be inclusive. Exploring Christianity has given me the chance to ask questions that I haven't given words to before, and helped me have engaging spiritual conversations with loved ones.

In class discussions, it became clear that students appreciated a trustworthy academic environment where they could acknowledge their socially-sanctioned isolation from the religious *other* and toxic stereotypes they had been taught. But they craved more than tepid tolerance, seeking deeper commonalities among our traditions. Reading about the Perennial Philosophy offered a conceptual template for these common bonds. Their efforts to practice cultural humility, while challenging perceived injustice, were evident in their explorations of Islam.

- A Caucasian American Protestant female wrote:

    Until now, I have held the notion that Islam is a radical religion emphasizing archaic rituals and religious ideals stemming from Biblical times. Generally, I was completely ignorant about Islam: its theology, rituals, and content. I based my opinions on extreme events broadcast in the media: news reports, movies, and documentaries depicting the fanatical sects who claim to represent Islam. In myriad of ways, Islam seemed primitive and overzealous, with no regard for human rights or common sense. With these notions in mind, learning about Islam, a religion so far removed from my Catholic Italian background, was appropriate. This exploration was enlightening. I discovered many commonalities between Islam and other traditions that brought home my great ignorance about this religion.

- A Latina American wrote:

    This assignment has pushed me to dig deeper than I have before into a religion beside my own Catholic religion. I chose Islam. It seems so different from what I grew up knowing about God, yet many of its practices are intriguing for me. I was curious if both religions lead me back to the same God. I discovered that they do.

    "Fasting calls one back to one's frailty and dependence. It sensitizes compassion." This statement [by Huston Smith] is profound. It resonates very deeply with me. I can only imagine the strength gained from such a practice. It also strengthens compassion and breaks down a sense of privilege. About the role of women, culturally, I see similarities concerning how submissive a woman is expected to be. Muslims are clear about a woman's place. In my Latino culture, it is more an undertone and unspoken rule. But as an American I have learned women are as capable, sometimes more capable, as men.

- An African American Protestant male wrote:

   My family and I attended a black Baptist church. Although we were dedicated to this tradition, we did not disdain the belief systems of others, or denigrate them as wrong or dangerous. My parents were respectful, and instilled the same respect in me.

   I had a brief affiliation with the Nation of Islam. Although unfamiliar, I adhered to its daily practices faithfully. But I did not learn enough about this tradition. I enjoyed further study through my course readings, which provided history and specific details of Islam. I have found certain aspects that resonate with me and my Christianity.

   I still have concern regarding the loosely defined term infidel and the concept of Jihad. The present reality is that certain Muslim factions refer to Israel, the United States, and "the west" as infidels, and vow death to them. Unfortunately, all religions have splinter groups and extremists that are abusive. Christianity has not been an exception.

- A Caucasian American Catholic female wrote:

   I attended Catholic school for my early education, and though we devoted a great deal of time to religious studies every day, I did not learn there were other religions. My first realization came when I watched the events of September 11th on TV while my teacher cried frantically into her cell phone trying to contact her parents in the city. Of the many things I learned, the lesson that stood out most was there was an "us" and a "them," and the "them" covered a whole city with smoke and sent bodies crashing to the ground.

   I feel guilty when I think about my reaction to 9/11. I remind myself that I was only 8 years old and didn't understand that the fear mongering was not based in reality. In the months that followed, we had classroom drills where we hid under our desks, but we never talked about why. We learned to fear men in head coverings with thick facial hair, and we were taught not to ask why. We were not capable of understanding institutionally enforced racism or reactionary anger.

   The readings helped me further separate Islam from the stereotypes I developed. What I learned contradicted the "otherness."

Another social teaching of Islam I was taught to think of as "other" was the treatment of women. I was taught that women who covered themselves were oppressed by savage men who hated them. These statements were followed by slogans like, "You're so lucky to be an American woman where you can wear whatever you want." I am lucky. But it is dangerous to apply "us/them" thinking to such a complex issue, when the "us" is a nation rooted in institutionalized sexism. The Koran teaches women should be covered "so that they may be recognized and not annoyed" (33:59). This made me reflect on our cultural norms for women's attire where girls as young as five learn to confuse sexualization and objectification with self-worth. We are taught that our appearance is to please others. The stereotypes I learned are excuses for sexist Americans to act like they care about the advancement of women.

- Another Caucasian American Protestant female wrote:

  I continued thinking about Islamic women wearing covering clothes, and decided not to wear spandex pants while working out. Recently, I felt very uncomfortable after I left my house wearing very tight pants. I ended up turning around, going home, and changing into more relaxed pants. It made a big difference in how I felt. I was mindful of how bare I usually felt and was happy making a change.

These thoughtful explorations extend into our experiential work. Because Islam is so unfamiliar to many students, we listen to a recording of the Muslim "Call to Prayer," with an English translation to allay fears about its content. In most cohorts, students are surprised by its melodic complexity, depth of feeling, and spiritual meaning. But during one class, two students said they *hated* hearing it. When another student asked why, they said it reminded them of a TV program in which suicide-terrorists chant this prayer before embarking. For a moment, there was stunned silence. Then a student expressed frustration with the negative stereotypes reinforced on this program, which many had watched. Then other students raised concerns about Jihad. The conversation became more heated and complex when one student added, "In my childhood, we sang *Onward Christian Soldiers* at church. Christians are filled with our own triumphalism and violence." After several voices of agreement, another student spoke in a plaintive voice, "Oh dear, I used to love that song SO MUCH." The child-like pathos in her voice broke the ice. We began to laugh, acknowledging the comedic absurdity in humanity's tragic chain of pain. As the conversation ended, I addressed the students who had expressed hating the Muslim prayer. I noted that they had initiated this fruitful conversation, thanking them for their courage. The class affirmed that learning requires an atmosphere that affirms the courage to be imperfect.

Exploring Conflict-Engagement Styles and Interpersonal Behavior During Stress

As follow-up to these often divisive issues, I reiterate that interpersonal and intergroup relations benefit when individuals can speak honestly and express overt disagreement, without fear of reprisal, thereby creating safe conditions for dialogue and mutual understanding. Because constructive conflict resolution is a core quality of psychospiritual maturation, the curriculum introduces several experiential activities to help students become aware of, and refine, their behavior during conflict. First, using anonymous sharing, students identify a broad range of responses to conflictual situations:

- When conflict arises, I have difficulty controlling my emotions. It is challenging for me to express my point of view without raising my voice. The emotions cloud my judgment and ability to communicate. I say mean things that aren't always true, especially when my feelings are hurt or ego is bruised. When I don't feel comfortable enough to argue, I bottle up my emotions and take them out on someone else.

- I tend to be direct and blunt. I have a hard time seeing how I contribute to the other person's reactions, through my tone of voice or my choice of words. I am starting to be mindful of my own presence when I'm angry, and to apologize if that is inappropriate.

- I have stayed quiet during crucial points in class discussion because I was nervous about how I would be seen. I regret this, and know it speaks to my larger fear of conflict.

- I HATE CONFLICT!! It makes me uncomfortable and anxious. I used to turn the other way. However, it is a fact of life. I've learned to face it rather than turn away from it. I've noticed that turns down the volume and allows for a more peaceful conversation.

- I need to remember not to run from conflict, pushing it away brings it that much closer.

- I am learning that being angry with someone or with a situation is not shameful and that naming that anger can help to work toward a resolution.

- I am learning to sit with the discomfort of the conflict. I often try to make things black and white, all or nothing, because I feel safer when I can categorize the issue into right and wrong. Leaning into the discomfort of not knowing the outcome is very hard for me.

- I need to learn how to voice my opinion while maintaining empathy and compassion for the counter view. Most of my life I have not stood up for myself in conflict. If others didn't stand up for me, then I was not defended. Learning to stick up for myself, I have found that when I do, I cannot fully see the other person's P.O.V. I am fighting blindly. I need to find a balance between the old me (flight) and the new me (fight).

- I have been growing braver with regard to conflict. In the past I often stayed silent. Now, at the very least, I take a deep breath and let my body relax. Then I consider what would be the wisest way for me to react. Sometimes it is still with silence, or until passions lessen and reason returns. However, more and more I am finding a wise way to respond in the moment. I no longer feel as afraid to make waves. I can better tolerate discord. As long as I keep breathing!

Anonymous sharing normalizes this broad range of responses. As we look for patterns and themes, students identify their fight, flight, and freeze tendencies, and specific ways their stress responses are disempowering.

Students then examine their interpersonal behavior during academic stress, specifically exploring its impact on others. They use an experiential approach, working in trios. Each student is invited, if comfortable, to serve as "the protagonist," while a second student role plays a close friend, roommate, or family member. The third student serves as facilitator/observer. First, the protagonist demonstrates her or his typical interpersonal behavior during academic stress. Using role reversal, the protagonist then becomes recipient of this behavior. Finally, the trios discuss their experiences and learning, and we conclude with anonymous sharing. The following examples illustrate key aspects of their learning:

- I become agitated and irritable. I get angry at others easily and focus on negative things they've done. I also take less responsibility and blame others for my problems. This response is associated with *fight*. I project onto others and become angry with them.

- During academic stress, I want to sell all my worldly possessions and live in the woods. I find myself demanding more alone time (not always respectfully), ignoring phone calls, and "going off the grid" as much as possible. I definitely think this is a *flight* response. When under a great amount of stress, I am always looking for the nearest exit.

- One thing I do is bottle up any feelings of being overwhelmed, frustrated or incompetent. I become snippy and short with others and make the assumption that they can't help me. Even writing this gives me the heavy feeling of holding all of that to myself. This feels like *freeze*, not knowing where to put emotions so doing nothing with them instead.

- I tend to feel overwhelmed. This leads to withdrawal socially. I also become easily annoyed by things my friends do. This annoyance can escalate into passive-aggressive behavior or crankiness. Either way, I end up in a self-induced isolation. This connects to *flight* as I try to distance myself from others, and *fight* when I push them away through passive-aggressive/cranky behavior.

- It was difficult to face myself when I'm experiencing academic stress. It's hard to know that I push loved ones away.

- My wife bears the brunt of my propensity to withdraw under stress. Experiencing how it feels to be on the receiving end demonstrated the need for constructive communication.

- I learned that when I am under stress, I think about my own issues and don't take the time or make the effort to think about others.

- Sometimes I feel like people just suck. My patience is very limited. I have a temper.

Students note the ethical implications of this exercise. When they experience stress, their empathic concern for others shuts down. Whether expressed through fight, flight, or freeze responses, their reactions are self-protective and rupture communication, often hurting others.

At the same time, students recognize that conflictual situations can require protective self-advocacy, including expression of anger and hurt. This recognition highlights the need to cultivate mindfulness and internal composure, to insure that their social engagement systems remain active and their responses to stress do not become destructive or malicious. Such awareness, they recognize, is particularly necessary when they have social power over others.

In Vivo Experiences of Conflict and Restorative Dialogue

As the community-building process proceeds, interpersonal conflicts periodically emerge. Two examples illustrate important areas of individual and group learning, and the role of faculty in these situations.

Example #1: Peer conflicts. As students began their self-inquiry projects, they joined small groups for discussions about their psychospiritual autobiographies and learning. In her essays, "Patty" described bonding strongly with these peers during their first meeting. However, a female student was absent and joined her small group at the next session. Patty had a strong negative reaction to "Michelle," experiencing her as an intruder. As Patty's antipathy grew, she began to ignore Michelle's comments and presence.

As the class practiced mindfulness skills, Patty became aware of her reactivity. Rather than letting her negative responses escalate, Patty used the self-inquiry project to investigate her reactions to Michelle. She explained her learning in a lengthy self-inquiry essay. It began with Patty acknowledging shame she had been carrying from a life-long physical disability:

> I was born with tumors on my retinas, which resulted in one eye turning inward. This has caused me a lot of pain and isolation and shame and helplessness.
>
> When I was little, children would call me names like monkey face or homely. People would laugh at me or do double takes. They often did not know where I was looking or that I was talking to them. I did not have dates in high school, and I attributed it all to this eye. This is a big part of what I bring to interactions with people. I am very wary.

It required considerable courage for Patty to examine her reaction to Michelle.

> When Michelle entered our group, I felt so disrupted… I felt intimidated by her presence, and resentful of the way she came into the group. I was jealous—and angry at myself for feeling that way.
>
> I saw her as beautiful…so in touch with her spirituality…and in touch with her body. She talked about going on dates. I felt unattractive…out of touch with my body and my spirit. My dating days seemed to be over.

Over the ensuing weeks, Patty became even angrier when Michelle began to speak about her own feelings of vulnerability.

> She spoke about the same insecurities I felt about my appearance—even touching on the fact that she too had a lazy eye. I got very angry that she was saying, with all her beauty, that she had a similar problem to me. I felt that she dared to go where no one had dared go before. How could she know anything about my situation? I practically cut her off verbally in order to not hear her pain. But after a while, I realized that…I had not wanted to see her for her, because of the jealousy and insecurity inside me about me.

Patty's realization shifted the focus of her self-inquiry work.

> This opened my experience…and helped me see that this whole thing was not about Michelle. It was about me. She had taken my lazy eye and made it common, and I couldn't handle it at the time. I was forced to see the falseness of my myth of being a defective self. I [had to] acknowledge that I am using it as another reason to ignore who I am, and to speak harshly to myself.

As these realizations took shape, Patty decided to talk about them in her small group.

> We were able to discuss the night that she joined us. I told Michelle that I had felt threatened. I realized that the problem I had was about my feelings. Through this discussion, I faced that it really was my insecurity and jealousy. For me to really see it, as it was inside me, felt good ultimately.

Eventually, Patty and Michelle discussed this experience with the whole class. Michelle had sensed and felt hurt by Patty's dismissive behavior. But she had not known what to do. She appreciated Patty's ability to speak openly and self-reflectively about her feelings. By the end of the semester, Patty and Michelle had developed a strong bond of mutual respect and caring.

Patty engaged in courageous and substantive inner work to achieve this resolution. She recognized her misplaced hostility and took responsibility for it. The significance of her learning was evident: hostility and exclusion can be transformed. Through psychospiritual growth, Patty had learned how to strengthen a peace-promoting culture in our community.

Example #2: Student in conflict with faculty member. Midway through the semester, "Peter" wrote the following statement in a self-inquiry essay:

> The chant we sing in class says that we are love. But my mind tells me that we are the potential for love, and many other things.
>
> When I hear those words… I fall into my awareness of what they have wrought. History's hell unfolds in my mind and I see what those who sing of love have done.

Initially, it appeared that Peter was addressing the hypocrisy and lack of spiritual congruence he experienced in his Catholic upbringing. But it quickly became clear that his statement was a critique of the class. He felt that the songs and curriculum required too much conformity.

> As I further contemplate this rage it becomes clear to me that I am fearful of this class in general. My fear centers around and stems from the dogmatic nature of spiritual teaching in general and the way dogma is used to control behavior… It is the singing of it that binds me to the past. I can't… avoid this interpretation while we sing.

Energized by the strength of his feelings, Peter expressed his anger and distrust in class. This was a moment when I, the professor, needed to listen carefully and maintain internal composure. Several weeks earlier, he explained, he recoiled during my introduction to chanting in class. It sounded as though the class was "required" to sing during our experiential work. This perceived demand made him feel angry and distrustful. The strength of his anger was visible in his tense facial muscles and loud voice.

I knew it was important to regulate my own reactivity to criticism. I thanked Peter for putting this issue on the table with strength and clarity. I turned to the class, reiterating my respect for Peter for having the courage to raise an important issue: the potential for a leader to exert social coercion, a dynamic that can generate justified, negative feelings. I asked if other students had felt similar responses when I introduced chanting in class. Two other students expressed feeling similar concerns, but had not felt confident voicing them. I thanked them for speaking now, and noted to Peter that by speaking for himself, he had spoken for others.

Thus, I realized that my introduction to chanting in class *had* been unclear, at least to some students. Requiring them to participate in this activity had certainly not been my intention. I apologized for the ambiguity I had created and took responsibility for not having clarified sufficiently their freedom not to participate.

Then I asked Peter and the rest of the class to challenge me immediately if any other issue raised their concerns. Peter had made an important contribution to our group process, and I asked them to recognize that I was demonstrating a respectful response to criticism. It was vital that I did not use my power as an authority figure to deflect or silence this interchange. While receiving criticism is not easy, it was important for the class to experience a nondefensive authority figure who could model an attachment solution to a relational rupture.

Ultimately, our classroom interchange had deeper ramifications for Peter. My acceptance of his anger and genuine consideration of his criticism were new experiences for him. In earlier life experiences, he had been silenced by significant authority figures. It had required significant inner strength for him to express his anger at me. My acceptance strengthened his ability to trust his internal locus of evaluation more fully. For Peter, this was a moment of psychospiritual courage and growth that strengthened his confidence in life and self.

At the same time, this experience enabled Peter to trust our community-building process more fully. In a subsequent self-inquiry essay about his psychospiritual growth, he wrote:

> The only way I can see continuing on this path is to find and become a part of a spiritual community that is capable of the kind of nonjudgmental guidance that I felt.

In addition to strengthening faith in himself, this experience helped Peter develop faith in the human potential to build trustworthy communities. In addition, he had learned to identify the qualities of leadership and group power dynamics that make such communities possible.

In summary, throughout the *Know Your Self* curriculum, students learn to approach sociocultural differences, intergroup tensions, and interpersonal conflict as meaningful catalysts for psychospiritual growth. Viewing conflict as an inevitable, potentially positive, aspect of human relations, they learn to approach it with composure, rather than responding destructively through their instinctive stress (or trauma) response mechanisms:

- Historically, I have shied away from conflict. But I was able to address a concern of mine in this class, and it was a positive experience. It is risky to confront conflict in everyday life. It was so helpful to get clarification in our class on how to find safe ways.

- I need to learn when and how to fight for the underdog in society. My experience with conflict has taught me to "mind my own business." I feel ashamed of this part of myself. For example, I didn't know that I was harming society with my inherited white privilege or that I was part of a racist system. I need to be more of an activist.

- I carry a great deal of fear in engaging in conflict. It often is a source of tremendous anxiety for me. I still need to process the whys and hows. But I want to thank each person in this room for modeling how conflict can be healthy and productive. You have given me a feeling of safety because of your bravery and thoughtfulness.

As these statements indicate, when conflict is approached proactively, the learning that students and communities derive engenders trust, respect, courage, and cohesive bonding. These positive group dynamics foster a culture of peace, on both interpersonal and intergroup levels.

From this perspective, the *Know Your Self* curriculum conceptualizes conflict as a manifestation of the *formative tendency*, in which a separation challenge creates the potential energy for human beings to develop enhanced forms of awareness, compassionate attunement to the *other*, and connective social systems. Approaching conflict as a catalyst for psychospiritual maturation can build Confidence in Life and Self, creating the resilience to break humanity's chain of pain, and facilitating movement towards secure existential attachment.

CHAPTER 9

From Self-Regulation to Psychospiritual Exploration: An Introduction to the Deep Structure of Contemplative Mind: Group Case Study #3

This chapter presents the third learning module of the *Know Your Self* curriculum, in which students develop an internal locus of existential meaning-making. First, they identify the existential worldview that fuels their destructive behaviors. Second, they shift the focus of their meditation practice from the development of self-regulation skills to its use as a method for psychospiritual exploration in the deep structure of the psyche. Using Frankl's logotherapeutic methodology, students engage in contemplative self-inquiry during meditation that helps them develop new insights about their attitudes and behaviors, while experiencing connection to a wise, core dimension of self. The chapter presents the meditative methods they use to explore the deep structure of contemplative mind, with narrative data illustrating this learning process.

IDENTIFYING THE EXISTENTIAL WORLDVIEW THAT FUELS DESTRUCTIVE BEHAVIOR

As discussed in Chap. 7, academic stress has already provided students with a concrete focus for the first stage of their self-inquiry projects. They used this focus to examine personal manifestations of the stress response, confront the inner critic, and develop self-regulation skills. In this next step, they identify the existential worldview that fuels their response to academic stress. For example, many students identified their procrastination as a form of avoidant flight. But many found that their newly developed mindfulness and relaxation response skills were not sufficient to break this habitual behavior. It had a stronger psychological grip than they realized.

To understand its tenacity, the curriculum introduces a paradoxical self-inquiry question: students are asked to examine the psychological *benefits* they derive from procrastination. Initially, many find this question confusing. Why look for something "good" in this behavior? But the assignment produces surprising insights. During class discussions, many acknowledge "loving the intense energy" and "focused attention" that they experience during last-minute all-nighters. They generate an exciting, positive state of mind where students describe themselves becoming immersed in the present moment and intensely engaged in focused writing. There is no time, they note, for the intrusive, perfectionistic demands of the inner critic. They must remain in the flow of one-pointed concentration. From a different perspective, other students extol the joyful, relaxed "sense of inner liberation" they experience on rebellious days when they avoid school work. These discussions highlight how much students value these positive states of mind. Some acknowledge that they often self-medicate with ADHD stimulants and marijuana to experience these positive states of mind regularly. In short, these self-inquiry discussions help students recognize that their procrastination catalyzes behavior that mimics a beneficial and highly desired state of psychological well-being.

We then identify the existential worldview that they temporarily achieve when they pull all-nighters, postpone school work, or self-medicate. Several themes emerge: anxiety is replaced by excitement; depressed heaviness is replaced by light-hearted happiness; rather than feeling contracted and tense, they feel expansive and relaxed; rather than feeling isolated and alone, they connect with others; rather than feeling unhappy and stressed, they feel joyful and content; rather than feeling embattled by life, they feel at peace with life. These themes, they recognize, specify the positive existential worldview they want to experience. This understanding helps them reframe their destructive coping behaviors as misguided efforts to achieve a positive existential worldview. By understanding their misguided efforts as a self-defeating cycle of impermanent satisfaction and repetitive suffering, students recognize that the root of their harmful behaviors is yearning for inner contentment, connection with others, and connection with life: secure existential attachment. Thus, students discover links between their problematic daily behaviors and their deepest psychospiritual needs.

This link provides a rationale for investigating meditation as a mode of psychospiritual exploration. The Perennial Philosophy posits a source of insight and wisdom in every person which can help them transform their existential worldview and cultivate behaviors that promote the well-being of self and society. Students are then invited to test this possibility empirically, by learning to practice meditation as a mode of access to their own inner wisdom.

The Deep Structure of the Psyche

As discussed in Chap. 5, meditation is a mode of intuitive awareness that can enhance learning about self and life. From the perspective of the Perennial Philosophy, meditation is an established method for intrapsychic self-inquiry and a replicable route to core dimensions of self.

The curriculum presents the deep structure of the psyche through a psychospiritual model that integrates maps of consciousness from Western spiritual traditions, Eastern traditions, and modern psychology. This model describes four increasingly interior dimensions of awareness: (1) an externally-focused dimension (challenges of daily life that require the development of survival skills and ethical behavior), (2) a subjective dimension (conscious and unconscious cognitive schema and emotions) that shapes daily actions, survival strategies, and ethical behavior, (3) an intuitive dimension (inwardly-directed knowing) that is receptive to insight and wisdom from the core self, (4) a core dimension of self, where the individual ego experiences attachment to a formless, all-pervasive Ground of Being.

In this maturation-oriented model, the individual ego gradually becomes aware of each dimension of consciousness. While the end point of psychospiritual growth is establishment in the fourth state of awareness, it is impossible to leapfrog the others. They are preparatory stages of refinement and growth. In the first dimension of being, the ego learns it is necessary to balance survival needs with ethical concern for the other. In the second dimension, the ego refines cognitive schema and emotional patterns that dysregulate daily behaviors destructively. It learns that these patterns are conditioned by the chain of pain and utilizes this knowledge to disempower their grip on its mental processes and actions. In the third dimension of awareness, the ego learns to draw intuitive sustenance and guidance from the core self, using this wisdom to break the tenacious grip of humanity's chain of pain on its subjective mental states. As growth proceeds, the ego gains increasingly regular access to the fourth dimension of being. Eventually, it becomes established in this fourth state, while remaining actively engaged in daily life.

This fourth state of being has different names in each spiritual tradition. For example, because Jesus lived fully in this state, he explained to his Jewish disciples, "My Father and I are one." Thus, Christianity calls this dimension of awareness Christ-consciousness. But Jesus did not claim sole access to this state. He taught that "the kingdom of heaven" dwells within (Borg 1997; Pennington 1986; Thurman 1971). The Perennial Philosophy teaches that this elevated state of is available to every person (Huxley 1945; Nasr 2007; Schuon 1984; Teasdale 1999).

With this introduction, students develop a meditation practice that is congruent with a meaning-making system or spiritual tradition of their choice. For example, to cultivate mindfulness, strengthen mental focus, and deepen receptivity to intuitive insight, secular humanist students can focus attention on their breathing as a basic rhythm of biological life, select a religiously-neutral word like *peace* as an anchoring phrase, and conceptualize the core dimension of self as a maturation-oriented, formative tendency in the human psyche. Observant Muslims, alternatively, can focus attention on their breathing as a physical expression of the transpersonal life force, select one of the 99 names of Allah as a mental focus, and conceptualize the core dimension of self as God/Allah.

Frankl's Transformative Method of Self-Inquiry

As prelude to meditation that explores the deep structure of the psyche, students read *Man's Search for Meaning* (Frankl 1959). As discussed (Chaps. 2 and 5), Viktor Frankl confronted evil on a catastrophic scale in the Nazi Holocaust. He nonetheless learned to develop a positive existential worldview. In the depth of suffering that he witnessed and endured, Frankl found himself asking, *why is life doing this to me?* But he realized this question had no value: it disempowered him, creating an adversarial rift between himself and *life*. He knew that *life* was not his adversary: human ignorance and ignominy were the cause of Nazi evil. To maintain his alliance with life, he changed the question. He asked, *what does life expect of me as I face this suffering?* Frankl allowed *life* to demand a response that would not degrade him to the level of the Nazis: a response that summoned his human capacity to elevate each moment morally and spiritually. He described brief moments of solitude when he turned within for dialogue with *life*. In this mental sanctuary, he experienced inner freedom beyond the Nazis' grasp. Frankl honestly acknowledged that he could not always maintain this elevating stance. He had no pretensions of sainthood, and described multiple episodes of selfish, self-protective behavior. Nonetheless, he developed a personal mode of contemplation that helped him maintain connection with his core self, inner wisdom, moral capacities, and *life* (Kass 1996a, b).

Meditation: Developing an Inner Sanctuary for Contemplation

Meditation, I explain to students, is the traditional method for creating an inner sanctuary to cultivate this interior connection. The curriculum employs this metaphor literally. Students begin this phase of meditation work by visualizing an inner sanctuary where they can engage in contemplative self-inquiry and cultivate receptivity to inner wisdom. To concretize this process, they begin by drawing an inner sanctuary of their own design. Their images range from special childhood environments to idealized places. We discuss their images as a group, personalizing their upcoming contemplative work.

Students then shift their attentional focus inward. Using progressive muscle relaxation and diaphragmatic breathing, they increase mental concentration. I lead a guided visualization to begin their imaginal work. Upon reaching their sanctuary, my directions become minimal and their contemplative experiences become increasingly spontaneous. This procedure helps them enter the third level of interior awareness, where receptivity to intuitive insights and archetypal imagery increases. After exploring their sanctuary, students locate a place to sit for meditation. During their first introduction to this method, they then practice mindful breathing in the present moment, having learned to use this visualization work as a foundation for meditative awareness.

In subsequent sessions, students further explore this inwardly-directed receptive mode of being. Returning to their inner sanctuary, they are directed to visualize a mentoring presence. This imaginal figure can be a living being, object, or felt presence that symbolizes wisdom for them. Using Watkin's imaginal dialogue methods (Chap. 5), which students had begun to use during their inner critic work (Chap. 7), they enter into dialogue with their inner mentor. To concretize this dialogue, they adapt Frankl's question. Students ask the mentor for guidance that can help them respond to academic stress in increasingly wise, mature ways. Their anonymous sharing illustrates the range and depth of this contemplative exploration:

- It was such a nice instruction to build our own place. We had space to create whatever little safe, warm, wonderful world we wanted, and so this sanctuary that I can return to whenever I want feels more like mine than anywhere I've traveled inside myself before.

- I was able to connect with this exercise because of the slow process we took through the field and down the wooded path. My chosen spot was more sacred and special because it couldn't immediately be accessed. I want to hang my drawing over my bed.

- This was my first experience. I could follow the instructions, but felt disconnected. I believe with practice, I will be able to find my sanctuary and speak with my inner self.

- I was able to see and feel my inner sanctuary. I could feel ocean sand in my hand. Cool and soft. I could feel sunlight on my face and I felt myself surrounded by white light. I saw a flame next to me where I sat on the sand. My inner critic seemed quiet. I had the urge to throw my critic into the flame, but then realized that I needed to be gentle with it. My godfather was my mentor. I could feel his hands on my shoulders. His hands were large and warm and so was his embrace, like when he was alive.

- There was a sense of safety walking through the grove of trees. I felt protected, excited. Then I started to feel myself falling deeper into a relaxed state. Sleep even. I continued to drift in and out... My mentor did not have a face, it was a feeling. It was the feeling I used to get when my grandmother hugged me: safe, protected, loved, and respected.

- I've been through guided imagery before. The difference this time was that I knew where I was headed. Creating the sanctuary ahead of time made it more real and personal when I arrived. Taking on the role of the mentor was the most powerful part of the experience. I was able to speak to myself in a way that I've always wanted someone to speak to me.

- My mind travelled to my sanctuary and when I arrived I drifted in sleep. But I awoke and was facing my mentor. I didn't need to tell him what my inner critic had said. He already knew and just looked at me and said, "You are loved."

- I was surprised to discover that my mentor appeared in an animal form, and that I could even imagine a mentor at all. When Jared asked us to picture a mentor, I had a moment of panic, but then, there she was. It felt strangely natural to have her by my right hand, and very calming. I sensed great wisdom. Later, when we switched places with our mentor, I realized all this was happening within me: a surreal moment of realization.

- When I finally got to my sanctuary, I was able to stay there. My mentor kept changing shapes, but stayed with me as well. I could not visualize the critic, but my mentor spoke to her and said, "It's not my fault." For a person who has a tough time with meditation, this is the most focused I have ever been. I didn't want to leave my sanctuary, but I know the exact path to get back.

- At the pond, I sat on the bank beneath the cherry blossom tree tossing pebbles into the water. I watched the ripples spread and at one point glanced across the water where I was surprised to see a small statue of the Buddha. But that is not where 'the voice' came from. It came from the ripples….

- I found myself somewhere between deep relaxation and sleep throughout this meditation. I had moments when pieces of my sanctuary would come into clear view: the water, the sun on my face. But the images faded in and out of consciousness. The most striking moment was when I saw, I felt, my grandmother's hand on mine. She always hated her hands. She said they were too thin, but to me they were beautiful. She held my hand. We were completely connected. She, my inner mentor, always made me feel secure and deeply loved. It was a privilege to be in this place with her.

As their narratives indicate, the focused attention required by this visualization process was difficult for some students to sustain. Anonymous sharing normalizes this difficulty, while showing students that this skill is achievable. For those who maintained focus, the spontaneous experiences were very meaningful. Symbolic images of the inner mentor assumed forms which were personal and poignant. Students understand that these imaginal images are symbolic. But as they describe their experiences anonymously, the archetypal real-ness of the inner mentor becomes clear. Within the deep structure of the psyche, in the domain Jung described as the collective unconscious, there is an abiding intelligence that can provide support and guidance. Symbolic representations of this inner wisdom never take a "standardized" form. The mentor appears in a representational form that has unique personal meaning for each person.

The Wisdom of the Inner Mentor

The following examples from students' self-inquiry essays illustrate the depth of these experiences and clarify their person-specific relevance:

- In one student's psychospiritual autobiography, he had recognized his stress response as an unyielding, highly competitive personality trait. He found himself standing in a swift mountain stream that was his inner mentor. In this encounter, the mentor challenged him in ways that were illuminating and painful:

  The stream seemed to point out leaves floating on top of the swift water. The lea ves were being carried from point to point on the stream's journey. They had a carefree easiness about them. These floating objects went with the flow of the stream. They were whirling and diving and dancing on top of the water.

  There is a part of me that wants to "dig my heels in" and stand up against the flow. As much as I enjoy feeling the power of the stream, I can't stop It—or slow It down. I am envious of the floating objects that are going with the flow into amazing places, while I stay stuck in the stream testing my strength.

- In her psychospiritual autobiography, another student explored loneliness and sadness that were interfering with her academic studies. Having moved to Boston to attend our program, she had few friends. Initially, she found herself in a place that did not feel like a sanctuary. But as she practiced internal composure, its mentoring presence became clear:

My space is a dark, cold cave. Above me, I see tree roots. They extend throughout the cave, but there is space for me to fit inside. I am cold and it is damp.

The roots attract my attention. I am drawn to their intricacy. They are delicate, yet strong. They nourish a large tree above me that I do not see, but know is there. I trust that the tree is healthy, and don't fear it crashing in on me. I am safe in the cave.

I become aware of the space around the roots, and notice that they have not firmly settled in. Some roots dangle, as they have not yet found their grounding, while others have just newly planted themselves into the earth.

I ask the roots "What does life expect of me?" The answer softly comes, "Be gentle with yourself settling in. Give yourself time and space to find your place, to extend, to grow." I feel lightened, as if given permission to be patient with and accepting of myself. This process causes me to recognize that I have been through a tremendous amount in the last two months. In reality, I, like the tree, have been transplanted.

- Another student explored low self-esteem. Her mentor took the form of a gardener who offered unconditional support, while challenging her tendency to rank herself against others:

He appears after I turn a row of high sunflowers. He's down on one knee digging and turning over the dark, moist dirt. I near him, and he looks up. The sun catches him in the eyes, but he doesn't mind. He smiles a warm greeting.

He doesn't seem surprised to see me. It's as though he knows something I'm not aware of. He goes back to digging with his spade, never saying a word. I bend down to sit on the grass and he says, "I know your question, but you yourself know the answer."

I remained still. I thought about his reply. I knew in my heart he was correct. It seemed so simple here, inside this walled garden. Then I said, "But you know how I begin to feel about myself, how I start thinking that I'm not good enough. I try so hard to overcome it, but it finds a way to catch me off guard."

He kept turning over the earth with his spade, then spoke again. "I am the gardener for this garden. I have seen many different kinds of flowers. Some are thin and tall; others full and bushy; some reach way up towards the sun, others remain close to the earth. Their colors are all different hues as well as their different petal designs and shapes... There are many different eyes who gaze upon them for all sorts of different reasons. Some enjoy the tall, brightly colored flowers. Others find beauty in the flowers who grow out from the earth. So, so many flowers and so many different people will see the beauty and joy in them for a variety of different reasons.

And so it is with you. You have your own unique way of growing towards the sun. A few will want to plant themselves around you but there will be others who will need less sun perhaps and require more shade. You understand?"

I understood. As I began to thank him, he stood up, reached out for my hand, helped me to my feet and he took me in his arms, hugged me with so much love, it enveloped me. "It's time for me to go." He turned to walk down another path of flowers.

When my eyes open, and I am back on my living room floor, my eyes well up with tears. The love remains in my heart, his hug lingers, and my heart is filled with love and joy.

- For another student, the inner mentor appeared consistently as Jesus. Writing her psychospiritual autobiography, she recognized that her stress response pushes her off-balance: she grows frustrated, loses task-focus, and behaves in hostile ways:

My place was a small wooden bridge over a brook that I often visited in high school. After I was able to relax and focus on this place, I sat and took in the surroundings. I listened to the babbling of the brook, breathed the fresh air, and felt the sun shine on my face. Then my inner guide, Jesus, came to me. As He always does, He enveloped me in His warm bright light; the light of truth, love and justice. I felt safe and loved in a way that no one and nothing else makes me feel.

When I asked my question, He smiled and told me the answer is "to love." God, and life, expect me to love myself and my fellows despite horrendous events and circumstances.

Then I left the bridge and came back to the world. When I get caught up in daily living, I forget how important it is to try to achieve, maintain, and project love in *all* areas of my life. I get caught up in relatively insignificant details. I begin to project feelings of anger, frustration and sadness.

This mentoring presence rarely limits itself to supportive statements. Quite regularly, it confronts students with negative or disabling aspects of themselves. It knows them intimately and pushes them to grow. I often note that if a person confronted them so directly, these students would likely become defensive, feeling hurt or humiliated. But they receive this maturational feedback differently. Its source is within them, a core aspect of self that helps them feel known, safe, protected, and loved. They accept its critical guidance non-defensively, with a growing sense of secure existential attachment.

While visualizing the inner sanctuary and mentor can be highly meaningful, I am careful to emphasize that it is an educational device that eventually can be discarded. When students become adept entering the interior dimension of being, the inner mentor can manifest directly as intuitive insight about self and life. Still, during periods of stress, when mental concentration is difficult, visualization work provides a concrete path to meditative states. These archetypes also provide a conceptual frame for understanding the deep structure of the psyche. In the imaginal dimension of being, students can locate a "place" where intuitive wisdom can be cultivated.

As the previous narratives show, this contemplative work helped many students make significant shifts in their existential worldview and experience of self. These shifts led some students to comment directly on Frankl's transformative existential question.

- One student wrote,

    Using Frankl's question often would provide a helpful and useful reframing of daily life difficulties, and major difficulties. It is so easy to get caught in the downward spiral of "why is this happening to me? The world is a bad place, I am bad, people are bad, what is the point?" To reframe the situation to find out what life expects of me, under the circumstances at present, whether I had control over them or not, would help to decrease self-blame and self-negativity, as well as outward blame and negativity. Frankl's question puts things into perspective.

Other students noted that the impact of Frankl's question had been heightened by the deep state of "contemplative mind" they had experienced.

- A student who suffered from a degenerative muscle disease wrote:

  > When I was in this safe place I felt physically and emotionally vibrant. I had no concept of time or space and did not feel pressured to be perfect. This is the first meditation experience I have had which made me feel completely integrated with my inner being and optimistic about life and goals for my future.
  >
  > I was encouraged because I used my mind at a higher level than ever before. I learned that I have the power within me to endure different experiences in life without destroying my self-esteem. This process made me feel confident, more connected to others, and it helped me gain insight into my spirituality. I felt closer to God through this experience because I had no fear of being rejected or punished by Him. This allowed me to have a safe connection and experience with Him without feeling distant or inferior to Him.
  >
  > Using my life as a vehicle for maturation and growth was certainly the first step in transforming my worldview; simultaneously I began to develop a deeper understanding of the meaning and purpose of life through meditation.

In summary, these visualization methods are useful in two ways. First, they strengthen inwardly-focused mental concentration. Second, they provide a framework for understanding the deep structure of the psyche. The intuitive level of awareness is a place within that can be located. Concentrating mental focus within this inner sanctuary, students become receptive to an integrative, maturation-oriented function of the psyche. When they become skilled at reaching this degree of receptive stillness, intuitive insights may arise with immediacy, without facilitation through visualization work, and without visual images. Still, as in dreams, intuitive insights often manifest through nonverbal images, including an archetypal inner mentor, assuming creative forms that have personal meaning for the individual.

Students also understand the paradoxical nature of these contemplative experiences. On the one hand, they are purely subjective and symbolic. On the other hand, these insights include unexpected guidance that they experience coming from a source outside their individual, ego-awareness. Whether they conceptualize this source in the language of science or metaphysics, its personal relevance and reality is clear.

MEDITATIONS ON THE *INNER HEART*

To complete their introduction to the deep structure of contemplative mind, students learn to visualize the *inner heart*. As discussed in Chap. 5, the spiritual traditions describe the heart as the psychospiritual center of being. It is the symbolic term for the core dimension of self where the individual ego experiences connection to the transpersonal Ground of Being: often experienced as radiant light or formless presence. However, the inner *heart* has another aspect. It is encrusted with knots and scar tissue: mental conditioning from humanity's chain of pain. This outer layer of the heart blocks access to its radiant inner core. Visualizing this outer layer and inner core facilitates two levels of psychospiritual work. First, students can have imaginal dialogues with their emotional scars and traumatic experiences. Second, they can pass through the outer layer, imaginally experiencing the innermost, core dimension of self.

Imaginal work with the outer layer, it should be noted, can release intense emotions and memories. These explorations require preparatory growth, as the curriculum gradually provides. Student narratives demonstrate their development of internal composure, helping them tolerate emotional distress without being overwhelmed. Further, the curriculum's psychospiritual model of the psyche provides a positive perspective for processing this difficult material: their traumatic experiences have not impaired their most essential self. *While they may feel shaken to the core by these traumatic experiences, their core self has not been wounded or altered.*

Students with a history of trauma often find it difficult to grapple with this possibility. Some insist there is no aspect of self that has not been harmed. As with all aspects of their contemplative work, I invite them to test these ideas experimentally by investigating the deep structure of the psyche, reaching their own conclusions. Most are open to this experiment.

- One student, a survivor of physical violence, described her first step in this experiment, while experiencing turbulent emotions and hyper-vigilant thoughts:

  I was fascinated by this week's meditation topic. I cannot imagine what it would be like to experience the Ground of Being, or creative source, as within.

> As I attempted to experience the inner depth of my heart, I couldn't quiet my anxious emotions. I leaped from one line of thought to another, without much order. I couldn't let go of errant ideas. I wondered, as I tried to meditate and found myself buffeted, "What would it be like to slow things down to a very slow pace, to truly quiet my mind and reach a peaceful state? What would that tremendous inner peace feel like?"

- Another trauma survivor experienced the outer layer of her heart as a repository of self-doubts. Her contemplation provided a new vantage for experiencing them:

> The word *vulnerability* came to my mind. [It] described the outer layer of my heart... *Vulnerability* describes how I feel about the confusion, insecurities, fear, and self-doubt that I have experienced over the years. But rather than just talking about these feelings, I was able to experience them while also remaining "apart from them," an observer and a participant at the same time.

This new ability helped her experience the inner core:

> I felt a sense of deep peace and relaxation. My whole being felt like it was engulfed in white light. My breathing slowed. I lost awareness of my environment. I lost awareness of my body and became aware of a place within me that is very good at *being*. Anxiety, fear, self-doubt and confusion left, and I felt whole.

- Another student recognized the need to be patient and gentle, while teaching her outer heart to soften its defenses:

> I could see my outer heart as kind of a tough, leathery skin, with scars and kind of dark. But it was protecting my inner heart, which is a bright light of innocence and happiness, and is not afraid to feel good. But my outer heart is afraid to feel good. This journey will take several times before I can release my hesitance: it is involuntary. I felt happy on this journey. If I try to tune into my inner heart more regularly, maybe I can be less afraid to access it, and see what it has to offer.

- For another student, the inner core provided an experience of protective safety:

When I began meditating on the inner depth of the heart, I drifted downward through many layers. Then, I came to a place that felt peaceful. I began to cry.

I didn't understand the tears because I thought I was going to be happy. I meditated on why the tears were occurring. I [realized] the inner depth of the heart was a place of joy and peace—but more important it was a place I felt safe… I would never feel afraid, scared, or be hurt as long as I was in this place.

- Another student experienced her outer heart as a bandage wrapped tightly around wounds. "The journey into my inner heart," she recognized, "will be painful."

I see its outer layers tightly wrapped and covered with gauze. The wounds still exist and are sore. [They] prevent me from "giving life my all." I sometimes feel like a wounded soldier tossed back into battle. I don't want to expose myself to the pain and to allow myself to be vulnerable. The gauze is reluctant to unfold itself and let me in. But the gauze knows it must be removed for the wounds to be properly cared for. With this awareness, I feel I have no choice but to continue to move inwards.

There, she experienced her inner core.

There is an everlasting ancientness to it, and, paradoxically, it is as new as it is old. I can barely contain the excitement within me. I want to dance, to jump, and sing. What a wonderful treasure I have found.

- Another student described a healing process that took place during this contemplation:

The concept of the heart with an outer and inner layer is new to me… The meditation on the heart brought [many]… feelings and images. The image I received focusing on the outer layer was an anatomical-shaped heart, with thick black around the edges. It was charred like burnt newspaper that looks crisp, yet crumbles when you pick it up. This is indeed the place of scars, wounds, and bondage.

When I began to move more inward, I remember having a thought of not really believing there was a place.

Then I received another image within the charred heart. There was a small red and pink flame in the center, reminding me of a candle in an underground cave. I suspended my censor, my critic, and my disbelief, to allow this image to unfold. I slowly brought more and more of my attention there, hearing words that informed me that this is a place of peaceful stillness that always exists in a state of wholeness.

- Another student wrestled with this concept during several contemplative sessions:

This "heart" was not the physical organ inside my chest cavity. It was a sort of seedpod. This seedpod definitely had an outside layer and an inside layer. The outside was a textured hard skin. The color was sort of a dark purple-black...

The outer layer of skin opened like a door and inside I saw a bright yellow gold energy ball. It was glowing and brilliant—very bright. The ball stayed inside the shell of the seedpod. The definition between it and the inside layer was clear. The outer layer looked like solid material and the inner layer looked like energy.

In her next contemplation, the same image appeared again:

Slowly, I began to relax and calm down. I looked for the outer layer of the heart. The same image appeared. I could see the outer layer. It all looked and felt familiar.

I stayed there for a time and then proceeded to the inner layer. Again, the outer layer opened like a door and the glowing, yellow-gold sphere was revealed. This time, I reached out to touch it. Just as I suspected, it was rubbery feeling. It pressed in where I touched it, but bounced back out as I let go.

Then for some unknown reason, I poked it with a pin. Out of the pinhole shot a whole bunch of gold sparkle dust. It looked like confetti. When I looked back to the pinhole, worried that I had done damage, I saw that it had "healed" itself. The hole was gone. There was no trace. "Wow!" I thought. "It really can't be hurt." There was my answer to why I had poked it. I didn't believe there is a part of me that isn't and cannot be hurt.

In subsequent sessions, or at home, students deepened this contemplative exploration through imaginal dialogue between these layers of the inner heart.

- One student wrote:

   It was easy to get in touch with the outer layer. I immediately became aware of pain and hurt I have experienced. I imagined myself holding my heart and comforting it. I could actually see it. It was smaller than I thought, and fit easily in the palm of my hand. As it began to tell me of its pain, I could see images flash before me. Most of the pain has to do with losses in my life. I had the image of being in the emergency room and hearing the doctors telling me my father had died of a massive heart attack. My dad never had a problem with his heart, so this was a complete shock to my family. Images kept coming of other losses. I could feel my heart crying and crying, actual tears were coming out of my heart, and I could feel pain in my chest. I focused on allowing the pain to release and just flow out, and I continued to comfort and hold my heart as it cried. It was quite a moving experience.

   Slowly I became aware of…the core of my heart. At once I saw a sparkling light, almost like diamonds, covering a very small heart inside my heart. This inner heart gave off a silvery, shiny light. The feeling was one of happiness and contentment and strength. The light from my inner heart completely surrounded my outer heart and slowly melted the pain, so that all I could see was my outer heart being covered in this sparkling light. I could still feel tension in my chest, but there was also a feeling of strength.

   After this meditation I was feeling several things all at once: tired, rested, sad, happy, and stronger. All these feelings were going on simultaneously, and it felt strange. I also had the feeling of "knowing" that my inner heart really exists, and is the part of me that keeps me going, that helps me to survive the pain and suffering. And the thing that stands out most is this overwhelming feeling of "strength" within me.

- Another student, after meditating at home, wrote:

   I did stretches and deep breathing exercises, shut off my light, laid down on my bed, and prepared for this journey. I allowed the painful feelings on the outer layer to surface. Sadness and loneliness paid a visit as well as fear of being alone. I could feel the pain in my heart as it rose to the surface.

My eyes began to tear. "This was why I didn't want to do this meditation," I thought. "There's so much here...so much."

I stayed with these feelings for a few minutes and began to comfort my heart. I became aware of the healing energy of my inner heart, and I began wrapping my heart in a ribbon of white light. This ribbon enfolded the sorrows and pains that lay at the surface.

But this nurturance was difficult to accept, as though "there was a war going on" within her.

[Then] I heard a voice, this time from my core, the Spirit of Life within me: "I am always here for you. I will never leave you. I love and accept you exactly as you are. I will never reject or abandon you. I am here whenever you need." I felt a sense of peace and relaxation, as though a loving parent was nurturing me, letting me know I am all right; that I am loved and held in secure and sacred arms. I felt held in a most profound way.

Other students recognized the need to inhabit their painful feelings more intentionally.

- One student, who was learning about the impact of her mother's death, wrote:

During this meditation, like last week, I had difficulty connecting with my inner heart. I am aware of its presence, but struggling with pain in my outer heart. The pain of losing my mother when I was younger has influenced communication between the two layers. I am afraid to access my painful heart for fear that the pain will go deeper, to a place where I cannot defend myself...

After last week's meditation I felt very sad. I realized that underlying my general state of anxiety is sadness. I wanted to escape this sadness by calling a friend to come over and distract me, but I decided to sit with it, as difficult as that was. I felt better afterward, but I am still left with a feeling of sadness and a deep longing...

If I am unable to feel anything but sadness, I must give myself over to that. There is no avoiding the moment. That is what was reinforced for me in this meditation. I am not yet comfortable accepting [her] death, but I feel this is part of my current journey.

Through these internal dialogues, students learned to experience and understand their emotions from a new perspective.

- One student wrote:

    These hurts and pains are part of me, but do not define me. Every one of those original dents is still there. They are simply integrated into a more healthy coping mechanism. I can never make those pains go away, but I can soften their impact on my life. I am who I am because of all these bumps and bruises on my heart. I have known on an intellectual level that I am who I am because of my life experiences. But it has never been as clear to me that my core being can integrate and comfort all of my hurts and pains. To know that I have the capability to go inside and connect with my core is a gift.

These contemplative explorations create opportunities for transformative psychospiritual growth. When students understand that their core dimension of self is radiant and unharmed, they can approach their psychological wounds from a new perspective. These wounds are very real, requiring acknowledgement and healing. But when students understand that they need not be defined or controlled by these wounds, they experience a new ability to integrate them. Over time, this process confers genuine perspective: these life experiences are never forgotten, but they are no longer triggering sources of dysregulation. As this internal composure gradually deepens, they can reside more fully in the attached experience of their core self.

I will note again that students understand the symbolic nature of these contemplative experiences. While they offer glimpses into the fourth level of unitive awareness, they take place in the third level of awareness, where intuitive insights and spontaneous archetypal images offer preliminary knowledge about the deepest dimension of self. Nonetheless, their imaginal explorations of the inner heart and glimpses into the fourth level of awareness are profoundly healing. As students understand and experience the deep structure of the psyche, they learn about a core part of self that can help them break their personal links in humanity's chain of pain. This new resource becomes a source of sturdy resilience.

As discussed in Chap. 5, contemplative work in the deep structure of the psyche requires caution. Imaginal experiences can be distorted by grief and anger inherited personally or collectively from humanity's chain of pain. Primitive protective responses and instinctive fear of the *other* embedded in the unconscious can be triggered. The spiritual traditions recognize this possibility. They insist that preparatory work is necessary, mentored by a teacher who has faced these challenges. Character development is required, prior to visionary experience, in which distorting cognitive schema and emotions are examined (second level of awareness) and individuals learn to balance their survival instincts with moral behavior and ethical concern for the other (first level of awareness). *Know Your Self* incorporates this awareness in its conceptual and experiential approaches to psychospiritual growth. Teaching meditation as a method for psychospiritual exploration into the deep structure of the psyche can facilitate important new capacities for resilience and secure existential attachment. But these deeper applications of meditation must be approached cautiously and mentored carefully.

When mentored through this ethically-oriented, character-developing perspective, contemplative experiences will not become exclusionary or distorted by anger and grief from past experiences. Rather, they become an inclusive force, strengthening compassion and community. Anonymous sharing highlights this inclusive quality of growth:

- I am learning that people are resilient. We seek loving attachments and have been hurt deeply by unhealthy attachments. You can create your own community of belonging. Unconditional love is our collective desire.

- I am taking in the humanity from this process. Whether devastatingly painful or immensely joyful, we share the same basic needs. We are all connected.

- Our experiences are our own, but we share a sense of commonality at the same time!

- Hearing from other people about their experiences is giving me a sense of belonging and less isolation with my own life events. I have felt warmth and respect for the bravery of my classmates not only for sharing, but that we are each here despite difficult odds. It has made me wish I could take a little more of a risk in what I share and how I trust others.

- My developmental timeline helped me visually see the factors that have contributed to who I am today. Hearing about others' positive and negative influences lets me know that I am not alone in this group, but also not alone in this world, even when my inner critic would like to make me think I am.

- Our group process affirms the power of sharing stories. Hearing my experiences, and reading those of others, dropped the group into a place where we could begin the work, and start the healing process. We are not alone, we have survived, and we will overcome.

Conclusions

Chapters 7–9 have illustrated three learning modules in the *Know Your Self* curriculum. These modules overlap, generating synergistic learning that contributes to person-centered psychospiritual maturation. While insights that occur during psychospiritual explorations in the deep structure of the psyche are profoundly transformative, their impact depends on disciplined commitment to probing self-inquiry; the cultivation of psychophysiological self-regulation skills; critical analysis of cognitive schema and socio-cultural narratives that distort perceptions of self and *other*; and the ability to approach conflict and differences as a catalyst for psychospiritual growth. Thus, writing a psychospiritual autobiography and participation in culturally-diverse learning communities are essential preparation for seeking contemplative wisdom and insight.

References

Borg, M. (1997). *The God we never knew*. San Francisco, CA: HarperSanFrancisco.
Frankl, V. (1959). *Man's search for meaning*. New York, NY: Simon and Schuster.
Huxley, A. (1945). *The perennial philosophy*. New York, NY: Harper Brothers.
Kass, J. D. (1996a). Coping with life-threatening illnesses using a logotherapeutic approach, 1: Health care team interventions. *International Forum for Logotherapy, 19*(Spring), 15–19.
Kass, J. D. (1996b). Coping with life-threatening illnesses using a logotherapeutic approach, 2: Clinical mental health counseling. *International Forum for Logotherapy, 20*(Spring), 10–14.
Nasr, S. H. (2007). *The garden of truth: The vision and promise of Sufism, Islam's mystical tradition*. New York, NY: HarperCollins.

Pennington, M. B. (1986). *Centered living: The way of centering prayer.* New York, NY: Image/Doubleday.
Schuon, F. (1984). *The transcendent unity of religions.* Wheaton, IL: Theosophical Publishing.
Teasdale, W. (1999). *The mystic heart: Discovering a universal spirituality in the world's religions.* Novato, CA: New World Library.
Thurman, H. (1971). *The inward journey.* Richmond, IN: Friends United Press.

CHAPTER 10

Individual Case Studies of Psychospiritual Maturation: Autobiographical Inquiry and the Deep Wisdom of Contemplative Mind

This chapter summarizes the psychospiritual growth of 10 individual students. They were selected to reflect the broad range of behaviors that students examined during their self-inquiry projects, and the diverse sociocultural identities and belief systems in the student cohorts. The qualitative analysis of students' behavioral change goals identified four domains that undermined their well-being and academic success: social-emotional impairments to academic performance, health-compromising attitudes and behaviors, impaired relational skills, existential struggles and spiritual alienation. The students presented in this chapter learned to use difficulties in these four domains as catalysts for person-centered psychospiritual growth. Chaps. 7–9 explained the experiential learning processes in the curriculum. This chapter will focus on two elements that were particularly significant for their individual work: writing a psychospiritual autobiography and practicing contemplative self-inquiry during meditation. Autobiographical inquiry examined personal, familial, and sociocultural factors (including religious upbringing) which helped shape their behavior. During this process, students developed the capacity for empathic self-reflection and learned to reframe harmful behaviors as unsuccessful efforts to develop a positive existential worldview. Using this autobiographical focus, they engaged in contemplative self-inquiry through meditation, cultivating access to the deep wisdom of contemplative mind. Each case study summarizes their autobiographical work and contemplative experiences. The chapter concludes with an analysis of their growth in the five dimensions of psychospiritual maturation.

© The Author(s) 2017
J.D. Kass, *A Person-Centered Approach to Psychospiritual Maturation*,
DOI 10.1007/978-3-319-57919-1_10

Social-Emotional Impairments to Academic Performance

Procrastination

"Mary Ann": Undergraduate, 25, White, Practicing Roman Catholic
Mary Ann was an undergraduate whose academic work had been interrupted by family crises. Having returned to school, she desperately wanted to complete her degree. But she was struggling academically. In her first self-inquiry essay, as she explored her reasons for taking this class, Mary Ann hypothesized a connection between her weak study habits and high stress levels. She noted that spirituality had been important to her periodically, though she now felt cut off from it. While Mary Ann did not consider herself lazy, she consistently procrastinated in her work. When trying to apply herself, she experienced physical and emotional tension. She also noted that whenever she got sick, it coincided with a period of stress.

Psychospiritual Autobiography
Writing a structured psychospiritual autobiography helped Mary Ann explore these issues systematically. She had begun college at age 18. Although academics were a struggle, she had managed to complete the first 2 years. Then two events interrupted her studies. In her junior year, her fiancé was diagnosed with a terminal illness, and she took a leave of absence to care for him. Soon after his death, her parents divorced. Disoriented by these painful events, Mary Ann extended her academic leave, taking an administrative job with a local business. She had finally returned to school, but procrastination was undermining her academic progress.

Mary Ann was a "practicing Catholic and a fairly regular churchgoer." She had loved "the ritual of receiving communion" as a child, but found church attendance less meaningful as an adolescent. When her fiancée became ill, she experienced a resurgence of spirituality, but the intensity of the connection she felt with God had gradually diminished:

> Losing a loved one was hard enough, but feeling I had lost God was devastating. I tried going to church to regain the feeling of connection with God, but that did not work.

Examining her procrastination through mindfulness and the relaxation response was a new experience for Mary Ann. She realized that she "avoids working on a task to forget about the pressures that I feel associated with it," but that "feelings of incompetence only intensify when I rush to meet a deadline." Visualizing a stressful academic situation deepened her mindfulness skills:

> I was never consciously aware of the feelings I have, until I looked within myself while we meditated. I was surprised to discover the level of intensity I felt associated with my procrastinating behavior. I could feel the same tension and anxiety in my body that often occurs when I am scurrying to complete a project. My bones stiffened, my skin seemed to shrink two sizes, and I felt as though I could burst into tears at any moment.
>
> The thoughts I experienced are what surprised me most. I consider myself a confident person. But during this meditation, all I could think about was how inadequate I was. When I experienced the anxiety associated with my procrastination habits, I thought things like, "I can't do anything right," or "What's the point anyway?" I was shocked, but at the same time knew they were my actual thoughts. It scared me to realize I could have such a low opinion of myself. I still feel that way.

Through meditation, Mary Ann was learning to recognize and tolerate her distress, rather than avoid it. Then she was assigned to explore the psychological benefits of her procrastination.

> The idea was strange. I was not going find good feelings. Isn't addictive behavior all bad? I never stopped to think that this addictive behavior must provide me with some gratification. I was surprised when I realized how much comfort I receive. I enjoy the control I have when I postpone a task to enjoy an activity of my choice. I feel a weight lifted from my shoulders. I am free for a while.

As Mary Ann shared these insights in class, she was surprised to learn that other students identified with her. This bonding reinforced her growing capacity for empathic self-reflection. She now understood that her procrastination truly was *not* laziness. Rather, it was an effort to experience a positive existential worldview. During her fiancé's illness and parents' divorce, she had lacked a feeling of inner freedom and calm. Her procrastination embodied this need. Mary Ann had previously tried to overcome this behavior with more disciplined study habits, but now understood why this strategy had failed. As her distorted and distorting perceptions about self and life changed through her self-inquiry process, Mary Ann was eager to engage in a deeper level of contemplative exploration.

Contemplative Self-Inquiry During Meditation
During the first meditation, her mind was in turmoil. She could not visualize an inner sanctuary. Nor could she believe that she had a wise presence within her. But this didn't matter, she explained in her self-inquiry essay. She "already knew" what life expected of her. "The answer seems crystal clear. Life expects me to stop feeling sorry for myself and do something about my procrastination." She did not express awareness of the harsh judgmental tone in this statement. But when she spoke about her experience in class, she realized that her mental turmoil and inner critic had undermined her meditation. Discussing this problem helped her approach the next meditation with greater composure and receptivity.

> When I began to see my safe place, I was very surprised to find it was not the place I intended to imagine. I had been thinking of the ocean, its exciting waves, the crashing noises they make. I had thought about sitting on a large rock, on a warm, sunny day.
>
> Surprisingly, I found myself imagining a small, quiet body of water. The entire image was dark—not dismal, but not bright—and the lake was so still it barely moved. I could feel myself wrapped in a large blanket, watching… Perhaps the image I have described sounds dreary, but it was actually very calming. I felt warm and safe…comforted…and empowered with a great deal of confidence.

It is not clear whether Mary Ann's inner mentor was the comforting blanket or the unseen presence that had wrapped her in it. In either case, she then wrote: "For the first time, I think I can work on this area of my life with a successful outcome."

Learning to rest peacefully in this sanctuary, Mary Ann began to explore her inner heart.

> I really enjoyed this meditation in which I concentrated on the Ground of Being within the innermost regions of my heart. I could feel my chest expand fully as I inhaled. It filled not only with air, but with love, peace, and

happiness. As I exhaled, I could feel the core of my heart pushing through the outer layers, as though struggling to emerge. It sounds strange but I felt a really powerful sense of control—and yet it was as though my thoughts and feelings were on auto-pilot.

This contemplation became an unexpected and important spiritual experience.

I could feel the inner part of my heart in my diaphragm, chest and throat. I expected it to feel smaller because I imagined it within my actual heart. But it was larger. It seemed to take over my insides. It was strong, powerful and bright. I could not see its brightness. It simply felt bright. It was a good force fighting for control over less positive influences.

I felt energized and on top of the world. I felt alive and whole. It is hard to describe how I felt. These words seem inadequate, as I put them on paper. It is difficult to describe such a strong feeling. There are no words to express what I felt. It was an incredible feeling. I really felt connected, yet I can only guess as to what I was connected.

Feeling this powerful energy within her, she also had a new experience of self:

I began to feel as though I were truly myself, only better. It was as though I was as good as I could possibly be. I did not feel bad for not concentrating as much as I should have, and I did not worry about all that was going on in my life. I simply relaxed and marveled in these wonderful emotions. I do not think that I have ever felt more positive or in control of my life.

In a subsequent session, Mary Ann engaged in imaginal dialogue between the core and outer layers of her heart.

[At first] I could not concentrate on the outer layer that has experienced my hurts and pains... Instead, I moved past it to the inner layer. I felt a great sense of energy. I felt happy and alive. [Then] I tried to speak to, and soothe, the outer layer of my heart. I tried to make a conscious effort to view my experience from an outside perspective. (I cannot believe that I just typed that. I am amazed to realize that I was once so skeptical about these experiential exercises and now I am suggesting to myself that I view my experience from an "outside" perspective.)

> It was as though I could look at my past through someone else's eyes. I was well aware of the situations that had caused me pain, but unaware of the pain. The only explanation that I can offer for not feeling the pain is that I was in the inner layer of my heart that is filled with love and untouched by this pain.

The inner resources and wisdom that Mary Ann was learning to tap had practical implications, as she learned in her next meditation.

> With final projects approaching, I have not been able to relax much lately. Trying to relax for this particular meditation was no exception. I had been thinking long and hard about topics that I would discuss in these papers. I was particularly worried about my "Fine Arts of Boston" final paper. Thoughts of tasks I needed to complete flooded my head. I concentrated harder until I managed to stop making mental "to do" lists.
>
> When I finally began to relax, I had a few moments where I experienced a quiet stillness inside. All was calm. I could feel my head drop slightly as though a weight had been lifted. I could feel my breath flow deeply from my head to my abdomen and back again, following the same cycle over and over. Then I realized that I had come up with an idea for my Fine Arts of Boston paper. For days, I had been racking my brain looking for a topic and now I had one. And it was good!

Self-Evaluation of Learning

In their closing self-inquiry essays, students assess their learning. Mary Ann began by reviewing her spiritual growth.

> This course far exceeded my expectations. I not only learned about other religions, I learned a lot about myself. When I began the meditation exercises, I was very skeptical. When you introduced singing and chanting, I felt so silly that I almost wanted to laugh. But each time I completed one of the exercises, I felt great inside. I felt alive and happy like I have not in a long time.
>
> This class and my meditation practice has taught me how to get back in touch with God. I have realized that God is a part of me and present all the time. Before, I would say my prayers diligently. But they felt empty. Now, I feel more like I am speaking with God. I feel like I am praying for a purpose and not just because, as a good Christian, I should.

Then she examined her behavioral learning goal: reducing procrastination. She now recognized the destructive impact of her unrecognized, deeply embedded, inner critic:

> This self-inquiry project has helped me tremendously. It has helped me to get in touch with feelings I did not know existed. I have trouble forgiving myself when I fall short of my expectations. This semester, I have made remarkable improvements in this area.

Through intensive autobiographical and contemplative self-inquiry, Mary Ann had identified and reduced significant social-emotional factors that were impairing her academic progress.

Pressure to Overachieve and Somatic Symptoms of Stress

"Kim": Graduate Student, 23, White, Alienated Roman Catholic
Kim was taking this class "to gain new perspectives." Although she enjoyed her studies in arts education, Kim felt overwhelmed by her program's performance demands. She described feeling despondent and exhausted, trying to "keep up with assignments, handle the professional responsibilities of a practicum, find time to work in order to pay rent, and attempt to spend time with family, friends, and boyfriend."

> There are always things to do, people to see, and work to complete. There are not enough hours in the day. This causes me stress. All these activities are great; I get satisfaction from each. It is balancing them that makes me crazy! Whether it is headaches, intestinal problems, or just plain exhaustion, my inability to smell the coffee has had a negative impact. I guess I should say I am in need of stress management.

Psychospiritual Autobiography
Exploring her life history helped Kim articulate a series of complex, interrelated issues. Her problems with stress had begun in college.

> During my senior year, filled with change, the chaos of applying to graduate programs, and stress fulfilling my BFA requirements, I developed intestinal problems. I had difficulty eating, digesting food, and was often up most nights with abdominal pain.

> Eventually I saw a doctor, went through a series of tests, and was told I had severe gall stones. Two weeks before my graduation, I had my gall bladder removed. Two weeks after that I moved to Boston. A week after that my family moved further away from me, to a new state. Needless to say "change" was a theme in my life.
>
> Unfortunately, my symptoms did not subside. Two years later, things have not really changed. Ultimately the doctors have diagnosed this as irritable bowel syndrome, a disorder that involves involuntary spasms in the intestines.

Kim was scheduled to take more medical tests. But her doctor had told her firmly that her current symptoms were stress-related. Kim realized that she needed to confront her stress more proactively. She already knew that deep breathing helped. She had taken this class to learn more about the mind-body-spirit connection.

Kim had another reason for taking this class: guilt about her "lack of organized religion."

> I was raised in the Catholic faith, but have had difficulty accepting some of its practices, well really most of them. I never felt comfortable going to church when I didn't feel anything spiritual in the experience. It was more of a duty that needed to be completed. At the same time, I really felt a void in my life, and still do.

As she reviewed her religious upbringing, in her essays and class discussions, Kim criticized the hypocrisy she had experienced in her church.

> Growing up Catholic meant going to CCD classes where teachers scared the shit out of you. I remember one teacher telling us that aborted fetuses were used in shampoos. It was terrifying to contemplate washing your hair with dead babies.
>
> Growing up Catholic meant I was dragged out of bed Sunday mornings to attend mass, hoping that there would be a cute altar boy, or at least some *cool* people in the pews. It was a social thing. What families were there? "Oh, Mr. O'Leary is here with his kids, but where is the Mrs.?" It meant being a Eucharist minister because I was popular, not because I had a strong sense of Catholic faith.

Growing up Catholic meant dressing up on holidays and leaving for church an hour early to ensure our family a good seat.

Growing up Catholic meant accepting my best friend's mother being refused communion after she divorced her alcoholic, abusive, adulterous husband. Another friend, who was pregnant, and told the priest she was not sorry for having premarital sex, continued to receive communion. Maybe because her mother ran an important church committee.

As Kim expressed outrage with strength and clarity, other students shared similar experiences. Feeling less alone and despondent, she affirmed, "It bothers me that I should feel guilty for not practicing a religion. I am more a Christian than these folks will ever be."

This shift toward a positive self-concept helped Kim explore her responses to academic stress. Practicing mindfulness, she noted thoughts that made her feel driven and anxious:

> I have this belief that I must, at all costs, accomplish everything on the day's agenda. It is so hard for me to allow myself time to just sit and be. In the back of my mind I know there are a million things I "should" be doing.
>
> It is hard for me to accept that there will *always* be things I *should* be doing… that the world won't end, people won't be disappointed, and I won't be a "bad" person, if I can't do it all. I guess I am a workaholic. An overachiever? Probably that, too.

Kim then explored how she developed this "overachieving" behavior.

> It comes from a belief that I can do a good job and trust myself to get the job done right. Does this mean I don't trust others? This *is* my belief, due to past experiences. I rely only on myself. Maybe I push so hard, so I won't let myself down.

These insights clarified that she was the source of her unrealistic performance demands, and the feelings of exhausted inadequacy they generated. They also helped her identify an avoidant coping behavior that she had never recognized:

> I am a Bargain Shopper. And proud of it! Since I can remember, people have either praised or joked about my ability to find cheap items. This has been a helpful skill. Even in junior high I remember friends coming home with two sweaters, two skirts, and two pairs of jeans to start off the new school year. I, on the other hand, would have a vast variety of items to mix and match, as well as to transition into the different seasons!
>
> Shopping helps me escape into aisles of colors and shapes. There are no expectations, no questions, and no time frame. No one will be hurt if I choose blue instead of red, and no one will be disappointed if I wait a week to buy the stereo system. Shopping allows me to make decisions that will not intensely affect my life. It's a nice escape from reality.

Then she added, humorously,

> What if I viewed life through the eyes of a Bargain Shopper, making thoughtful decisions along the way, but not worrying that the world will end and others will be disappointed by what I choose. I never knew I had a reason for my "Bargain Shopper's Syndrome!"

As the self-inquiry project helped Kim achieve such novel insights, she became increasingly engaged in the process.

Contemplative Self-Inquiry During Meditation

Kim had begun to combine self-inquiry and meditation effectively as a means to cultivate mindfulness. Nonetheless, the existential orientation of Viktor Frankl was new territory. Still, she approached this contemplative exercise with receptivity and intense mental concentration.

> I really tried to allow the images to come forth. At times I caught myself questioning them—even trying to change them. My "ego" didn't understand the process. But, I allowed the images to answer my question, and I was amazed, and deeply touched by what I saw, heard, and felt.
>
> I envisioned a fort I had built as a child when I lived in Maine. It was my safe place, nestled in the green of the pine trees and the song of the birds. It had rock steps leading to the entrance and soft moss pillows that I used to lay on. I waited for a guide to appear.
>
> I heard the wood quietly crack behind me. Without turning around, I felt the presence of Lester, our next door neighbor lobsterman. He seemed old and wise to me, smelling of fish, with something gentle to say. At first I was

startled by this image. What the hell was an old smelly man doing in my meditation? I was even a little scared so I asked—to whom I don't know—if I could have Max, my old cat, instead of Lester.

She appeared around my neck and provided a deeper sense of safety. I then allowed both Lester and Max to be my guides.

Max's presence provided the secure attachment that enabled Kim to follow Lester.

> No one spoke as we walked through the wood to the lobster shack Lester had built right next to my home. We stood amongst the empty traps, as he started to rummage in his small garden. Then I asked him, "What does life expect of me?" He did not answer. So I asked him for any advice. Still nothing. So I asked him what life had expected of him. He replied in his strong Maine accent, "Well, to go fishing, to be a good man, ya' know family and such, and to go pick blueberries once and awhile." I then looked to Max and asked her the same question. She did not move her mouth, but I heard her thoughts say, "Silly, I'm a cat, I can't talk!" Then she wrapped her arms around my neck and gave me a hug. She always used to do this.
>
> I was left with a sense of peace and fulfillment, and it wasn't until I was coming out of the meditation that I realized the magnitude of what I had just experienced.

Then Kim began to reflect on the meaning of her contemplative experience.

> The simplicity of fishing, the connection to nature, the flow of water…are my thoughts about Lester's first statement. His second statement about family is self-explanatory. It fits very well with my own beliefs. Maybe I need to focus more on fostering my family relationships, to be able to take the time for those I care about. Picking blueberries is something Lester did with my Dad and brother…and something I did recently.

These rich family memories felt connected to her recent experience. The previous summer, visiting her aunt in Maine, Kim had a constant "desire to pick blueberries." These hours of solitude in nature "brought me closer to the Ground of Being." Then she realized that she had recently purchased "blueberry face scrub, something I have never done before." Kim then understood that her shopping purchases might have deeper symbolic meanings she had not understood. Then she unpacked it further.

> I wonder if Lester's suggestion wasn't so much about blueberries, but rather a symbol for the experience I had [in Maine]. It could be a reminder to allow myself to "transcend," for lack of a better word, every once and awhile.

Taking the form of Lester, the wise presence within Kim had answered Frankl's question, *What does life expect of me?* She realized that she needed to transcend her stressful life periodically, nourishing relationships that were important to her and communing with the Ground of Being.

In subsequent sessions, Kim explored the inner heart in the imaginal dimension of self.

> I focused on my breathing. Once I was stable and relaxed, I let the images come. [Then her mind asked]: Am I creating these images? Or is something providing them for me? Part of myself or a Higher Power? I tried not to judge, and just see what was before me.
>
> I imagined the outer, painful layers. I felt the feelings that corresponded to my memories of painful events. I felt regret about the loss of my dancing career. I experienced the loss of my family moving away, the sense of abandonment. I felt my boyfriend's betrayal, and saw myself lying on my bed crying hopelessly. I felt the weight of my daily stress.
>
> I struggled to push myself through these layers. It was very tough. I never thought I'd get through! I imagined a person walking around a ring, chopping at it, stomping her feet, as if she was trying to break through to find the center of the heart. Then I heard a voice, a voice I've heard before that is my own, yet it is also empowered by something else. It is a clear voice, one of wisdom and strength. It said, "Don't try to fix things. You have the strength to accept the pain and simply move on." It kept saying, "You have the strength, you have the strength, you have the strength." It was interesting because each time I felt a painful situation, I thought of ways to "fix" them; join an adult dancing group, write a letter to my family, confront my old boyfriend.
>
> But once I allowed myself to let it all go, I felt silent tears drip down my face. I'm not sure why, but there was this feeling of release, as if a large weight had been lifted. I couldn't change what had happened, so why should I try to hold to these things anymore.

Kim realized she had the strength simply to bear her painful emotions: "I felt like a doorway was opening in the ring. I would be let through to the inner heart."

It grew quiet and still. I fell into a deeper inner place. Then I began to see a yellow sphere. It was a core, glowing with warmth and hope. Little people were dancing around it, their faces filled with happiness. They began to raise the sphere to a higher place for all to enjoy. Then it became the sun.

Slowly, I came out of the meditation, catching the last glimpses of the sun as the images dissipated. I wanted to stay there. Nevertheless something had changed.

Self-Evaluation of Learning
Kim began by examining her behavioral change goal: stress reduction.

As the semester winds to a close, the work piles higher and my stress usually increases. Yet, this year, it feels a little different. I have a quiet sense of calm about me. I know there is a load of work to do, but I'm assured it will get done. Actually, the less I stress about it, the more productive I seem to be.

She also commented on her avoidant stress coping behavior:

I haven't been shopping in a long while. I'm not sure if it's because my needs are being fulfilled by other means, or if I just haven't had the time. Whatever the case, I have been able to reduce my stress. I turned in a paper late, and the world didn't end! I am coming to accept that I can't do it all, and no one is expecting me to.

Finally, she reflected on her psychospiritual growth.

I think I'm learning to take life less seriously, but also to view life as a serious thing. It is a great opportunity not meant to be missed out on because I spend time worrying and struggling to get everything completed. This awareness has become clearer as I allow time for relaxation and enjoyment, especially through meditation.

Through proidance of conflict, she realized, access to her inner wisdom, Kim reduced her internal pressure to overachieve, developing internal composure, resilience, and a more engaged relationship with life.

Health-Compromising Attitudes and Behaviors

Unhealthy Diet

"Deanna": Adult Undergraduate, 34, African American, Inactive Baptist
Deanna was studying African cultural history. She took this class to learn about health education and address personal health issues. She hoped "to prevent the occurrence of high blood pressure and stroke prevalent in my family." She wanted "to change her diet radically," reducing her intake of high-fat foods and sugar.

Psychospiritual Autobiography
Deanna was raised as an African American Baptist. But as she explained in class, and her first self-inquiry essay, she no longer attended church. She was searching for a "spirituality that felt right" for her. This search was "private," she explained emphatically. Her primary focus for this class was learning about health.

Deanna used the structured assignments of the psychospiritual autobiography to develop new insights about stress in different areas of her life.

> I experience stress in three major areas of my life: my family, my partner, and work. These separate areas have one thing in common, my relationships with other people.

In relationships, she had begun to realize, she had difficulty expressing her "true needs."

> I am more concerned with how others will see me and how my behavior will affect them, than how their behavior is affecting me.

Rather than expressing her needs, she would retreat. As Deanna visualized this behavior, practicing mindfulness, she noted that she became "frustrated and angry with myself."

> My physical response is to internalize the stress which results in upset stomachs, and headaches. Behaviorally, I shut down and remove myself from the situation. I become sullen and non-communicative, causing people to describe me as moody and avoid me. Their response leads to more anger and

frustration, as I do not want to be silent and brood, yet cannot tell them how I feel. This is especially true in my family.

Exploring the roots of this behavior, Deanna realized she had learned to turn her anger inward as a child. Her family avoided conflict.

In my household, which consisted of my parents, siblings, grandmother and two aunts, the motto was, "For a peaceful life, do this or that," or "Why make a fuss?" We had to accept what was dealt to us, and make no fuss over it. Disagreements and anger were patched over without resolution. Sometimes they were forgotten. But sometimes they erupted into fierce quarrels which created rifts in the family. As a result, my family communicates on a superficial level. They are more concerned with outward appearance of unity, rather than true communication and heartfelt solidarity.

Deanna's avoidance of conflict, she realized, was also connected to her family's legacy of racial trauma. Watching white classmates "stand up for their beliefs" without fear, she became aware that she "envied" them. But she also "distrusted their sincerity." It was unfair that they had learned to assert their needs, and she had not. She described hopeless feelings, shaped by her experience as a woman of color with limited financial means and constant stress.

My distrust of people and their motives is amplified when I am under stress. At these times I feel that life is unfair and not worth the effort. Then I begin to focus on all the negative aspects: working in jobs you hate just to pay bills, dealing with people you don't trust and who don't trust you, going through the motions of living only to eventually die.

As Deanna began to examine these reactions in class, students joined her by discussing ways that social inequality and systemic racism create hopelessness, anger, and feelings of isolation. Deanna also recognized how these feelings affected her health.

I care less about eating healthy during these periods and find that I do eat more junk, skipping healthy meals. I did not realize that my moods affected the way I ate.

Based on the stressors in my life and my reaction to them, my existential worldview is one of distrust in people and a lack of hope that we can ever change the way the world is today even to save ourselves.

Deanna noted that hopelessness and distrust had been governing her attitudes for many years. She wanted to change their impact on her daily behavior. She examined her behaviors and history with probing honesty and deep insight.

> I am addicted to running away when faced with conflict. My running could at first be described as simply withdrawing from interaction when I was younger. As I have grown, it has become more pronounced. At the age of eighteen, I moved out on my own. My relationship with my family was not good, nor my relationships with other people.
>
> But I did not see this at first. I spent many years on the move, changing addresses and roommates or partners, frequently. After the breakup of a painful relationship, I left the state. My thinking at the time was that I needed new surroundings. The real reason was to get away from my past. I changed states three times, ending up back where I started, in Boston. My reason for returning was feeling cutoff from my family. Deep down I missed them. How ironic. But I felt that I was stronger and could now be myself and create the kind of relationship I needed with them. Presently I am involved in conflict with them, and have resorted to my old way of coping—minimal communication.

Nonetheless, Deanna could identify psychological benefits from her avoidant style.

> It allows me the space I need to regroup. I feel a certain respect for myself that I know when to withdraw. This demonstrates and reaffirms a sense of inner strength and control over my life. My anger also forces me to examine these events, and find a reason.

This reframing helped Deanna see herself more positively. Her ability to withdraw from conflicts, and her commitment to self-examination...

> ...shows my resolve to use these experiences as tools to find a better way of dealing and communicating. Otherwise, they become unproductive, futile. Traveling around the country, experiencing other communities, people and

cultures I found a new strength within myself. I found confidence and the ability to care for myself and others in new situations. I found that I could rely upon myself to be responsible, caring, and productive.

But her positive self-concept and worldview felt fragile.

I have allowed my old ways of dealing overshadow all that I learned about myself to the point where I am beginning to wish that I could be someplace else. I do not know how to find this person again, without the old behaviors, but this self-inquiry work has helped.

Contemplative Self-Inquiry During Meditation
Deanna was familiar with meditation as a tool for self-regulation. Though not familiar with Victor Frankl's work, she also understood reformulating stressful situations into potential sources of meaning. She had also practiced visualization techniques. As contemplative self-inquiry began, she moved rapidly into imaginal dialogue with an inner mentor she already knew:

The image of a house came into my mind—a place I created several years earlier. In this place, safe from intrusion by others, there is my teacher—who is neither male nor female, young nor old, black nor white—but any and all, depending on the situation. A gentle person who takes time to make sure that I understand as I learn.

I tell my teacher what has been going on in my life with my family and my feelings of frustration, anger, and loss of hope. I ask the question "What does life expect of me as I face this challenge?" And my teacher responds, "What do you think life expects of you?" My teacher has often explained that my truest learning comes from within me, that I already know the answers to the questions I ask.

However, after a few moments, her inner mentor surprised Deanna by challenging her directly:

My teacher points out that my reluctance to look at this problem means I am afraid of seeing the part I play in my family dynamics. I am afraid to see myself through my family's eyes, or face being responsible for some of the miscommunication.

> My teacher asks me to replay the last event and look at how I failed to express myself in a way my family would have understood. If I had, maybe they would have respected my feelings and I would have retained my dignity.
>
> I express feeling that my family is robbing me of my adulthood and returning me to childhood. My teacher asks why I am afraid for my family to see me as an adult.

This unexpected confrontation precipitated a seismic shift in Deanna's worldview.

> I began to realize that Life expects me to be true to myself, take the risk, speak my feelings, stand up for myself.

As her contemplation ended, Deanna realized that her mindset had shifted.

> I feel refreshed and reborn. I am usually a positive, optimistic, and hopeful person, and this exercise helps me to reclaim that state of mind. It helps me confront myself and sort out my feelings. There will probably be times in the future when I will need the guidance of my teacher. I am glad that I have remembered where to find it.

A week later, she was still reveling in this contemplative experience:

> I reread the last paper. Part of me was amazed at the depth and clarity with which I spoke about my feelings. Never before have I had such insight, or I should say, never before have I expressed with such honesty the feelings I keep inside.

Later, Deanna explored the inner heart. This symbolic representation of her psyche was new to her, but made sense. She began "peeling away the layers of the heart, and became aware of hurt, anger and pain." Then she realized she was having difficulty moving "beyond the layer of pain," demonstrating her psychological insight and mindfulness skills:

> I want to linger. It is necessary for me to acknowledge the events that created this layer. They have created the person I am today. But I urgently feel it is

important to get beyond them, to experience the core of my being. Still, I am reluctant to disturb this layer. It serves as a protective armor.

Finally, after focused concentration, she found herself in stillness at the core of the heart.

Once I envision the center of my heart, I realize that it does not need protection from the outside. It is beyond the reach of this mortal world. I feel totally at peace here.

When I think about life after experiencing this joy, I see how senseless many of my worries and cares really are. If we could all know the inner core of our being and experience the joy and peace that emanates from it, life in this world would be different. I realize that I allow myself to become distracted by the everyday grind.

Then Deanna engaged in imaginal dialogue between the layers of the heart:

As I examined the outer layer I found that I had no choice but feel the pain and relive the events that caused them. I had always thought before that, in order to heal, one should let go of the past. That included bad memories of times when I was hurt by others. Reliving these events usually caused me to remain trapped in their power. I had to reassure myself that this process was a way to grow beyond the pain. This was probably the root of my reluctance to undergo this self-inquiry process.

On some level, I use this layer of pain as protection for my inner core. I see the layer of pain as a hardened shell around the most vulnerable part of me. Any examination could find cracks and chinks that would leave the core unprotected.

Deanna realized that her defensive stance was no longer necessary or helpful.

Many of the thoughts and ideas expressed in this class leave me reassessing the way I have looked at things for many years. Finding strength within the place I thought needed protection makes me realize I am stronger than I had thought.

This realization prepared her for another level of healing. In a subsequent meditation, she experienced early memories and wounds.

> I found scars that were very old—too painful to touch. But I could allow myself to look at them and know their source. These scars were placed on my heart during childhood. The pain they represent is very strong and present in my life to this day. These scars surround my memories and experiences with my father. He was not violent, but would resort to verbal abuse and critical comparison. His coldness left me hating him and myself. He died when I was 11, leaving me insecure and angry. That insecurity has followed me all my life, and is the basis of my personality.

But in a subsequent contemplative exercise, she experienced the possibility of healing.

> As I allow the warmth from my core to melt this scar, I have a sense of the person my father was—and I understand better what his life was like. The pain and anger melt as the scar melts. I feel a sense of well-being enveloping me. I feel that my father is at rest and that I can let the pain of our relationship go. As a child I had no voice and missed the opportunity to ask my father why he did not love me. As an adult I have used that misplaced chance to withdraw from situations when I feared confrontation, when I feared seeing myself through someone else's eyes.
>
> I will draw on the strength which comes from the spirit of life within me to develop my skills of communication, accepting conflict as healthy and necessary in relationships.

Self-Evaluation of Learning
Deanna noted that she had planned a "radical change" in her diet. But when she cut out all high-fat, high-sugar comfort foods, she felt "deprived." She associated many of these foods with her sociocultural identity. As her self-inquiry work diminished the power of her inner critic, she recognized that her "radical" approach was self-punishing. She began to eat these foods "in moderation," feeling "new respect for the person I am becoming."

Deanna also affirmed her psychospiritual growth:

> I have made great steps in my journey to myself by experiencing the inner core of my being. I learned not to fear laying open old scars that exist upon

the outer layers of my heart and revisiting events that caused their formation. This allowed me to hear what my heart had to say through its layers of pain. Some of this was very painful and I resisted the attempt to go beyond the surface. I now know that I am a being of energy and light which radiates from the Spirit of Life. I am part of the spirit of life.

These multiple areas of growth had helped Deanna develop new relational skills and a more resilient worldview, characterized by confidence in self and life.

Cigarette Smoking

"Jessica": Undergraduate, 21, Caucasian, Inactive Protestant
Jessica was an International Studies major. Exploring her reasons for taking this class, she noted that she grew up in a Protestant home and "went to Sunday school every week." But she stopped attending church regularly in high school. She still considered spiritual development an important goal. "Without it, life could turn out to be unrewarding." But spiritual growth was not her primary goal for this class. "My spirituality will happen when I'm ready." Rather, she wanted to understand why she could not stop smoking cigarettes.

Psychospiritual Autobiography
Jessica reviewed her smoking history, explaining that she had tried to quit and relapsed numerous times. She wanted to identify the underlying factors that kept her addicted.

> I have been smoking for about six years now. My main reason for starting was the social aspect. I smoked with friends. Now, smoking has become a stress and coping habit.
>
> I find it impossible to quit. I know the damage that smoking causes, but I often overlook those dangers. Smoking already has a huge impact on my daily health. There are times when I can't stop coughing or sneezing. Also, it decreases the efficiency of my immune system. Most winters I'm sick for the entire season. Sometimes I'm not able to complete my school assignments or go to work, because I get ill. But I continue to smoke.

> My addiction happened so slowly and sneaky, that I didn't even know I was addicted until I found myself not being able to live without smoking. I have tried to quit several times, but all attempts have failed. I always tell myself, "next month," or "as soon as I graduate." This is only putting off the problem until later. I've tried hypnosis, cold turkey, and weaning myself down. None of these methods have worked. I'm starting to feel hopeless and helpless.

Examining her current stressors, she had several important insights:

> The stressor which impacts me most is schoolwork. But if it was my only stressor, I could deal with it. I work two jobs each week, 30-40 h, and take six courses.

> These stressors have a definite impact on my health-related behavior. I'm so busy that I don't have time to care about quitting. Quitting takes an enormous amount of energy. I also use cigarettes as a reward system. I often say, "I have worked so hard all day, I deserve to smoke more than I usually do!"

Jessica also recognized that these pressures affected her cognitive and emotional functioning.

> When I'm bombarded with many stressors all at once, I have a hard time focusing. Everything in my life will constantly race through my head...

> I feel as though life is passing me by, that there is no way I can catch up with myself. I can't find the time to do anything. Often, I can't even find the time to sleep. This makes me view life as unfair. Sometimes I ask myself, "Why am I putting myself through this? I feel as though I'm not going anywhere!"

Still, Jessica thought she had a positive worldview, in contrast to her mother.

> I try hard to be an optimistic person. A smile on my face. This makes me feel better, as well people around me. I take things as they come and deal with them from a relaxed perspective. There are too many pessimists in this world, like my mother. She is an extremely stressed out person. Organized, on the go, has to get everything done ASAP.

Jessica did not note dissonance between her harried description of her stress-filled life and her self-concept as an optimist. But as she explored the psychological benefits she derived from smoking, she realized that her optimistic worldview was, in fact, fragile.

> I often have feelings of inadequacy and depression. I am alone, reaching for the comfort I find in my cigarettes. I could ask a friend for comfort. But they are under the same amount of pressure as myself. I could reach for a chocolate bar. In the end, I always feel worse because chocolate will make me gain weight. I could seek comfort in a significant other. But, to tell you the truth, I don't have the time or energy to invest in anyone except myself. I give myself no other choice but to find comfort in my cigarettes.
>
> From the information I have just gathered, the positive feelings I receive from smoking suggest the worldview I would like to have. I'm continually trying to obtain a feeling of comfort and understanding. I try to hold on to something that is constant, such as cigarettes, to give me this feeling. When I don't have this comfort, I reject myself—which then leads me toward a path of depression.

Exploring these issues in her psychospiritual autobiography and class, Jessica recognized the relational and existential isolation she was experiencing at college. In my role as faculty mentor, I spoke with her individually during a class break to determine if she was in a genuine psychological crisis. She was able to assure me that she was not. She explained that the self-inquiry writing and group-sharing provided a structured format that helped her examine her feelings of loneliness. They also helped her understand her addictive behavior.

Contemplative Self-Inquiry During Meditation
Meditation, visualizations, and Viktor Frankl's existential perspective were new concepts for Jessica. Still, she approached them receptively. Mindfulness and elicitation of the relaxation response helped her stay centered while exploring her autobiographical material and smoking addiction. Perplexed that she could not break her own chain of pain, she was intrigued to think she could gain access to a wise part of herself.

> What does life expect from me as I face this difficult semester? This is one of the most puzzling questions I've ever had to ask myself. The meditation had interesting results.

Her description of her encounter with an inner mentor, recalled in the present tense, suggested how vibrant this meeting became for her: On a road in the woods…

> A rabbit comes hopping by. This is no ordinary rabbit, more like an Easter bunny rabbit. The creature is extremely cute and furry, and hops around with spunk. He greets me with a warm smile, but before I can reply he summons me to follow. I'm completely down on myself, following his footsteps sluggishly. After a couple of seconds I begin to cheer up because of the rays of sunshine and happiness that illuminate from my friend.

Despite being "cute and furry," the actions and guidance of this rabbit were hardly childish.

> I have a feeling he already knows the question I'm going to ask him. My friend brings me to a spot where I can see myself, as well as bits and pieces of my life. Both of us stare down in amazement. I start to panic, and my rabbit friend can see it in my eyes. If he didn't start to talk, I would have started to cry.
>
> My friend had me look at everything going on in my life. Then he said, "Take every piece of your life one step at a time. Take it slow and you will be able to accomplish everything you set your mind to. You will learn a lot when this semester is over. But remember, only do it for yourself! You are the only person you need to please."
>
> I understood what the rabbit was saying, but I had one burning question. "What if I fail everything I've worked so hard to achieve?" My friend gave me an answer to that, as he had done for the first question. He said, "You will not fail! You are completely capable of every task you have taken on. Just remember, you are the only person you need to prove yourself to." After his last words he hopped away ever so cheerful and confident.
>
> I walked back down the peaceful narrow road. The most exciting part was the smile that radiated from my face. I felt a warming sensation inside, almost as if a heat wave came over my body.

Jessica had experienced an unexpected challenge to her need for external approval and support.

The inner heart was another completely novel idea. Yet she understood intuitively the symbolic meaning of exploring its outer layer and inner core.

> The outer layer of my heart is rough and weathered, torn and well used. It's been through a lot. It's a stern old person who has spent years dodging, absorbing, and experiencing pain. It has kept up a stern face because it's afraid to let down its guard and reveal it is soft inside. It doesn't want to be rough and up tight, but a child who is free and lovable.
>
> The outer layer can hear the child pleading, "Come let's play. Please play with me." The child splashes around in the water, hidden in a sea of sunlight and mist. The child can't feel the pain the outer layer feels, but only joy, everlasting love, and friendliness.
>
> The outer layer is mad because it is the one who has had to endure and experience the pain. But, as it listens to the inner layer, it realizes that it too can experience happiness… It can hear the child saying over and over again, "We will always be together. We will be best friends forever and ever. We will never be apart."

Later, Jessica wrote about the emotional turmoil she had endured. The inner heart metaphor helped her begin to put words to her life experience, for the first time.

> I have always had the ability to keep my outer layer strong and tough, as though it were leather hard. I don't acknowledge when I feel pain. I let the pain bounce *off* me as though my outer layer was water resistant.
>
> I never gave the inner layer permission to come forward, because I assumed the outer layer could take care of itself. It didn't need help. The outer layer and the inner layer never connected, though the inner layer tried. But every time the inner layer tried to comfort the outer layer, the outer layer shot it down. The inner layer didn't even try to help anymore. They became separate entities, unable to help each other.
>
> Until recently, this was always the case. Until the outer layer couldn't deal with the pain and suffering it dealt with for so many years. The outer layer was so sad because it had worked so hard to become strong. It had never anticipated that a breakdown would occur, or that it would ever need the help of the inner.

But it was bound to happen at some point... The outer layer was not as strong as it had once thought. Because of this, all the pain that it had felt over the years, all the pain that it had kept deep inside was let go. The outer layer was now extremely vulnerable to pain and suffering. It could never get by without the help of the inner layer.

Recognizing the significant emotional pain that Jessica was now accessing, I consulted with her again after class. Jessica demonstrated resilience once again. I heard confidence in her voice, as well as sadness. Nonetheless, I suggested that she consider contacting the university counseling center, explaining my concern that this one-semester class would not provide enough time or opportunity for her to complete the important learning process she had begun. Jessica acknowledged that the outer layer of her heart was feeling very vulnerable, but didn't know how she could start to explain this to a counselor. I suggested that she share her self-inquiry project with the counselor, assuring her that the professionals at our counseling center would understand the psychospiritual elements of this learning process, and support her in drawing strength from the inner layer of her heart. Jessica agreed to consider this, but asked if I thought that she needed to leave our class. "Absolutely not," I replied. She was handling this self-inquiry project very well, making wonderful progress in her learning, and contributing to the group learning process in important ways. Jessica was relieved.

In the next contemplative dialogue, Jessica continued to grow in strength and insight:

> The inner layer spoke soft and calm, realizing the pain the outer layer was suffering. The inner layer knew that the outer layer had been suffering for years, but until the outer layer accepted help, it couldn't have done much. Why do people allow this pain to build until it is too late and a breakdown occurs? The outer layer and inner layer would have been so happy if they had worked together. Now they are there for each other, together as one. They will never be separate, only friends.
>
> It isn't too late for the outer layer to gain back the confidence it once had. It just needs to accept what has happened and graciously take help from the inner layer. How hard can that be? But it seemed so impossible before.

In the final dialogue of the heart, Jessica continued her courageous healing journey.

The link on the chain of pain that I chose to dissolve was one that has been with me for way too long. I have been deeply hurt by this link.

As I brought the flame from my inner core toward the scar, it began to melt. I felt great joy and happiness. My heart felt stronger than ever.

The scar didn't want me to become the person that I want to be. It held me back as long as possible. But now I have hold of the scar. It can no longer make me feel bad or inadequate. It doesn't have the power it once did, and will never have that power again.

The scar never thought that I could do that. It never believed I was strong enough... Instead of the scar laughing at me, I can now laugh at it. I actually did, out loud, in my meditation. And the scar didn't even try to fight back. It knew its time was up.

These contemplative experiences, of course, were not the completion in Jessica's healing journey. Rather, the self-inquiry project had provided her with an important first step.

Self-Evaluation of Learning

I did not stop smoking. I wish I had, but I didn't. What was most helpful for me was realizing where my addiction stems from. I have an empty spot that needs to be filled, that smoking helps to fill. Smoking helps me see the world in a positive light. Now I know that I don't need to smoke to have a positive view of the world.

I learned a lot from this course. Most important, I learned that I am able to melt the scars that have formed on my outer layer. The inner heart is much more pure and powerful than the outer. The inner heart has not been hurt, and has the power to mend.

I want to continue to develop a positive worldview. I still have a lot to work on. It will be a long process. Still, my overall ways of thinking have changed. I now look at life's problems as, "What can I do to make the best of my situation?" My old way of thinking has changed. Before this semester I would always ask myself, "Why is this happening to me?" I will not do this to myself any longer.

I have learned that I am an extremely spiritual person. Being spiritual was an aspect of my life that I have fought with for years. My inner self has congratulated me on the great job I have done this semester. It knew that I could do it, even when I doubted it myself.

Jessica had begun a new and empowering learning process. She discovered a core place of strength within herself, building confidence in life and self. Though she did not stop smoking, she had begun to build internal resources for future success.

Alcohol Dependence

"Erin": Graduate Student, 25, Caucasian, Inactive Presbyterian
Erin was training as a mental health counselor. She worked in a community program for teenagers, attending classes at night. Her first self-inquiry essay indicated that she felt a great deal of confusion about her spirituality and wanted to explore it.

Psychospiritual Autobiography
Erin began her self-inquiry work by reviewing her limited religious upbringing.

> As a child, my only churchgoing was for familial milestones, which generally occurred at a Presbyterian Church. In my house, God's name was generally used only in vain, and there wasn't a sense of spirituality. I struggled with this issue in my interactions with friends. I didn't understand *how* they could believe in God, and they wondered how I couldn't. Still, I felt envious of their faiths, their families, and whereabouts on Sunday mornings. I felt like I was missing out on something, especially since my home life wasn't offering anything really positive to believe in.

> Once in a while I tried to believe in God. I joined a religious charity group in high school, vowing that I believed in "the one, true, and living God." But I never did. And I often wondered how, if there was a God, he could let this world be so terrible.

Several years earlier, her nephew had been killed by a drunk driver. Since then, "Existential confusion has dominated my life."

Erin was very quiet during the first class. In the second meeting, she mentioned the death of her nephew. After class, I expressed condolences for this tragedy and asked to check in with her. Based on the learning agreement for self-inquiry, I wanted to see if this class might be too intense for her. Erin indicated that she had been in counseling since her nephew's death and was coping reasonably well. She agreed to discuss this issue with her counselor. They decided she could handle the class; and Erin managed this self-inquiry process very well.

Interestingly, Erin hadn't chosen a behavioral change goal in her first essay. She wanted more time. She didn't reach clarity until she completed reviewing her religious upbringing.

> These topics seem to be coalescing. While thinking about my spiritual development, I have relived some pretty unhealthy things I have done in my life. Fortunately, I am in a better place than years past. I have never thought of these issues in terms of spirituality, rather as reactions to family problems, societal pressures, and depression.
>
> My topic will be cigarette smoking. I quit smoking six weeks ago. I have smoked off and on for seven years. SEVEN YEARS!!! I'm having a hard time even writing this! Obviously I'm in a bit of denial about the whole thing!
>
> Smoking cigarettes has been a habit of many family members. My grandfather smoked for years and died of lung cancer. In high school I smoked with friends, but never bought a pack. In college, I smoked occasionally—until my "summer from hell." Then I *really* started, smoking "non-socially," and feeling like I "needed" them.
>
> I often describe myself as a "stress" smoker, a "while drinking beer" smoker, and a "peer pressure" smoker. I have used this to minimize it. But I have been fooling myself.

In the next essay, Erin explored family and sociocultural identity factors which have shaped her psychological development and stress coping mechanisms.

> My family is an ongoing source of anxiety. Our relationships have been tumultuous—filled with intense alliances, coalitions, and triangles. We live from crisis to crisis. This is connected to our working-class, Irish background. We live with secrets, emotional distance, shame, and alcohol—all of which create stress. Of course, in keeping with our ethnic heritage, we have always maintained a good sense of humor.

I hold a lot of muscle tension in my neck, shoulders, and back. My behavioral responses have been to drink alcohol and smoke cigarettes. My sister and I talk a lot about this. We feel like we are victims in many situations. I think this is part of our Irish, working-class paranoia that "everyone is trying to screw us!!!" We often joke about this.

This worldview is pretty understandable given our lives. We have been hurt by our father and oppressed by economics. My trust in my family declines by the year as new secrets are revealed. My trust in men has been shattered several times. After my first major heartbreak, I set myself up for even more bad decisions about dating. My basic distrust has affected my ability to have faith and to establish trusting relationships with people. I explored this issue in my counseling.

Exploring the psychological benefits of this behavior, Erin made a courageous choice. "While my chosen addiction is cigarettes, I really need to look at how I use alcohol."

Alcohol has had an enormous negative impact on my family. My father's alcoholism caused me a lot of pain as a child. He wasn't a staggering drunk. But his temper was unpredictable and authoritarian. As a child, I didn't connect it to alcohol. When my father told me that he is an alcoholic, when I was nineteen, I was surprised. Even I was in denial. His relationship with alcohol allows him to distance himself from issues that he needs to work on. When I talk to him, he is in a kind of fog, unaware and uninterested in the conversation. The bottle keeps him from dealing, keeps him from feeling.

I began drinking when I was around seventeen, mostly wine coolers. It was fun, it tasted good, and it made me feel silly. I liked that. In college I discovered cheap beer and vodka. I liked that too. I liked going to parties and getting silly with new friends.

Now, I like to come home from work and open a beer or bottle of wine to unwind. At twenty-five, my drinking has changed. I party a lot less and drink more to relax.

Then she identified the positive worldview she sought in her life.

How do I feel while engaging in this addictive behavior??? Good question. I guess I feel happy. I feel more focused and easygoing. I don't like being uptight and grumpy. When I drink socially, my attitude is that the world and its people are fun and enjoyable. I feel like I am funnier, more competent, and more attractive. When I drink alone...I feel looser, freer. I like to kick back with a beer while I clean and listen to music. I guess my worldview during these times is that the world is fun and my troubles can disappear for a little. I feel like there is order and meaning to life. I feel more calm and secure.

Erin's autobiographical work catalyzed a difficult process of probing self-inquiry. As the normalization of the group learning process helped diminish her inner critic, she became more honest with herself, shifting her self-inquiry focus to alcohol dependence. This process also helped Erin identify the positive worldview she sought. She wasn't sure it could be attained, but understood the value in trying.

Contemplative Self-Inquiry During Meditation
Meditation was difficult for Erin. Her mind often felt too tense and distraught. But as she developed an intellectual understanding of the mind-body relationship, she worked hard at developing self-regulation skills. She appreciated eliciting the relaxation response through mental concentration. Mindfulness was more difficult because she experienced turbulent negative emotions from childhood. But Erin was motivated to deepen her meditation practice, as a way to access inner wisdom. She was intrigued by Frankl's existential orientation because she and her sister often asked, "Why has life done this to us?"

> As I discussed before, I have found myself playing the victim and am working hard to change that. On a day to day basis, maintaining a positive attitude is difficult.
>
> With my group [of adolescents at work], I often leave school driving like a maniac, and swearing at passersby. It's difficult to calm myself down. In my last group meeting, I got very upset with the guys.
>
> This is the scenario I focused on during our meditation. The group was still very fresh in my mind. I visualized a flat rock hidden in a cove near the ocean in my hometown. I used to visit this spot often with my dog, who recently died. He was the logical choice to ask my question, "What does life expect of me as I face this very difficult challenge?"
>
> His response was relayed through his eyes as he looked at me with understanding and love. This is something he always gave me in his short life. His love and understanding had always been therapeutic for me. And this was my

answer for my group: Love and understanding. That is what these kids need, not my futile, angry reactions.

But reducing reactivity and maintaining internal composure were difficult for Erin to sustain. When she tried meditating at home, her mind and body often felt too tense and turbulent.

The metaphor of the inner heart gave Erin hope. She was intrigued to consider that she had an inner, unharmed core—that her emotional scars did not define her. But exploring the deep structure of her mind was not an easy process.

> I tried it three times, but only once got close to feeling what I was looking for. I dissected my heart, layer by layer. Each piece I broke away from the outer layer represented a painful experience. It took forever. I kept peeling and peeling, breaking and breaking, waiting for a breakthrough to the inner layer. I didn't know what I would find if I got there—or if I would know when I got there.
>
> Then I felt a burst of light. It was strong, radiating. And it was still and calm.
>
> I stayed there for a short period of time, until layer by layer, the external world returned to recapture and obscure the inner core. I haven't been able to get back to this place. I have been so stressed and anxious. I just can't concentrate.

The following week was the anniversary of her nephew's death.

> It's difficult to get to the inner layer when one's life is in an emotional uproar. Every one of my nerve endings are standing up and screaming. I am a wreck. I have too much schoolwork. I am hating my job. I feel overwhelmed, angry, anxious, lonely, and confused. I want to crawl into bed and suck my thumb. I'm having a difficult time with this so-called Ground of Being. It sounds like bullshit today. I know I have found it before, but it is eluding me. And I'm mad at it. I'm mad at the world.

Ultimately, it was important for Erin to touch this depth of anger about her nephew's death. While this self-inquiry process was difficult, it created a structure to explore the impact of this traumatizing tragedy. Unable to sustain these feelings alone, Erin went to church.

> I needed to find community yesterday. I knew I had to leave my job for a few hours and go to church. I lit a candle to celebrate his short life. I needed to hear spiritual wisdom from other people. Fortunately, I met a friend, an older woman who is a member of this church, so I was able to sit with her and not be alone.

When Erin tried meditating again, she had a minor breakthrough. Instead of trying to witness her thoughts and emotions non-reactively, she decided to use her mind actively to analyze what she was experiencing.

> I start to feel a fleeting sense of doom, of death—an overwhelming fear that I have to push away really quickly. Sometimes the images are bloody or violent.

> While trying to get to my safe place, a weird feeling comes over me that doesn't want me to be there. It's hard to explain. I just want it to go away.

As she spoke about these frightening experiences, Erin realized this was the first time she had become cognizant that her nephew's death was triggering traumatic reactivity. This understanding helped her continue to meditate.

> I found time and calmness to meditate today—and had a pretty good experience. That black shadow of darkness came over me, and wouldn't let me go to my safe space alone. So I gave in and allowed this black cloud to follow me there. Instead of fighting it, I just sat with it. I didn't like it, but I knew I couldn't fight it. I decided that if I just let it sit there with me, it wouldn't hurt me. So we sat there, me and this black cloud. It wasn't very comfortable, but at least I stayed there and became more relaxed.

> If this darkness was my inner guide, I'm not really sure what it was telling me. It just sat there. I didn't let it intimidate or scare me. I didn't try to push it away. That was a new experience. Maybe this doom thing just needs to be "sat with" every once in a while.

From one point of view, Erin was developing a stabilizing mindfulness practice. She was learning to observe and tolerate her dark emotions and thoughts. From another point of view, the dark cloud was an inner mentor.

> I became aware in the past few days that this darkness needs to be dealt with. It needs to be acknowledged and experienced. Otherwise, it isn't handled productively.
>
> My alcohol vice makes my problems go away temporarily. But the reality is that my pain and anger are real. When I drink away my problems, that's probably when the darkness enters my meditations and my life.

Erin realized that she had been trying to use meditation as she had been using alcohol: as an escape. By allowing these emotions into her place of contemplation, she could finally *be* with herself. If she let herself experience them gradually, as she was now learning to do, she would not need to run away from them. This was a healthier way to learn to detach from them.

Self-Evaluation of Learning
Erin recognized that this process was incomplete. While she had not smoked a cigarette in more than a month, her drinking had continued. Nonetheless, she was aware of her progress:

> I have examined the stress in my life, dissected my worldview, and understood my issues with pain and anger. I know myself better. At times I have gotten discouraged...but that is just part of the process.
>
> This summer, I plan to hike the Appalachian Trail. I am thinking about Forrest Gump. He ran and ran and ran until he figured out his problems. I want to hike and hike and hike, and re-enter the working world as a stable, connected, focused adult. Hiking will be a great opportunity to practice my spirituality—and incorporate it into my new life.

In combination with personal counseling, Erin learned a great deal from her self-inquiry project, demonstrating impressive psychological insight and strength. Her growing confidence in life and self reflected the resilience she had begun to develop.

Negative Body Image and Depression

"Karen": Graduate Student, 26, Caucasian, Ambivalent Southern Baptist
Karen named two reasons for taking this class. For much of her life, she had felt strongly connected to her Southern Baptist spiritual roots. She

wanted to examine the disconnection she now felt, and renew her sense of spirituality. She also wanted to explore low self-esteem. This problem was connected to an important feminist issue: the pressure to be thin.

Psychospiritual Autobiography
Karen described growing up in a loving, stable Southern Baptist family. Throughout her youth, religious life had great meaning for her.

> I always liked church. I enjoyed the community. I'm a social creature, so it provided an outlet for that. I was loved there. I was a member of the youth group. I played the piano for the children's choir...

Church life provided a deep sense of spirituality in which she would "sometimes feel the Spirit." Deeply immersed in spirituality, Karen was "baptized at age 11." But as she grew older, Karen experienced dissonance between the values of her family and church.

> I began to claim my beliefs and to argue for them in church. I never just accepted what people said. I knew what was true in my heart, my gut, my intuition. My mother taught me that. And I thank her for it... When my Sunday school teacher came back from a mission trip in Poland and called the Catholic Church a work of the Devil, I got up and walked out. I stopped going to church regularly after that.

But Karen's spirituality and attachment to her Baptist tradition endured. At college, she experienced a resurgence of commitment, though from a different perspective:

> My roommate took me to the open house at the Baptist Student Union. Coincidence? Nothing is. I found a worship community.
>
> Most of the students were questioning their heritage like I was. We communed with one another in Christ. These activities produced new awareness about prejudice and social justice. I saw another side of religion. The side you have to wrestle with, just like Jacob... My journey became clearer and more difficult. How was I to accept, to claim my heritage and embrace my religion?

Although college introduced Karen to the possibility of engaging with social justice issues through her Baptist tradition, and despite building strong friendships in this community, she again became disaffected from her religion. She stopped going to church at graduation, 4 years ago, and "I haven't been active in church since."

Reviewing her spiritual development, Karen clarified her goals. Her previous religious activities had been oriented primarily toward her social needs and commitment to social justice. While these were important, she wanted to explore her spirituality more personally.

> I want to find my religious self and nourish her… Why is this important to me? Because I am a Christian. And that to me means to be Christ like.

Further, she had become aware of psychological turmoil that previous religious activities had not helped her explore. Spirituality had always been "her strength." But she needed "to renew that strength" in a deeper way. She wanted to "learn how to heal wounds that are buried too deep within for any x-ray to find." Karen had begun to acknowledge "my own force of destruction: depression. Not just sadness, but feeling utterly morose. I've never contemplated suicide. But I have often felt a desire to live within myself. To stop interacting with the world."

Observing Karen's participation in class discussions, I was not concerned that she was experiencing a psychological crisis. She listened and responded empathically to other students, and was clearly able to step outside her own life story. Speaking about herself, she demonstrated clarity and keen self-awareness.

Karen began a deep exploration of developmental "wounds" related to her feelings of depression. They focused on "being a woman, being feminine, feeling loved." Throughout childhood, she remembered people telling her she was pretty.

> Then came adolescence! Does anyone come out unscathed!? I didn't. I was sooo tall. I had my growth spurt in the 6th grade. I was 5'6"…and the boys were all 5'!

High school and college were difficult for her socially.

> I could never figure out the relationship thing. I had a few boyfriends, but it never lasted very long… In college it just got worse. Everything was about sex appeal and that meant short skirts, tight clothes. Not me at all… I still struggle with this issue. I have learned that how I feel is more important than

what I think I look like. But I still base so much on looks... This whole thing still confuses me.

Despite the love she received from family and friends, Karen's self-esteem had been wounded by the social construction of female beauty. Further, her religious upbringing had avoided these developmental and sociocultural issues. Karen sought a more integrative form of psychospiritual growth, and began to explore her behavioral responses to the stressors in her life.

I like to eat comfort foods. That temporarily eases the situation, but it makes for more stress in terms of body image.

Extending this exploration to her psychological responses to stress, she noticed a pattern:

I also tend to seek comfort from people... I realize that I am addicted to certain people and the way they make me feel. I find myself needing to hear from or talk to certain people. I experience the high, the withdrawal and the rationalizations. Scary!

Karen began to recognize her external locus of evaluation and the lengths she would go to feel comforted. This exploration identified an underlying negative aspect of her worldview.

When I feel lonely or hurt...all my insecurities kick in and I feel as if I am in some way not good enough for the world.

Then Karen explored how she felt about God during stress. She had an unexpected insight.

I forget about God at these times. I just ignore God because I know if I seek that source that I will have to deal with the real issue or pain and that seems much too difficult.

Karen saw that her depression and alienation from God were interconnected parts of a negative worldview that felt "overwhelming and unfulfilling." She knew that a stronger relationship with God could help her overcome it. "I think it is my faith in a greater source of love that gives me the hope to continue to persist against this negative worldview." But she did not know how to build this relationship: "I just wish I could get a mirror made by the greater source of love!"

Contemplative Self-Inquiry During Meditation
While meditation was not part of her Baptist upbringing, prayer had introduced Karen to the experience of wise inner presence. Elicitation of the relaxation response and mindfulness were useful new tools for cultivating inner calm. Visualizing an inner sanctuary to build concentration and receptive awareness was also congruent with her religious worldview.

Karen began a series of rich contemplative explorations. After walking a forest path to her inner sanctuary, she had a spontaneous, unexpected imaginal experience. She climbed through kudzu "and jumped into a large hole," sliding down a wet surface. "The tunnel kept getting curvier. I was filled with adrenaline: the rush of the speed and also the thrill of what might lie ahead." She landed in…

> …an underground lake. The water was cool and very clear… and came up to about my thigh. I began to wade ahead. After a while I saw a beam of light shining toward me, like the way the moon casts its rays across the ocean to you on the beach… As I came closer to the light I could see the shore and an opening. I walked through the opening and was standing at the front gate of a large, white, Victorian farmhouse. Somehow I knew that this was my house. I walked through the gate into a quaint flower garden. I saw rockers and swings on a porch decorated with ferns and red geraniums.

This farmhouse became her inner sanctuary.

Karen found Frankl's existential question a meaningful focus for addressing life issues and seeking an inner mentor. In the next contemplation, she returned to the garden outside her farmhouse where she noticed… "many people, family and friends, gathering around me."

> Then a man approached and touched my hand. He said the most beautiful things to me. It touched my heart. I wish I could remember the exact words. It was something like, *Sing. They have come to hear you sing. It is the music that brings them here. It is your love that you share through your song. Sing for them. Sing for me… Then you can begin to connect to the ultimate song of us all. Sing.* I was truly moved by what happened.

During the next class, Karen sang a sacred song she had learned in church as a child. She sang with a strength that surprised us. Her face rippled with emotion, warmth, and energy. This was an aspect of her we had not met before. She explained that she sang in church often when a child. But she had lost touch with "the singing part" of herself. Her meditation had reconnected her. She had been singing all week. The more she sang, she reported, the more confident she felt about herself and her attractiveness to others. She spoke for several minutes about the profound meaning of this meditation, and how glad she was to have met, in her place of contemplation, this unknown man who knew that she needed to sing.

In the following weeks, Karen interacted in increasingly self-confident ways. She spoke forcefully about commitment to a life of service and egalitarian social values. She responded to others with thoughtfulness and compassion. Moreover, her contemplative experiences became increasingly meaningful. Her inner sanctuary was both a haven and point of receptivity for profound insights. During one meditation, she reported: "I felt within myself a swelling light…"

> —light energy… I felt care, love, joy, pain, hurt, and suffering in my chest. Then this light filled my hands. It was so pink. It was alive and beautiful.

> This image was telling me of this place I am at in my life. I feel empowered. I feel the strength I need to accomplish my dreams. I feel loved and I am not afraid of being alone.

She also had a deeper recognition. She felt…

> …secure, and somehow known. I was not alone. I never felt as if I was separate. And whether the light energy was in my hands or all around me, it was all through me. That is how I see God in my life—ever present, knowing, sensing, being, loving, light energy. Maybe this is the product of the faith I've begun to embrace.

Karen wanted to practice anchoring herself in this awareness of connection throughout her day. In the next contemplation, she sought an anchoring prayer.

> This time when I went to the house. I went inside from room to room shouting, "Is anyone home?" Finally, I went through this door under the

staircase. It led into a study and there sat a man in a large chair, legs crossed, smoking a pipe. I said, "I should've known you'd be in here." It was the same man that had told me to sing in the first meditation, but he seemed older this time. I still didn't really see his face. I told him you'd sent me to find a centering prayer. After speaking with him, it came to me, *Sing to me the song of us all*. I felt a wonderful sensation all over. I knew these were the words.

She clarified the meaning of her anchoring prayer in her written reflections. During stress, she "gets lost, and loses touch with God's presence." At those moments, "I need to stop and listen to God's music more deeply." *Sing to me the song of us all* became a prayer asking God to guide her in a moment of doubt.

Karen noted that this contemplation was also a reminder to stop and listen to God's music, to feel God's presence. In her first meditation, the wise man had told her to sing. This time, he reversed the message. He told her to anchor herself by listening to God's music. She didn't need to nurture herself all the time. She could let God nurture her. All she needed to do was ask, and listen. Once again, the inner mentor had given her a great gift, and she knew it.

> I ran to him and hugged him and asked how he always did that. He just smiled.
>
> Then I said, "What would I do without you?"
>
> He replied (and I'll never forget this part), "You'll never know."

The tenderness of this moment moved Karen deeply.

> I told him I was going to play. I went out the back door and started picking flowers. I lifted my arms, and I felt all the energy of God flow through me into the sky. I let go of my loneliness and sorrow. I'm not sad anymore. So I picked one daisy, ran through the field across the road, and dove into a lake of water. Then I opened my eyes.

Self-Evaluation of Learning
Karen wrote about her learning in detail.

> I feel as if I've found myself again. Writing about my experiences in and through this class have had an overwhelming and profound effect on how I exist in the world every day. Because of choices in my life over the past four years I had gotten further and further away from my spiritual practices which I now see was breaking down my self-confidence and my feelings of purpose, joy and peace. It was a gradual loss so it was hard to pinpoint the culprit, but through this process I have come to find the many pieces of myself that were causing decay or lying dormant. I have again found a place within myself where I can "be." That is a sacred experience.

She also noted the particular way the self-inquiry project helped her develop stress-coping skills.

> It forced me to be present. It forced me to find stillness. It forced me to enjoy myself again. I have spent a lot of time alone dealing with the issues presented in class. Typing at my computer, drawing, meditating, dancing, singing. Those moments have been some of the most precious moments this semester. I enjoy me again."

Moreover, she had developed an effective end-of-semester stress-coping skill:

> I've been stressed lately about how I'm going to finish everything before I go home for Christmas. I feel as if I've done well in my classes thus far and I don't want to lose that because of the stress of the final products. So I've been trying to sing. Sometimes I say the prayer, but it usually just makes me want to sing. So when I get overly stressed I say the prayer and then listen for the song that comes to mind. It's funny what songs pop up!

Karen also wrote poignantly about her sense of spiritual renewal:

> I go to church again. I pray. I see god in those around me. I know God's love and feel the energy as I move through the world. I don't have profound epiphanies every day, but I have joy. I can't begin to express how good it is to be home again. The journey of the prodigal daughter has come to its fruition. She is home and she knows the blessings it has to offer. She will be a better witness to its abundance because of her journey.

Karen ended with mature acknowledgment that the inner critic was not fully silent. But she knew how to disempower its destructive message. Looking in the mirror...

I sometimes still tell her that she's not pretty enough, or needs to lose a few pounds, but she still keeps smiling and if I stare at her long enough I can find her beauty.

I am centered now. I have a home within myself where I know love. And I make sure to draw on the love and support of friends and family in my life. I see beautiful things in my future now.

Through her self-inquiry work, Karen developed confidence in life and self, overcame socially-constructed pressures to be thin, affirmed her social values, and developed a connection to the Ground of Being that was personally meaningful and sustaining. This growth enabled her to return to her Southern Baptist faith tradition with a robust internal locus of evaluation.

Impaired Relational Skills

Sexual Promiscuity

"Alexander": Graduate Student, 25, Caucasian, Atheist
Alex's interpersonal style in the opening weeks of class was memorable: self-assured, funny, and superficial. But it was clear in his first self-inquiry essay that this style did not reflect his internal experience of himself. Inwardly, he had serious professional goals. Alex wanted to teach at-risk youth how to write clearly and creatively, developing positive aspirations for their lives. He considered "creativity sacred." Alex also referred to "a dark night of the soul" that he needed to explore: his repetitive pattern of "sexual infidelity." Conscious of his social power as a man, Alex recognized that he had hurt several women. He also recognized that he had been hurting himself. He wanted to understand and change this pattern.

Psychospiritual Autobiography
Alex's autobiography wove disparate elements of his life story into a coherent whole. Initially, these connections were not clear to him, reflecting a lack of self-awareness that would eventually emerge as a central theme. Before his graduate program, he had worked at a hospice for AIDS patients. This job helped him develop career goals. He had been fortunate, he explained, to fall into the job after several years of painful confusion about his life.

Alex described becoming an atheist. His parents were practicing Protestants, and he was "baptized Lutheran." He attended church until he was 20, "yet rarely felt a spiritual presence at church," valuing only the social community. His father and mother were working professionals. They gave him "a beautiful life, full of love and devotion, where material needs have always been met with generosity." Yet, he noted bitterly, they were rarely at home. His childhood had passed "as mere formality." He saw little reason to believe in God.

> I learned over the first 12 years that I would need to be self-sufficient in areas of my life due to the perpetual absence of my parents. I began to write when I had to come to terms in some way with being a latch-key kid.

Alex also noted the compliant, happy, false persona he had created by age six. At that time, he described having severe nightmares:

> I would wake each night for a whole year screaming, clutching the blankets until Mom and Dad could relax my body and tuck me back in for the remainder of the night. They were dark dreams of being buried alive in gruesome ways, of being followed on a shadowy, vacant landscape by an unknown, terrible power. [But] each morning, I was a model child: smiling, happy, laughing, respectful, and generous to the rest of the family.

This discontinuity between inner life and outward behavior was not yet a clearly articulated theme. At this point, Alex was simply describing seemingly disparate elements.

He hardly mentioned his college years. His only reference concerned the girlfriend he had dated during junior and senior year. When they graduated, she had returned home to India.

After graduation, Alex moved to Canada. He attended a Zen Buddhist monastery several miles outside the town where he lived, immersing himself in meditation practice.

> I would walk four miles every morning and do zazen for two hours. Through the sub-zero winter I showed up each day at five in the morning. The monks were already be in the temple room, sitting or lighting the altar candle. The non-temple residents would file in silently, bow upon entering the main room, find their mat, and sit. In this absolute quiet, except for the wind outside, I found doors to myself that let in peace and serenity.

But during these grueling 8-months, he also discovered that he was emotionally lost.

> I was exercising my body and mind to such an extent that by the time spring rolled around I was aware of only one thing: I had lost my ground in reality. During this time I engaged in a love affair with a woman ten years my senior, and obeyed the limits of a strict, vegan diet. After eight months, I lost twenty-five pounds. I was emotionally vacant and abrasive to be around. I was suicidal and my relationship with my woman friend crumbled. I would walk ten miles a day. I would sit out on a frozen lake all night hoping my life would begin or end.
>
> Then, one day, while I was sitting in the temple, I opened my eyes, stood up, bowed, and left. I never went back to the temple, nor did I practice zazen again. The ritual had lost meaning, along with everything else in my life.

He returned home, lost, and entered counseling with a minister trained in Jungian psychotherapy.

> I realized that what I had done the previous year was not altogether healthy. I had almost succeeded in abandoning my body for some sort of higher consciousness. But my body wasn't ready to let me go. It was still in love with the world, while I, decidedly, was not. Since then, two and a half years ago, my spiritual tradition has had everything to do with service to others. After therapy, I worked in a hospice for AIDS sufferers. This brought me back to the blinding light of reality.

Writing this autobiography, Alex began to see the pattern of emotional loss he had experienced in his life. Then he turned to a more direct exploration of his behavioral change goal.

> The health-related behavior that I have chosen to work on, in conjunction with my own spiritual orientation, is that of sexual contact with others. I have had a hard time drawing boundaries with members of the opposite sex.
>
> I have had a couple of significant relationships in recent years. But throughout that time I have adopted behaviors that now appear to me as less than dignified—and much less than safe for my own mental and emotional health, as well as the health of others.

But while he knew this pattern was not healthy, he felt the need to rationalize it:

> I am a sensual person and find myself attracted to many women. I am not drawn towards infidelity. I am drawn towards making contact with others.

Further, he added, even when he tried to be faithful, relationships don't work out. He "had been involved with a young woman last year." He had found "monogamy a blessed and a rewarding foundation for our relationship." This year-long effort had been "one of the hardest in his life." For the first time, he was able "to express to another person my deepest joys and fears, my hopes for the future and my unfailing committed love." Still, the relationship hadn't worked out.

Alex was perplexed. He was now in love with another woman. So far, he had remained "totally faithful." But he wasn't sure he could hold on. His feelings of internal fragmentation and conflict frightened him. They heightened his determination to explore the issue more fully.

> My health-risk behavior has to do with drawing boundaries between myself and others—around sexual intimacy. I have a mottled past of botched relationships because of infidelities I committed in what were supposed to be monogamous relationships.

As he wrote, Alex had a personal insight:

> [These] relationships were destined to crash because I was fragmenting myself in ways that made each intimate interaction emotionally destructive. After beginning sexual relations with someone, there was no easy way to backpedal. I wonder all the time why my behaviors became so entrenched in these short, stormy, love affairs.

The next self-inquiry assignment shifted Alex's focus. As he examined his typical responses to stress, he entered a new area of awareness.

> I realize that I go along with things and don't stand up for what I want. Sometimes I feel like more of a placating presence in the lives of my friends than a buddy. I shouldn't be going out for coffee at midnight with a friend who "has nothing better to do."

Then he realized that his compliant behavior and infidelities were both forms of flight.

> I seem to entertain the flight mode much of the time when I'm feeling strained by stressful situations. These responses have had a direct effect on my health-risk behavior, for it was in the act of taking flight that I found it easy to begin other incomplete relationships that would further push me from facing the music of my stressful situation.

Alex began to suspect that his core problem might be avoidance of interpersonal stress. Then he examined the psychological benefits of his infidelities.

> By not creating safe boundaries with people, my commitment to them, and to my mental health, can be put aside. This is good if you're running away from wounds to the soul.

Alex then made a first attempt to connect this behavior to his chain of pain.

> Perhaps I've always been afraid of losing people, for I recognize a slew of abandonment issues from childhood. I want to float through friendships, sexualize them, and move on, without resolving the deep, emotional conflict that would result after such episodes.
>
> There was something pleasant about not drawing lines between platonic and romantic interactions. I don't think it was youthful exploration that drove me to extremes with this behavior. It was fear of getting close to someone, or rather, hesitance to do the work of getting closer to someone on an emotional, intellectual, and spiritual level. It's fun to be sexual. When one is young, the rules around proper behavior are not yet fully learned. But on some level, I knew what I was doing. I knew deep down it was destructive.

Writing these words, Alex touched a pool of sadness. He began to mourn his isolation.

> I've moved so many times in the last six years that I don't have a place I can firmly call home. I haven't found a healthy, lasting relationship with another person. Or, rather, I haven't found a place in me that is willing to commit

to something so vast and sacred. Part of me that still obeys this addictive behavior, but I get depressed thinking I won't find a place to call home. I feel terribly uncomfortable writing about this—because I think I've just come up with something new about myself.

Contemplative Self-Inquiry During Meditation

Alex was already familiar with Zen Buddhist meditation, and no longer trusted it. But he found the approach to meditation in this class sensible. Mindfulness helped him become aware of his emotions, thoughts, and habitual pattern of flight. Eliciting the relaxation response was calming. Exploring the psychophysiology of stress and neuroscience of meditation grounded meditation empirically. Accessing inner wisdom was congruent with his atheist worldview.

Alex reframed Frankl's question, asking, "What does my wise self expect of me in this stressful situation?" But he was unprepared for the images that emerged spontaneously. He had a flood of memories about his "romantic partner through the second half of my undergrad years."

> She is living in India but we still keep up contact. From day one we had a strong psychic connection. At times we will telephone, after we both have been thinking about each other. Though we may never be with each other again as romantic partners—that doesn't matter. She is my best friend. In my meditation I remembered an afternoon in college. We took a picnic to a Japanese garden designed to look like a monastic village. We sat under cherry blossoms and ate avocado and cheese sandwiches, drank apple juice and read to each other. My world-view is simple like that garden. My challenge is to understand why being simple is almost impossible for me right now.

This meditation opened a floodgate of sadness that Alex had suppressed. In the next contemplative session, he explored the inner heart, noting the suffering of its outer layer and the beauty at its core. Then he wrote a poem that expressed his sadness, hope, and incipient spirituality.

> The heart is an unknown quantity,
> the flypaper where Buddha's cries turn to dust.
> The heart is a chain of disaster,
> both the reason we speak and why we are silent.

> The heart, both inner and outer, is the chariot
> of what we were meant to become, and the horses that drag us over the brink.
>
> It is thanksgiving. You sit over a table of groceries for an imaginary family,
> each member full of abused love and the tiny remembrances
> that egg us on, saying yes god will recognize you
> and that you do not breathe in vain

In the next session, Alex took another step toward owning and understanding his role in these relational failures.

> I am beginning to discover what I have been doing to lengthen my personal chain of pain. My lack of sexual boundaries, compounded by lack of commitment to relationships, articulate a certain resistance to becoming better acquainted with myself.

Infidelity was a strategy to block intimacy and avoid emotions he had been suppressing. He experienced sharp neck pain during this meditation which deepened his insights:

> In this meditation, and my daily practice of mindfulness, my body is becoming an active focus. I have had chronic neck problems. Through guidance I have received from my own Ground of Being, I have found that the pain really belongs to my inner heart. My heart, not my neck, not my sexuality, not my acne, not my fears, is my challenge.

This insight reflected a poignant, integrative breakthrough into self-understanding. Alex's physical pain, emotional pain, relational losses, fear of abandonment, and protective escape through infidelity were connected. His growing capacity for honest, empathic self-reflection and his growing ability to consult his own inner wisdom helped him explore this labyrinth of seemingly disconnected themes and discover a coherent connection among them.

Self-Evaluation of Learning
Alex affirmed his substantive progress and appreciation for our learning community. At the same time, he continued to be realistic about the fragility of his new relational behavior.

> I have opened a can of psychic worms this semester. Making friends who are striving to understand themselves has been a great factor in becoming more comfortable turning my attention inward to discover my own true self. Making strong connections with people shows me that I can, just maybe, develop safe boundaries with others. But when it comes to relationships with women I am attracted to, that is another story, and it is the heart of the story, as my self-inquiries have put forth.

Alex also noted the new tools he had developed for self-awareness and growth:

> The self-inquiry process has been a surgical tool, and I have been the persistent-surgeon-who-seeks-understanding-of-what-lay-sick within my own body, mind, and spirit. I'm beginning to see a thread connecting back to my childhood, back to germinal moments whose illumination give clarity to what my health-risk behavior means to me.

> These self-inquiries started as little stepping stones across a river to a place I didn't figure on being so packed with memory, some of which is emotionally and physically painful. As time passed, the stepping-stone nature of these inquiries changed, as a direct result of my own psychic changes. Now, at this point, these inquiries serve more as handholds on the face of a sheer rock, which is the place in me I am now exploring. This is a place of extreme emotions, extreme pain, and extreme compassion for others.

This growing capacity for compassion had become evident in his interpersonal behavior in class. Throughout the semester, he shared minimally about the subject of his self-inquiry work, needing to keep it private. But he became increasingly engaged and compassionate in his responses to others. His deflective, humor-laden behavior was gone.

Reviewing the new stress-coping skills he had developed, Alex expressed a new sense of confidence in self and life.

> These inquiries have made dealing with stress easier. I see a multi-dimensionality in myself that offers tools to my problems, tools I never knew I had. These are not just coping mechanisms. Instead they are dormant surgical

tools that allow me—and push me—to address my chain of pain. I guess I just see a bigger picture, a clearer vision of how so much, everything, is in mutual relation to everything else. I am still on this rock face, but the valley looks great.

Alex ended by reflecting on his spiritual growth and our learning community:

> Spiritual learning has been twofold: my meditation practice has grown measurably, as well as my ability and willingness to hold and acknowledge painful issues within myself.
>
> The community of this class has been special. I've made a couple of close friends here, and in these friendships, including my friendship with the group of the class, I have found another reason to survive and grow. The people in this class care about their lives, their health, their evolution. That's spiritual to me: community. I take refuge in this spirit.

Alex made substantial strides in his behavioral change goal through intensive self-inquiry in the five dimensions of psychospiritual maturation. Four years after completing the class, Alex contacted me. He had a teaching job and was married. His self-inquiry project, he said, had helped him commit himself to a monogamous relationship and the emotional work it required.

Fear of Intimate Relationships

"Christopher": Graduate Student, 28, Caucasian, Gay Male, Alienated Roman Catholic

Christopher worked as a medical researcher, and was studying to become a counselor. In itially, his behavioral change goal was vague. Relationally, "I want the best for myself now...

> I hope this class can help me further to develop my potentials. I want to be able to connect to, not to mistrust and fear the judgment, of others.

Psychospiritual Autobiography

Chris reviewed his religious upbringing in an Italian, working class, Catholic family.

Like most Italian children, I was thrown into the religious culture of Roman Catholicism. Religious ritual was the center of my large extended family's life. For [each family] supper, I sat at the 'Lord's Table.' There were no elbows on the table at Uncle Joe's house. Grace was always said, often by me. The Sacraments were performed, religious holidays were celebrated grand opera style, and Mass was attended each Sunday.

Chris "was sent to Catholic school for 12 years." He described strict family life where "the Bible was read regularly," characterized by a punitive worldview.

The family interpreted misfortune—and there was a lot of that—as a curse by God and penance for their sins. I feared and tried to please a punishing God.

Nonetheless, as "an altar boy," he felt great affinity for ritual and religious life:

I aspired to become a priest. I fondly remember myself adorned in my father's oversized robes conducting Mass to an empty living room. I recited the priest's lines, answered for the congregation of stuffed animals, and always delivered a meaningful sermon.

However, his trust in the Church was betrayed. This theme emerged as he explored how his psychospiritual growth had been impacted by multiple strands of his sociocultural identity.

My cultural identities fostered an image of God as an Italian, white, male, heterosexual, able, and lower-class person. This was beneficial for my spiritual development because God was like me.

Being male and physically able furthered my personal ability to practice this patriarchal religion. I could rise to the top and be Pope. Thus, my identities of ethnicity, race, class, gender, and ableness made it possible for me to cultivate a sense of spirituality in a then dominant, accepted, religious sector of American culture. In fact, my cultural identities expected that I be a good practicing Roman Catholic.

By age 17, however, Chris recognized that he was gay, precipitating a painful crisis:

I could identify with God, until I knew I was gay. Unable to reconcile my sexuality with the Church, I felt unworthy of God's love. I was unacceptable. I was damned to Hell.

[This conflict] heightened feelings of alienation, isolation, and the need for redemption. It meant something was inherently wrong with me. Something I could not change. I felt shut out and oppressed by my religion's prejudice—rejected by the community that formed, nurtured, and loved me.

Chris also began to acknowledge that he was "a survivor of childhood sexual abuse."

Both experiences have had a monumental impact on my development...These intertwined issues have taken me nearly 10 years to clear out. I have worked hard through a lot of felt pain, anxiety, depression, and addictions.

Struggling to recover from the complex trauma he had experienced, Chris lost faith in God:

In the early years, I looked for God. I wanted God. I needed God. Yet, I felt God had deserted me. Where was He to protect me? What did He say of homosexuals? God rejected me, so I rejected God. Where was the Church for this abused gay adolescent who had such dedication to it as a heterosexually assumed child?"

I abandoned religion because it abandoned me. I left the Church hurt and angry! I turned to science, existentialism, and philosophy in college. I reached within me for the strength to pull through. I did not pray. I did not ask for God's help. I was wary of others.

Chris expressed deep residues of anger. He held the Church accountable for creating a culture of intolerance, conformity, power-protecting hierarchy, and abuse. But it was clear from his class participation that Chris was not becoming overwhelmed. The self-inquiry project was helping him organize this material into a coherent life narrative that affirmed his gay identity and facilitated empathic self-reflection.

As part of his recovery process, Chris explained, he developed a "private spirituality."

> I needed something to guide me to the light. I found connection alone in remote beautiful areas. Alone in nature, I found peace in my most troubled times. It was there that I found connection to the life force—alone.

Despite the isolative stance Chris adopted, personal therapy and his work as a medical researcher led to interest in psychology, the mind-body relationship, and spirituality. His current studies "have taught me much about this relationship... I can now take [better] care of myself."

> My culture, church, and family forced values on me that were not congruent with my inner experience of being gay. I failed to achieve in comparison to these forced ideals. My self-esteem collapsed.

Chris then began to explore his responses to stress.

> I find myself lonely and over-engaged in responsibility: work, family, social life, school, practicum, maintaining my condo building and car, and taking care of myself. I am the good medical researcher, son, brother, student, counselor, homemaker, building manager, bill payer, BMW driver, fag, gym bunny, disco queen—you name it. It is too much to do and too much to be.

> Physically, I get symptoms of the stress response. My muscles and digestive system suffer. Behaviorally, I get the craving to smoke, drink, or escape the situation. Mentally, I become anxious, irritable, and angry. Later, I become tired and depressed.

Chris' behavioral change goal had initially been vague. Identifying cigarette smoking as a primary stress buffer, he decided that smoking should be his focus. He then added, "My sexual life is not satisfying. I also want to work on it."

> I have trouble when intimacy is coupled with sex. I know this is largely because I'm gay, male, and a survivor. However, I feel that my spirituality is an important piece of this. I do not know how or why. I just sense that it is. I hope to move this block. In so doing, I believe I will be a more complete and available person to others.

Chris sensed that his cigarette smoking was "linked" to these issues. By focusing on smoking, he hoped to reduce it, and understand more about his fear of relational intimacy.

In the next self-inquiry essay, Chris noted that "most role models in my family smoke." Then he examined his smoking history.

> I started smoking when I was about age 15 with my best friend, Sam, whom I loved. I smoked about one pack every three days until I was 17. Then I smoked a pack a day until I was 21. Then I went back to a pack every three days until I was 26. Since then I have smoked only two cigarettes each day (one pack every 10 days).
>
> Ages 17–21 were the most troubling time of my life. This was when I broke the silence on my abuse. This was also [when] I was discovering that I was gay and in love with my best friend who was confused about his sexuality. In fear of losing the love of those I cared about, my sexual expression was stifled. In these years, I smoked the most.
>
> Ages 21–26 were also an important and difficult time. These were also sexually "prime" years. I smoked the second most during those dark years of incest recovery and sexual identity development.
>
> I cut down to two cigarettes a day after age 26. I became more aware of the relationship between health and behavior. I also had more knowledge and self-esteem. So I could no longer justify my self-destructive habit. Today, at 28, I would like to stop smoking.

Next he reviewed his cessation efforts, noting "I have tried to quit many times."

> My most successful time was when I was 17. I stopped for 10 months. I tried again at 19. I stopped for 8 months. I tried once again at 23 and stopped for 5 months. Over the years, I have gone without smoking 2 months here and there. I seem to always go back.

Chris understood the health dangers. He didn't need information. He also recognized his withdrawal symptoms accurately. "I get extraordinarily anxious when I try to stop. That state is very uncomfortable, almost unbearable." He was benefiting from meditation practice in class, learning to elicit the relaxation response and to witness uncomfortable feelings mindfully. But these self-regulation tools were not sufficient. Chris recognized that smoking served a deeper function. Thus, he was receptive to explore the psychological benefits he derived.

> I *like* smoking… I enjoy the process. I smoke two cigarettes each night before I go to sleep. It's the last thing I do each day.
>
> Smoking calms me down. It takes the edge off. It soothes me. In the brain, nicotine stimulates the release of dopamine into the synapses. Dopamine is the neurotransmitter most closely associated with feelings of euphoria and satisfaction. Addicts, like myself, become accustomed to high levels of dopamine. The high is pleasurable.
>
> In this way, my nicotine addiction has a biological basis. It is not a failure of character. Perhaps all of the psychological trauma in my life has led to physiological changes in my brain functioning. On some physical level, I may need this high.
>
> On a psychological level, it makes me feel good. It takes away painful emotions and soothes core wounds. Increasing my dopamine levels can push my depressing negative worldview away. I don't like myself when I have a negative worldview, when I'm depressed, when I'm not nice to people. Smoking keeps all that more manageable.
>
> I am laughing because it seems so absurd. Like, smoking two cigarettes each night before bed really does anything. But it does.

Chris then made connections between his bedtime smoking behavior and his sexuality. "The more sexual I feel the more I [need to] smoke." Then he experienced frustration that this pattern had a meaning "I am unaware of at this time." But Chris persisted in his search.

> This pattern has something to do with not having sex, and smoking when I am feeling sexual. I seem to push my sexual feelings down with cigarettes! (I just learned this!)

This discovery surprised Chris. It presented a new way to think about this pattern.

> I found pause on this one. Smoking is a way for me to calm and soothe myself under stress. Withdrawing from sex is a way to protect myself from people when I am under stress. Of course, I am always under stress. So, I smoke and never have sex. In this way, smoking and abstinence are comforting behaviors.

But, sex isn't ultimately what I'm after: it's a loving relationship that I want. In this light, my "comforting" behavior is better described as *withdrawal*, not abstinence.

This realization felt momentous to Chris. Then he reviewed his "personal chain of pain," identifying factors that had shaped his relationship-avoidant interpersonal style. He discussed his extended family, which was "abusive, dysfunctional, and chaotic." He described being an "isolated child" who felt different from his peers, "spending a lot of time with [his] family." But both of his parents were "somewhat unavailable," and so he "spent a lot of time with relatives."

> These factors gave my uncle the opportunity to abuse me from ages 6 to 12. He hurt and betrayed me by sexualizing my needs. Then my family hurt me by withholding support when I broke the news. In denial of their own abused childhoods, they were unable to give me the love and support that I needed from them.

In pain-filled words, Chris described the transgenerational transmission of trauma that is a figural dynamic in humanity's chain of pain.

> Despite all this shit, there were and are many positive aspects of my life. Using these pieces of information, I realize that my negative worldview is in many ways inaccurate.

> At the same time, I now understand better why my negative worldview formed. I know its power to color objective reality.

By combining critical analysis of autobiographical material with an increased capacity for empathic self-reflection, Chris was identifying the need to reframe his negative worldview, relationally-avoidant behavior, and cigarette smoking in a manner that respected their originally protective intentions: "I need to befriend this negative worldview, understand how it emerged, how it influences me, and how it distorts reality."

Contemplative Self-Inquiry During Meditation

Chris was intrigued to explore the deep structure of contemplative mind, seek inner wisdom, and determine if he could develop a genuinely positive worldview. In his second exploration, his inner mentor challenged him in an unexpected way:

> I focused on my loneliness and unmet desire to share life with a husband. I asked what life expected of me [to achieve this goal]. The answer came clearly. I immediately knew that if my world was to be a more loving place, than it was I who must look lovingly at myself and make loving change.
>
> Love is not going to find me. Love has to be found by me. Some prince isn't going to appear at my doorstep. I need to be more open and loving toward others.

Chris then contemplated the ramifications of this challenging message from his wise self.

> The key is the realization that this can only happen in relationship. Relationships are the vehicle through which I love and am loved. Relationships are a source of connectedness, love, solidity, and stability. Yet, relationships can also be painful. It is in relationship that I can be most hurt by others. This is the challenge! Only in relationship can I find love, but can I bear the pain of relationship? I cannot have one without the other. This realization is a big breakthrough for me.

Chris recognized that he had been protecting himself from "emotional pain by staying out of relationship. I have been shielding myself from love to protect myself from further pain."

> I was wondering why love hasn't found me. It is I who haven't found love, because I have kept myself out of relationship. I must make the change to actively engage in relationship. It is time to leave the disciplines of withdrawal and contemplation born in the loneliness of gay childhood and adolescence. It is time for reordering my worldview and the spirituality that underlies it.

This contemplative exploration helped Chris feel "more positive about myself, others, life, and the creator." Using Frankl's question, he "no longer felt helpless or hopeless." Rather, he felt "empowered to affect my situation. I saw that I was not just a victim of life."

> I am not saying my worldview has been completely transformed in this one meditation. But it will be useful for me to use this self-inquiry process, and this question, more often.

In the next class, Chris chose not to meditate. He wanted to experiment with spontaneous drawing, an alternative mode for receptivity to inner wisdom. Contemplating the inner heart, he drew the face of a person in meditation, superimposed on a vast natural expanse. "The face is a part of nature, just as nature is part of the face." For him, this drawing expressed growing reconnection with the spirit of life. He noted, with excitement,

> I am coming out of isolation and establishing a sense of connection and belonging through the heart we all share. This is important for me because I cannot recall 10-15 years ago, a single positive image or role model that mirrored my own experience as a gay young man. This created a dire sense of isolation that was emotionally and spiritually damaging. The cumulative effect of this work is that in my inner heart, I feel I am now a part of the circle of life. My inner heart is unfolding its potential more and more as the darkness surrounding it recedes. I am more fully my core self.

During his next contemplation, Chris consulted his inner mentor, seeking an anchoring phrase to use during meditation or in stressful situations. He had entered his inner sanctuary through a dark cave that opened "a long narrow cliff that overlooked the open ocean." Then they had a humorous exchange in which his inner guide would suggest different aspects of nature that Chris loved. But Chris kept rejecting them because they didn't hit the mark.

> Then it hit me. In my places of contemplation, I am always before a vastness. Ocean, sky, space, plateaus, prairies, canyons. Their commonality is vastness! My guide spoke the phrase, "Nature, the vast land." Yes, this was it!

At the end of this essay, Chris noted that this meditative experience reminded him of powerful lines from William Wordsworth's poem, *Tintern Abbey*.

> "I have felt a presence that disturbs me with the joy of elevated thoughts; a sense sublime of something far more deeply interfused, whose dwelling is the light of setting suns, and the round ocean and the living air, and the blue sky, and in the mind of man; a spirit that impels all thinking things, all objects of all thought, and rolls through all things."

In his final contemplation, Chris experienced a reality check. He encountered the emotional vulnerability he would need to risk.

> I imagined myself at bedtime, lying alone, lighting up my two cigarettes for the day. I was overwhelmed with sadness and aloneness. I tried to heal this core wound, but the scar felt too deep. The aloneness had a density that I could not penetrate. It had a gravity that pulled me into its sadness and desperation. I felt down for three days after.
>
> I asked, "What does life expect of me now?" The answer was to [develop] deep self-love and to have faith, Paul Tillich's type of faith. My ultimate concern is love. Yet, I cannot be sure to experience it as I wish. Uncertainty cannot be removed. It must be accepted. The element of faith that accepts this uncertainty is courage.
>
> Healing this wound is a process-oriented, chipping away, or deconstruction, occurring slowly over time. I will stay open and pray, becoming, living the question.

Self-Evaluation of Learning
Chris first noted the importance of his community experience:

> Participating in this class resurrected my inherent, formerly stifled, spirituality [and introduced me to] a safe, sensible, enjoyable way to express that spirituality. I would like to belong to a person centered spiritual community. In such a community, I am taken as I am — gay. Diversity is celebrated. I am empowered not disempowered. Goals of the community include weaving sustained relationships, constructing a community actively engaged in caring, and sharing a sense of life purpose.

Then Chris reviewed growth in stress-coping skills. He was practicing meditation "with vigor."

I am practicing at least three times a week. I want to work toward a daily practice. I am now centered and mindful more of the time. I also experience a more positive, unwavering worldview and mood, that is sustained more of the time.

Chris then summarized key areas of learning, progress, and challenges he faces:

My health risk behaviors are Band-Aids on my spiritual wounds, comforting behaviors to numb pain. I focused on two behaviors. My goal was to quit smoking and to become more satisfied with my sex life. I achieved neither. But I now understand the dynamics of [these] behaviors. I first withdraw from relationship to numb and avoid the pain of being hurt by others. Then, I smoke to numb the pain of being alone. The clarification of the connections will enable me to move forward toward change.

I learned that I feel sexual, but I am without a partner. On a deeper level, the power of sex is the intimacy it brings. But I keep myself out of relationship, because I fear being hurt. I crave intimacy, yet I block it. The solution is in the willingness to bear the pain of relationship. Vulnerability and hurt are risks in love. The challenge is that one does not come without the other. I sit with that for now.

Despite these challenges, Chris affirmed his positive experiences and growth.

I feel not so alone now. I, like all else, am a part of the creative energy. The creative energy is also a part of me.

This spiritual experience has opened my heart more to others. I recovered my intense emotions. Most notable is a renewed sense of compassion. I am not so wary of others. If people are mean to me, I try to ask myself, "I wonder how they're hurting inside?"

Most important, I feel more like my core self. I have wanted to recover this for a long time. I am in a process of becoming whole: experiencing wholeness. The process of these self-inquiries has been an invaluable piece of my life's inner work.

Chris' courageous and thoughtful self-inquiry work helped him affirm his sexual identity as a gay man, and confront challenges that gay men encounter in a homophobic society which undermines their deepest needs for wholeness and healthy relational intimacy.

EXISTENTIAL STRUGGLES AND SPIRITUAL ALIENATION

Existential Coping with a Chronic Illness

"Anna": Graduate Student, 24, Caucasian, Practicing American Baptist
A Fine Arts major in college, Anna planned to become an arts educator. But over the past two years, her Christian spirituality had become increasingly important. She contemplated transferring to a divinity program that supported creativity. In this class, she wanted to deepen her spirituality, explore its relationship to her health, and integrate artistic expression.

Psychospiritual Autobiography
Anna wrote a probing narrative about her religious upbringing and spiritual struggles.

> For as long as I can remember I have had some sort of relationship with a "spiritual other" and I have always placed great importance on my well-being. This is due to two factors: my struggle with a chronic illness and the strong presence of religion in my family.
>
> I was born with a nervous system disorder that was not diagnosed accurately until I was 12 years old. The symptoms include waves of pain throughout my body, headaches, and insomnia. I learned early on that no one and nothing could bring me comfort, let alone a cure, so my chosen way to cope was to look to God to transcend the pain.
>
> Another way to escape the pain and to feel like a "normal" kid was to block it out as much as possible. This was difficult and took a great deal of energy and focus. I can remember humming songs to the clouds during the carpool to and from kindergarten imagining that I was flying high above myself in the presence of God. To me, God and nature have always been one and the same. I find great comfort in both, especially animals.
>
> I was not your usual carefree active child. I constantly monitored my body's symptoms to be prepared for what might happen next. Spirituality was a way to maintain hope that someday I might feel better. Today, I have a diagnosis and medications that have changed my life considerably for the better.

Her parents, she explained, helped her develop crucial coping skills.

> My father was a deacon and my mother was very active in our Baptist church. Turning to God when things seemed overwhelming is something I learned from them. In addition to relentlessly pursing a diagnosis, my father prayed with me to find comfort when nothing else worked. My Winnie-the-Pooh bear became an ambassador of God. He absorbed many tears and has since gone the way of the Velveteen Rabbit in becoming real.

But "the fact that religion was so intertwined with family relationships has been both positive and negative." In college, she began to wonder if her parents' forceful beliefs, coupled with her need to escape from physical pain, had convinced her to believe in God. This initiated a long period of spiritual questioning. Still, her parents helped her understand that spiritual crises often produce new understanding. While probing the foundations of her belief system, she retained a deep sense of loyalty to her Christianity.

> I cannot deny the importance spirituality has had in my survival. In my personal life, I look for people who can identify with the experience of spirituality even if they are of a different faith. When I can't share these experiences with those closest to me, it's as if there's a big empty rift between us.

> This is not to say that spirituality is always roses. I'm interested in learning from the crises that are part of spiritual life. For me, it is an active maintenance of trying to live what I believe and not just go through the motions. I run into many brick walls and unanswerable questions. It's like a journey, and change is constant. It is a foundation for my life that sometimes feels like a rock, and sometimes there are earthquakes.

Anna's exploration deepened as she examined her dependence on authority figures.

> While dealing with my illness, I didn't have the energy to question the authority figures in my life and what they believed. I was very dependent on my parents because they were my only advocates in finding a diagnosis and cure. This didn't start to change until early college when I got the medication which freed me up considerably. I was finally able to start breaking out of survival mode and discover all the things I might be. The joy of individuation. Sometimes I feel like I have to make up for lost time.

> I have finally started to gain perspective on the religious upbringing of my childhood. Religious ritual, jargon, and rules were pervasive in our family. It often felt suffocating. On the other hand, my parents had enough insight to encourage me as I began to define my own faith after leaving home.
>
> Most difficult was sorting out the enmeshment of the parent/child-spirituality/faith relationship. Asserting myself as an individual in front of my parents also meant that I rejected my faith and religious rituals. I felt that I needed to fight extra hard, since I had always felt so bound.

Anna also struggled with core beliefs that she had been taught in her childhood church.

> The church was small and predominantly white lower-middle class, but our members welcomed people of any walk of life and country. We were taught that Christianity was the only true faith and that others, despite being "good" people, would not go to heaven if they had not accepted Christ as their Savior. It didn't matter what your social status was. It was whether you were a Christian, and whether you lived as such, that was important.
>
> How can there only be one correct perspective on God? Just because I dress one way doesn't mean that the way someone else dresses is wrong. I have a lot of trouble with the history of the Christian church and the many terrible things that were done in the name of God. I have difficulty supporting missionary work because who am I to go into some area where things work perfectly well and say, "Excuse me, but you've got it all wrong."
>
> I am slowly coming to terms with these issues, not by figuring out all the answers, but by being content with not knowing and leaving room to change my mind.

As Anna gained her footing as a separate person, she reconnected to her faith. Her parents' nondefensive response to her individuation was an important source of support.

> Gradually I was able to come back to my faith and the church without it feeling like I was giving into my parents. Of course the process continues, but at least now I sense myself to be an individual instead of an extension of my parents.

Anna celebrated her hard-won autonomy. She lived in a different city than her parents; her Christianity felt authentic. She attended church and social activities "fairly regularly."

Still, over the past year, Anna realized her spiritual commitment was "a bit deceptive." The problem crystallized during a silent retreat 1 month before this class. During a solo nature walk, usually a source of spiritual inspiration, something important was missing:

> The distraction of awe inspiring experiences helps me fly above the struggles life sends. These experiences are like dessert—often delicious, memorable and truly beautiful. Unfortunately, what is missing is the main course—faith in God which helps me weather life instead of escaping into some random beautiful experience. I did not realize this until I went on silent retreat. It was me and God—and sometimes it felt like just me.

Throughout the retreat, God's presence and love "hadn't seemed accessible."

Her emerging awareness of spiritual emptiness signified, for Anna, a need to embark on a new stage of growth. Immersion in nature had become a distraction, an escape rather than an encounter. Her religion had taught her to believe that "God lives in me and loves me." As she completed the first segment of her autobiographical work, she committed herself to look within herself, rather than outside, for God's presence.

> Feeling God's presence [in nature] is an awesome experience that words often cannot describe. It is very powerful and unforgettable.

But recognizing God as a loving presence within herself "is often difficult for me to fully acknowledge." Anna wanted to examine "the various reasons" for this difficulty.

The self-inquiry project then shifted to exploration of her responses to stress. Anna's stressors included her chronic illness, spiritual emptiness, and high academic expectations. Her typical response, she noted, was becoming very anxious. She selected anxiety as a health-compromising behavior that she wanted to reduce as part of her self-inquiry project.

The health-related behavior I choose to explore is my anxiety. I've learned a lot about anxiety disorders, and I'm slowly coming to grips with the fact that learning to live with the tendency to be overly anxious, sometimes to the point of panic attacks, is a lifelong task. This makes me sad, but that's ok.

Anna also knew she had learned to block awareness of pain through intellectual activity. Art became a nonverbal way to express herself that did not dilute emotions.

I tend to use words as a way to distance myself from emotions. Intellectualizing makes it less likely that I'll feel overwhelmed by them, but I'm realizing this class is about feeling and connecting. I've decided to challenge myself by making art part of the self-inquiries.

Anna created a series of collages. Selecting pictures cut from magazines, she created striking images symbolizing the physical pain she had endured. To clarify the personal meaning of her images, she wrote a brief orienting statement.

Starting in the lower left corner is the picture of a little girl with a needle being aimed at her head. It means pain and the doctors probing for clues. The tornado behind her (me) is the nightmares she has. Next there is a rabbit almost hidden by camouflaged fur. She identifies with it because rabbits say little, always watching and listening, and fearful...

My teenage years [are] represented by the young woman in the black dress getting ready for a celebration. She was beautiful on the outside, but hated what was inside her, because it held her back. The leech's mouth is the monster she feels inside her. The volcano is anger, usually kept inside. The ice is the feeling of being trapped in an anxious state. A monster is inside there, too, represented by the little dinosaur baby. On top is a picture of a serene beautiful sunset which is about me trying to transcend all the unpleasant stuff.

My goal is to challenge myself to feel and connect, knowing when not to push myself too much. My goal is not to make my anxiety go away. I know that doesn't work.

After sharing the collage with classmates, Anna examined her responses to stress.

> The first thing that happens is my mindset changes. I go into ultra-efficiency mode where everything must be done as perfectly and efficiently as possible. My view of the world begins to narrow as I try to focus on the tasks at hand. Physically, I feel anxiety in my upper abdomen and tension across my chest and shoulders. Psychologically, I start hating myself for having a defective body. This leads to feeling helpless and hopeless.

These responses clarified the negative components of her worldview:

> Defensive protection against a world that doesn't believe [in] me. My world hurts more than it helps. Life is a struggle which I'm never sure if I'm going to have the strength to make it through. God is the rope from which I swing, holding on for dear life. Or maybe God is what my rope is attached to. I forget that instead of dangling at the end I could climb up and sit with God (really trusting him). Trust is very difficult for me.

This examination helped Anna recognize that her anxiety also had some psychological benefits. It was an automatic protective response that helped her "feel prepared to face a world that is going to harm me." But Anna found it difficult to re-frame her anxiety as protective.

> It's hard for me to see many positive aspects. The old ways of thinking and feeling are so familiar and comforting in a sick, pathetic way. My eyes are tearing now, but I need to write through this. It's amazing how quickly my mind and heart cloud over. When I feel like this, I don't want to see anybody, or burden them with my baggage, to use a nice word for it. This is a hard place to be in. It hurts. I don't have a positive worldview yet.

Contemplative Self-Inquiry during Meditation
Anna had practiced meditation as a mode of self-regulation. She knew many mental techniques for relaxation and self-distraction. However, psychologically and spiritually, they left her feeling empty. Mindfulness, she noted, offered a different approach: a method for observing her pain without reacting. But she did not feel ready for the intensity of this practice. Her pain felt intolerable, as her collages showed. In the first module of the class, I supported her choice to create symbolic art as mindful observation of her feelings. But meditation and imaginal work resonated with Anna's desire to find God's presence within.

As she created her inner sanctuary, Anna chose academic stress as a focus for using Frankl's existential question to develop new perspectives on her anxiety.

> I asked, "What does life expect of me as I face this difficult stress? I have a research paper due next week. I am anxious. I am afraid I won't be able to finish it. What if I can't do it, what if I fail? What if, what if, what if?" My heartbeat quickens. "Surely something must be DONE in order to relieve the stress. I must DO *something*."
>
> As I looked out across the horizon, the ocean answered softly but without hesitation, "Just keep going. You're doing fine. Nothing needs to be done. It's ok. This is life."
>
> "But I hurt, I'm uncomfortable, things aren't smooth, I'm scared."
>
> "That's ok," said the sea. "You are alive and that's why you feel. You CAN feel and that makes you special. Sometimes you will be uncomfortable, but that doesn't mean that a disaster is around the corner. Just keep going. You'll be ok."

Speaking through the symbolic image of the ocean, her inner wisdom told Anna she did not need to keep blocking her emotions. She could tolerate them. Further, they did not portend doom. Anna knew this insight could guide her to a new stage of awareness.

> Someday, I hope to feel strong enough to embrace all of living—the joy, the despair, and everything in between. Until then I will walk with one foot in the old and one foot in the new. Some days I will feel strong enough to really live; on other days, I will slip into survival mode. But I will continue to ask the question, "What does life expect of me at this moment in time?" I suppose it takes time to adopt new ways of viewing the world and living in it. The ocean suggests that I be patient.

Then Anna explored the inner heart, journeying deep inside herself.

> I was so relaxed that I almost fell asleep - unusual for me. I felt safe with myself - also new. Going deeper, I imagined a glowing place that was warm, soothing, yet powerful.

Then the images became more spontaneous.

> I envisioned sitting near a bonfire on the shore of my safe place in Maine. I also recalled an image I once drew: a small yellow dot where my heart "would" be.

The dot designated where Anna's inner heart could be found, *if* she could experience it. This image felt hopeful. It evoked a sustaining image of God "who does not give up on me even when I have given up on myself." Then the spontaneous contemplation deepened further.

> I envisioned my whole body filling with light, life, and energy. I suppose I also felt love for myself. This is hard to say.

Another image appeared, one that she had also painted earlier.

> [It] was a window into my heart, depicted as a whole world with little people doing lots of work. They kept the stone wall surrounding the heart strong, but most of their energy was focused on an excavating project. The huge pile of dirt looked like a pile of shit (pardon my French) being dug up.

As she contemplated this image, it did not remain static.

> I got to see what they dug up out of that big hole. Everyone stood around as a huge glowing jewel was uncovered from the pit. It was alive and breathing and strong.

After class, Anna spoke with me about the excitement she felt. She had never had a meditation experience like this before. The inner mentor had revealed "an image of her soul," unwounded and strong! For days, she reveled in this experience:

> Each day, I keep thinking about these new ideas and feelings and I try them on. What would it be like to imagine myself strong? What would it be like to actually feel love and actually have Life inside me? I am life and life is me—what is that like?

During her next contemplation, Anna could not meditate. Turbulent emotions surfaced, and she needed to write about them.

> I am learning to love me. I am learning to feel God's love for me and to accept it. That's as far as I've gotten. I know that alone is a big step. But what is difficult for me to understand is why [another person] might choose to love me. I feel very unlovable despite the consistent attention I receive from the opposite sex.

Anna often experienced men being physically attracted to her. But, she noted archly, they rarely make the effort to know who she is. If they really knew, she feared, they would lose interest.

> This isn't just about romantic relationships. It applies to friendships with women as well. I don't feel I deserve someone else's love. They could do better. As I write, I'm noticing anger welling up inside. I don't know where it's coming from or why. I do deserve to be loved, not just by myself and by God. Everyone deserves to be loved.

The following week, she was able to meditate again, and sought an anchoring prayer.

> I found myself in an unfamiliar place, a tiny garden on a cloudy day. It was very quiet, as if everything had left town. The phrase that came to mind this time was "let it be." This reminds me that, as I let go, life will come together on its own. It reminds me of the wonder of living in the ambiguity instead of being afraid of it.

In her final contemplation, she experienced a complex symbol which illuminated the transformative, but still transitional, process she was experiencing.

> An image that I had painted earlier came to mind. It was a desert with high mesas that bordered the sea. Through these mesas ran a new river. After thousands of years the river had eventually cut through the rock. Undaunted by the desert, it flowed all the way to the sea. The mesa wasn't sure what its purpose was anymore. It had always held back the river. Now what was it supposed to do? It felt abandoned and left out of the action.
>
> I think these rocks might be old ways of viewing the world and coping/blocking which I'm now learning to at least negotiate with and at times discard. There is a feeling of wanting to hold onto the old ways because they did their job so well and are so familiar.

Self-Evaluation of Learning

Anna summarized her substantive learning during this self-inquiry project: growth in self-confidence, reductions in anxiety and defensive fears, and strengthening of a newly robust, internally-experienced, relationship with the Ground of Being.

> I need a very large trunk in which to place all of what I have learned in this class. These past 13 weeks have been a particularly amazing part of an on-going process of personal growth. I've been working mostly on developing a 'grounded sturdy sense of personal self' and my capacity to know my core self—and how I am connected to God, The Spirit of Life. I am slowly learning to unfold.
>
> I am learning that I can feel alive and feel wounded at the same time: there is space, and energy, and strength for both.
>
> I used to view the world from a defensive stance, positioned for whatever catastrophe might befall me next. It was me against Life. I am learning to experience myself as being part of Life, I am Life. Thinking of it in this way I can share in that power that the idea of Life used to hold over me.
>
> When I began this class, I described an image that had come to me earlier this summer regarding my spiritual relationship with God. The Lord loved me. I knew that, but I couldn't feel it or be it. The Lord's love was grand and plentiful like a huge banquet table full of luscious food and drink. I had been invited to the feast, invited to receive God's love, but I could not eat. I had no mouth, no way to even partake of the feast.
>
> In these months, I have found my mouth and I am beginning to nibble on the love of God available to me. It is a wonderful feeling. The spirituality I experience now is far greater than ever before. It can be overwhelming sometimes, but it's ok to feel overwhelmed.
>
> Another important piece has been learning about my core self which I see as being intimately connected with my spirituality. That fiery jewel that burns inside me is a gift from God, and the fact that after hiding for so long underground it is still intact is also thanks to God. God created me strong and sturdy, loveable and caring, with a core that will somehow be present in me from now into eternity. I am part of something larger. I am Life. I am the Ocean. And God invites me to be in Him and of Him as well.

As she noted, Anna experienced substantial growth in the resilient worldview, confidence in life and self, and poignantly robust movement toward secure existential attachment.

Alienation from God and Religious Tradition

"Hasna": Adult Undergraduate, 27, Algerian American Female, Inactive Muslim

Hasna hoped to become a human resource specialist. Introducing herself to the class, she explained that she is Muslim, an American citizen whose family emigrated from Algeria when she was a child. Hasna had been intrigued to find a course that addressed spirituality from a multi-faith perspective, and looked forward to meeting her fellow students. It quickly became clear that this thoughtful, articulate young woman would contribute to our class significantly.

Psychospiritual Autobiography
In her first essay, Hasna stated that she felt disconnected from God and her Muslim spirituality. She identified three learning goals. She wanted to understand her current alienation from Allah, increase the frequency of her daily prayers, and "increase the peace within myself." Hasna used the words *God* and *Allah* interchangeably, throughout her essays and our class.

Writing a psychospiritual autobiography provided Hasna with an opportunity to review and analyze the life experiences that had shaped her current alienation from Islam. During an escalation of violence and political turmoil in Algeria, her father's clothing store was destroyed in a fire. Though not a target of harassment, the loss created financial and emotional strain, and his health deteriorated. Seeking a stable life for their four young children, her parents sought refuge in the United States.

Hasna identified two issues that led to her alienation from Islam. In childhood, she had developed a strong sense of spirituality. Her observant parents prayed regularly. Hasna remembered praying for her father's health "almost every night, before sleep." Each prayer began by imagining herself "on a journey" that reached "over the clouds."

Now comes the prayer…deep down from the hidden corners of my soul. A prayer for rescue, help, so that my sisters and I should not feel so much pain. A prayer to hold onto my dad. "O Allah, I have come from you and I shall return to you in the end. Please hear my prayers and accept them. Keep my father safe. Do not let me bow my head to anyone. End our sufferings."

But when Hasna was 17, her father died from a painful illness. His loss undermined her belief in Allah as her protector. It felt like a betrayal.

The second source of alienation was conflict between American and Algerian-Muslim social norms. During adolescence, she felt deep confusion. After her father's death, her teenage boyfriend convinced her to have sex. "I kept a special relationship with Allah for a long time. The break happened with my first sin." She had not intended to have sex. Too frightened and confused to speak with her mother, she told her school counselor she had committed a terrible sin. Hasna described feeling profoundly shamed by the counselor's response:

> She was supposed to be multicultural. She asked me what made "sex" a sin in my religion. She told me to do some research on it. In her smug smile, there was a winning and devaluing of my religion and traditions. My feelings and my shame were never addressed. I never went back to her.

Hasna's emotional turmoil and isolation coincided with severe psychosomatic reactions.

> I suffered from all kinds of ear infections, colds, and allergies. My allergies were so severe that I was not able to sleep at night. Tiredness, not being able to breathe well, combined with the guilt was a burden I had to carry all on my own.

Despite medical treatment, the allergies and colds persisted. The feeling that she was carrying a terrible burden intensified.

However, the burden was not related only to shame about having had sex. It was also related to a rift she had begun to experience in her spiritual faith. God had not protected her.

> I was angry because there is the concept of *kader* in Islam. It means that everything in one's life is already known to Allah. There are choices given to you, yet Allah knows which one you will pick.

If Allah had known she would commit this "shameful" act, yet had not intervened to prevent it, then her illnesses seemed like unfair punishment.

> Why was I being punished for something I had not planned to do to begin with? How could Allah punish me in such a cruel way? I had not hurt anyone knowingly.

Angry and disappointed, Hasna began to think that God might be no more than a superstition. Further, "all the new information I was learning in the academic world of science, philosophy, and anthropology" added to these doubts.

Nonetheless, one night as she prayed before going to sleep, she sought clarity about her boyfriend. Despite feeling compromised, she had attempted to remain loyal. Now it seemed she had "hung on for all the wrong reasons."

> I asked for guidance from Allah. The answer was very clear. I broke up from my boyfriend almost immediately.

Hasna was relieved to experience that Allah remained a guiding presence in her life. Following the breakup with her boyfriend, to her great surprise, her "allergies ceased to exist."

But "this divine guidance did not help me to get back to my old close relationship with Allah." Hasna's sister, who she loved dearly, "was struck by cancer," and her spiritual anguish deepened. This new crisis undermined the stable belief system of her youth. "Once again, in shock, I questioned the existence of Allah." Despite her sister surviving painful surgery and ultimately recovering from the cancer, Hasna's faith system had broken down. "I could not bring myself to prayer every night, or accept that there is something divine out there."

It had been nearly a decade since these events. In recent years, Hasna had felt a growing spiritual vacuum and a yearning to reexamine these events. Despite rejecting her childhood image of God as protector, she sensed that her anger and disappointment, reinforced by secular society, had cut her off from the spiritual dimension of her life. Writing about these events helped Hasna organize her thoughts and feelings about those stressful times and helped her look at them from a new perspective.

> What am I hoping to learn in this class? To find a way back to that old feeling of comfort. The comfort of knowing there is something out there, which wishes me good and is willing to listen and take good care of me.

Despite yearning for the simplicity of her childhood relationship with God, Hasna recognized that her questions required a deeper answer: Could relationship with Allah withstand awareness of life's pain, disappointments, and uncertainties?

Sensing this possibility, and longing to intensify her relationship with Allah, Hasna set a goal for herself. This goal became the specific behavioral focus of her self-inquiry project:

> In Islam, there is the concept of remembrance. There are probably many different ways of describing it, but I am going to pick one particular description. One needs to stop everything he/she is doing and pray, physically and mentally, five times a day. This prayer includes thanking Allah for all that you have and asking for the things you need. I wish to accomplish at least three times a day, this particular prayer.

Her goal also included psychological growth. "I am hoping to find more peace within myself."

Reviewing her complex history and articulating these concrete goals energized Hasna. The following week, she asserted her sense of empowerment by altering the self-inquiry assignment. She decided to write a personal letter to God. She began with an explanation:

> I have chosen to express myself through a one way conversation with Allah. [In this letter], I have described what God is to me. I feel that what I am, and what I have been, was my responsibility rather than any other role model's manipulation. I feel strongly that I have chosen to be in a relationship with Allah, today, through the trials and errors of my past. People in my life have had influences on me. However, I was the one who made the decision to keep or ignore this friendship.

Then she included the letter:

> There is no other God but Allah. It has no beginning and no ending. It was not begotten nor does it beget. It simply says be, and it is. I came from you and I shall return to you.

Forgive me, because I have denied your existence. As I have denied my own wisdom. Leave the doors, and my heart, open to you. This soul is trying to get back to the same feeling again; the full, the complete, the loving, and the one that is loved. I yearn to be back with you. I have passed from a dark corridor. In this pathway, there was danger, anxiety, love, passion, anger, knowledge, and choices.

This soul has been searching for herself. How is it that we have so much distance between us? Is it because I have made a journey of insecurity, and disbelief? Hold on to me, as I would like to hold on to you. I need the strength that you have always supplied me with. I am angry you know. You let me down, as I have let you down too. I am sorry for the pain I have caused both of us. I need answers! I have questions, thirsty for knowledge. Where are you among all this dismay?

Will you give me [someday] the parts of me that are silenced? Let them speak, and break the walls—because once they are broken I will know who I am.

Thank you for all I have: the sun, my friends, family, a warm home, and a loved one. Thanks for all the protection and choices.

In the next self-inquiry essays, the meaning of the closing section of her letter became clear. Hasna examined her identity as a woman in Muslim culture. This aspect of identity felt complex. While she valued this role, it included important aspects of self that had been silenced.

I come from a culture that is patriarchal. However, there is a strong religious and cultural component which speaks to the importance of respecting women and elders. Respecting elders is such an important part of community that anyone who does not take care of the elders—and their extended family—is looked down on. Within the family, a woman comes to the role of superiority through motherhood. In the religious texts, it is said that heaven is beneath the feet of mothers. In the eye of Allah, the best person is the man or woman who does the best deeds and who follows the prescribed life.

The image of a good woman still lingers in my mind. She is someone able to manage a household with ease, have complete satisfaction with raising well behaved children, and somehow, if they are poor, be able to stretch her husband's earnings to the next month.

Hasna recognized the constraints of this traditional role, as seen through a modern, feminist, Western perspective. But she did not consider the role demeaning. She affirmed the respect that women receive in Muslim culture, as she had experienced these dynamics. Hasna also noted that Allah is not conceptualized in Islam as male.

> In Islam, Allah is not in the likeness of humankind. It does not have gender. It is a power source, a light called *Noor*. There are no human bodies, such as priests, between a person and Allah. One asks for what she/he wishes directly from it. Although prayer with a community is encouraged, one can pray where ever one may be.

At the same time, she disagreed with certain aspects of her religion. Although she considered Islam tolerant, life in the United States had introduced her to many different spiritual traditions whose value she now recognized.

> As far as looking at different groups and religions, [in Islam] there is tolerance of others, as long as they believe in God. However, multi-Gods, or believing in nature to be God, is forbidden. For a long time I have struggled with this idea. How was I to rationalize the notion of so many peoples' beliefs as not being fitted into my world of Islam?

Recently, she had begun to find her own way to resolve this dilemma.

> I have discovered a sweet surprise. There are 99 other names that are listed for Allah within the Quran. Here are some: The giver of life, The taker of life, Protecting Friend, Creator of the Harmful, The Preventive of Harm, The Maker of Order, All Compassionate, The Patient One, The Avenger, The Forgiving, The Just—and the list goes on. Perhaps the message is clear. There is no need to look elsewhere for a creator, when it is present in everything.
>
> Every culture is holding on to a different part of the elephant. We all describe it to be something else. Perhaps we need to gather all the information we have and see what we can piece together. As far as who I am now, I still am piecing it together.

Hasna also sought greater empowerment and clarity for her emotional life—an aspect of being a woman in which she felt most silenced by her family upbringing and Muslim cultural norms.

> I want to work on accessing my feelings. I have found that, on many different occasions, I do not know what I feel. Changing this behavior is very important to me. It will allow me to be whole once again. To my dismay, many times I experience a blank wall, not knowing how I feel. I am not sure when this behavior began. Most probably, when I was very young. It was never considered, and I had no right to verbalize it, in my family.

Hasna had also begun to recognize the negative impact of emotional stress on her physical health, interpersonal behavior, and relationships.

> Throughout college, I have been discovering and confronting my different parts. This journey has enabled me to feel more confident, aware, and whole as a person.
>
> However conscious or unconscious this behavior is, [stress] has a great amount of effect on my mental and physical health. I know that when I am angry, hurt, frustrated, or rushed, I get strong stomach aches which can last a whole day. In certain situations, if I am very stressed, it may evoke a migraine headache.
>
> In my personal relationships of the past, not acknowledging my anger, frustrations, and displeasure has caused some of my close friendships to suffer.

In her letter to God and subsequent essays, Hasna discovered three parallel themes. First, to deepen her relationship with God, others, and self, she needed to know her emotions. Second, she needed the strength to express them. Third, locking these unexamined feelings inside was unhealthy and isolating. Excited, Hasna wanted to risk discussing this learning in class. This degree of vulnerability felt like a big step. But she wanted to break through this self-isolation.

> I am nervous and excited about sharing this with others. I have been working on it for a while now, yet not as actively as I would want it to be. I have learned that I have many walls to break through in order to reach my own truth.

As this self-reflective process helped Hasna understand the sources of emotional turmoil and inner silence, she became less self-critical. She experienced inner relief, and liberation, noting, "I am learning to empathize with myself through this project."

Exploring the psychological benefits of remaining emotionally unaware, Hasna reached another layer of self-awareness.

> I numb my feelings to function with the rest of my world. This negative behavior helped me a lot at one point in my life. I do not feel that I would have been able to cope. I still am able to shut off a part of me that is hurt, and go on with daily living. If I had to deal with the pain and stress at all times, there would be no room to breathe. I could not concentrate on school, work, or friendships. My numbness gives me a sense of control over my life.

Writing a psychospiritual autobiography helped Hasna in two distinct ways. From the perspective of content, she learned how she had become alienated from herself, her culture, and her religion. From the perspective of process, she learned to become mindful of the events, memories, emotions, and thoughts that were sources of her psychological turmoil.

Contemplative Self-Inquiry During Meditation
While writing her autobiography, Hasna was introduced to meditation as a tool for self-regulation, eliciting the relaxation response and developing mindful awareness of sensations, thoughts, and feelings. But as she conducted her life review, her anger at God grew increasingly visceral and intrusive. During one class, her agitation completely hijacked these self-regulation practices. After this class, Hasna wrote her passionate letter to God, filled with anger and grief.

Writing this letter was constructive, helping her name her emotions concretely. It also helped Hasna begin listening to herself, identifying specific causes of her agitation. By writing feelings that she experienced as nearly intolerable, they became more specific and manageable. This writing strengthened her use of meditation as a self-regulation skill.

Hasna approached our next learning module eagerly. Seeking guidance from an inner mentor was consistent with her experience of prayer in the Muslim tradition. Frankl's existential question seemed meaningful as a guidance-seeking focus, particularly as follow-up to the issues she explored in her psychospiritual autobiography. But this contemplative process confronted Hasna with new obstacles. As she observed the images that arose spontaneously during imaginal work, the inner sanctuary that took form in her mind was frightening:

> The space looks kind of empty, made of marble, cold. There are other darker rooms as well. I am overwhelmed. Scared. It is as if all these images are going to drown me.

The rooms were filled with images of fragmented, contorted bodies. They were "sad looking, broken, not very human at all." One body was "covered with scars, half of her body that is. She is very sad, yet it is me."

Initially frightened, Hasna explored their meaning in her essays. These symbolic images expressed suppressed grief: bouts of terror before her family left Algeria, anguish at her father's illness, anger with an absent God who had abandoned her. One image had particular meaning:

> She says, "Shish! Don't say anything, don't talk." I know very well what this means. My silent part for years to come.

This image symbolized frightened silence: a traumatized figure who had internalized intense emotions in speechless horror.

Hasna no longer felt frightened by this contemplative process. She recognized that these meditations were releasing memories and emotions which had been buried in her silenced self. She no longer needed to numb her emotions or avoid the fragmented, broken parts of herself. During one contemplation, her inner wisdom took the form of a female figure, disfigured with scars from Hasna's life history. But this figure was not defeated or constrained by these scars. She became an inner mentor who asked Hasna to love her as she was, while at the same time offering Hasna guidance and strength for releasing the pain from these wounds.

> She gave me two words to say when I am scared, 'Free yourself!' I have been using them constantly. [They remind me] that I have control over my life and feelings. I can change my behavior. [My past] does not have to rule me.

Hasna's mentor became a numinous, trustworthy, inner presence. She realized that these symbolic encounters with wounded figures representing her past were guiding her in a process of healing, in which she could incorporate these memories. With new confidence, she wrote,

> I somehow feel more whole. I know what is in there, and I have access to it. I am not completely frozen after all. There is a great hope in being able to erase some of the scars that were created beforehand. I have a great urge to draw this being. It is me.

Hasna had begun to construct a new image of herself, gradually experiencing an intact "part of me that is untouched [by my painful life experiences]....I am whole after all." Then Hasna envisioned herself transforming the somber environment of her inner sanctuary: "Perhaps I will bring pots of flowers, maybe even plant some, in this cold home."

At the same time, Hasna developed new insights about the impact of her chain of pain on her interpersonal behavior:

> ...the parts from the past come in whenever they need to, usually without my invitation. I know this because I become very sensitive whenever I feel someone does not listen or care for what I say. I get hurt and angry.

This important recognition reflected Hasna's dawning recognition of her interpersonal reactivity: prickly behavior she had begun to observe in herself during the community-building activities. But rather than turning these insights against herself, a self-defeating pattern from the past, she was learning to view them through an emerging capacity for empathic self-reflection. This empathic perspective, in turn, created pathways for resilient growth:

> Now I know why my need to be heard and understood is so deep. It is my little child that is screaming. My job is to realize this, and perhaps feed my soul the strength it needs.

In a subsequent meditation, her inner mentor embodied a previously unfamiliar part of herself: an unwounded core. The mentor first appeared as a disfigured body, then she "shed her shell of hurt and scars." Hasna noted with undisguised pleasure:

> I have not been able to get her back into the shell again. This [meditation process] gives a different picture of myself. I am an adult, not a scared child any more. So much of me was made by others. I can love them, without being afraid. I thank God for this opportunity.

Self-Evaluation of Learning

This self-inquiry project, Hasna affirmed, had helped her to examine herself with a new degree of non-defensive clarity and empathic self-understanding.

> I was able to write down my self-defeating behaviors. I understand that these behaviors do not make me a lazy, stupid, or useless person. I am able to go back to different stages of my life when these behaviors began and understand the reasons for them.

She also noted reduced interpersonal reactivity and less fear of being shamed by peers:

> I am able to share my inner world with more than one person, for the first time, without being so afraid of what they will think.

Hasna highlighted the importance of her contemplative experiences: both her exploration of emotional scars from her chain of pain and her discovery of an unwounded core self.

> This process has made me aware that I do have a part that is not touched by all the hurt and scars. I have ventured into my [inner] self, discovered different parts of me—the scary, the child, the helpless—and I know that I have access to them now. I can have conversations with them, and ask what they need in order for us to heal.

Hasna also reflected on growth that had taken place in her spirituality. She had found many parallels between her Muslim worldview and key elements of the Perennial Philosophy presented in the curriculum, noting, "Many things I used to believe got repeated in class." In addition to feeling her worldview accepted, the self-inquiry project provided her with structured assignments and experiential tools to explore and resolve her alienation from Islam.

> Overall, I feel a lot closer to Allah. I feel more at peace with myself. I have been reading and practicing my religion to a greater extent. I wanted to get closer to Allah. My wish was to pray daily, three times. I am close to this goal.

Hasna closed with several insights about the inner heart, and its outer layer of scar tissue.

It can be a veil over our eyes and being. It can take us to a place where we continue to repeat a pattern of hurt and anger, and not see what is underneath the hard cover of our hearts. It can also become a vessel, which enhances our inner beauty and lets the core be known to the rest without being afraid. It lets us know ourselves completely—where we do not feel incomplete and wronged.

This learning had begun to transform her worldview:

Eventually everybody can find their inner core where they are in complete sync with the rest of the cosmos. Cosmos is not dark and lonely. Once we remove the veil of hurt from our vision, world and everyone changes—including ourselves.

These poignant statements summarized her substantive growth developing a resilient worldview and secure existential attachment.

Concluding Analysis

Growth in the Five Dimensions of Psychospiritual Maturation

The 10 case studies presented in this chapter illustrate substantive growth in the five dimensions of person-centered psychospiritual maturation. As reported in Chap. 6, the narrative material from each student in the experimental group ($N = 127$) was analyzed for growth in these five dimensions. The 10 students in this chapter were selected to exemplify the full range of their learning. Following the development of each case study, a detailed analysis was written, examining their growth. The following explication of Hasna's learning in the five dimensions of psychospiritual maturation is a representative example of these analyses:

Bio-Behavioral At the beginning of this class, Hasna reported a high degree of anxiety and confused feelings about her prolonged withdrawal from Islam, providing initial indicators of the psychophysiological distress she was experiencing. This distress was illustrated further in her anger at God, turbulent emotions during meditation, and interpersonal reactivity. By the end of class, Hasna had developed important new stress-coping skills: mindfulness, elicitation of the relaxation response, and the capacity for empathic self-reflection. Growing internal composure was evident in her ability to sustain meditative concentration and to explore traumatic aspects of her personal history. Further, Hasna achieved her self-selected goals for behavioral change: increased frequency of daily prayer and a greater degree of inner peace.

Cognitive-Sociocultural : This growth process required significant maturation in Hasna's thought processes. Writing a psychospiritual autobiography helped Hasna identify specific areas of stress reactivity, develop a coherent narrative about her sociocultural identity and relational tensions created by her family's immigration to the United States, understand her current alienation from Islam through a developmental perspective, challenge Muslim female social norms that undermined emotional self-awareness and empowerment, and affirm positive aspects of her Muslim identity by deconstructing introjected shame from a culturally-insensitive counselor. In addition, Hasna's childhood conception of God as external protector evolved to a more mature understanding of Allah as a mentoring inner presence. These investigations produced growth in cognitive flexibility, stress tolerance, internal locus of evaluation, and empathic self-reflection.

Social-Emotional : Participation in a community that combined in vivo interpersonal learning with autobiographical writing helped Hasna develop emotional self-awareness and repair insecure attachment templates. She identified emotional numbing as a primary stress-coping strategy, developed access to suppressed emotions and memories, and integrated painful aspects of her life history, achieving a new degree of emotional integration and congruence. In addition, Hasna reduced her interpersonal reactivity, learning not to fear presumed negative judgments. Further, she deepened her capacity for emotional bonding by sharing details about her Muslim identity, personal life, and psychospiritual growth process.

Existential-Spiritual : Developing intuitive access to her own inner wisdom through a robust process of contemplative practice played a key role helping Hasna develop a greater degree of secure existential attachment. As her inner mentor became a trustworthy source of guidance, this female figure helped Hasna engage in empathic self-reflection, heal wounds from her traumatic past, counter Hasna's upbringing as a woman by affirming her emotions, develop self-regulation skills, and learn to maintain a significant degree of internal composure during these difficult explorations. The particular form in which this mentor appeared was uniquely suited to the particularities of Hasna's life, providing robust support and unexpected challenge during this learning process. In addition, the increasingly numinous quality of her inner mentor increased Hasna's experience of being securely attached to Allah.

Integrative Consolidation of a Resilient Worldview : Through these learning processes, Hasna developed a more resilient worldview, characterized by increased confidence in life and self. Initially feeling emotionally overwhelmed by her difficult life circumstances, she had learned to grow from them, discovering that she had the strength to integrate these experiences positively into her life and future behavior. This learning increased her internal locus of control and self-confidence during stress. Hasna's confidence in life also increased substantively. Initially feeling betrayed and abandoned by God, she now experienced Allah as a trustworthy, inner guiding presence. This sense of robust attachment deepened her confidence in life, as expressed in her notable statement that "cosmos is no longer dark and lonely."

Unifying Constructs : Through synergistic growth in these five dimensions of person-centered psychospiritual maturation, Hasna demonstrated movement toward *secure existential attachment*, evidenced in her growing capacity for *connective awareness*. Rather than feeling isolated from self, she grew more congruent, deepening an internal locus of evaluation. Rather than feeling socially isolated from others, she developed relational confidence. Rather than feeling existentially alienated, she felt connected to *life*, an attachment that she experienced as relationship with Allah/God. This holistic growth strengthened Hasna's capacity for internal composure, a defining characteristic of secure existential attachment.

In closing, this analysis provides a detailed evaluation of Hasna's psychospiritual growth in the five dimensions of person-centered psychospiritual maturation. Similar growth is evident in the case studies of each student in this chapter. These 10 case studies have illustrated the substantive degree of person-specific psychospiritual growth that was facilitated through participation in the *Know Your Self* curriculum.

CHAPTER 11

The Learning Community: An Inclusive Environment for Person-Centered Psychospiritual Growth: Group Case Study #4

This chapter completes the presentation of results and case study material from this research project. It highlights the central role of the inclusive learning community as a catalytic, prosocial holding environment for growth in the five dimensions of psychospiritual maturation.

STUDENT REFLECTIONS ON COMMUNITY-BUILDING AND EXPERIENTIAL LEARNING

In their final self-inquiry essays, students often commented on the value of experiential learning and community-building. The following examples present key themes:

- I have seen how profound experiential learning can be. I learned that journaling can be a powerful way for things buried to come to the surface. I learned the power of anonymous sharing as a way to share intimate parts of ourselves without fear or shame. I learned the power of having thoughts, feelings, and behaviors normalized by seeing parts of ourselves in other group members. This reduced isolation and stigmatization that can occur when we struggle with stress. I learned how exercises that seem simple can create profound meaning. They allow us to feel deep realizations rather than just thinking about them cognitively, creating *aha* moments. Group learning adds a dimension to wellness that I had not realized. Being part of a group allows one to experience community, to realize the commonalities we share, to see that we are not just waves but part of the ocean.

- It was comforting to hear from others using anonymous sharing. It was reassuring to find that so many students were going through similar types of experiences whether we were discussing the inner critic, responses to stress, reactions to meditation activities or work in small groups. Every person had an equal voice during the anonymous sharing which was important to creating group cohesion. It expedited the group's openness and allowed us to share personal feelings in an open yet confidential way. Had we shared in a more traditional hand-raising style, we would not have reached the same depth and honesty.

  As we continued to use anonymous sharing, I noticed that more people willingly pointed out which comment was theirs. I found this interesting because at the beginning of the class, no one identified their submission. I attribute this in some part to the respect and patience that was given to each person's writing. A rapport was built that created a nonjudgmental, affirming atmosphere.

- Initially, I was skeptical of the self-inquiry project because previous "failures" at mindfulness, meditation, and journaling had led me to believe I would never find true success or meaning in these practices. Now, I know that these "failures" were projections of my own fears of profound connections.

Learning-in-Community: The Five Dimensions of Psychospiritual Maturation

Community-building followed a consistent developmental arc. Initially, students felt vulnerable and cautious. During this introductory phase, the instructor modeled reflective listening, empathic understanding, emotional congruence, and unconditional positive regard. As group cohesion developed, students became less guarded and their bonds facilitated constructive explorations of sociocultural differences. Still, as the group evolved, conflicts emerged that required self-inquiry and restorative dialogue. Group bonding also helped students share their highly meaningful contemplative growth experiences. Over time, as students developed trusting relationships, there was a shift in the interpersonal atmosphere. They demonstrated a growing capacity for interpersonal attunement, compassion, and unconditional positive regard: attitudinal indicators of secure existential attachment. During higher-order analysis, the impact of learning-in-community was evident in each dimension of psychospiritual maturation.

Bio-Behavioral Dimension

The community-building experience provided interpersonal challenge, feedback, and support that helped student's develop self-regulation skills. Using experiential work that ranged from the peacock feather exercise, inner critic work, exploration of stress coping mechanisms, and discussions of sociocultural factors affecting their psychospiritual development, students learned to increase resilient modes of stress coping.

- A Caucasian American female, who had strengthened self-empowerment skills, wrote:

    I was able to name my physical, mental, and emotional reactions to stress. When things pile up (papers, readings, work), I start feeling overwhelmed. I have been noticing a pattern of feeling manic. I abandon regular sleeping patterns, eating healthy, and exercising, putting work first, at all costs. When the assignments are submitted, I am depleted. It takes a while before I can regulate my body and mind, and sometimes I am not back in a healthy routine before the next wave of responsibilities piles up. On the flip side, when I feel intense stress, I sometimes shut down. I get flustered, can't prioritize, get easily confused, and frozen. Trying to navigate between these two reactions is difficult, especially in freeze mode. The most helpful realizations took place during anonymous sharing. My reaction felt normalized. I felt connected and understood.

- Another Caucasian American female, a survivor of physical and sexual abuse, found meditation difficult in the early stages of self-inquiry. Agitated feelings and painful memories surfaced. After sharing her life story and receiving peer support, she began to consider the concept of an unhurt core part of self. She decided to participate in meditation work on the inner heart. Her final self-inquiry essay reflected substantive and poignant learning:

    I am beginning to heal my memory a little. I let bad or scary memories (which the meditation stirred up) simply drift past me. For example, I have a painful childhood memory that I still have difficulty believing to be true. When it comes up, I think I'm remembering wrong—that I'm *crazy* for thinking it. This week, I didn't fight it coming up, or contemplate whether it was true or not. I just let it be and quietly moved past it.

I am able to tolerate my memories better than I was able before I began this semester. I am also better able to experience and accept my feelings. Sadness bubbles up in me after a meditation, even when it's a good experience. Maybe it's a sadness I need to feel in order to learn from my meditations. It's always accompanied by hope. My unexplored or unresolved memories, and my difficulty letting myself feel things, is the root of the anxiety, hypervigilance, and physically aroused state I set out to work on in my self-inquiry topics. I am now working at a better, deeper level than I originally expected.

- An African American male wrote:

Group work has helped me see that my reaction to stress is two-fold. Physically, the muscles in my body tense and my blood pressure rises. I even have tension in my face. Emotionally, I get confrontational. I tend to fight first and then resort to flight. When faced with conflict, I want the problem to go away, and frequently get annoyed with the other person. To overcome these natural tendencies, I have implemented tools from this course. My goal is to find productive, peaceful ways to manage conflict and stress.

Practicing mindfulness has been very helpful. I use this tool to recognize stress in the early stages of its inception, before it escalates. I am becoming more aware of triggers that contribute to my stress, such as being overtired, overworked, feeling overwhelmed, and breakdowns in communication. Meditation has also been helpful. When I begin to feel stressed, I use deep breathing to slow my heart rate, reduce my blood pressure, and release the stress from my body.

- A Caucasian American female, who examined her rigid upbringing, explored a different form of self-regulation. During experiential community-building with music and circle dancing, she watched others, becoming aware of her self-constricting behavior:

Singing. Dancing. Holding hands. The singers, some of them, sing different notes. The dancers, some of them, dance different steps. But I cannot. I keep the original steps, the steady beat, the first melody, while others play. I always had to stay home and take care of things while others played. I have taken this role again and again in my life, while others get to play, relax, change the tune, and vary the steps.

This student experimented with releasing her energy through creative self-expression. Affirmed by group members, she experienced new autonomy and self-confidence.

- Students also learned from the example of positive role models:

    I appreciated the vulnerability others have shown discussing their self-inquiry process. It has helped me feel less alone and isolated. Observing others model their vulnerabilities provided me with important knowledge: I am not so different from everyone else in my struggles, weaknesses and successes. I am also more aware of a sense of compassion that I feel toward others which allows me to connect easier.

Thus, community building contributed to self-regulatory and connective behavioral skills.

Cognitive-Sociocultural Dimension

Exploring the impact of sociocultural identity and social dominance hierarchies on their psychospiritual development, while also investigating spiritual traditions they had learned to consider *other*, inclusive community-building provided a forum for students to deconstruct harmful narratives about self and others. This learning process required a thoughtful mixture of empathic self-reflection and critical analysis, catalyzing honest dialogue and introspection about these challenging subjects. Chapter 8 presents many examples. Students developed positive self-narratives that countered messages from the inner critic and learned to identify these negative scripts as a destructive inheritance from humanity's chain of pain.

- A Caucasian American female wrote:

    Empathic self-reflection was a new concept for me. I now understand that a starting point is examining my developmental process. I saw how interwoven my religious, family, social and cultural experiences were. All of these factors, positive and negative, have made me who I am today.

- Another Caucasian American female wrote about the impact of her ethnicity:

When we looked at our family histories and positions of power or oppression that we hold and dissected ways that these intersections influence how we react and treat ourselves in times of stress, I began to understand my inner critic as something separate from myself—I don't need to hold onto the harsh messages that run through my mind. When I looked at where these messages originated, I saw that some came from several generations of family dynamics and cultural values, others came from my position in society as a woman. Unpacking and unraveling the origins of the inner critic allowed me to create space for more compassionate self-talk to come through.

Among students from a socially-conservative Caucasian American Christian background, the community experience contributed to increased cognitive flexibility and inclusion of the *other*:

- A big part of this class was learning about our different spiritual and cultural identities and how we all, with our differences, can still be a community. I think the integrated community is stronger than one that is homogeneous. A lot of me wants to believe in the connectedness of all the world's religions, but a little voice from my upbringing still says, there can be only one that is "right." This view presents a problem because it does not allow us to meet on common, equal ground. So, until I can come to a more complex understanding of these two views, I will continue to sit with both feelings but listen mostly to the one which connects humanity rather than alienates and discriminates.

Among students of color, the community experience reduced internalized negative attitudes about self. This shift was evident in their self-inquiry essays where they commented on the anonymous sharing process. These comments reflected an internalized sense of inadequacy and how anonymous sharing helped them overcome this socially-reinforced myth.

- A Latina American wrote:

This class about spirituality and well-being was a chance to find out that the stress I am going through is not only because of all the cultural barriers I confront on a personal and professional level. It is also because being a student at any level is stressful. During the first weekend, I felt surprise during one of the anonymous readings when a high number of my classmates expressed having the same reaction and hard time I have with academic stress. It is clear that the outcomes are shared by every single student, regardless of any situation or personal environment. Taking this relevant piece of information has helped me to adopt new techniques learned and practiced in this class.

- A Latino American undergraduate, who emigrated to this country, wrote:

For a long time I saw myself as a student who has more problems than others. I never put myself in somebody else's situation regarding the academic stress and the personal issues that they may have. Through this class, I found out that, like me, other students are dealing with very difficult situations.

- Another Latina American student wrote:

The journey through the self-inquiry process was eye-opening. My own response to academic stress and interpersonal conflict has not been brought to my attention at such a deep level. I have known how easily I can get "stressed out" whenever there is a lot demanded from me in school and work. Before this class, I believed I was the only one who handled academic stress in a negative way. To my surprise, most of us in class have dealt with stress negatively. I appreciated having our group discussion on academic stress because it completely normalized my experience.

The positive changes can be attributed to building a trusting community in order to discuss our difficulties with academic stress which has normalized the experience and lessened my shame. I started feeling like I was not alone. The shame kept my reaction to stress hidden and only reinforced them.

Students also deconstructed persistent stereotypes separating Jews and Christians. For example, a Latina American examined negative stereotypes among Catholic Dominicans against Jews who came to her island homeland escaping the Nazis. Conversely, Jewish students wrote about overcoming stereotypes about Christians.

- A Caucasian Jewish American wrote:

Doris (fictitious name) was raised Catholic, and I Jewish. Our upbringings were quite different. But we have connected through our goals in this class. We both have self-worth issues displayed through overeating and negativity.... We are compassionate towards one another's problems, and I have learned that our differences are really just similar struggles with different faces.

In addition, Christian students of color, from countries with a history of colonialism, deconstructed stereotypes about religious traditions native to their culture. For example, a South Asian Christian developed new respect for Hinduism. An African American deepened his understanding of Islam. A Latina American developed new respect for Santeria.

Thus, as discussed in Chap. 4, when a learning community inhabits a sufficiently deep level of sociocultural awareness, the discovery of similarities can be profoundly transformative.

- A Caucasian American student, for whom inclusive community was new, wrote:

The experience of being in a class and witnessing all of the differences among the members while at the same time experiencing such a profound coming together and connection that unifies us all is very powerful.

- A Latina American student wrote:

Each person in our class is richly complex with their own life paths, stories, thoughts, beliefs, spirituality, talents, and vulnerabilities. I appreciated the globe exercise to learn where we come from. My bias of Caucasian people was that there is no cultural diversity or richness to their Whiteness. As I look back now, I scoff at my ignorant bias. This activity enhanced my experience and respect for my Caucasian peers. We all come from remarkably diverse cultures and countries. The United States of America is a land of immigrants. People of color are not the only immigrants in this country. Once this epiphany occurred, I felt my heart and mind open to our community.

Social-Emotional Dimension

Community-building provided an in vivo laboratory for students to examine and repair their relational attachment templates. This learning took many forms.

Many students learned to listen to others receptively, with the intention of understanding their perspectives. Developing mindful self-awareness, they overcame reactive tendencies to dispense advice, feel defensive, or become argumentative:

- One ability I've developed, especially through classroom discussions, is to hear another's perspective and not feel that I have to agree with it, but also not feel that I have to argue with it. Simple acceptance is the key.

- I think back to the earliest classes and remember my "reaction" to another student's comment—feeling strongly defensive. That experience, coupled with the entire semester of hearing different individuals' opinions on the readings and/or the self-inquiry process itself, has helped me be more accepting of others' ideas and perspectives and worldviews, and less likely to feel the need to defend myself. I was surprised to find myself saying, recently, that disagreement does not equal troubled relationships.

Students also strengthened emotional congruence and self-advocacy skills:

- I have learned the importance of speaking out for myself when things don't feel right. I would like to expand this into all of the areas of my life. Speaking out is about taking my feelings seriously and respecting them. That is what the safety [in this class] is about.

- During a circle dance, I found myself feeling restricted by holding hands and the pressure to move in only one direction. After some inner debate, I let go. I am still thinking about how liberating it felt. It was a new experience for me.

Others, learning from peer role models, recognized their need for further growth:

- A person with a different behavioral style impacted me with her openness. I was impressed with her candidness. I can't share deeply in class, afraid of being overcome with emotion. I also can't engage in conflict in class, but she seemed to take it in stride.

Interpersonal conflict, as discussed in Chap. 8, can be approached as a catalyst for maturational growth. Community building had an important role in this learning process.

- Learning to be at peace with encountering conflict is a skill I'm working on. It's an area where I feel vulnerable and insecure. During explorations in class, I was reminded that my passive-aggressive behavior stems from being hurt by others' "insensitive" behavior, and feeling that my dignity or identity is threatened. The exercise where we experienced the receiving end of our stress response was a powerful way to gain perspective. It's one thing to write down your behaviors and understand why they happen. But to experience them in real time and be forced to confront the intent and impacts of lashing out was eye-opening. It wasn't difficult to imagine how other people feel when I behave this way. It was an exercise that gave me a lot to think about.

- I still hurt people and am grouchy at times. What has changed is my awareness of when and how this seems to happen. I have noticed that several factors contribute to biting moods and actions. When I feel threatened, unloved, unaccepted, and unheard, I get mean. When I feel anxious and unsafe, I lash out. Being physically tired exacerbates my response. I have engaged in this behavior less than before this class. I am able to recognize situations which result in nasty behavior.

As described in Chap. 8, some students had in vivo experiences of conflict, developing and modeling restorative dialogue skills:

- Two adult undergraduates had a complex experience that led to important learning:

In an early meeting of our small group, "Yvonne" disclosed that she was divorced from her husband and they were unable to have children because he was sterile. We knew very little about each other, but she did know that I was married, my husband had died, and I have an adult daughter. I attempted to share stories of friends who had experiences similar to hers, but clearly that was not what Yvonne was looking for. She said I could not understand because I HAVE a daughter. What she did not know and what I [later] told her is that my daughter is not my birth child. She is my husband's natural daughter from a previous marriage. This came as a surprise to her. In her pain, Yvonne made an assumption that was incorrect. It was a lesson for both of us. I have learned from this class that we are connected in so many ways, and it is only in sharing that we learn just how deeply we are connected. I have made the same mistake that she did. I have made assumptions about people based on their outward appearance that were incorrect.

- Another student wrote:

   Our community gave me a chance to connect with a student I thought I did not like, and who got on my nerves. I was pretty sure she felt the same way about me. We barely spoke the first half of the semester. I am happy that I was proven wrong and proud of myself for remaining open to getting to know her in a different way. We are now supportive classmates and Facebook friends.

Other students, examining their relational styles, identified fear of attachment:

- I realize how rare it is, if ever, that I have felt like part of a community. In the past weeks I have discovered many things about my worldview: a recurring need for isolation due to lack of trust. This was created by early links in the chain of pain. Mistrust and fear of closeness reinforce my negative worldview. I have watched loneliness come up again and again. I don't allow myself to take chances with relationships. No one gets too close. I'm glad I no longer feel the pain of my father's death or my past poor judgments. But now I'm sick of feeling lonely and want to break down this shield. I am fighting a battle within myself, trying to be close to someone, but keeping my distance. Whenever I see the slightest chance of my emotional bond becoming too strong, I run.

- A student with a visible physical disability undertook a poignant exploration:

   Something sad was stirred up deep within me. It began when we sang *love each other as yourself*. [I remembered] my past attempts trying to do this and began to feel sorry for myself — as I realized how much work I had ahead of me to attain this love for myself.

She was relieved when the singing stopped. In the silence, she could push her feelings away.

My reaction does not surprise me when I consider my addiction [to being alone]. But something different was present in this space: the other people who surrounded it and the love that emanated from them. There was my goal, right before me, yet unattainable. I was also unattainable to them physically, my body position crouched up and contained. I wonder what might have happened if I had opened myself up to the group and allowed their love to fill my space. Would I have been welcomed and received?

In each cohort of students, there were many interpersonal interactions that generated experiences of reparative attachment:

- Old behaviors resurfaced in the group: panic, fear, insecurities. Being better and worse than others. But it sorted itself out as the semester went along. It became easier to really listen to others, and the need to have people listen to me lessened considerably. I spent a good deal of time feeling un-liked—and "in the way" of the group. That feeling too is lessening. One time, a classmate indicated that she felt safer doing the group [activities] if I was there. Then I started to feel that maybe I had a place.

- In class, a Latino adult undergraduate was explaining his discomfort discussing religion, a topic he had written about extensively in a self-inquiry essay:

    I grew up in a country where the religion that influences society is Christianity and the Bible is the book with the rules we were supposed to follow to obtain eternal salvation. Writing the first [class] assignment, I was concerned. In previous experiences, I have learned religion can bring a lot of controversy. Many of us have been influenced by our families, and religion has an enormous impact on our daily life.

As he spoke in the group, he alluded to emigrating from his country of origin because his family and religion did not accept him. Students responded warmly. But I sensed they were not hearing his statement fully. After indicating that I sensed the depth of his statements, I asked if there was more he wanted to say. Showing visible relief for being heard, he explained that he was gay. The students then responded with greater understanding. As conversation deepened, he noted that this was the first time he had affirmed his gay identity in an academic class. Later, he wrote:

Sharing in class was one of the most wonderful experiences in my life. I couldn't believe I was able to open my heart. I broke the chain I had for many years.

These experiences of reparative attachment and collaborative self-inquiry had a strong, positive impact on community cohesion and interpersonal bonding:

- For many years, I had been familiar with my inner critic. Its voice dominated the space between my ears. In fact, its voice had become so overwhelming that it became difficult to decipher these harsh condemnations from truth. In many ways, it was dictating reality. As the class engaged in anonymous sharing, it became evident that the inner critic existed in many forms, simultaneously managing the room's moods, feelings and actions. It was truly tremendous to see the impact of the critic outside my own personal experience. As this inner critic was brought to light, a profound experience occurred. Suddenly, a sense of community took shape at the hand of the inner critic. As a group, we bonded in our suffering, our vulnerability, and our shortcomings. Compassion seemed like the only reasonable attitude with which to approach anyone, including myself.

In summary, community building provided an in vivo laboratory for social-emotional development in which students identified and repaired insecure attachment templates, strengthened interpersonal skills, and developed greater compassion for self and others.

Existential-Spiritual Dimension

Meditating as a community deepened student explorations into the deep structure of contemplative mind. Chapters 9 and 10 have illustrated the value of spontaneous visualization work and imaginal dialogue, as sources of intuitive insight and wisdom. This section focuses on a final phase of meditation work, in which students cultivated awareness of the pre-conceptual, core dimension of self. These meditations often began with contemplative chanting, as a method for opening the heart, deepening mental concentration, and anchoring the mind in stillness.

We generally chant in English, to demystify this practice, using two chants that evoke core principles of the Perennial Philosophy. Secular humanists and American Buddhists find the first chant particularly salient, because it highlights mindfulness practice: *I am the watcher of the unfolding; I am the unfolded and the unfolding.* Students who identify with their Christian, Jewish, Muslim, or Hindu traditions, find the second chant particularly salient, because it highlights relationship with the Ground of Being: *We are opening to the light within, to the wisdom and love of the Holy One.* Students are invited to approach this activity as an experiment (in which they can assess the benefits of contemplative chanting or remain silent, if they prefer). Periodically, we also sing wordless contemplative melodies and tone the Sanskrit mantra Aum. I play guitar or harmonium to provide melodic and rhythmic structure. Afterwards, we meditate silently. Students use practices that currently work best for them, including mindfulness, mental concentration on the breath or a prayer/mantra, visualization methods, or anchoring themselves in relationship with the Ground of Being. Cultivating a receptive state of "active non-action," they learn to let meditation experiences unfold through a person-specific developmental process.

As their self-inquiry essays and anonymous sharing indicate, contemplative chanting contributed to an intensification of students' meditation experiences:

- I am the watcher. This is the first time I chanted in English. What a different experience. Though I find Eastern chants to be powerful and moving, understanding the words as they are chanted connected me in a way that felt more genuine.

- I felt centered in myself, while connected to a greater whole. The experience was initially strange. But I soon found my inhibitions released. There was a sound only I could contribute to the harmony. The energy emitted from the depths of our throats began to take on a life of its own; the vibrations made me feel calm and sustained.

- As I sit in centering prayer, I can feel the anxiety replaced by calm and well-being. I no longer feel the tension and fear. I do not feel alone or sad. I feel connected to an inner strength which supports me, and that has been there all along, masked by intense feelings.

- I was accustomed to the benefits that meditation/mindfulness provide in terms of stress reduction and feeling more attuned with my body and mind. However, I always felt as though my practice was lacking, as if something were missing. I would long for a connection to something greater than myself and something bigger than just noticing my thoughts and noticing my body. To be honest, I felt alone and lonely. I felt as though I just was directionless and had no foundation to what it was I was trying to connect with.

Meditating in this class has given me the opportunity to experience the connection I was looking for. It highlighted the sense of interconnectedness that is always present, but maybe not always felt. The most impactful moment came on the last day of class, when we were chanting and singing. I felt a visceral connection to everyone in the room, everyone in my life, and even all those I have not met. [Inwardly], I felt like I was greeting an old friend again, who was really myself–maybe even my Wise Self. I realized that we all at times can feel so lost, disconnected from who we truly are, or could be, and what a treasure it was to feel that strength inside of me again.

Students who had difficulty with this contemplative practice also described their experiences:

- As the chanting continued, my inner critic began to speak which stifled me. I grew self-conscious. My voice was shaky. Listening to others chant, I was able to feel connected and calm again. I gained confidence and my chanting became clearer.

Others reported dynamic experiences that included feelings of unitive awareness:

- I felt a "melting" into the chant and a sense that as we all sang, we rejoiced as one. I could feel pure love within me and had a strong desire to share it with everyone and everything. There were no boundaries, no delineations, which separated and divided us. We were all one joyous being, with many voices. I need to keep this awareness alive inside of me. Without [it], I lose my center and my worldview is negatively affected. [That is when] I contribute to the chain of pain, whether intentional or not.

- The music of the harmonium and the chanting touched a part of my heart I can't express with words. I had tears in my eyes when I realized the strength I need to face my life is always there, deep down inside. My place of contemplation changed. There was a spring bubbling and overflowing. "I am peace, I am light, I am love." I realized that this mantra came from my source of strength. So thankful for the loving support in this community.

- The simplicity of the music helped me relax and get into a deep meditative state. I felt all of us connected by light. I actually saw the light. There were arcs of light connecting each person through their hands. We were each in a lotus position. The light traveled from hand to hand, connecting us until we were a complete circle of light. Then the light traveled to the center of the room, shot upwards, and a sphere of light appeared. It exploded, enveloping us with love. I have never felt so peaceful and still in all my life.

- For much of the meditation, my mind was completely clear of any thought. I was still and peaceful. Towards the end, an image came into my head. There was a huge hill ahead of me and all I could see was the light coming from the sun, but I could never completely see the sun. As much as I tried to get up the hill, I couldn't get there. I was frustrated, [but] I knew I would eventually get there. So I sat in peace. Then [when Jared rang the closing bell], a blast of light filled my eyes. I was there at the top seeing the sun in full.

- I found myself contemplating the phrase "I rest in God." I found my heart with all of its pains and sorrows being embraced by these words. My felt sense of separation between my small self and my big Self begin to dissolve. This sense of Oneness with the Presence grew and I did not want to leave. I felt full—full of love, full of compassion, full of grace.

- The [Jewish] sacred names I repeated were *Raḥamim* (Compassion) and *Ruaḥ* (Breath; Spirit). I reflected on God as a presence beyond language and the limited forms and names we ascribe to the Ground of Being. I thanked *Ruaḥ* for each stretch of my lungs as I took in the breath of life. I prayed that all the other ways I stretch myself might be healthy ones. I prayed for the inner heart walls to stay tender while the outer walls pulsed me steadily onward in growth.

- My grandmother appeared. She greeted me in French as she did when I was a child, wrapping her arms around me in a full embrace. "Ma belle jeune fille!" I cleared my mind by settling into my grandmother's arms. I went deeper inside to connect with my heart center. I asked for a prayer, [and] clearly received "My soul doth magnify the Lord." Where did this come from? I was surprised. As I repeated this phrase I became aware of the light growing in my heart. I felt great joy and an almost physical sensation of connection—as if a cord of light was reaching from my heart to the heavens.

In summary, chanting and meditating in community intensified students' contemplative experiences. It helped them deepen an internally-directed perceptual orientation and become receptive to dynamic experiences that are available in the deep structure of contemplative mind. For many, these meditations introduced the felt experience of secure existential attachment.

Integrative Consolidation of Resilient Worldview

Community-building provided peer learning that helped students consolidate the resilient worldview, Confidence in Life and Self. These positive attitudes empowered them to transcend limiting cognitive schema and distorted perceptions about self and others. Community learning played an important role by helping them overcome interpersonal isolation and low self-esteem:

- I always thought everyone else had it together better than I did. It was invaluable to hear others' fears and insecurities. In realizing my basic commonality with others, not only have I realized that there's not that much wrong with the way I am… but also it has strengthened my empathy with others. Other people are just as fragile as I am!

- Hearing about struggles that others have gone through was very touching and at the same time I felt stronger from it. I felt the strength within the hardships. This is part of the connection. There is joy in sorrow. There is also power in what is Real. This class was real, and I feel empowered from the class and the people.

- I have learned how much I can learn from other people's experiences. My spiritual development is in its beginning stages, but this class and the people have really opened up a lot more avenues that I am willing to investigate, both internally and externally.

Many students strengthened resilient attitudes through the peacock feather exercise and inner critic work. Several women of color, having discussed how anonymous sharing reduced their internalized negative attitudes about self (see "Cognitive-Sociocultural Dimension"), later discussed how their new stress-coping skills were helping them build resilience:

- [Before this class] my life was a constant fight to keep myself up. [I was] always on the run, not able to say "no," even to myself. This exercise created a big positive experiment. To keep the feather up and find balance at the same time was very difficult, like my own existence. I found out how easily I can spend all my energy trying to find steadiness, without any luck, if I do not embrace a practice like mindfulness. I am still working hard, though a little differently. Like the peacock feather, I will fall many times. But I will be able to get up and keep working, until I find a way to be stable and balanced.

- Group discussion about our progress provided a forum for different methods on how to handle stress. I took away one of the many powerful messages shared in the group: "Stress is about perspective." If I am able to alter my perceptions to a more positive or even practical standpoint ("I'll be okay even if I don't complete all of my assignments perfectly"), the power of academic stress decreases significantly.

- It made a big difference to go inside my thoughts and heart to explore my inner critic, because this ultimately led to my spiritual self, my inner mentor. I learned through this journey that I can have control over how I respond to stress and interpersonal conflict. The major change that I continue to adopt is to create motion in order to shift my energy and change my emotion. In the past, I would try to sleep it off (i.e., freeze mode) and look forward to a better day. How empowering it is to notice my problem and move forward. My confidence comes from strengthening my relationship to my spiritual self.

- An impactful exercise that helped me understand myself better concerned the role of the "inner critic" and "inner mentor" in psychological health. Exploring how much influence the inner critic has on my self-perception and how these negative thoughts translate into my external behaviors was powerful. Through class discussions, it was also interesting to see how much of ourselves we define by this inner critic, how irrational these thoughts really are, and not conducive to a positive approach to life. Finding an inner mentor was also thought provoking. The realization that I have tools within myself to face life's challenges is reassuring. It creates hope for areas of insecurity and doubt I still struggle with. This class was truly one of the most enlightening, empowering experiences I have had in this academic program.

In a similar vein, a white student examined her internalized subordination as a woman:

- It was helpful to name my inner critic's voice and discuss my personal stress responses when faced with the need to assert myself during interpersonal conflict. My inner critic tells me that I will always be alone, that I am not good enough. When needing to speak my voice [with my boyfriend], I shut down and avoid the situation, feeling exposed and afraid of being disregarded. I experience feeling worried about hurting another person's feelings so much that I am not fully honest. These responses make it challenging to have genuine relationships. For a long time, I've been trying to find my confident voice, but have had difficulty expressing it. I realized that other women in class felt the same, and I appreciated this being reiterated through anonymous sharing.

Other students showed evidence of increased resilience as they healed emotional wounds during contemplative group work. A white student, daughter of an alcoholic father, wrote:

- An image came to my mind's eye: a pinkish-red glowing ball of light. I remained within this light and meditated on my childhood, my loneliness, and anger at my father. Sadness welled up inside my heart. While reviewing these wounds, my inner heart center said: "Forgive him, for he could only give what he had. It wasn't you who was not good enough to love back." I held those words in my heart, and meditated on forgiveness—for my father and for myself. I had been blaming us both. I felt heat radiate out of my heart center, moving down my arms, down my legs, and then I was breathing deeply, taking "in" this warm glow throughout my whole body. Then I was filled with an incredible amount of love. I understood that my father was just a man with his own life's wounds, his own chain of pain; and I had unknowingly become linked to it. I was able, during this meditation, to move beyond the pain to feel a separating and a healing within myself.

Another white student, who had seen her mother beaten by an alcoholic father, and who had felt guilty that she was not able to stop this violence, wrote:

- In a previous self-inquiry, I said that I feared being damaged in my core. I know when this fear developed: the night that I saw my mother damaged. The two are no longer connected. In my core, I know that I am not damaged. This wound just made me feel like I was. In my core, I know I am strong and safe. I love having the flame burning there. It is the eternal flame. It will always be there. I feel strong with the flame in my core. The flame protects me and tells me that I am full—of fire and life. It gives me a sense of peace and joy. My tears will never extinguish the flame.

Other students showed evidence of greater resilience as they described new inner resources that were helping them respond to interpersonal conflict more constructively:

- I realized that many of the conflicts I face are made more difficult when I don't feel connected to something greater than myself. I have been learning to maintain the core belief that beneath the chaotic surface of the ocean, I am okay. By holding this core belief I can approach whatever life throws at me with a peaceful intention.

- The more I feel attached to my own strength and wisdom, and allow myself to be humbled, the more creatively and faithfully I can approach and engage with conflict.

Other students expressed new confidence in self and life in their growing capacity for connective, relational behavior:

- I could have sat silently feeling alone with my fear but chose to share my burden because I want to break the isolating cycle. I was surprised to see that because I spoke out, it helped others speak out as well. I learned I did not have to be alone with my problems and that I could trust others in the group to support my feelings of sadness, guilt, and regret. I also learned that my vulnerability and strength affects others. We are the compassion, the truth, and the strength of our community.

Other students spoke about developing a new sense of confidence in life and self through the psychospiritual knowledge and resources they were developing. A white female student, who had begun to renew her Jewish spirituality, wrote:

- My anchoring prayer provides a connection to an inner place of calmness and control. Once settled, I see options and possibilities. This helps me feel better about myself and my worldview. This seems too easy. I have had the power all along—inside myself. I knew this, but wasn't aware how to tap into this power. I cannot change every external event that affects me. But I can change my reaction to them. My centering prayer, "Blessed be my light," connects me to a calm, unscarred, healthy place of possibility.

Other students showed evidence of greater confidence in life and self by discussing the personal spiritual foundations they were building, and knowledge they had gained about how the chain of pain replicates itself. This confidence was reflected in greater personal commitment to personal and social transformation, and greater confidence that they could succeed:

- My personal journey through this class has been enlightening, therapeutic & constructive. I learned about contemplative and transformative practices for community-building, restorative dialogue, and a deep understanding of the ways in which we impact and have been impacted by our role in the chain of pain.

  Ultimately, what will stick with me most is knowledge that this chain lives on through us — unless we learn to forgive ourselves and each other, and stop perpetuating this cycle. Now that my eyes are open, I'm going to try to compassionately hold myself accountable, as I move forward in my growth.

- This has always been my struggle with religion: how can the concept of God exist, a God with intentionality, alongside all the suffering that occurs in this world? This is where the notion of the chain of pain pulled everything together. We have lost our way. It feels so profound. I feel like I have so much to explore now within myself. I also feel inspired to turn back to Judaism. I'm on the right path.

Unifying Construct—Movement Toward Secure Existential Attachment

As students experienced a growing sense of confidence in life and self, their attitudes and behaviors reflected movement toward secure existential attachment, a construct that embodies mature spiritual awareness. In a world where change, uncertainty, and suffering are constants, secure existential attachment helps individuals remain anchored in awareness of connection to the Ground of Being, helping them encounter these challenges with internal composure and the ability to derive maturational growth.

Some students expressed evidence of this mature attitude in their contemplative experiences. One student's inner sanctuary was a cottage in the woods:

- It was late November, the end of the afternoon, and rather cold. I gathered kindling, and brought in wood, and got a fire going in the wood stove. I next got a couple of pails to walk down to the well to get water. As I left, I admired a leafless silver maple silhouetted against the sky. There was no wind, just cold, crisp, quiet. I felt a kind of sadness or emptiness. I sat down next to the tree and started saying the Hail Mary prayer. Then I got up and headed to the well. I bent to lift the cover of the well and noticed my own reflection coming back from the depth of the well water. I became aware of the presence of someone and saw the reflection of Christ in the water.

I drew water from the well and together we headed back to the camp. As we got closer, there was a merging into one. I finished the walk alone carrying the two pails of water, went into the camp and carried on, warmed by the heat from the fire in the stove.

Other students expressed movement toward secure existential attachment through their reflections on the community-building activities. These reflections often included reference to the circle dances that became a closing ritual at the end of many sessions. Students with a secular humanist worldview affirmed the human capacity for attuned interpersonal relationships and appreciation for the unconditional altruistic love that emerged as the groups bonded:

- Being a part of this community has strengthened my belief in the sacredness of being human. Our gathering together has allowed me to develop meaningful relationships with others and nourished my need for a deeper connection to what is meaningful in my life. When I shared my deepest fear in the large group, I was shocked to find out later that my reaching out had helped others reach out as well. During our [circle] dance... "Trish" and "Anne" joined hands with me... Trish squeezed my hand as if to say, "I'm really with you," and Anne held my other hand tightly as if to secure me. I feel a deep sense of commitment and genuine caring for and from this learning community.

- In the dance that followed, I looked into the eyes of those in the classroom that offered deeply rendered tenderness and compassion. I felt loved and supported. That evening and classroom experience was exemplary. As a community, we offered faith, hope, love, and understanding. We also implicitly addressed the question, "What does life expect of me during these stressful circumstances?" We danced, we cried, we laughed. We completed a circle.

For other students, movement toward secure existential attachment fused interpersonal and transpersonal elements.

- I learned that as different as we seem on the surface, we all carry common fears and hurts along with intense yearning for connection to the sacred. In our small group I discovered that others were as frightened as I to reveal vulnerabilities and to share the private places our self-inquiries took us. I learned that even though we are not at the same place, we can still offer each other help along the path. The nod of a head to acknowledge a powerful revelation. A gentle request to say more. An invitation to share one's wisdom. To teach and be taught. To safely contain a powerful secret or awesome fear. I am grateful for the dance. The dance connected us to spirit and to each other. For it was in the dance, sometimes just for a very brief moment, our souls broke free and soared. Not always at once, sometimes not at all. But it happened.

- I felt accepted for who I was. I learned that many seek and have pain along the way. There was always respect and time given for each individual to express themselves. This indicated that I was wanted as part of the community. A sense of community, mutual respect, dignity and positive regard for all were the ingredients that fed my soul. Dancing together, meditating, sharing our thoughts, laughing and crying…working together, making a conscious effort to respect and honor one another as God's children…was one of the most wonderful experiences of my life.

CONCLUSIONS

The culturally inclusive learning community provided a prosocial holding environment that catalyzed and supported substantive learning in the five dimensions of person-centered psychospiritual maturation. Learning-in-community created a dynamic, experiential vehicle for transformative and reparative growth in which students learned to value self and *other*. The bonds and secure attachment templates that they developed—with each other, with a core dimension of self, and with life—suggests the critical importance of inclusive community-building in higher education, as well as in clinical work that promotes mature behavior in individuals and social systems.

PART III

—Discussion of Results—
Applications of the *Know Your Self*
Curriculum In Prevention-Oriented Mental
Health Practice and Higher Education

CHAPTER 12

The *Know Your Self* Curriculum: An Effective Template for Mentoring Psychological Resilience and Culturally-Inclusive Community

Implications for Prevention-Oriented Mental Health Practice

This chapter discusses results from this study of the *Know Your Self* curriculum, and explores their implications for prevention-oriented mental health programs. First, it reviews student learning outcomes: culturally-inclusive community, reductions in harmful behaviors, and growth in the five dimensions of person-centered psychospiritual maturation. Then it examines structural components and learning modules of the curriculum. Third, it discusses implications of these results for prevention programs, including a bio-cultural evolutionary perspective on person-centered psychospiritual maturation as an emergent and teachable human phenomenon. Finally, it discusses the curriculum as a conceptually-integrative reformulation of humanistic psychology, acknowledging Carl Rogers' pioneering contributions.

STUDENT LEARNING OUTCOMES

Culturally-Inclusive Community: Narratives in Chaps. 7, 8, 10, and 11 illustrate the learning process through which students developed inclusive community. They were written by students who were female and male; white, black, Latino and Asian; ethnically and religiously diverse; gay and straight; physically able and challenged; from middle-class and working-class backgrounds. Their narratives illustrate multiple ways that students explored their sociocultural identities and differences, examined the impact of group-based social dominance hierarchies, systemic forces, and historical trauma on their psychospiritual development, discussed the broken attachment systems and relational ruptures they had experienced, and learned that they can affirm cultural pride, while acknowledging oppressive chapters in their culture's history.

These explorations did not minimize, or equalize, the suffering of particular groups. Rather, they created an empathic environment where students learned to know each other as vulnerable human beings, building bonds of attachment, and repairing impaired relational skills. Examples in Chaps. 10 and 11 include a white female who explored alcoholism and emotional abuse in her working class family; a white male who explored his pattern of sexual promiscuity and infidelities, recognizing its roots in family dynamics and male privilege; a black female who explored connections between her family's history of racial trauma and her impaired relational skills; a black male with a similar family history who explored his magnified stress-reactivity; a gay male who explored the despair he experienced when his Catholic family disputed his report of being sexually abused; women of Jewish and Christian backgrounds who developed emotional bonds as they discussed common life struggles; a Muslim woman who explored the cultural and religious alienation that she experienced when her family emigrated to the United States; and Christians from socially-conservative denominations who questioned biased perceptions they had developed about people outside their traditions. Two particularly poignant narratives are presented in Chap. 11: a gay Latino male who experienced unexpected acceptance from his predominantly white learning community and a Latina student who described a new level of acceptance for her white peers. The chapter concludes with powerful student narratives affirming the human potential to build culturally-inclusive community.

Reductions in Harmful Behaviors: Each student conducted a self-inquiry project that revolved around changing a self-identified attitude or behavior that is harmful to self or others. Qualitative analysis organized these behaviors ($N = 127$) into four categories (see Chap. 6). Chapter 11 presents 10 illustrative case studies of students making substantive progress on these behavioral issues. Each case study describes an intensive process of psychospiritual self-inquiry that included writing a detailed psychospiritual autobiography, developing a meditation practice as a tool for self-regulation and access to the deep wisdom of contemplative mind, and relevant participation in the learning communities:

Category 1: Social-Emotional Impairments to Academic Performance. Two case studies illustrate these issues. The first student, Mary Ann, examined her procrastination. This 25-year-old undergraduate was convinced she was lazy. Psychospiritual self-inquiry helped her develop a more accurate understanding of her procrastinating behavior, modulate her stress reactivity, and experience a core dimension of self which had the strength to heal the emotional wounds at the heart of her inaccurate self-concept. Developing greater confidence in life and self, she overcame procrastination behavior. The second student, Kim, examined internal pressure to overachieve. Suffering from stress-related gastrointestinal problems, this 23-year-old graduate student used psychospiritual self-inquiry to outgrow an avoidant mode of stress-coping, which she called "Bargain Shopping," modulate her stress-reactivity, and experience a core dimension of self that helped her heal emotional pain and overcome the external locus of evaluation that drove her internal pressure to overachieve.

Category 2: Health-Compromising Attitudes and Behaviors. Four case studies illustrate these issues. Deanna, a 34-year-old adult undergraduate, examined her unhealthy diet as a focal point for intensive psychospiritual self-inquiry. She discovered connections between her low self-concept, relational patterns of conflict-avoidance, and her African American family's history of racial trauma, experienced a core dimension of self that was unharmed by her personal links in humanity's chain of pain, and made "moderate" (i.e., not self-punishing) changes in her diet. Jessica, a 21-year-old undergraduate, examined difficulties quitting cigarette smoking. Her self-inquiry produced the insight that smoking soothed an emotional vacuum in her life. Jessica also discovered a core dimension of self with the strength to confront her emotional wounds. While she did not quit smoking, she identified emotional healing that would be necessary for success. Erin, a 25-year-old graduate student, examined her alcohol consumption, identifying its roots in her father's alcoholism and emotional abuse. During meditation, she was challenged by her inner mentor to face her emotions, rather than avoid them through alcohol. Karen, a 26-year-old graduate student, conducted an intensive, highly courageous, self-inquiry project. She examined the negative impact of socially-constructed pressure to be thin on her self-esteem, dissonance between her social justice values and her religious tradition, and experienced a numinous inner mentor who helped her resolve these issues positively.

Category 3: Impaired Relational Skills. Two case studies illustrate these issues. Alex, a 25-year-old graduate student, examined sexual promiscuity and relational infidelities. Aware of the male privilege that reinforces this behavior, he committed himself to an intensive process of psychospiritual self-inquiry. He learned that this behavior reflected his emotional wounds and self-protective lack of commitment to emotional intimacy, clarified ways a previous meditation practice had reinforced a pattern of social isolation, developed a new form of contemplative practice that deepened his capacity for emotional engagement, and ended his promiscuous behavior. Christopher, a 28-year-old graduate student, examined fear of intimate relationships. Intensive psychospiritual self-inquiry helped him explore the rejection he experienced from his family and church, identify cigarette smoking as a mechanism to numb relational isolation, and experience an inner mentor that challenged him to risk emotional vulnerability. These two self-inquiry projects were conducted by courageous young men who confronted emotional armoring sanctioned by male-socialization patterns, and developed contemplative practices that increased their capacity for positive attachment with self, others, and life.

Category 4: Existential Struggles and Spiritual Alienation. Two case studies illustrate these issues. Anna, a 24-year-old graduate student, examined the impact of a chronic illness on her existential worldview. Psychospiritual self-inquiry helped her explore her relationship with her family and religion as sources of both healthy and disabling coping mechanisms, replace stress coping methods that numbed her emotions with alternative artistic and contemplative methods that increased her emotional vitality, and experience a core dimension of self that was unharmed by her long history of physical disability, and that anchored her in relationship with a Ground of Being. Hasna, a courageous 27-year-old adult undergraduate, examined her alienation from Islam. Through intensive psychospiritual self-inquiry, she explored cultural and religious dislocations that she experienced after her family's immigration to the United States and, later, her father's death, identified a pattern of emotional numbing she had developed in response to traumatic life experiences and socially-sanctioned behavioral expectations for women in her family, experienced a numinous female inner mentor who helped her heal traumatic wounds, and re-established a sense of secure existential attachment with Allah, as her Ground of Being.

Growth in the Five Dimensions of Person-Centered Psychospiritual Maturation

The self-inquiry process through which students reduced harmful behaviors produced growth in the five dimensions of person-centered psychospiritual maturation. Chapters 10 and 11 include detailed analysis of this growth. In the *bio-behavioral* dimension, students identified patterns of stress-reactivity; developed self-regulation skills through mindfulness and elicitation of the relaxation response; and eventually (with synergistic growth in the other dimensions of self) reduced their harmful behaviors. In the *cognitive-sociocultural* dimension, they employed critical analysis and empathic self-reflection to identify cognitive schema, sociocultural identity narratives, and positionality in group-based social dominance hierarchies that reinforce distorted perceptions about self and *other*, and trigger destructive stress-reactivity. In the *social-emotional* dimension, autobiographical writing and culturally-inclusive community-building helped them examine and repair insecure attachment templates created by family dynamics, ruptures in personal relationships, and systemic forces that undermine positive intergroup contact. In the *existential-spiritual* dimension, meditation helped them explore interior layers of the psyche; identify conscious and unconscious emotional residue from humanity's chain of pain; and deepen access to a core dimension of self where they could experience the deep wisdom of contemplative mind. In the *integrative, worldview-forming* dimension, synergistic learning in these five dimensions helped them develop a resilient worldview, Confidence in Life and Self. Developing new insights and skills in bio-behavioral, cognitive-sociocultural, social-emotional, and existential-spiritual dimensions of self, they experienced greater self-efficacy and more robust relational bonds which strengthened confidence in self. Learning to approach challenging life circumstances as potential catalysts for individual and systemic maturation, they developed deeper confidence in life as a coherent process.

As expected in a one-semester introduction to this self-inquiry process, student learning was not uniform. The qualitative analysis avoided excessively positive interpretations of their written narratives. Quantification of the qualitative results indicated substantive maturational growth in the following percentages of students: bio-behavioral (68%), cognitive-sociocultural (51%), social-emotional (55%), existential-spiritual (48%), integrative formation of a resilient worldview (57%). Quantification of maturational learning in each student indicated that

93% showed substantive improvement in at least one dimension; 7% showed minimal learning; 33% showed substantive improvement in one or two dimensions; and 60% showed substantive improvement in three to five dimensions, considered *substantive introductory maturational learning*.

These results were corroborated by statistical comparisons of pre-post outcome scores from control ($N = 138$) and experimental ($N = 127$) groups. Statistically significant effect sizes indicated 15–21% greater improvement in the experimental group on multiple measures. These robust results were notable for a one-semester introductory course.

The control group was particularly suitable. These students resembled the experimental group demographically and educationally; and participated in a course on Counseling Theories that used many engaged learning methods: intensive writing, small group work, and substantive faculty-student interactions. They also studied concepts and methods relevant to person-centered psychospiritual maturation. However, notably, the control group did not practice these methods experientially. Thus, it was justified to attribute the positive outcomes in the experimental group to experiential participation in the *Know Your Self* curriculum.

There was also clear convergence between the quantitative and qualitative results. The statistical comparisons measured change in two key dimensions of psychospiritual maturation. The Inventory of Positive Psychological Attitudes (IPPA) measured the integrative dimension of psychospiritual maturation: formation of a resilient worldview, Confidence in Life and Self. The results confirmed that experimental group participants experienced increased confidence that life has meaning and purpose. The qualitative analysis explicated this growth: students reframed their cognitive, emotional, and existential understanding of life stressors, learning to approach them as potential catalysts for psychospiritual growth. Further, these results confirmed their growth in self-confidence, also explicated by the qualitative analysis: students learned to confront stressful situations with greater internal composure, increased self-efficacy, and improved abilities to seek and receive support.

The Index of Core Spiritual Experience (INSPIRIT) measured the existential-spiritual dimension of psychospiritual maturation: contemplative experiences of inner peace and/or relational connection with the Ground of Being. The results confirmed that the experimental group experienced significant growth in the depth of these experiences. The qualitative analysis explicated these results. Initially, students used meditation to develop autonomous self-regulation skills. As their practice deepened, they learned to experience the deep wisdom of contemplative mind and took introductory steps toward *secure existential attachment*.

INSPIRIT scores on Q7 and written student narratives indicated that students interpreted their contemplative experiences through either a secular humanist or transpersonal/religious lens. This confirmed that the curriculum does not privilege or impose either worldview; rather, it supports student development of an internal locus of existential meaning-making.

In summary, these learning outcomes indicated that the curriculum mentored person-centered psychospiritual maturation effectively, helping students build inclusive community, achieve behavior change goals, and consolidate a resilient worldview, Confidence in Life and Self. While these results require replication, they are more than exploratory, offering convincing evidence that university students are capable of impressive maturational growth when mentored by a structured curriculum.

STRUCTURAL ANALYSIS OF CURRICULUM: COMPONENTS AND LEARNING MODULES

The qualitative analysis also identified four key structural components of the curriculum: First, students engaged in a written self-inquiry project. Second, during these guided assignments, they explored their psychospiritual development, including family, sociocultural, and religious factors that influenced identity formation. Third, students deepened their introspective work by engaging in contemplative self-inquiry through meditation. Fourth, they examined and refined interpersonal communication skills experientially as they participated in a group process of inclusive, person-centered, community building.

These four components worked synergistically. Writing a psychospiritual autobiography and sharing this material in a culturally-inclusive learning community had particular value. As students discussed the impact of sociocultural identity, family history, and religious upbringing on their stress-coping skills, they developed a more coherent, empathic understanding of themselves, often for the first time. As they learned about each other at increasingly deep levels, a bonding process took place which helped them repair insecure attachment templates and strengthen their capacities for altruistic, unconditional love.

Structural analysis also identified three interwoven learning modules:

The first module (Chap. 7) created foundations for person-centered learning and inclusive community-building, utilizing extensive experiential work. For example, during an introductory session, students learned to sing a simple round with polyphonic harmonies. This exercise served three purposes. *First*, by inducing mild stress, it became a vehicle for developing self-regulation skills: mindfulness, the relaxation response, and mental concentration. *Second*, it introduced themes central to culturally-inclusive community building. The round required students to divide into two subgroups. As singing began, they experienced intergroup tension as multiple voices sang variant melodies. To stabilize their singing, subgroup members needed to focus on each other, creating a firm subgroup identity. Afterwards, they began to hear the dynamic harmonies created by their polyphonic singing. Through analysis of this experience, they learned that groups can intentionally nurture diversity and unity simultaneously. *Third*, the exercise introduced key themes of the Perennial Philosophy. Each spiritual tradition has developed its own unique melodic approach to the maturational goals and contemplative practices that facilitate individual and social well-being. But there are distinct similarities in these goals and practices. They can coexist in a multicultural society, generating polyphonic harmony.

In other experiential exercises, students explored their responses to academic stress, using *anonymous sharing* to reduce their emotional vulnerability and help them engage collaboratively in person-centered learning. In summary, this module introduced self-regulation skills, inclusive community-building, and collaborative learning that created foundations for subsequent stages of person-centered psychospiritual maturation.

The second module (Chap. 8) taught students to approach sociocultural differences and interpersonal conflict proactively. They learned that these issues are engines of humanity's chain of pain, triggering individual and collective stress reactivity (fight/flight) that often escalates to traumatic levels (vicious attack/protective numbing) and protective regression into "tribal" identities. Rather than deflecting these volatile issues, or denying the significance of historical trauma on self and society, students learned to engage with them actively as potential catalysts for psychospiritual maturation and inclusive community. The module included psychoeducation about religious and sociocultural groups considered *other* and examination of systemic dynamics that reinforce group-based social dominance hierarchies, perpetuate inaccurate perceptions of self and others, foment intergroup tensions, and prevent humanizing intergroup communication.

The module also included challenging self-inquiry work, in which students explored their sociocultural identities and relevant developmental history, wrote a psychospiritual autobiography, and participated in community-building discussions about their family histories and sociocultural identities. These discussions revealed reservoirs of distress, trauma, and victimization that had shaped key elements of students' self-concepts. The discussions acknowledged each student's story and burdens. They did not equalize the suffering that different groups have endured, or minimize the toxic effects of racism and white male privilege. Rather, this inclusive approach recognized each student's links in humanity's chain of pain, helping individuals from diverse sociocultural groups develop personal bonds. Chapters 8 and 11 present many examples.

During this self-inquiry work, students also examined their interpersonal behaviors during stress and conflict. Courageous exploration of these sensitive issues was rewarded when students discovered normalizing similarities in their negative behaviors. They could then recognize that these behaviors were destructive variations of protective stress-coping mechanisms (fight/flight; vicious attack/protective numbing) which hurt people they love. These explorations strengthened commitment to changing these behaviors, and provided concrete tools for helping them succeed.

In summary, this second learning module, which was integrated throughout the curriculum, taught students that it is possible to approach sociocultural differences and interpersonal conflict as catalysts for psychospiritual maturation; and to recognize when stress reactivity undermined their individual and collective ability to approach these issues constructively and collaboratively.

The third learning module (Chap. 9) explored the existential-spiritual dimension of self. After practicing meditation as a tool for self-regulation, many found that reduced reactivity was not sufficient to interrupt habitual stress-coping mechanisms. These attitudes and behaviors (e.g., procrastination, unhealthy diet; cigarette smoking, interpersonal withdrawal or hostility, existential despair) were tenacious. Students developed deeper understanding of these issues in this module, through critical analysis, empathic self-reflection, and development of a meditation practice that helped them consolidate an internal locus of existential meaning-making and tap the deep wisdom of contemplative mind. (Chap. 10 presents detailed examples through individual case studies).

This learning process included several stages of critical self-analysis: recognition of their harmful behaviors as a self-defeating cycle of temporary satisfaction and repetitive suffering, identification of the positive existential worldview they tried to simulate through these behaviors, and reframing their life struggles through Viktor Frankl's transformative logotherapeutic question. The insights they developed provided a clear personal focus for their contemplative work.

This approach to meditation began by examining maps of consciousness developed by neuroscientific studies of meditation, Jungian psychology, and the spiritual traditions. As explained in Chaps. 5 and 9, these maps identify four increasingly interior strata of human consciousness: (1) externally-focused environmental scanning; (2) cognitive-emotional processes (conscious and unconscious) that shape the ego's responses to external experience; (3) a receptive mode of intuitive awareness oriented inwardly for insight and guidance from a core stratum of self; (4) a core stratum of awareness not conditioned or limited by the ego's external life experiences.

It is important to reiterate that the curriculum explicates this core dimension through both a secular humanist and nonsectarian transpersonal lens, and encourages students to conceptualize their contemplative experiences through a lens congruent with their personal belief systems.

Two approaches to meditation were taught. In its most distilled form, meditation can be practiced as inwardly-focused, undistracted attention that witnesses each stratum of consciousness mindfully, until awareness rests in the core dimension of being. Students already committed to this method were encouraged to continue. However, this approach to meditation can minimize the maturational value of life's developmental challenges by overemphasizing the illusory nature of daily experience. Thus, meditation was chiefly taught as a method to refine each stratum of consciousness until they serve the maturational purposes for which they evolved. For example, externally-oriented consciousness serves two dynamically-opposed maturational goals: developing vital survival skills and cultivating ethical behavior that supersedes self-interest. The second stratum has self-reflective maturational capacities: the ability to refine conscious and unconscious cognitions, emotions, and sociocultural narratives that fuel destructive behavior towards self and others. The third, intuitive stratum also requires refinement. It shares internal space with unconscious forces in the cognitive-emotional mind (primitive stress-coping mechanisms, instinctive fear of the *other*, and personal and collective residue from humanity's chain of pain). These psychological forces can distort intuitive knowing, infecting it with destructive impulses. They require vigilant awareness and healing before the intuitive stratum can accurately receive insight and guidance from the core stratum of self. This fourth, deepest dimension of self does not require refinement. It is not conditioned by humanity's chain of pain, or limited by the restrictive boundaries through which the ego perceives self, others, and life. However, this core dimension cannot be experienced fully until the other three strata have been refined. This non-dualistic approach to meditation provided a framework for students to conceptualize the deep structure of contemplative mind. It explicated the dual focus in person-centered psychospiritual maturation on enlightened individual awareness and collective social responsibility.

Chapter 9 presents student narratives as they developed these contemplative skills, using visualization methods that facilitate psychospiritual exploration: creating an inner sanctuary where symbolic imagery and insights could arise intuitively, including imaginal dialogues with an inner mentor. These were followed by contemplative explorations of the inner heart: a symbolic representation of the psyche with an outer layer of emotional scars and an inner core that is unconditioned by humanity's chain of pain. Students learned that this meditative mode of receptive awareness yielded symbol-filled experiences with deep personal significance. Their experiences are further illustrated in Chap. 10. Hasna's inner mentor took form as a contorted silent figure who represented the trauma and emotional numbing she had experienced. As Anna explored the inner heart, she had an imaginal experience in which little men, who were excavating a pile of "shit," uncovered a fiery jewel, her unharmed core self. Deanna also had an intuitive experience of this core dimension of self: a momentary spark of illumination in which she felt at-one with life and filled with compassionate love.

While experiences of inner wisdom were figural in this transformative learning, they cannot be divorced from the other structural components and learning modules of the curriculum. The clarity and depth of their illuminative experiences was catalyzed by students' intensive self-inquiry work. They wrote autobiographies that investigated ways their sociocultural identities, families, and religious upbringing had affected their psychospiritual development. They examined their stress-reactivity and its impact on self and others, probing the meaning of habitual behaviors through which they tried to cope with stress, and shared their self-inquiry work (both anonymously and transparently) with peers. They encountered insecure attachment templates through interactive community-building and challenged themselves to overcome sociocultural barriers.

Thus, the primary conclusion that emerged from the structural analysis of the curriculum was the synergistic nature of this learning process. Person-centered psychospiritual maturation was facilitated through integrated learning in the bio-behavioral, cognitive-sociocultural, social-emotional, existential-spiritual, and worldview-forming dimensions of self. This integration took place as students participated in the four components (and three learning modules) of the *Know Your Self* curriculum, through a combination of personal self-inquiry and collaborative community building, as they strengthened skills in critical analysis and empathic self-reflection.

THE DEEP WISDOM OF CONTEMPLATIVE MIND: OBSERVATIONS

At the same time, the structural analysis of the curriculum pointed clearly to the profound impact of these contemplative experiences on student learning. These experiences had two distinct dynamics. Many were predictably supportive and comforting. For example (Chap. 9), one student had a distinctly visceral experience of her grandmother holding her hand, assuring her that she is loved. However, in many other instances, the inner mentor did not provide comfort. Rather, it challenged students by confronting harmful attitudes or behaviors. For example (Chap. 9), one student found himself standing in a swift mountain stream, the symbolic form of his inner mentor and an expression of the life force. He experienced himself bucking the force of the stream, while many objects floated past him, supported by life's flowing energy. This inner mentor challenged him to recognize his rigid, unyielding, competitive traits. Similar confrontations were described in Chap. 10. Kim was challenged to feel her emotional pain. Deanna was challenged to examine her conflict-avoidant personality. Jessica was taken to a place where she had to "see all of herself." The dark cloud in Erin's gloomy sanctuary challenged her to learn to tolerate her pain, rather than numb it through alcohol. Karen's inner mentor confronted her low self-esteem by challenging her to sing publicly. Chris was challenged to risk emotional vulnerability. Hasna was challenged to face the traumatic experiences and social norms which had silenced her.

The consistent occurrence of these meaningful confrontations between the "inner mentor" and "daily ego" required thoughtful consideration during higher-order conceptual analysis, yielding three observations. *First*, symbols generated by the core dimension of self are person-centered: uniquely and exquisitely shaped for each individual. This observation is not really surprising. The core self knows the ego intimately because they are part of a unified psyche. *Second*, more surprisingly, these confrontations suggest that the core self has a significant degree of autonomy from the daily ego. It speaks from an elevated, mature perspective, from a domain of being that is not conditioned by the individual's personal wounds, and not restricted by distortions in the cognitive-emotional templates that shape the ego's perceptions and actions destructively. *Third*, the daily ego accepts this challenging guidance non-defensively because it feels known and held by this foundational dimension of being. The core self was indeed experienced as an inner mentor with a wiser, more expansive identity than the ego.

These observations cannot be construed as proof of a transpersonal dimension of existence. As science probes the structures of physical reality and consciousness, clear understanding about this core stratum of awareness may emerge. I will surmise, however, that this scientific model will describe the cosmos as a multidimensional unified whole, in which consciousness exists as a fundamental element in the fabric of reality. However, until science confirms such a cosmology, conclusions about the deep wisdom of contemplative mind must remain in the domain of a phenomenologically-oriented humanistic psychology.

From this humanistic perspective, four conclusions can be proposed. *First*, the consistent occurrence of these meaningful confrontations suggests that the human psyche contains a core dimension of self that is intimately connected to, yet autonomous from, the daily ego. *Second*, this core dimension of self is not conditioned by the cognitive-emotional schema and experiences of the daily ego. In essence, it is unharmed by humanity's chain of pain. *Third*, the confrontations and guidance the core self offers to the daily ego have demonstrable maturational value, seen in the narrative student data from this study (Chaps. 9, 10, 11). This core dimension of self challenged harmful attitudes and behaviors, strengthened confidence in life and self, and offered introductory (albeit brief) experiences of secure existential attachment, a developmental goal of person-centered psychospiritual maturation. *Fourth*, these observations provide evidence of the formative tendency that Carl Rogers hypothesized. This core dimension of self promotes maturational growth that increases awareness, compassionate understanding of self and *other*, constructive stress coping behaviors, and the capacity to build human communities that transcend divisive differences. While further research is required, this study affirms the existence of a formative, maturation-oriented tendency in the human psyche, without minimizing or dismissing the toxic reality of humanity's chain of pain. It offers grounds for a soberly positive humanistic psychology.

Implications for Prevention-Oriented Mental Health Practice

The results from this effectiveness study of the *Know Your Self* curriculum have several significant implications for prevention-oriented mental health practice with young adults.

1) *The curriculum teaches students to understand their dysfunctional behaviors as symptomatic expressions of dysregulation in normal stress-coping mechanisms.* As discussed in Chap. 5, there is growing recognition that dysregulated autonomic stress reactivity is a common trigger or underlying cause of psychopathology. Hyper- and hypo- arousal of ANS and HPA-axis responses have negative effects on metabolic, cognitive, and emotional functioning, increasing vulnerability to many medical conditions and harmful behaviors. Individual and group case studies from this project illustrate students experiencing a diverse range of these harmful effects: a toxic inner critic, anxiety, depression, somatic symptoms of stress, academic procrastination, internal pressure to overachieve, unhealthy diet, cigarette smoking, alcohol dependence, negative body image, sexual promiscuity, fear of intimate relationships, anxious coping with a chronic illness, existential and spiritual alienation, conflict-avoidant behavior, interpersonal hostility and passive-aggressive social withdrawal, and fear of the culturally *other*.

Typical diagnostic and treatment procedures differentiate these diverse behaviors into separate categories of dysfunction. While symptom differentiation (and assessment of severity, frequency, and disruption of daily functioning) are clinically meaningful, this approach tends to disguise the underlying, shared dynamic of these behaviors—the dysregulation of normal stress coping mechanisms. When students discovered this commonality, which began with anonymous sharing, shame and stigma associated with these behaviors was reduced. By humanizing and normalizing them, the curriculum helped students develop essential insights about their behaviors, strengthened motivation and confidence to make positive change, and reinforced their ability to employ empathic self-reflection during this necessary process of self-inquiry.

The common underpinnings of these behaviors were further clarified, normalized, and humanized when students explored the psychological benefits they derived from these harmful behaviors, and identified the positive existential worldview that these behaviors mimicked. These insights deepened motivation to develop a genuinely positive existential worldview.

Thus, results from this study suggest the clinical utility, in prevention-oriented approaches, of a unifying approach to dysfunctional behaviors that helps young adults understand them as normal reactions to the difficult challenges of being human. This humanistic approach cannot be dismissed as simplistic or naïve. It recognizes the complex roots of dysfunctional behavior in multiple dimensions of self and systemic elements of humanity's chain of pain. Rather, this unifying model provides an accurate, concrete, humanizing construct for emerging adults to address these problems before they escalate into serious clinical syndromes.

2) *The curriculum utilizes a person-centered approach that helps students recognize and repair the five dimensions of self that have been dysregulated by their personal links in the chain of pain.* This project has identified multiple dimensions of self that can be disrupted by individual links and systemic elements in humanity's chain of pain: bio-behavioral, cognitive-sociocultural, social-emotional, existential-spiritual, and integrative worldview formation. In addition, it has investigated a multidimensional process of psychospiritual maturation for repairing these dimensions of self. Many psychotherapeutic approaches target only one or two dimensions, and fail to recognize the interactive synergy that links multiple dimensions. For example, while building self-regulatory capacities in the bio-behavioral dimension is a basic therapeutic goal, it is important to recognize that this dysregulation is often driven by a chaotic worldview that reflects existential-spiritual alienation, impaired social-emotional attachment templates, and residues of historical trauma, current social subordination, and ongoing systemic victimization that undermine the formation of positive sociocultural identity narratives.

Interactions among these dimensions were particularly evident in the individual case studies (Chap. 10). Chris' cigarette smoking was the visible surface of an iceberg that included a hopeless worldview, alienation from his religion, traumatically-shattered attachment templates, and a legacy of rejection and denigration in his family and society as a gay man. It would have been counter-productive to focus his self-inquiry work solely on reducing smoking. He needed to develop a coherent narrative that incorporated an understanding of his impaired functioning and wounds in each dimension of self. Further, he needed to contact a core dimension of self, where he could receive challenging guidance nondefensively, in order to take necessary emotional risks to repair his broken attachment systems, affirm his gay sexuality, and seek relational intimacy. Similarly, Deanna's unhealthy diet, Erin's alcohol drinking, Karen's depression, Alex's sexual promiscuity, Anna's existential anguish, and Hasna's disconnection from Islam were the visible manifestation of subsurface icebergs. Each student needed to develop a coherent self-narrative through probing self-inquiry, interactive group learning, and meditative access to the deep wisdom of contemplative mind in order to make substantive behavioral change. While multidimensional learning of this kind may seem a formidable task, this study of the *Know Your Self* curriculum demonstrates the feasibility of addressing these issues holistically, through an integrative approach, that is particularly effective in prevention-oriented work with emerging adults.

3) *By helping students recognize the positive existential worldview that their harmful behaviors seek to mimic, the curriculum motivates students to develop an authentically positive worldview and mature behavior through person-centered psychospiritual maturation.* This normalizing process introduces students to the maturational potential in their lives. Further, the curriculum teaches a process of psychospiritual development and self-inquiry through which they can achieve these maturational potentials. As results from this project demonstrate (Chaps. 6–11), the curriculum facilitated the development of a resilient worldview, Confidence in Life and Self, that helped students respond to stress with increased internal composure, learning to treat self and others with empathic understanding in circumstances that previously would have triggered their stress reactivity.

4) *By introducing students to the deep wisdom of contemplative mind, the curriculum helps students address their need to develop an internal locus of existential meaning-making.* Figural in these psychospiritual explorations is the discovery of an unwounded core self that has not been harmed by humanity's chain of pain. As their narratives in Chaps. 10–11 indicate, this learning provided students with a conceptual and

experiential framework for understanding that the chain of pain can be broken, at the personal and systemic levels, despite its toxic, replicative power. These recognitions help students experience the fabric of life as coherent, despite humanity's long history of self-replicating trauma.

5) *Psychospiritual maturation is a teachable, emergent phenomenon of bio-cultural evolution.* Chapter 5 discussed the five dimensions of psychospiritual maturation as emergent phenomena of bio-cultural evolution, in which cultural niches created trait selection pressures for mature forms of stress-coping, social identity formation, relational attachment, and psychospiritual awareness. This evolutionary process produced sequential development in the bio-behavioral, cognitive-sociocultural, social-emotional, existential-spiritual, and integrative worldview-forming dimensions of self. For example (Chap. 5), as humans evolved from our reptilian, mammalian, and primate ancestors, social attachment systems became increasingly complex. By providing profound survival advantages, increased needs for attachment created trait selection pressures that altered brain structures and reproductive physiology, reinforcing stable pair-bonding, cooperative survival strategies, social units with a group identity and specialized roles, the capacity for emotionally-rich relational engagement, and expansive perceptual capacities for critical analysis and psychospiritual awareness. Thus, biological and cultural elements of human evolution have become increasingly intertwined.

As further discussed in Chap. 5, mature capacities evolved in each dimension along a continuum. For example, in the *bio-behavioral* dimension, fight-flight-freeze mechanisms which developed in the early vertebrate brain provided distinct survival benefits for reptiles, mammals, and primates. However, as human culture has evolved, instinctive recourse to fight-flight-freeze stress coping mechanisms is often destructive. In response, as Porges explains, the human brain evolved new vagal circuits that enable resilient coping. But primitive coping mechanisms were retained because they still provide survival advantages in specific circumstances. Thus, humans have a continuum of stress-coping responses that range from primitive to mature. Depending on the level of maturity in other dimensions of self, individuals and groups regress into primitive stress-coping mechanisms or utilize their mature capacity for resilient coping.

Each dimension has its own version of this continuum. In the *cognitive-sociocultural* dimension, kin- and group-based social hierarchies were an advanced form of social organization in early human societies.

However, as humans developed the capacity for personal individuation and the need for self-determination, permanent hierarchies became destructive: a primitive form of organization. In the *social-emotional* dimension, when early humans developed transactional pair-bonds with specialized gender roles, they were an advanced mode of attachment. But as humans developed the capacity for emotionally-rich relational intimacy, these rigidified roles became a primitive mode of attachment. In the *existential-spiritual dimension*, many early human societies developed religious belief systems that ascribed spiritual authority to dominant members of social hierarchies. These belief systems mediated existential insecurity and developed meaning-making mythologies that created a sense of coherence. But as these political-religious hierarchies resisted advanced meaning-making systems and cosmological models developed by empirical science and highly-developed contemplatives, these systems became regressive.

Thus, as mature capacities have evolved in each dimension, the limited survival value of the structurally-primitive coping mechanisms has become clear, though humans still regress to them under stress. Human culture has reached a stage of complexity in which the primitive modes have lost substantial value and credibility, but our mature capacities have not been consolidated.

This study suggests that mature individual and social behavior can be mentored through an intentional learning process that engages young adults in person-centered psychospiritual growth. While psychospiritual maturation is an emergent human phenomenon, it can be taught. Although this effectiveness study cannot be considered definitive, it has demonstrated that the *Know Your Self* curriculum provides a practical template for this prevention-oriented mentoring process.

THE LEGACY OF CARL ROGERS:
AN INTEGRATIVE HUMANISTIC PSYCHOLOGY

When Carl Rogers first formulated his humanistic philosophy and methods, he was on the cusp of a movement in which the field of mental health would commit itself to promote social justice, transformative learning, and a positive model of human nature which located a maturation-oriented *formative tendency* in each individual's psychological core. Rogers recognized the constraints that poverty, social inequality, rigid hierarchies, historical trauma, and impaired family systems placed on self-actualization. But his formulation of the human potential to develop mature individual and social behavior did not highlight these constraints.

Humanistic theory required substantive reformulation through feminist, multicultural, social psychological, and systemic social justice perspectives. Research in neuroscience added further refinements. By clarifying mind-body connections, this research became the basis for cognitive-behavioral therapies, health psychology, and the assimilation of attachment theory into somatic and experiential approaches to therapy that are relevant in trauma treatment. Trauma studies had a profound impact on humanistic philosophy, challenging Freud's intrapsychic model of dysfunction, providing compelling evidence that cycles of trauma are pervasive and systemic; and generating essential connections between social justice theory, substance abuse treatment, and recognition that racial and historical trauma have self-replicating intergenerational effects. At the same time, contemplative psychology explored interior dimensions of the psyche, assimilating models of the unconscious developed by Freud and Jung, but extending them toward recognition of a core dimension of self, unconditioned by wounds that distort the perceptions and behavior of the daily ego. These contemplative insights provided additional support for Rogers' conclusion that unconditional positive regard is a natural human capacity and a necessary interpersonal condition for therapeutic growth. These contemplative insights also highlight new areas of psychospiritual development that must be addressed when training mental health clinicians.

However, while Rogers' work required trenchant criticism and creative developments in many subfields of psychology, these contributions have only strengthened the foundations of his positively-oriented humanistic philosophy. When clinicians have engaged in a thorough process of psychospiritual development, their mature, attuned, compassionate presence becomes a relational force for therapeutic healing, which they express in empathic understanding, personal congruence, and unconditional positive regard. Such presence may not be sufficient to facilitate therapeutic growth. Each new theoretical contribution has added concepts and methods to the integrative humanistic psychology which has emerged. The *Know Your Self* curriculum has incorporated these conceptual and methodological refinements.

Having known Rogers personally, I can state unequivocally that he relished and affirmed new therapeutic developments. I have never met a thought leader who was less defensive, more open to criticism, and more fully supportive of substantive refinements to his ideas. Rogers never created a school (or social hierarchy) to espouse his philosophy. He believed that such reification would stifle the creativity necessary to promote the human potential to achieve mature individual and social behavior. He believed in the wise, creative capacities of human beings, and encouraged clinicians who worked with him to pursue their specific methods for bringing therapeutic presence and skillful means to this work.

The contributions of Carl Rogers to the field of mental health have been transformed into a soberly positive, conceptually rich, integrative humanistic psychology. This reformulation offers an optimistic perspective on humanity's evolving capacity to mature, while recognizing the toxic constraints created by humanity's chain of pain. Developing and testing the *Know Your Self* curriculum reflects my professional efforts to formulate an integrative humanistic psychology that can promote mature individual and social behavior. While we have advanced beyond his original formulations, our appreciation for Rogers' contributions should be nothing less than profound.

CHAPTER 13

Person-Centered Psychospiritual Maturation: Strengthening Campus Cultures of Health, Social Justice, and Peace

Implications for Engaged Learning in Higher Education

This concluding chapter discusses person-centered psychospiritual maturation as a learning process that can strengthen campus cultures of health, social justice, and peace. It reviews behavioral dysregulation, psychological distress, and lack of cohesive community on our campuses, as well as the failure of current engaged learning practices to solve these problems. It frames these problems through the lens of humanistic psychology, viewing them as evidence that higher education has become a mirror of systemic forces that fuel humanity's chain of pain. Based on results reported in Chap. 12, it suggests that these issues can be addressed more effectively by mentoring undergraduate and entry-level graduate students in a person-centered, nonsectarian approach to psychospiritual maturation within culturally inclusive learning communities. It reviews the five dimensions of psychospiritual maturation, and discusses how faculty and student life professionals can integrate this learning process into the core curriculum and co-curricular activities.

HIGHER EDUCATION: PATHWAY TO CAREER SUCCESS, MIRROR OF HUMANITY'S CHAIN OF PAIN

There is little doubt that post-secondary education is a vital step in career development (Kena et al. 2015). Simply compare median earnings of young adults age 25–34 with a master's degree or higher ($59,600), bachelor's degree ($48,500), associate's degree ($37,500), and high school diploma ($30,000). Families recognize these benefits. In fall 2015, approximately 20.2 million students attended American colleges and universities: 40% of the country's young adults. Students in postsecondary education include a growing proportion of young adults who are female (43%), Black (34%), Hispanic (34%), and American Indian (32%). However, these promising numbers do not tell the full story: completion rates are problematic. Of young adults who began undergraduate studies in fall 2007, only 59% earned degrees by 2013 (6 years). Completion rates were lower for males (56%) than females (62%). Among students of color, completion rates were more alarming. While 34% of Black young adults enrolled, 17% of males and 23% of females earned degrees by 2013. While 34% of Hispanic young adults enrolled, 13% of males and 19% of females graduated by 2013. While 32% of American Indian young adults enrolled, 1% of males and 16% of females completed degrees by 2013 (Kena et al. 2015).

Further, as discussed in Chap. 3, while higher education is a critical pathway to career success, students' psychological and behavioral dysregulation undermines their academic achievement and well-being. Many become vulnerable to affective distress (e.g., feeling overwhelmed, depressed), self-defeating behavior (e.g., academic procrastination, binge drinking), and behavioral misconduct (e.g., alcohol-related vandalism, sexual harassment and violence, racial discrimination) (ACHA 2014). These problems affect graduation rates and impair campus culture. They are demonstrable evidence that the systemic forces that fuel humanity's chain of pain impair the lives of these young people.

HIGHER EDUCATION'S INEFFECTIVE RESPONSE

As discussed in Chap. 3, the Association of American Colleges and Universities has attempted to address these issues. Because many students have become disengaged from their academic studies, initiatives have been developed for *engaged teaching and learning*. However, results from current efforts have been mixed. While engaged learning practices strengthen academic achievement and civic involvement (through service learning), current methods have not been effective at reducing these psychological and behavioral issues.

These current practices do not address psychological and behavioral well-being directly. Rather, they assume these problems can be solved indirectly, through more engaged academic work. Two recent publications from Project LEAP (Liberal Education and America's Promise) highlight this limitation. In *General Education Transformed: How We Can, Why We Must*, Paul Gaston summarizes current formulations of engaged learning: a coherent academic curriculum, challenging students to develop intellectual autonomy, intensive advising, service learning, co-curricular activities, and integrative capstone projects (Gaston 2015). In *Faculty Leadership for Integrative Liberal Learning*, Ann Ferren and David Paris advocate engaged learning that addresses complex intellectual issues through problem-based inquiry, integration of curricular, co-curricular, and community experiences, and pedagogy that promotes "inclusive excellence and equitable outcomes." They recommend education of the whole student, "catalyzing... intellectual and personal growth" by providing "opportunities and guidance to make sense of the world and their place in it" (p.2) (Ferren and Paris 2015). While the pedagogical methods these authors propose are excellent, they assume that necessary psychosocial development will occur *indirectly* through academic, civic, and co-curricular activities.

This indirect hypothesis is also evident in the mission statement of Bringing Theory to Practice (BTtoP), an initiative that explores the relationship between engaged learning and "the resilience and health of students." The project encourages "faculty and academic leadership to strengthen an essential focus on learning, and thereby to strengthen the health...of today's college students" (BTtoP 2015). BTtoP's recent publications highlight the positive shift in civic engagement that this project has supported through advocacy of service learning and community-based internships (Finley 2014; Harward 2012a, 2013; Levine and Soltan 2014; Reich 2014). However, as its mission statement indicates, BTtoP assumes that active learning and civic engagement will "thereby" contribute to the psychological well-being of students. The research reviewed in Chap. 3 highlights the inaccuracy of this hypothesis. A more direct approach is necessary to address these issues.

The Missing Element: Person-Centered Learning that Mentors Psychospiritual Maturation

Person-centered has a different meaning than *student-centered*, which refers specifically to intellectual development. Person-centered learning engages students in maturational growth necessary for the well-being of self and society. This learning is not psychotherapy in disguise. When students require clinical treatment, this learning process can alert faculty to these issues, enabling appropriate referrals. Case studies in Chap. 10 illustrate proactive faculty assessment of these issues. *Psychospiritual maturation* is a non-sectarian term that connotes developmental learning in five dimensions of self (bio-behavioral, cognitive-sociocultural, social-emotional, existential-spiritual, and worldview formation) commonly impaired by humanity's chain of pain. These impairments fuel the psychological distress and behavioral dysregulation evident in our students. A person-centered approach to psychospiritual maturation is an engaged pedagogy that integrates intellectual and experiential learning, teaching students to recognize and repair the impact of these negative systemic forces. We cannot expect students to develop psychological resilience without directly teaching them how to engage in their psychospiritual development. Nor can we expect them to repair sociocultural tensions and inequities rampant in our society, unless we teach them how to build culturally-inclusive community.

THE *KNOW YOUR SELF* CURRICULUM: RESULTS FROM THE EFFECTIVENESS STUDY

The research results and case study material presented in this book demonstrate that these skills can be mentored effectively and responsibly in higher education. These results (from a quasi-experimental, mixed-methods study) have been summarized thoroughly in Chap. 12. They identified substantive learning outcomes. Students learned to build strong relational bonds in culturally-inclusive learning communities, a challenging process that included learning to approach sociocultural differences and interpersonal conflict proactively as potential sources of psychospiritual growth. They learned to cultivate a resilient worldview, Confidence in Life and Self, which helped them approach stress-inducing problems with internal composure. They explored four life-domains that they considered problematic (social-emotional impairments to academic performance, health-compromising attitudes and behaviors, impaired relational skills, and existential struggles and spiritual alienation), strengthening positive attitudes and behaviors in each of these domains. These positive learning outcomes were the result of growth in the five dimensions of person-centered psychospiritual maturation.

As reported in Chap. 6, statistical comparisons between the control group (N=138) and experimental group (N=127) were highly significant, with effect sizes that ranged from 15–21% greater improvement in the experimental group. These effects were considered notable and robust for a one-semester introduction to this learning process, and suggest the potential for much greater effects in a sustained program of person-centered psychospiritual learning.

Engaged learning specialists will note that the control group was not a traditional lecture class. As discussed (Chaps. 6 and 12), the control group was a course that employed well-established methods of academically-oriented engaged learning: intensive writing assignments, small group discussions, and substantive faculty-student interactions. Further, the control group course studied concepts and methods related to psychospiritual maturation. Critically, however, students in the control group course did not practice these methods experientially. Thus, the positive growth in the experimental group was attributable to their experiential engagement in *person-centered* learning.

Breaking Humanity's Chain of Pain: Prosocial Motivation for Person-Centered Learning

The *Know Your Self* curriculum is presented to students as a method for learning how to break humanity's chain of pain in their personal lives and in the social systems they will inhabit. This conceptualization highlights the prosocial function of person-centered learning, and invites students to participate in a socially-responsible, rather than a self-centered, maturational process. By combining didactic and experiential learning, the curriculum helps them develop intellectual understanding of the systemic and personal forces that undermine healthy functioning in five key dimensions of self and society, while learning to confront and repair these impairments in their own lives. This explanation of person-centered psychospiritual maturation provides meaningful prosocial motivation for engagement in this learning process.

This explanation also normalizes and destigmatizes the harmful behaviors that they will explore in their self-inquiry projects. Rather than framing these behaviors through a model of individual psychopathology, the curriculum frames them as evidence that key elements of self have been impaired by toxic systemic forces. Further, as discussed in Chap. 12, the curriculum helps them recognize a unifying theme among their diverse forms of impaired behavior. These harmful behaviors are triggered by dysregulation of normal stress-coping mechanisms. This conceptual framework reduces shame and promotes collaborative efforts to make positive changes in their attitudes and behaviors. This framework also helps them understand behaviors that harm *self* and *others* holistically, as mirror images. In typical educational settings, these behaviors are examined separately, creating unnecessary bifurcation between our educational efforts to promote behavioral health and social justice. This bifurcation overlooks connections in the systemic and psychosocial dynamics that drive health-compromising and socially-destructive behavior, and fails to identify both as shared consequences of humanity's chain of pain.

The dynamics that affect psychological and social well-being are linked more fully than we often understand. When groups and individuals perceive threats to their identity, dignity, emotional and economic well-being, or physical survival, they experience psychophysiological reactivity which triggers primitive stress-coping mechanisms. The neurobiological pathways underlying this reactivity are explained in Chap. 5. When groups or individuals perceive threat and believe they can improve their chances for survival by dominating others (social power or physical force), they treat them in destructive ways, disregarding rational evaluation of the moral implications. Ethical considerations are further eroded by legitimizing narratives that justify group-based social dominance hierarchies. When groups or individuals perceive threat with diminished hope they can improve their chances for survival, they experience despair and frustration, striking out at others vengefully or soothing themselves with activities or substances that numb their agitation temporarily. Groups and individuals often ricochet between moral disregard for the well-being of others and self-soothing activities that offer temporary relief. Traumatic violence, of course, escalates reactivity. These patterns provide an operant model for the self-replicating dynamics that fuel humanity's chain of pain.

When students conceptualize personal behaviors that harm self and others through this framework, they are motivated to participate in community-building person-centered learning.

THE FIVE DIMENSIONS OF PERSON-CENTERED PSYCHOSPIRITUAL MATURATION

As students' written narratives indicate, they found this maturational learning process highly salient and deeply satisfying. While I have presented these five dimensions of learning in several chapters, a summary in this concluding chapter is appropriate. This summary should be supplemented by discussions in Chaps. 5 and 12 that examine psychospiritual maturation from a bio-cultural evolutionary perspective, as an emergent phenomenon that reflects humanity's growing capacity for mature individual and social behavior, and as evidence of a maturation-oriented, *formative tendency* in the bio-cultural evolutionary process. While an emergent phenomenon, this maturational process can be facilitated through intentional learning in five dimensions of self. The findings from this study demonstrate the capacity of university students to participate in this person-centered pedagogical process which includes intensive self-inquiry writing assignments and experiential work in culturally-inclusive learning communities.

Bio-Behavioral: The curriculum presented material about the neural and physiological pathways that regulate metabolic processes through which people respond constructively or destructively to life challenges, stress, and perceived threat. Through self-inquiry, students became aware of their own psychophysiological stress-reactivity, developed behavioral self-regulation skills, and cultivated internal composure when confronted with stressful situations.

Cognitive-Sociocultural: The curriculum presented material about psychosocial and systemic dynamics that create cognitive schema and sociocultural identity narratives which condition perceptions about self and *other*, legitimizing group-based dominance hierarchies. Through self-inquiry, students examined their cognitive schema and identity narratives, using critical analysis and empathic self-reflection to correct distorted perceptions about self and *other*.

Social-Emotional: The curriculum presented material about attachment theory and trauma psychology, exploring ways that insecure attachment undermines family dynamics and social systems, increasing vulnerability to relational ruptures, attachment disorders, and regression into "tribal" group identities that impair healthy interpersonal relationships and inclusive community. Through self-inquiry, students learned to repair insecure attachment templates, deepen reflective listening skills that facilitate relational bonding, respond to conflict and sociocultural differences as gateways to psychospiritual growth, and experience attuned, altruistic caring for peers.

Existential-Spiritual: The curriculum presented material describing the negative impact of ontological insecurity on individual and social well-being, and examined contemplative practices that facilitate an internal locus of meaning-making and secure existential attachment. Through self-inquiry, students explored the interior structure of the psyche, using meditation to experience the deep wisdom of contemplative mind. This learning increased internal composure, reduced existential alienation, and facilitated movement toward secure existential attachment.

Integrative Worldview Formation: The curriculum presented neuroscientific material about the integrative process of worldview formation, locating this process in the medial pre-frontal cortex (which integrates data from right and left cortical hemispheres, subcortical limbic areas, cerebellum, and brainstem). Through self-inquiry, students synthesized learning in the four previous dimensions of self, developing a resilient worldview, Confidence in Life and Self. This worldview reinforced mature responses to life challenges, supporting constructive and compassionate behavior towards self and others.

In summary, these five dimensions of synergistic learning are an operational definition of person-centered psychospiritual maturation, as facilitated by the *Know Your Self* curriculum.

The Deep Wisdom of Contemplative Mind: Teaching Contemplative Self-Inquiry with a Non-Sectarian Pedagogy that Affirms Diverse Belief Systems

As the case study material in this book illustrates, contemplative growth in the existential-spiritual dimension of self is a central feature of person-centered psychospiritual maturation. As I have reiterated, these transformative contemplative experiences can be understood through a secular humanist or a transpersonal/religious conceptual lens. The curriculum encourages students to frame their contemplative learning through a lens that is congruent with their philosophical belief system and/or sociocultural identity. This inclusivity is not evasive. The central goal in this dimension of learning is to help students develop an internal locus of existential meaning-making through which they can experience life as a coherent process, while also learning to respect the existential meaning-making systems of their peers. The curriculum does not privilege or impose a secular humanist or transpersonal/religious lens, nor does it privilege contemplative practices from a particular tradition. When discussing the spiritual traditions, the curriculum invokes the Perennial Philosophy: the distilled constellation of maturational goals and contemplative methods that are shared by these traditions. It has been my distinct pleasure to guide meditation sessions in this class where Catholics, Protestants, Jews, Muslims, Buddhists, Hindus, Atheists, and Agnostics have described their experiences of contemplative mind through their own meaning-making systems, with confidence that they will be respected, and with the ability to offer this same respect to others.

Incorporating Person-Centered Psychospiritual Learning in Higher Education

I will now shift this discussion to consider academic and administrative strategies to incorporate person-centered psychospiritual maturation in higher education. As faculty and student life professionals review the five dimensions of this learning process, it will be evident that they already integrate various elements in their academic programs and co-curricular student activities. However, in many cases these efforts are not well coordinated and do not facilitate the synergistic, multidimensional learning that students require (see Chap. 12). Many universities have established Centers for Teaching and Learning that can provide a venue for student life professionals and faculty to develop a coordinated model and action plan.

The Need for Faculty Engagement: It is essential to emphasize that this learning process should not be limited to co-curricular activities. My work with the Higher Education Center for Alcohol and Other Drug Abuse Prevention (Chap. 3) revealed the extent to which faculty are disengaged from these issues, placing the burden on understaffed Student Life Offices to facilitate these vital areas of student development. Faculty often remain curiously disconnected from their students as persons. It is problematic that programs in every academic discipline do not offer students opportunities to cultivate psychospiritual maturity that is essential to socially-consequential practice in our professions, as well as genuine success in their careers and lives. Students in every academic discipline could benefit from foundational courses like *Know Your Self*, in which they learn to cultivate person-centered psychospiritual maturation and build culturally-inclusive community. This maturational learning is sorely needed in undergraduate programs and entry-level graduate studies. It is relevant to a broad range of academic and professional training disciplines, including STEM programs, the humanities, the social sciences, education, medicine and nursing, law, government, business, and religion.

Introducing the Know Your Self Curriculum (and Adaptations) into Academic Programs: The *Know Your Self* curriculum is a template, not a manual, for teaching students how to engage in a person-centered process of psychospiritual development. Its current, one-semester format was developed and tested for use with entry-level graduate students, adult undergraduates, and traditional undergraduates in their senior year. These students were capable of engaging in an intensive introduction to this learning process that required reasonably rapid assimilation of the intellectual material and self-inquiry work. When specifically taught to undergraduates, as I will discuss at greater length, it will be beneficial to create a year-long learning community seminar where students have more time to assimilate and consolidate this material.

The course is designed to be taught by faculty with background in the integrative humanistic psychology that I have described in this book. Most departments of Counseling and Psychology already have faculty with appropriate background and skills. They could begin to offer this course through their own departments with cross-registration from other academic disciplines that recommend the value of this maturational learning process. Each campus, academic program, and student population will require adaptations of the curriculum. Even among student cohorts that I have taught, the timing and sequence of learning experiences has required variations. Presenting this curriculum, as I have done in this book, as a template rather than a manual, is meant to empower faculty to shape this material to meet the psychospiritual maturational needs of their students, and to assimilate this material into their own teaching styles.

As students from other disciplines benefit from participation in this course, opportunities will be created for these disciplines to invite Counseling and Psychology faculty to adapt the *Know Your Self* curriculum more specifically to the developmental needs of their students. This will create the possibility for Counseling and Psychology faculty to have a larger impact on campus culture, eventually co-teaching this class with faculty from diverse disciplines.

Introducing the Know Your Self Curriculum into Co-Curricular Programs and Activities: Person-centered psychospiritual maturation is highly relevant to Offices of Student Life and their developmental goals for students. This learning process can be adapted for use by mental health counseling center staffs, chaplaincy teams, service-learning programs, residential life staff, and co-curricular activity directors.

The curriculum could be incorporated into a Leadership Training Program for Cultures of Health, Social Justice, and Peace. Under such an umbrella, it could be offered as a one-semester or a multi-semester class (with or without academic credits). Alternatively, the five dimensions of person-centered psychospiritual maturation could be addressed separately in weekend workshops. These *Know Your Self* trainings could be offered by various student life programs, ranging from spiritual and religious life to service learning.

Service learning would be an important focus. As reported in the BTtoP research (Chap. 3), students find service learning valuable, but consider it demanding and stressful. Creating a coordinated approach where service learning activities become a modular component of person-centered psychospiritual maturation would help students develop skills in stress reduction, self-regulation, interpersonal relations, culturally-inclusive community building, and contemplative self-inquiry that would deepen their ability to have successful service learning experiences. In addition, a leadership training program could provide supervision to students during service-learning activities.

A Leadership Training Program for Cultures of Health, Social Justice, and Peace could also be co-led by student life professionals and faculty, becoming the foundation for an academic specialization relevant to many disciplines. Centers for Teaching and Learning are an ideal vehicle for creating research projects in which student life professionals and faculty from many disciplines collaborate to develop a coordinated approach to student development and learning.

A second important co-curricular focus would be the introduction of material from the *Know Your Self* curriculum into intramural arts and sports programs. Effective development of self-awareness and internal composure skills can be heightened through somatic approaches. Dance, choral singing, ensemble music, art, theater, and sports are meaningful venues for active mentoring. In Chap. 8, I presented two experiential exercises (polyphonic singing and the peacock feather exercise) that illustrate concrete ways that intramural arts and sports programs can be utilized to mentor psychological resilience and culturally-inclusive community.

I would like to offer an additional sports example from my early work with high school students. During my first professional experience in residential student life, I worked as a dorm advisor in a high-school enrichment program. As a founder of the team sport, *Ultimate*, I taught these highly-competitive adolescents a game that required them to develop new self-regulation skills (Herndon 2003; Leonardo and Zagoria 2005). This nimble, disc-throwing sport has unique characteristics. There are no referees. Players call fouls on themselves. This unusual discipline requires a high degree of sportsmanship. Players acknowledge their fouls immediately, and the other team takes control of the disc. Rather than engaging in acrimonious debate, or depending on the outside authority of a referee, player self-regulation keeps the focus on the flow and the joy of the game. *Ultimate* players eventually named this highly-ethical form of sportsmanship *the spirit of the game*. I am delighted it has remained a prevailing value (Leonardo 2007).

The story of the genesis of this sport has already been told, as referenced. However, here is a summary of what I taught these adolescents. When you play with all of your energy and concentration and enter fully into the flow of this dynamic game, you can discover an "ultimate" experience of joyous engagement that makes winning or losing inconsequential. These were new ideas for a group of competitive young men, who initially begged me to serve as referee. I adamantly refused. But once they understood this rule, they began to play in a different way. They played hard. They played fair. They tried to win. However, they also learned that winning mattered less than having a taste of the *Ultimate* experience: the near selflessness that can be achieved effortlessly when fully engaged in the flow of this game.

I often reflect on this early teaching experience, and recognize it as the first time I taught an active form of contemplative practice. *Ultimate* requires undivided concentration and full engagement in the mental and physical flow that is characteristic of peak experiences (Csikszentmihalyi 1996; Maslow 1964). Meditation, of course, is a far more distilled form of this practice, with a more clearly designated psychospiritual purpose.

However, just as I have learned that the peacock feather exercise is a useful introduction to meditation practice, *Ultimate* can serve a similar purpose: providing a highly engaged, physical introduction to the mindfulness required during meditation, and the peak experiences that meditation can elicit.

In summary, I have described several ways that student life professionals can introduce the *Know Your Self* curriculum, or aspects of the curriculum, into many forms of co-curricular activity. These activities could be integrated into a unified Leadership Training Program for Cultures of Health, Social Justice, and Peace, when conceptualized through the five dimensions of person-centered psychospiritual maturation. The prosocial value of such a program would justify it becoming an academic specialization, taught by student life professionals and faculty.

Integrating the Know Your Self Curriculum into Undergraduate Education: As noted, while the current one-semester curriculum was effective with advanced level undergraduates, entry-level students will require a longer period of sustained learning. As the BTtoP research reported in Chap. 3, learning communities are one of the few current approaches to engaged learning that have a positive impact on psychological well-being. This book supports the value of community. Chap. 11, in particular, highlights the positive role of the learning community as a holding environment for maturational learning. With appropriate adaptations, the *Know Your Self* curriculum could be incorporated into a year-long "learning-community seminar" that could reduce the behavioral dysregulation so common during this entry-level year.

As discussed in Chap. 3, campus life presents young adults with a maturational challenge. They have begun a process of individuation in which they separate from most of the attachment figures and meaning-making activities that have played a stabilizing role in their lives. Campus life catalyzes an intensified state of ontological and relational insecurity, although students may be only intermittently aware of their internal turmoil. Like Kate in Chap. 2, or the students in Chap. 7, they require a developmentally appropriate, structured curriculum to develop this awareness, while building community bonds that decrease their attachment anxiety. Without such a curriculum, they become vulnerable to highly dysregulated behavior. Sadly, this behavior often recapitulates the worst aspects of humanity's chain of pain.

I propose a change in our approach to first-year seminars. We should focus on helping students become aware of the maturational challenges that campus life presents, their reactions to these challenges, and conceptual connections between their reactions and the chain of pain. Like the *Know Your Self* curriculum, the seminar can focus intellectually on the five dimensions of self that are impaired by the chain of pain, introducing students to multiple disciplines of knowledge and inquiry. At the same time, the experiential learning component in these year-long seminars will introduce students to person-centered psychospiritual maturation and teach them how to build culturally-inclusive community. If successful, this approach will contribute to student growth, strengthening campus cultures of health, social justice, and peace.

A 4-year experience of participation in a sustained learning community could be expected to have an even more profound impact on student development. The sequence could incorporate service learning experiences and identification of a personally-meaningful area of academic focus and potential career direction during sustained psychospiritual growth and community building. From a developmental perspective, a 4-year sequence would become a robust holding environment for integrative personal and professional identity development.

Breaking the Chain of Pain: A Deeper Purpose and Unifying Theme for Higher Education

When I speak with colleagues from many academic disciplines about the need to break humanity's chain of pain, I am not surprised that most consider this goal an essential thread in their academic commitments. Virtually every discipline sheds light on processes that contribute to, and could repair, this toxic cycle. Yet we rarely speak openly and conceptually about this thread, with colleagues or students. Nor do students understand, as they enter college, that the choice of a major can be more than a career direction, but a gateway to a socially-consequential life and profession. As our disciplines become increasingly isolated, this thread could enhance connections, creating a more coherent university curriculum and opening new avenues for multidisciplinary collaboration. When we lose this connective thread, we weaken the university as a force and role model for social and systemic maturation.

Conclusions

The higher education campus, as this book shows, could become a laboratory for developing methods to facilitate person-centered psychospiritual maturation and culturally-inclusive community. This study has demonstrated its benefits to students. How can we expect them to develop these skills, or break humanity's chain of pain, if we do not mentor this learning process? We need to teach students far more directly and intentionally how to develop skills that will contribute to a culture of health, social justice, and peace, on our campuses and in society.

Perhaps we fear to undertake this challenge because we know these toxic patterns are deeply embedded in systemic forces and the human psyche. They impact bio-behavioral, cognitive-sociocultural, social-emotional, existential-spiritual, and worldview-forming dimensions of self and society. Each time we think we have made progress toward mature individual and social behavior, events set us back. Individuals and systems regress into primitive stress reactivity, tribal protectionism, and group-based dominance hierarchies that rupture the fragile bridges of attachment we have tried to build between people with long histories of inter-group trauma. These repetitive patterns of rupture sow profound existential doubt about life's coherence and ultimate meaning, reinforcing a sense of chaos in our worldview.

But when we recognize that this process can be understood through this five-dimensional model of individual and systemic dysfunction, we can recall that humanity has developed a continuum of potential behaviors in each dimension which range from regressive to mature. While individuals and our social systems are fragile and highly vulnerable to regressive forces, the very complexities of the bio-cultural evolutionary niche that humans inhabit has wired us for mature psychospiritual awareness and behavior. Our task as educators is to embody the directionality we can intuit in life's formative tendency, and join this process of co-creation by investigating and teaching effective ways to mentor these emergent mature capacities.

Undeniably, the task is formidable. Among the Talmudic sages whom Maimonides valued so highly, there is an ethical dictum that I will paraphrase. *It is not our responsibility to complete the task of healing the world. But we cannot refrain from engaged participation.* We cannot wait to discover if life is a coherent process before we engage. Rather, as Viktor

Frankl learned, we must use the challenges we face to discover the coherence in the fabric of life.

This book has described a modest experiment in higher education. It has reported positive, though necessarily tentative, results. In this experiment, I created a curriculum that could become a laboratory for students' maturational learning and psychospiritual development. I discovered that the curriculum can mentor this learning in an effective, responsible, inclusive manner. My goal for the course has been to help students learn to approach life as an evolving curriculum for their own psychospiritual maturation, to understand life as a learning environment that confronts us with a series of maturational challenges, as individuals, sociocultural groups, and as a society. In a sense, I wanted students to understand that life itself is a university, and that when we live intentionally with this understanding, as individuals and as a society, we will derive the greatest benefits from the experiences we encounter.

References

ACHA. (2014). *American college health association: National college health assessment II, 2014 executive summary.* Hanover, MD: American College Health Association.

BTtoP. (2015). *Bringing theory to practice: A project addressing depression and substance abuse among students through engaged learning.* Washington, DC: Bringing Theory to Practice, Association of American Colleges and Universities, Charles Engelhard Foundation.

Csikszentmihalyi, M. (1996). *Flow and the psychology of discovery and invention.* New York, NY: Harper Collins.

Ferren, A. S., & Paris, D. C. (2015). *Faculty leadership for integrative liberal learning.* Washington, DC: Association of American Colleges and Universities.

Finley, A. P. (Ed.). (2014). *Civic learning and teaching.* Washington, DC: Bringing Theory to Practice.

Gaston, P. L. (2015). *General education transformed: How we can, why we must.* Washington, DC: Association of American Colleges and Universities.

Harward, D. W. (Ed.). (2012). *Civic provocations.* Washington, DC: Bringing Theory to Practice.

Harward, D. W. (Ed.). (2013). *Civic values, civic practices.* Washington, DC: Bringing Theory to Practice.

Herndon, W. (2003). This is how it all began. Ultimate News, *23*(Winter), 16–17, 28.

Kena, G., Musu-Gillette, L., Robinson, J., Wang, X., Rathbun, A., Zhang, J., et al. (2015). *The condition of education 2015 (NCES 2015-144)*. Washington, DC: U.S. Department of Education, National Center for Education Statistics.

Leonardo, P. A. (2007). *Ultimate: The greatest sport ever invented by man*. Halcottsville, NY: Breakaway Books.

Leonardo, P. A., & Zagoria, A. (2005). *Ultimate: The first four decades*. Los Altos, CA: Ultimate History Inc.

Levine, P., & Soltan, K. E. (Eds.). (2014). *Civic studies*. Washington, DC: Bringing Theory to Practice.

Maslow, A. H. (1964). *Religions, values, and peak experiences*. Columbus, OH: Ohio State University Press.

Reich, J. N. (Ed.). (2014). Civic engagement, civic development, and higher education. Washington, DC: Bringing Theory to Practice.

INDEX

A
Afflictive emotions, 11, 91, 111
African American church, 72
Agnosticism (*See* Secular humanism)
Atheism (*See* Secular humanism)
Ainsworth, Mary, 6, 12, 89, 98
Allport, Gordon, 12, 41, 96, 100, 102. *See also* Attachment (Intergroup contact theory)
  extrinsic religious orientation, 41, 102
  intrinsic religious orientation, 41, 102
Altruistic love, 141, 142, 143, 330
American College Health Association (ACHA), 3, 36, 37, 140, 356
Antonovsky, Aaron, 101
  sense of coherence, 101, 352
Armstrong, Karen, 8, 91
Arnett, Jeffrey, 4, 42
Association of American Colleges and Universities (AAC&U), 3, 13, 35, 38, 356
Association of American Universities Campus Climate Survey, 36
Astin, Alexander, 35, 37, 42

Cooperative Institutional Research Program, 37
Input-Environment-Output Linear Regression, 37
UCLA Higher Education Resource Center (HERI), 37
Astin, Helen, 42
Attachment, 5, 10, 11, 44, 60, 61, 63, 68, 70, 89, 90, 98, 101, 104, 142, 182, 200, 205, 308, 316, 320, 338, 348, 367, 369. *See also* Autonomic dysregulation in stress and trauma; Ainsworth, Mary; Bowlby, John; Schore, Alan; Secure existential attachment
  adult attachment style, 99
  attachment theory, 6, 89, 100, 353, 361
  attunement, 6, 7, 14, 22, 61, 94, 99, 101, 142, 143, 170, 171, 201, 310
  broken relational networks, 87, 336, 349
  insecure attachment, 27, 34, 99, 103, 104, 143, 307, 339, 341, 346;

anxious attachment, 98, 99, 306
avoidant attachment, 9, 98, 99, 337
disorganized attachment, 98, 99
intergroup bonds, 100
intergroup contact theory, 100
secure attachment, 11, 12, 44, 89, 94, 99, 100, 101, 103, 112, 143

Attunement. *See* Attachment; Empathic attunement

Autonomic dysregulation in stress and trauma, 26, 57, 68, 92, 341, 348. *See also* Cannon, Walter; Porges, Stephen; Resilience; Selye, Hans
animal aggression, 65
ANS hyper- and hypo-arousal, 26, 65, 92, 93, 95, 180, 182, 348
Autonomic nervous system (ANS), 57, 64, 65, 92
cortisol levels, 65
Hypothalamic-Pituitary-Adrenal Axis (HPA), 65, 348
stress response and inhibition
fight-flight response, 64, 182, 312, 318, 342, 343
Parasympathetic Nervous System (PNS), 93
Sympathetic Nervous System (SNS), 93, 94; vagus nerve, 93, 94
trauma response; freeze response, 65, 67, 94, 196, 197; hyper-aggression, 66
intrusive memories, 66
protective numbing, 9, 66, 182, 342, 343
vicious attack, 9, 65, 182, 342, 343

Awareness, 225. *See also* Contemplative mind (models); Neuroscience of meditation; Person-centered psychospiritual maturation (five dimensions); Secure existential attachment
attraction and aversion, 104
connective awareness, 105, 111, 112, 308
differentiating awarness, 104, 105, 112
daily ego, 347, 353
ego consciousness, 104–106, 108, 111
proto-self, 104
reverie, 61

B

Ballou, Mary, 6, 57
Belief in God, 68, 69, 137, 138
Bell, John, 34, 90, 108
Benson, Herbert, 64. *See also* Relaxation Response
Benson-Henry Institute for Mind-Body Medicine, Massachusetts General Hospital (BHI), 66
Section on Behavioral Medicine, Beth Israel-New England Deaconess Hospitals, 14
Bio-cultural model of evolution, 5, 10, 11, 12, 87, 88, 89, 94, 96, 97, 199, 101, 111, 188, 335, 351, 361, 369. *See also* Fricchione, Gregory; MacLean, Paul; Rogers, Carl
changes in reproductive physiology, 100, 351
cooperative hunting, 97
dominance hierarchies, 5, 7, 10, 90, 95–98, 103, 149, 164, 181, 185, 187, 313, 336, 339, 342, 360, 361, 369
niche construction, 11, 90
phylogenetic model of brain, 90
trait selection pressures;

formative tendency, 352, 361, 369
most fit, 88, 89
most mature, 89
separation challenge-attachment solution dialectic, 89, 100
Bohm, David, 12
Borysenko, Joan, 64, 67, 91, 92
Boston Clergy and Religious Leaders Group for Interfaith Dialogue, 14, 71, 73
Bowlby, John, 12, 89, 98
Boyer, Ernest, 3, 33, 34, 35, 38
  student disengagement, 33, 37, 356
Brown, Laura, 6, 57
Bryant-Davis, Thema, 65

C

Cannon, Walter, 6, 64. *See also* Autonomic dysregulation in stress and trauma
Centers for Teaching and Learning, 363, 365
Chain of Pain, *See* Person-Centered Psychospiritual Maturation (Five Dimensions); Trauma
Chiao, Joan, 97, 100
Chickering, Arthur, 35, 42
Cognitive-behavioral methods, 6, 14, 66, 67, 68
Confidence in Life and Self (CLS) *See* Resilient worldview
Congruence *See* Rogers, Carl (Interpersonal conditions for therapeutic growth)
Contemplative mind (models), 105, 141, 205, 344
  collective unconscious, 110, 111, 210
  core self
  autonomy, 60, 137, 163, 347
  challenge, 70, 72, 89, 91, 346, 347

deep wisdom, 225, 337, 339, 341, 343, 346, 347, 350, 362
unharmed, 221, 256, 337, 338, 345, 347
unwounded, 292, 304, 305, 350
deep structure of contemplative mind, 141, 149, 203, 215, 281, 321, 325, 345
four levels/strata of consciousness, 105, 205, 206, 221, 344
Maimonides' model of the psyche, 105–107, 110
personal unconscious, 110
Contemplative practice, 7, 11, 12, 28, 61, 63, 88, 102, 108, 111, 156, 164, 307, 323, 338, 342, 362, 363, 366
Contemplative psychology, 6, 353
Contemplative self-inquiry, 141, 150, 203, 207, 225, 228, 231, 234, 241, 247, 255, 262, 271, 290, 302, 341, 362, 365
Corbin, Henry, 106, 136

D

Damasio, Antonio, 104
Davidson, Richard, 64, 141
DeLoria Jr., Vine, 35
DiClemente, Carlo, 92

E

Eck, Diana, 8, 14, 71, 157
Emerging adulthood, 3, 30, 42, 44. *See also* Arnett, Jeffrey
Emerson, Ralph Waldo, 8, 102
Empathic attunement, 6, 7, 99
Empathic self-reflection, 96, 98, 141, 180, 225, 227, 272, 280, 304, 307, 313, 339, 343, 346, 349, 361

Empathy *See* Rogers, Carl (Interpersonal conditions for therapeutic growth)
Engaged teaching and learning, 5, 9, 33, 34, 35, 37, 38, 39, 40, 41, 42, 133, 135, 136, 147, 355, 356, 357, 359, 367. *See also* Harward, Donald; Kuh, George; Learning communities; Swaner, Lynn
    Bringing Theory to Practice (BTtoP), 13, 38, 357
    civic engagement, 38, 39, 41, 155, 357
    faculty-student interaction, 135, 340, 359
    Fink, John, 41
    Finley, Ashley, 39, 357
    first-year seminars, 36, 40, 368
    flourishing, 40, 59
    Freeman, Scott, 38, 135
    high-impact teaching, 40
    limitations to current methods, 33
    Low, Kathryn, 41
    need for person-centered learning, 3, 13, 38, 55, 58, 66, 148, 155, 342, 357, 359, 360
    Pascarella, Ernest, 38
    service learning, 35, 40, 166, 168, 356, 357, 365, 368
    Terenzini, Patrick, 38
Equanimity *See* Resilience
Erikson, Erik, 12, 101
Evolution *See* Bio-cultural model of evolution
Existential Psychology, 12. *See also* Allport, Gordon; Confidence in Life and Self; Inventory of Positive Psychological Attitudes; Frankl, Viktor; Tillich, Paul
    existential anomie, 34, 45
    existential despair, 102, 343
    existential worldview, 141, 146, 149, 203, 204, 206, 213, 225, 227, 240, 338, 344, 349, 350
    fabric of life, 24, 29, 45, 59, 351, 370
    life purpose, 101, 112, 283
    ontological insecurity, 12, 27, 45, 103, 104, 173, 362
    subjectively-experienced relationship with *Ground of Being*, 102
Experiential learning exercises
    academic stress, types and student responses, 148, 165
    anonymous sharing, 165, 166, 168, 173, 175, 176, 177, 178, 183, 184, 195, 208, 209, 222, 309–311, 314, 322, 325, 327, 342, 348
    birthplace of great-grandparents, 183, 189
    conflict engagement styles, 181
    group meditation and chanting, 199, 200, 230, 321, 322, 325
    inner critic work, 148, 169, 172, 173, 178, 203, 204, 207, 311, 325
    interpersonal behavior during stress, 194
    in vivo conflicts, 181, 197, 318
    peacock feather exercise, 170, 173, 175, 311, 326, 366, 367
    polyphonic singing, 8, 342, 366
    restorative dialogue, 8, 142, 181, 197, 310, 318, 329
    self-regulation skills, 7, 67, 99, 143, 149, 175, 178, 203, 223, 255, 308, 311, 342

F
Faust, Drew Gilpin, 37
Feminist theory, 6

Frankl, Viktor, 28, 29, 101, 102, 203, 206, 207, 208, 213, 344, 370
 crisis of meaning, 134, 253, 297
 logotherapeutic philosophy, 29, 344
 Man's Search for Meaning, 28, 206
Fredrickson, Barbara, 113. *See also* Resilience
Freire, Paolo, 35, 56
Fricchione, Gregory, 11, 66, 89, 100. *See also* Bio-cultural model of evolution
Frustration tolerance, 67. *See also* Ogden, Pat
Thetford, William, 57, 67

G
Gallardo, Miguel, 72, 73, 96
Gendler, Everett, 72
Germer, Christopher, 65, 91
Gestalt theory, 61
Giles, Cheryl, 65
God images, 107. *See also* Maimonides, Moses; Moore, Diane
 anthropomorphic God images, 105
 childhood representations of God; compensation for relational deficits, 103; protector, 103, 296, 297, 307
 gender- or racially-dissonant, 103
 shame-inducing, 103
 transformation; psychospiritual mentoring, 45, 103; spiritually-integrative counseling, 103
Goodman, Lenn, 62, 73, 90, 105, 107
Ground of Being, 8, 12, 28, 60, 61, 70, 71, 102, 103, 107, 108, 164, 205, 215, 228, 235, 256, 266, 272, 294, 322, 324, 329, 338, 340

H
Hartman, David, 62, 92, 105
Harward, Donald, 14, 35, 38

Herman, Judith, 6, 66
Heschel, Abraham Joshua, 61, 62, 73
Higher Education, 3, 4, 30, 33, 114, 140, 331, 355
 career success, 355, 356
 change in approach to first year seminars (chapter 12), 368
 deeper purpose, 4, 368
 incorporating person-centered psychospiritual learning, 363
 mirror of humanity's chain of pain, 33, 42, 355
 unparalleled success, 33
Higher Education College Life Surveys, 36–37
 Columbia University Center on Addiction and Substance Abuse, 36
 Core Institute Alcohol and Drug Surveys, 36
 Harvard School of Public Health College Alcohol Surveys, 36
 National College Health Assessment (NCHA), 37
 National Study of Living-Learning Programs, 41
 National Survey of College Counseling Centers, 36
 UCLA Higher Education Research Institute (HERI), 37
 University of Southern Maine Center for Prevention of Hate Violence, 36
Holland, Jimmie, 29
Hood, Ralph, 102, 108
Humanistic Psychology, 6
 integrative humanistic psychology, 353, 364

I
Imaginal dimension of awareness, 106, 110, 111, 207, 210, 213, 215, 221, 236, 262, 290, 302

Index of Core Spiritual Experiences (INSPIRIT) *See* Spiritual/mystical/religious experience
Interfaith dialogue, 14. *See also* Boston Clergy and Religious Group for Interfaith Dialogue
Conde-Frazier, Elizabeth, 8
Kazanjian, Victor, 35
Kujawa-Holbrook, Sheryl, 8
Spretnak, Charlene, 8, 103, 107
Tutu, Desmond, 8
Internal composure *See* Resilience
Internal locus of evaluation, 56, 60, 140, 200, 266, 307, 308
Internal locus of existential meaning-making, 8, 63, 149, 203, 341, 343, 350, 362
Internal perceptual orientation, 104
Intuitive dimension of consciousness, 107
Inventory of Positive Psychological Attitudes (IPPA) *See* Resilient worldview

J
James, William, 73, 107, 161
Jung, Carl
 active imagination, 109, 110
 archetypal dream symbolism, 107
 fragmentation of psyche, 110
 transcendent function, 107, 110

K
Kabat-Zinn, Jon, 64. *See also* Mindfulness
Mind-Body Stress Reduction Clinic (MBSR), University of Massachusetts Medical Center, 64
Kazanjian, Victor, 35, 241

Keeling, Richard, 13, 35
Kelman, Herbert, 6, 95, 96
Keyes, Corey, 40. *See also* Engaged teaching and learning (Flourishing)
 Mental Health Continuum, 40
King, Jr., Martin Luther, 72, 156
Kirschenbaum, Howard, 6, 56, 57
Kuh, George, 7. *See also* Engaged teaching and learning
 National Survey for Student Engagement (NSSE), 35
Kujawa-Holbrook. Sheryl, 8

L
Lazar, Sara, 8, 66
Leadership training for cultures of health, social justice, and peace, 365
Learning communities, 33. *See also* Engaged teaching and learning
Life Purpose and Satisfaction (LPS) *See* Resilient worldview

M
MacLean, Paul, 91. *See also* Bio-cultural evolutionary model of evolution
 triune model of the brain, 91
Maimonides, Moses, 27, 62, 63, 102, 103, 105–108. *See also* God images; Contemplative mind (models)
 Guide of the Perplexed, 27, 62
 Mishneh Torah, 62
 Salah al-Din Yussuf ibn Ayyub (Saladin), 62
Marlatt, Alan, 65, 92
Maslow, Abraham, 366
Mature relational love, 101

Mature stress coping skills (taught in spiritual traditions), 168
Meditation, 66. *See also* Contemplative mind (models); Mindfulness; Relaxation Response
　diaphragmatic breathing, 66, 93, 163, 207
　mental concentration, 7, 66, 69, 141, 175
Mental conditioning (terminology of spiritual traditions), 106
　attachment, 111
　ignorance, 28, 103
　mental formations, 106, 110, 111
　nafs, 106
　polluting moral qualities, 106
　samskaras, 106
　sankharas, 106
　scars, 215
　spiritual imperfections, 106
　veil, 61
Merton, Thomas, 28, 61, 107, 108
Mikulincer, Mario, 99, 100
Miller, William, 64, 65
Mindfulness, 7, 42, 64–67, 69, 91, 92, 96, 111, 141, 155, 164, 168, 170, 180, 203, 227, 247, 322, 339, 342, 367. *See also* Germer, Christopher; Giles, Cheryl; Kabat-Zinn, Jon; Marlatt, Alan
　Buddhist Psychology, 65
　Santorelli, Saki, 65
Moore, Diane
　cultural studies approach to religion, 103
　religious literacy, 103
Multicultural skills and learning, 6, 134, 155, 166, 353. *See also* Anonymous sharing; Social justice and systemic inequality; Social identity development; Trauma (Historical and Racial trauma)
　building culturally-inclusive community, 3, 8, 11, 12, 15, 70–73, 133, 141, 181–202, 313–316, 336, 339, 342, 358, 364, 365, 368, 369
　cultural humility, 73, 188
　cultural *other*, 91, 98
　multicultural competence, 56, 57, 147
　overcoming bias and prejudice, 73
　pro-social development, 139
　religious *other*, 95, 191
　value of anonymous sharing, 178
　vulnerable – building human connections, 148, 155, 180, 336
Multicultural theory, 6, 353

N
Neuroscience of meditation
　deep sleep (Delta), 109
　default mode network, 108, 109
　Electroencephalogram (EEG), 109
　　alpha waves
　　beta waves, 109
　　delta waves, 109
　　gamma waves, 108
　　theta waves, 109
　Green, Elmer and Alyce, 109
　meditation and unitive awareness, 109
　neurological correlates of spiritual experience, 90
　neurophenomenology, 109

O
Ogden, Pat, 58, 65, 67, 92, 99
　window of tolerance, 67

P
Palmer, Parker, 26, 35
Pargament, Kenneth, 6, 12, 41, 102, 103, 134

Parks, Sharon Daloz, 45
Peace psychology, 6
Perennial Philosophy, 8, 15, 102, 206, 342, 363. *See also* Spiritual Traditions
   Huxley, Aldous, 8
   Schuon, Frithjof, 8, 102
   Smith, Huston, 8
   Teasdale, Walter, 8
Person-Centered Approach Project, 6, 14, 56, 58, 63. *See also* Rogers, Carl
   Bowen, Maria Villas-Boas, 14, 58
   Rogers, Natalie, 14, 58
Person-centered psychospiritual maturation (Five Dimensions)
   bio-behavioral dimension of learning, 5, 9, 26, 44, 91, 306, 311, 339, 361
   cognitive-sociocultural dimension of learning, 5, 10, 26, 44, 95, 306, 313, 339, 361
   existential-spiritual dimension of learning, 5, 11, 27, 45, 101, 307, 321, 339, 362
   integrative worldview formation, 5, 13, 30, 45, 112, 307, 325, 339, 362
   social-emotional dimension of learning, 5, 10, 27, 44, 98, 306, 316, 336, 361
Person-centered theory, 6, 352
Porges, Stephen *See* Resilience (Polyvagal theory)
Pratto, Felicia, 10, 72, 95–97, 100
Pro-social development, 43. *See also* Multicultural skills and learning
Psychodynamic attachment theory, 6. *See also* Attachment
Psychological well-being *see* Resilience
Psychospiritual, 3. *See also* Contemplative Self-Inquiry; Person-Centered Psychospiritual Maturation
psychospiritual crisis, 21
psychospiritual exploration, 7, 111, 149, 203, 205, 222, 223, 345, 350
psychospiritual self-inquiry, 11, 43, 103, 134, 149, 336–338

Q
Qualitative analytic procedures
   Grounded Theory, 136, 148
Quantitative measures for statistical comparison, 137

R
Racial trauma *See* Trauma
Relaxation response, 42, 64, 66, 67, 70, 92, 111, 141, 149, 170, 175, 182, 203, 227, 247, 255, 262, 271, 278, 302, 307, 339, 342
Religious literacy, 181. *See also* Moore, Diane
Resilience, 12. *See also* Autonomic dysregulation in stress and trauma; Fredrickson, Barbara
   cardiovascular recovery, 93, 113
   equanimity, 42, 69, 70
   internal composure, 11, 25, 29, 67
   Polyvagal theory (Porges, Stephen), 92–94
      dorsal vagal complex, 94
      heart-rate variability (HRA), 68, 92
      three-tiers of resilient coping, 94
      vagal brake, 93
      vagal tone, 93
      ventral vagal complex (smart vagus), 92
   psychological well-being, 37, 40, 63, 93, 137, 204, 357

resilient stress-coping, 9, 88, 92, 94–96, 168, 265, 273, 283, 307, 325, 337, 341, 343, 344, 351, 359, 360
Resilient worldview, 12, 14, 30, 45, 68, 112, 113, 137, 143, 144, 145, 146, 307, 325, 339, 340, 341, 350, 362. *See also* Secure existential attachment
  Confidence in Life and Self (CLS), 12, 13, 14, 30, 45, 69, 112, 113, 137, 143, 144, 146, 200, 201, 258, 266, 295, 308, 325, 328, 329, 339, 340, 341, 347, 350, 358, 362
  Inventory of Positive Psychological Attitudes (IPPA), 14, 41, 68, 137, 144, 340
  Life purpose and satisfaction (LPS), 137, 144
  Self-Confidence during Stress (SCDS), 137, 144
  Spirituality and Resilience Assessment Packet (SRA), 14, 17
Rockefeller, Laurance, 68
Rogers, Carl, 6, 14, 22, 55–59, 61, 63, 67, 68, 70, 89, 96, 101, 107, 335, 347, 352, 353, 354. *See also* Bio-cultural model of evolution (Formative tendency)
  A Way of Being, 59
  China Diaries, 56
  interpersonal conditions, 6, 56; congruence, 56, 58, 96; empathy, 56, 96; unconditional positive regard, 56, 96
  reflective listening, 22, 29, 56, 57, 310, 361
  self-actualizing tendency, 59

S
Sapolsky, Robert, 65, 92, 93, 95, 96, 158
Schore, Alan, 6, 58, 95, 99, 110, 112
Secular humanism, 7, 8, 11, 12, 69, 102, 134, 137, 146, 206, 321, 330, 321, 330, 341, 344, 362, 363
  agnostic, 160, 190, 363
  atheist, 117, 266, 267, 271, 363
Secure existential attachment, 12, 30, 108, 111, 112, 113, 137, 143–145, 146, 188, 201, 204, 213, 222, 295, 307, 308, 310, 325, 329, 330, 331, 338, 341, 347, 362. *See also* Attachment
Self-Confidence during Stress (SCDS) *See* Resilient worldview
Self-directed group process, 58
Self-regulation *See* Experiential learning exercises
Selye, Hans, 64. *See also* Autonomic dysregulation in stress and trauma
Shaver, Phillip, 99, 100
Sidanius, Jim, 10, 72, 90, 95, 97, 110
Siegel, Daniel, 6, 13, 58, 65, 90, 91, 99, 104, 110, 112
Social identity development, 72, 73, 164
sociocultural differences (student explorations), 201, 342
sociocultural identity narratives, 5, 10, 95, 143, 149, 155, 181, 182, 310, 339, 343, 349, 361
Social justice and systemic inequality, 3, 4, 6, 8, 14, 15, 34, 35, 55, 56, 63, 70, 71–74, 90, 155, 159, 165, 188, 352–355, 360, 365–369. *See also* Bio-cultural model of evolution; Gendler, Everett; Heschel, Abraham Joshua; King, Jr., Martin Luther;

Pratto, Felicia; Sapolsky, Robert; Person-centered psychospiritual maturation (Five dimensions); Sidanius, Jim
- group-based stress reactivity, 181
- own-group preference vs. egalitarian, 97
- privileged access to the Divine, 7, 71
- social dominance hierarchies, 5, 7, 10, 72, 90, 91, 95–98, 100, 103, 110, 149, 164, 181, 185, 187, 188, 313, 336, 339, 342, 360
- social dominance orientation, 91, 97, 110
- social stratification, 6, 65, 72
- sociocultural stress, 65

Somatic memory, 61, 66, 91
- armoring, 58
- bio-energetic theory, 61
- segmented musculature, 61
- somatic residues of trauma, 99, 110

Spiritual/mystical/religious experience, 12, 107. *See also* Awareness (Connective and Differentiating); Contemplative mind (models); Neuroscience of Meditation; Secure existential attachment
- core spiritual experience, 14, 141
- critiques (non-mystical explanations), 35, 107–108
- emergent capacity for connective awareness, 105
- Hood, Ralph, 138
- Index of Core Spiritual Experiences (INSPIRIT), 14, 68, 137, 144, 146, 340
- James, William, 107
- Stace, Walter, 102

Spirituality and Resilience Assessment Packet (SRA) *See* Resilient worldview

Spirituality in Higher Education, 41. *See also* Astin, Alexander; Chickering, Arthur; Equanimity
- Astin, Helen, 42
- Keen, James, 42
- Lindholm, Jennifer, 42

Spiritual traditions (Scholars, teachers, traditions), 7. *See also* Mature stress coping skills (taught in spiritual traditions); Maimonides, Moses; Merton, Thomas; Perennial Philosophy; Thurman, Howard
- Angha, Nahid, 61
- Borg, Marcus, 206
- Buddha, Gautama, 28, 101, 209
- Buddhist spirituality, 8, 65, 105, 106, 107, 158, 160, 267, 271, 321, 363
- Christian spirituality, 8, 56, 61, 62, 105, 106, 107, 135, 156, 157, 158, 160, 161, 186, 188, 189, 190, 192, 193, 206, 230, 233, 259, 260, 265, 284, 285, 286, 287, 288, 314, 315, 316, 320, 322, 336
  - Protestant, 69, 135, 160, 186, 189, 191, 192, 193, 245, 267, 363
  - Roman Catholic, 69, 135, 157, 160, 161, 184, 185, 186, 188, 189, 190, 191, 192, 199, 226, 231, 232, 233, 259, 274, 275, 315, 316, 336, 363
- Greek Orthodox, 135
- Dalai Lama (Tenzin Gyatso), 106
- Deloria, Vincent, Jr., 35
- Dharma teachings (Buddhist and Hindu), 8, 105, 160
- Easwaran, Eknath, 28, 104, 105, 107, 108, 109
- Green, Arthur, 61, 108, 109
- Hanh, Thich Nhat, 101

Hindu spirituality, 8, 105, 106, 107, 158, 160, 316, 322, 363
Indigenous spiritual traditions, 8, 35
Jesus, 105, 160, 161, 186, 189, 190, 206, 212, 330
Jewish spirituality, vii, 8, 27, 61, 62, 63, 69, 72, 73, 105, 106, 107, 135, 156, 158, 184, 188, 189, 206, 315, 316, 322, 324, 328, 330, 336, 363
Muslim spirituality, 8, 61, 62, 71, 105, 106, 107, 135, 183, 188, 191–194, 206, 295, 296, 298, 299, 300, 302, 305–307, 316, 322, 336, 338, 350, 363
Nasr, Seyyed Hossein, 8, 28, 102, 104, 105, 106, 107, 108, 206
Pennington, M. Basil, 107, 108, 206
Prager, Marcia, 61
Santeria, 316
Secret of the Golden Flower, 106
St. John of the Cross, 106
St. Teresa of Avila, 28, 105, 107
Taoist spirituality (China), 106, 161
Yoga Psychology (Buddhist and Hindu), 8, 19, 60, 61, 106, 109, 142
STEM disciplines, 38, 364
Stress – complex forms, 87. *See also* Autonomic dysregulation in stress and trauma
Student Life
 environmental management, 13
 initiatives to change campus culture, 35
 National Association for Student Life Personnel and Administrators (NASPA), 13
 Offices of Student Life
  overburdened, 45
  understaffed, 363

Student Life Issues
 Behavioral Change Goals, 139–140
 existential struggles/spiritual alienation, 285, 338
 health-compromising attitudes and behaviors, 238, 337
 impaired relational skills, 266, 338
 social-emotional impairments to academic performance, 226, 337
 psychological and behavioral dysregulation, 33. *See also* Autonomic dysregulation in stress and trauma
Sue, Derald Wing, 6, 56
Swaner, Lynn, 3, 13, 35, 37–39

T
Thetford, William, 57, 67, 68
Thurman, Howard, 72, 206
Tillich, Paul, 12, 27, 45, 101, 102, 108, 283. *See also* Existential psychology (ontological insecurity)
Trauma, 4, 6, 14, 57, 60, 65, 66, 67, 87, 94, 104, 110, 161, 175, 182, 215, 216, 256, 276, 303, 307, 338, 342, 343, 346, 350. *See also* Autonomic dysregulation in stress/trauma; Herman, Judith; Ogden, Pat; Resilience; Siegel, Daniel; van der Kolk, Bessell
 collective trauma, 27, 95, 198
 destruction of relational networks, 98
 historical trauma, 336, 349, 353, 369
 intergenerational transmission of trauma, 95, 280, 360
 racial trauma, 65, 70, 71, 239, 336, 337
 replicative dynamics (Humanity's Chain of Pain), 4

U

Ultimate, 366
  spirit of the game, 366
  self-regulation, 366
Unconditional positive regard *See* Rogers, Carl (Interpersonal conditions for therapeutic growth)

V

van der Kolk, Bessel, 6, 65, 94

W

Walsh, Diana Chapman, 26
Watkins, Mary, 110. *See also* Imaginal dimension of awareness
  imaginal dialogues, 110, 215, 219, 229, 241, 243, 321, 345

Y

Young Adulthood, 3. *See also* Arnett, Jeffrey; Emerging Adulthood

Made in United States
North Haven, CT
28 July 2025